To

J. R. Wallin

Master Craftsman

BORN IN BLOOD

THE LOST SECRETS
OF FREEMASONRY

JOHN J. ROBINSON

M. EVANS
Lanham • New York • Boulder • Toronto • Plymouth, UK

Published by M. Evans
An imprint of The Rowman & Littlefield Publishing Group, Inc.
4501 Forbes Boulevard, Suite 200, Lanham, Maryland 20706
www.rlpgtrade.com

Estover Road
Plymouth PL6 7PY
United Kingdom

Distributed by NATIONAL BOOK NETWORK

Library of Congress Cataloging-in-Publication Data

Robinson, John J.
Born in blood : the lost secrets of freemasonry / John J. Robinson
   p. cm.
Includes bibliographical references.
1. Freemasons—History. 2. Freemasonry—History. I. Title.
HS403.R64 1989   89-23703
366'.1—dc20

ISBN: 0-87131-602-1 (cloth : alk. paper)
ISBN: 978-1-59077-148-8 (pbk. : alk. paper)
ISBN: 978-1-59077-149-5 (electronic)

♾™ The paper used in this publication meets the minimum requirements of American
National Standard for Information Sciences—Permanence of Paper for Printed Library
Materials, ANSI/NISO Z39.48-1992.

Manufactured in the United States of America.

Contents

Acknowledgments

Special thanks are due to the Reverend Martin Chadwick, M.A., Rural Dean of Chipping Norton in Oxfordshire, who obtained permission for me to use the Bodleian Library and its Radcliffe Camera at Oxford University in England. In that same locale, special thanks must also be expressed to Dr. Maurice Keen of Balliol College, who took time from his crowded schedule for a tutorial session with an amateur American historian. His insights into aspects of the Peasants' Revolt and of the teachings of John Wycliffe and of the Lollard Knights provided fresh starting points for research. The willing assistance of librarians is too often overlooked, so I would like to express appreciation for the helpful attitudes of the staff members of the libraries in Oxford and Lincoln in England, as well as those of New York's Forty-second Street library and the public library of Cincinnati. I was also given most gracious treatment at the county archives of Oxfordshire and at the Lincolnshire County Museum.

Recognition should also be given to a number of Freemasons of various degrees who shared with me not the "secrets" of the order, but rather their understandings of the origins and purposes of the fraternity as expressed to them by Masonic writers and lecturers.

It should be noted that although I received a great deal of generous help, the opinions expressed and the conclusions reached in this book are my own.

As for the contributions of my wife, they are difficult to enumerate. The manuscript was not just typed but reviewed for clarity as well as for accuracy of dates and geography. She assisted in four years of research and enthusiastically discussed the outline and content of each chapter. Her knowledge of French eased that aspect of the research, and most of the sources in England came as a result of the friends and contacts she had made over a period of years as an educator in Oxfordshire.

Finally, a word of explanation about the dedication of this book. J. R. Wallin is not a "Master Craftsman" in the symbolic Masonic sense but is literally a master worker in iron and steel. During working hours his forge turns out decorative iron gates and brackets and furniture, but in his spare time it gives way to his fascination with the medieval period by producing such items as a mace, a dagger, or a jousting helmet. The hours spent with him talking about the Crusades and the Templars helped to keep up my enthusiasm for the project. I chose to dedicate this book to him because I think we should all encourage rare breeds, and there can't be many people left on this earth who spend winter evenings interlocking thousands of handmade loops to create a coat of chain mail.

John J. Robinson
Twin Brook Farm
Carroll County, Kentucky

Introduction

In Search of the Great Society

The research behind this book was not originally intended to reveal anything about Freemasonry or the Knights Templar. Its objective had been to satisfy my own curiosity about certain unexplained aspects of the Peasants' Revolt in England in 1381, a savage uprising that saw upwards of a hundred thousand Englishmen march on London. They moved in uncontrolled rage, burning down manor houses, breaking open prisons, and cutting down any who stood in their way.

One unsolved mystery of that revolt was the organization behind it. For several years a group of disgruntled priests of the lower clergy had traveled the towns, preaching against the riches and corruption of the church. During the months before the uprising, secret meetings had been held throughout central England by men weaving a network of communication. After the revolt was put down, rebel leaders confessed to being agents of a Great Society, said to be based in London. So very little is known of that alleged organization that several scholars have solved the mystery simply by deciding that no such secret society ever existed.

Another mystery was the concentrated and especially vicious attacks on the religious order of the Knights Hospitaller of St. John, now known as the Knights of Malta. Not only did the rebels seek out their properties for vandalism and fire, but their prior

was dragged from the Tower of London to have his head struck
off and placed on London Bridge, to the delight of the cheering
mob.

There was no question that the ferocity unleashed on the crusading Hospitallers had a purpose behind it. One captured rebel
leader, when asked the reasons for the revolt, said, "First, and
above all . . . the destruction of the Hospitallers." What kind of
secret society could have had that special hatred as one of its primary purposes?

A desire for vengeance against the Hospitallers was easy to
identify in the rival crusading order of the Knights of the Temple
of Solomon in Jerusalem. The problem was that those Knights
Templar had been completely suppressed almost seventy years
before the Peasants' Revolt, following several years during which
the Templars had been imprisoned, tortured, and burned at the
stake. After issuing the decree that put an end to the Templar
order, Pope Clement V had directed that all of the extensive
properties of the Templars should be given to the Hospitallers.
Could a Templar desire for revenge actually have survived underground for three generations?

There was no incontrovertible proof, yet the only evidence suggests the existence of just one secret society in fourteenth-
century England, the society that was, or would become, the
order of Free and Accepted Masons. There appeared to be no
connection, however, between the revolt and Freemasonry,
except for the name or title of its leader. He occupied the center
stage of English history for just eight days and nothing is known
of him except that he was the supreme commander of the rebellion. He was called Walter the Tyler, and it seemed at first to be
mere coincidence that he bore the title of the enforcement officer of the Masonic lodge. In Freemasonry the Tyler, who must be
a Master Mason, is the sentry, the sergeant-at-arms, and the officer who screens the credentials of visitors who seek entrance to
the lodge. In remembrance of an earlier, more dangerous time,
his post is just outside the door of the lodge room, where he
stands with a drawn sword in his hand.

I was aware that there had been many attempts in the past to
link the Freemasons with the Knights Templar, but never with
success. The fragile evidence advanced by proponents of that
connection had never held up, sometimes because it was based

on wild speculation, and at least once because it had been based on a deliberate forgery. But despite the failures to establish that link, it just will not go away, and the time-shrouded belief in some relationship between the two orders remains as one of the more durable legends of Freemasonry. That is entirely appropriate, because all of the various theories of the origins of Freemasonry are legendary. Not one of them is supported by any universally accepted evidence. I was not about to travel down that time-worn trail, and decided to concentrate my efforts on digging deeper into the history of the Knights Templar, to see if there was any link between the suppressed Knights and the secret society behind the Peasants' Revolt. In doing so, I thought that I would be leaving Freemasonry far behind. I couldn't have been more mistaken.

Like anyone curious about medieval history, I had developed an interest in the Crusades, and perhaps more than just an interest. Those holy wars hold an appeal that is frequently as romantic as it is historical, and in my travels I had tried to drink in the atmosphere of the narrow defiles in the mountains of Lebanon through which Crusader armies had passed, and had sat staring at the castle ruins around Sidon and Tyre, trying to hear the clashing sounds of attack and defense. I had marveled at the walls of Constantinople and had strolled the Arsenal of Venice, where Crusader fleets were assembled. I had sat in the round church of the Knights Templar in London, trying to imagine the ceremony of its consecration by the Patriarch of Jerusalem in 1185, more than three hundred years before Columbus set sail west to the Indies.

The Templar order was founded in Jerusalem in 1118, in the aftermath of the First Crusade. Its name came from the location of its first headquarters on the site of the ancient Temple of Solomon. Helping to fill a desperate need for a standing army in the Holy Land, the Knights of the Temple soon grew in numbers, in wealth, and in political power. They also grew in arrogance, and their Grand Master de Ridfort was a key figure in the mistakes that led to the fall of Jerusalem in 1187. The Latin Christians managed to hold onto a narrow strip of territory along the coast, where the Templars were among the largest owners of the land and fortifications.

Finally, the enthusiasm for sending men and money to the

Holy Land waned among the European kingdoms, which were preoccupied with their wars against each other. By 1296 the Egyptian sultan was able to push the resident Crusaders, along with the military orders, into the sea. The Holy Land was lost, and the defeated Knights Templar moved their base to the island kingdom of Cyprus, dreaming of yet one more Crusade to restore their past glory.

As the Templars planned a new Crusade against the infidel, King Philip IV of France was planning his own private crusade against the Templars. He longed to be rid of his massive debts to the Templar order, which had used its wealth to establish a major banking operation. Philip wanted the Templar treasure to finance his continental wars against Edward I of England.

After two decades of fighting England on one side and the Holy Roman Church on the other, two unrelated events gave Philip of France the opportunity he needed. Edward I died, and his deplorably weak son took the throne of England as Edward II. On the other front, Philip was able to get his own man on the Throne of Peter as Pope Clement V.

When word arrived on Cyprus that the new pope would mount a Crusade, the Knights Templar thought that their time of restoration to glory was at hand. Summoned to France, their aging grand master, Jacques de Molay, went armed with elaborate plans for the rescue of Jerusalem. In Paris, he was humored and honored until the fatal day. At dawn on Friday, the thirteenth of October, 1307, every Templar in France was arrested and put in chains on Philip's orders. Their hideous torture for confessions of heresy began immediately.

When the pope's orders to arrest the Templars arrived at the English court, young Edward II took no action at all. He protested to the pontiff that the Templars were innocent. Only after the pope issued a formal bull was the English king forced to act. In January, 1308, Edward finally issued orders for the arrest of the Knights Templar in England, but the three months of warning had been put to good use. Many of the Templars had gone underground, while some of those arrested managed to escape. Their treasure, their jeweled reliquaries, even the bulk of their records, had disappeared. In Scotland, the papal order was not even published. Under those conditions England, and especially Scotland, became targeted havens for fugitive Templars from continental

Europe, and the efficiency of their concealment spoke to some assistance from outside, or from each other.

The English throne passed from Edward II to Edward III, who bequeathed the crown to his ten-year-old grandson who, as Richard II, watched from the Tower as the Peasants' Revolt exploded throughout the City of London.

Much had happened to the English people along the way. Incessant wars had drained most of the king's treasury and corruption had taken the rest. A third of the population had perished in the Black Death, and famine exacted further tolls. The reduced labor force of farmers and craftsmen found that they could earn more for their labor, but their increased income came at the expense of land-owning barons and bishops, who were not prepared to tolerate such a state of affairs. Laws were passed to reduce wages and prices to preplague levels, and genealogies were searched to reimpose the bondage of serfdom and villeinage on men who thought themselves free. The king's need for money to fight his French wars inspired new and ingenious taxes. The oppression was coming from all sides, and the pot of rebellion was brought to the boil.

Religion didn't help, either. The landowning church was as merciless a master as the landowning nobility. Religion would have been a source of confusion for the fugitive Templars as well. They were a religious body of warrior monks who owed allegiance to no man on earth except the Holy Father. When their pope turned on them, chained them, beat them, he broke their link with God. In fourteenth-century Europe there was no pathway to God except through the vicar of Christ on earth. If the pope rejected the Templars and the Templars rejected the pope, they had to find a new way to worship their God, at a time when any variation from the teachings of the established church was blasted as heresy.

That dilemma called to mind the central tenet of Freemasonry, which requires only that a man believe in a Supreme Being, with no requirements as to how he worships the deity of his choice. In Catholic Britain such a belief would have been a crime, but it would have accommodated the fugitive Templars who had been cut off from the universal church. In consideration of the extreme punishment for heresy, such an independent belief also made sense of one of the more mysterious of Freemasonry's Old

Charges, the ancient rules that still govern the conduct of the fraternity. The Charge says that no Mason should reveal the secrets of a brother that may deprive him of his life and property.

That connection caused me to take a different look at the Masonic Old Charges. They took on new direction and meaning when viewed as a set of instructions for a secret society created to assist and protect fraternal brothers on the run and in hiding from the church. That characterization made no sense in the context of a medieval guild of stonemasons, the usual claim for the roots of Freemasonry. It did make a great deal of sense, however, for men such as the fugitive Templars, whose very lives depended upon their concealment. Nor would there have been any problem in finding new recruits over the years ahead: There were to be plenty of protestors and dissidents against the church among future generations. The rebels of the Peasants' Revolt proved that when they attacked abbeys and monasteries, and when they cut the head off the Archbishop of Canterbury, the leading Catholic prelate in England.

The fugitive Templars would have needed a code such as the Old Charges of Masonry, but the working stonemasons clearly did not. It had become obvious that I needed to know more about the Ancient Order of Free and Accepted Masons. The extent of the Masonic material available at large public libraries surprised me, as did the fact that it was housed in the department of education and religion. Not content with just what was generally available to the public, I asked to use the library in the Masonic Temple in Cincinnati, Ohio. I told the gentleman there that I was not a Freemason, but wanted to use the library as part of my research for a book that would probably include a new examination of the Masonic order. His only question to me was, "Will it be fair?" I assured him that I had no desire or intention to be anything other than fair, to which he replied, "Good enough." I was left alone with the catalog and the hundreds of Masonic books that lined the walls. I also took advantage of the publications of the Masonic Service Association at Silver Spring, Maryland.

Later, as my growing knowledge of Masonry enabled me to sustain a conversation on the subject, I began to talk to Freemasons. At first I wondered how I would go about meeting fifteen or twenty Masons and, if I could meet them, would they be willing to talk to me? The first problem was solved as soon as I started asking friends and associates if they were Masons. There were four in one group I had known for about five years, and many more among men I had known for twenty years and more, without ever realizing that they had any connection with Freemasonry. As for the second part of my concern, I found them quite willing to talk, not about the "secret" passwords and hand grips (by then, I already knew them), but about what they had been taught concerning the origins of Freemasonry and its ancient Old Charges.

They were as intrigued as I was about the possibilities of discovering the lost meanings of words, symbols, and ritual for which no logical explanation was available, such as why a Master Mason is told in his initiation rites that "this degree will make you a brother to pirates and corsairs." We agreed that unlocking the secrets of those Masonic mysteries would contribute most to unearthing the past, because the loss of their true meanings had caused the ancient terms and symbols to be preserved intact, less subject to change over the centuries, or by adaptations to new conditions.

Among those lost secrets were the meanings of words used in the Masonic rituals, words like *tyler, cowan, due-guard,* and *Juwes.* Masonic writers have struggled for centuries, without success, to make those words fit with their preconceived conviction that Masonry was born in the English-speaking guilds of medieval stonemasons.

Now I would test the possibility that there was indeed a connection between Freemasonry and the French-speaking Templar order, by looking for the lost meanings of those terms, not in English, but in medieval French. The answers began to flow, and soon a sensible meaning for every one of the mysterious Masonic terms was established in the French language. It even provided the first credible meaning for the name of Hiram Abiff, the murdered architect of the Temple of Solomon, who is the central figure of Masonic ritual. The examination established something else as well. It is well known that in 1362 the English courts officially changed the language used for court proceedings from French to English, so the French roots of all the mysterious terms of Freemasonry confirmed the existence of that secret society in the fourteenth century, the century of the Templar suppression and the Peasants' Revolt.

With that encouragement I addressed other lost secrets of Masonry: the circle and mosaic pavement on the lodge room floor, gloves and lambskin aprons, the symbol of the compass and the square, even the mysterious legend of the murder of Hiram Abiff. The Rule, customs, and traditions of the Templars provided answers to all of those mysteries. Next came a deeper analysis of the Old Charges of ancient Masonry that define a secret society of mutual protection. What the "lodge" was doing was assisting brothers in hiding from the wrath of church and state, providing them with money, vouching for them with the authorities, even providing the "lodging" that gave Freemasonry the unique term for its chapters and their meeting rooms. There remained no reasonable doubt in my mind that the original concept of the secret society that came to call itself Freemasonry had been born as a society of mutual protection among fugitive Templars and their associates in Britain, men who had gone underground to escape the imprisonment and torture that had been ordered for them by Pope Clement V. Their antagonism toward the Church was rendered more powerful by its total secrecy. The suppression of the Templar order appeared to be one of the biggest mistakes the Holy See ever made.

In return, Freemasonry has been the target of more angry papal bulls and encyclicals than any other secular organization in Christian history. Those condemnations began just a few years after Masonry revealed itself in 1717 and grew in intensity, culminating in the bull *Humanum Genus,* promulgated by Pope Leo XIII in 1884. In it, the Masons are accused of espousing religious freedom, the separation of church and state, the education of children by laymen, and the extraordinary crime of believing that people have the right to make their own laws and to elect their own government, "according to the new principles of liberty." Such concepts are identified, along with the Masons, as part of the kingdom of Satan. The document not only defines the concerns of the Catholic Church about Freemasonry at that time, but, in the negative, so clearly defines what Freemasons believe that I have included the complete text of that papal bull as an appendix to this book.

Finally, it should be added that the events described here were part of a great watershed of Western history. The feudal age was coming to a close. Land, and the peasant labor on it, had lost its role as the sole source of wealth. Merchant families banded into guilds, and took over whole towns with charters as municipal corporations. Commerce led to banking and investment, and towns became power centers to rival the nobility in wealth and influence.

The universal church, which had fought for a position of supremacy in a feudal context, was slow to accept changes that might affect that supremacy. Any material disagreement with the church was called heresy, the most heinous crime under heaven. The heretic not only deserved death, but the most painful death imaginable.

Some dissidents run for the woods and hide, while others organize. In the case of the fugitive Knights Templar, the organization already existed. They possessed a rich tradition of secret operations that had been raised to the highest level through their association with the intricacies of Byzantine politics, the secret ritual of the Assassins, and the intrigues of the Moslem courts which they met alternately on the battlefield or at the conference table. The church, in its bloody rejection of protest and change, provided them with a river of recruits that flowed for centuries.

More than six hundred years have passed since the suppression of the Knights Templar, but their heritage lives on in the largest fraternal organization ever known. And so the story of those tortured crusading knights, of the savagery of the Peasants' Revolt, and of the lost secrets of Freemasonry becomes the story of the most successful secret society in the history of the world.

PART 1

THE
KNIGHTS
TEMPLAR

CHAPTER 1

THE URGE TO KILL

In 1347, over a thousand miles from London, the Kipchak Mongols were besieging a walled Genoese trading center on the Crimean coast. Kipchak besiegers were beginning to die in large numbers from a strange disease that appeared to be highly infectious. In what may be the world's first recorded instance of biological warfare, the Kipchaks began to catapult the diseased corpses over the walls.

A few months later, Genoese galleys from the besieged city put in at Messina in Sicily, with men dying at their oars and tales of dead men who had been thrown over the side all along the way. The sailors ignored the efforts of authorities to prevent their landing, and the Black Death set foot ashore in Europe. Carried by ships' rats, it moved onto the continent through the ports of Naples and Marseilles. From Italy it moved into Switzerland and eastern Europe, meeting the spread through France into Germany. The plague came to England on ships landing at ports in Dorset and spread from there. Within two years it had killed off an estimated 35 to 40 percent of the population of Europe and Britain.

As in all times and places, famine, malnutrition, and the resultant lower immune defenses put out the welcome mat for the epidemic. A change in climate had produced longer winters and cooler, wetter summers, which had shortened and thwarted the growing season. From 1315 to 1318 torrential summer rains ruined crops, and mass starvation followed. Succeeding harvests were sporadic, but at least the people could survive. Then, in 1340, there was almost universal crop failure, and thousands perished in the worst famine of the century.

Even under what they would have considered ideal conditions, the general population was undernourished. Their diet was chiefly of wheat and rye, with few vegetables and a minimum of meat and milk—partially because, even if they could afford them, there was no refrigeration or other means of preservation. Vitamin and mineral deficiencies in winter were a part of life. Hunting could provide fresh meat, but hunting rights belonged to the manor lords. A beating was a light punishment and death not uncommon for taking a deer, or even a rabbit, from the lord's forests. That so many took the risk speaks to the intensity of the biological craving for fresh food.

Disease generally finds its easiest victims among children, who do not develop a mature immune system until about the age of ten or eleven, and among the elderly, whose immune systems decline with advancing years, and so it was with the Black Death. Although people of all ages and all stations died in the tens of thousands, the very young and the very old dominate the statistics. It was the very opposite of a "baby boom," leaving few young people to enter the work force during the next generation.

The Black Death was not a single disease, but three, and the source of all three was a flea. A bacillus in the blood blocks the flea's stomach. As the flea rams its probe through the skin of its host, preferably the black rat, the bacillus erupts from the flea's stomach and enters the host, introducing the infection. As the rats died off, the fleas took to other animals and to humans.

In one form, the bacilli settle in the lymph glands. Large swellings and carbuncles, called *buboes,* appear in the groin and armpits, which give this form of the disease the name "bubonic plague." The term "Black Death" comes from the fact that the victim's body is covered with black spots and his tongue turns black. Death usually comes within three days.

In another form—septicemic—the blood is infected, and death may take a week or more. The fastest death comes from the most infectious form, the pneumonic, which causes an inflammation of the throat and lungs, spitting and vomiting of blood, a foul stench, and intense pain.

No scientific identification was made of the plague diseases at the time, nor was anything known of the method of transmission. This permitted all manner of wild theories to be promulgated, of which the most common was that the Black Death was a punishment from God. Some even cursed God for the great calamity, and Philip VI of France took steps to prevent God from getting any angrier than He apparently already was. Special laws were passed against blasphemy, with very specific punishments. For the first offense, the lower lip of the blasphemer would be sliced off. For the second offense, the upper lip would go, and for the third offense the offender's tongue would be cut out.

Groups of penitents sprang up, publicly doing penance for sins that they could not specifically identify, but that were obviously serious enough to anger God to the point of destroying the human race. Only the most severe penance would do to expiate such horrible sin. Self-flagellation turned into group flagellation as penitents walked the streets, often led by a priest, and beat one another with knotted ropes and whips tipped with metal to lacerate their flesh. Some carried heavy crosses or wore crowns of thorns.

Others found their own answers in uninhibited rites and sexual orgies. Some acted on the theory that since the world was ending shortly every possible pleasure should be indulged; others believed an appeal to Satan was the only alternative, now that they had been abandoned by God.

As always in the Middle Ages, some communities put the blame on the only non-Christians in their midst, the Jews. Even though the Jews were dying from the Black Death themselves, they were accused of poisoning wells and causing the plague with secret rites and incantations intended to wipe out Christianity. Bloody pogroms were mounted in France, Austria, and especially—as had been the case during the Crusades—in Germany. In Strasbourg over two hundred Jews were burned alive. At one town on the Rhine the Jews were butchered, then their remains were sealed in wine barrels and sent bobbing down the river. The Jews at Esslingen who survived the first wave of persecution thought that their own world was coming to an end and gathered in their synagogue. They set the building on fire, burning themselves to death. Those Jews who weren't killed were frequently expelled, leaving their homes to spread their culture, and often the plague, to other areas. Poland saw its own persecutions in scattered areas, but that country was generally much safer than Germany, and German Jews streamed into Polish territory. This was the origin of the Ashkenazic (German) Jewish communities in Poland. They kept their German language, which gradually evolved into a vernacular called Yiddish.

Because of their crowded conditions and almost total lack of sanitation, the towns and cities were hardest hit at first, but as the townsmen dispersed to avoid the plague, they took it with them into the rural areas. As the farmers died off, fields went to weeds, and untended animals wandered the countryside until many of them died the same way their owners had. Henry Knighton, a canon of St. Mary's Abbey in Leicester, reported five thousand sheep dead and rotting in a single pasture. It has been estimated that the population of England when the plague first crossed the Channel was 4 million. By the time it subsided, the population had been reduced to less than 2.5 million.

News of the ravages of the plague in England reached the Scots, who concluded that this decimation of their ancient enemy could have come from no source other than an avenging God. They decided to assist the Almighty in His divine plan and attack the English in their weakened state. The call went out for the clans to gather at Selkirk Forest, but before they could begin their march south the plague struck the camp, killing an estimated five thousand Scots in a few days' time. There was nothing to do but abandon the invasion plan, so the still healthy, with the sick and dying, broke camp to return to their homes. Word of the gathering had reached the English, who moved north to intercept the invasion. They arrived in time to intercept and slaughter the dispersed Scottish army.

Incredibly, while the greatest death toll the world had ever known was in progress, the war between England and France kept right on going, each weakened side hoping that the other side was even weaker. Armies needed supplies, the products of craftsmen and farmers, of whom over a third had died. Armies needed money, and the population and products usually taxed for that purpose were declining. When the plague died out after a couple of years, the world was different than it had been before. It would never be the same again, because the lowest classes of society suddenly experienced a new power.

What had happened was that the one law that can never be broken without consequences, the law of supply and demand, was in full force and effect—this time to the benefit of the farmer, the common laborer, and the craftsman. In the recollection of the landowning class, there never had been a time when farm labor or farm tenant supply did not exceed the demand for it. Now the foundations of a way of life that had worked for centuries were beginning to crack. In the dark ages of anarchy the individual had been helpless. The preservation of life itself was the major consideration, and men freely pledged themselves in servitude to a stronger man who would provide them with protection. These strong men pledged themselves to even stronger men, and the result was the feudal system. Men at all levels pledged military service, often for a specific campaign or a specific period, such as forty days a year. The warrior class became the nobility, and they required wealth for war-horses, weapons, and armor. They needed still more wealth, partially in the form of labor, to build fortified places where their followers could come for protection. These gradually grew from moated stockades and fortified houses to lofty stone structures requiring an army of stonecutters, masons, carpenters, and smiths. All this had to be paid for, and although some revenue might be generated by the loot of warfare or the ransom of wealthy captives, the primary source of that wealth was the land, and the labor of the people who worked it.

As the armored horseman came to dominate the field of battle, there came an "arms race" of knights. The pledge of a local baron to his count might now include his obligation to respond to a call to arms by bringing with him anywhere from a single mounted knight to dozens, depending upon the size of his holdings. A knight was expensive to equip and maintain. He needed at least one trained heavy war-horse, a lighter horse for ordinary travel, and more horses for his squire, servants, and baggage. He required personal armor, which was very expensive, as well as some armor for his horse. To support him in all this, in exchange for his services he was provided with land, and the people on that land.

The status of serfs had changed over the centuries. Some were gradually able to become tenant farmers, tilling farmland assigned to them on shares while still making payments to the manor lord in fixed terms of service in the manor fields. Customs varied from one manor to another, but generally the tenant farmer paid in many ways for his tenure. On his death, his best farm animal went to the lord as a fee (the "heriot"), and his second-best animal to the parish priest. Neither he nor any member of his family could marry without permission, which usually required a payment. In addition to his prescribed days of labor for the lord (often two or three days a week), he might be called upon to give extra service without pay, a requirement with the unlikely name of "love-boon." He was subject to restrictions on gathering firewood, taking wood to repair his house, and even collecting the precious manure that would drop in the roads and byways.

If the manor lord owned a mill, the tenant had to use that mill and pay for the privilege. The same applied to manor ovens, frequently creating a monopoly on the baking of bread. In view of his rights and obligations, the tenant was not a serf, who was a man bound almost in slavery, but neither was he totally free. The greatest barrier to his liberty was the old law that took away his freedom of movement. These tenant farmers were required to stay on the manor to which they were attached by birth, where they lived in a cluster of houses called a "vill" (the obvious forerunner of "village"). For this reason the tenant was called a villein, pronounced almost the same way as the more disparaging term *villain* which was sometimes applied to him by his lord.

What most dramatically changed the status of many villeins was the manor lord's need for cash rather than a share of a crop that could not easily be transported to market for sale. There were almost no wagon roads, and grain crops could not be economically transported by packhorse, as was done with wool. The king needed cash to fight his French wars, and the nobles needed cash to pay mercenaries and to acquire transportation and supplies on the continent. Villeins began to make deals in which a ha'penny or penny might be given instead of a day's labor and a fixed cash payment in lieu of a share of crops. Their attitudes changed as they found themselves "renting" the land rather than trading their time and muscles for it. They *felt* free in the absence or reduction of the old customs of humbling servitude.

By the time of the Black Death, many of the English manors were held by the church. Some had been purchased, and many had been gifted. The extensive manorial holdings of the Knights Templar had been conveyed to the Knights of the Hospital of St. John of Jerusalem (the Hospitallers) after the Templars were suppressed by Pope Clement V in 1312. All of the monastic orders had manorial properties with thousands of serfs and villeins attached to them. Even the substitution of cash for villein services often didn't meet the lord's or bishop's need for cash, and a prosperous tenant would be permitted to purchase his freedom for a lump sum. Unfortunately, such men usually did not foresee a need for documentation that would stand up in court and so recorded the manumission improperly, or not at all. The attitude of the church was simple: No manumission was valid unless it was a recorded part of a business transaction. Any other act of freeing a villein was treated as embezzlement of valuable church property.

Now the Black Death had taken away a third or more of the work force. With labor shortages, prices went up, especially for the products of a greatly reduced work force of craftsmen. There were far fewer bootmakers, weavers, carpenters, masons, and smiths. There was less money being generated, and it bought less in the face of rising prices.

This was a golden time for the previously oppressed villein. Manors were lying fallow and their owners needed the income. For the first time in his life the tenant farmer's services were in short supply and he could bargain for, and get, a better share of the harvest and generally better living and working conditions. For his spare-time labor he could get double or triple the wages he was used to. Tenants began to leave their vills for better opportunities, much to the anger of their old landlords.

To put a stop to all this and restore things to comfortable normalcy, the English Parliament passed a Statute of Labourers in 1351. Primarily the statute tried to fix prices for labor at their preplague levels but it contained several extraordinary provisions. The rates for farm laborers were not just spelled out (two and a half pence for threshing a quarter of barley, five pence per acre for mowing, and so on), but, to enforce the rule, farm workers were to show themselves in market towns with their tools in their hands so that labor contracts would be made in public, not in secret. The statute forbade any extra incentives, such as meals. Farm contracts were to be made by the year and not by the day. Farm workers were to take an oath twice a year before the steward or constable of their vill, swearing that they would abide by the ordinances. They were forbidden to leave their own vills if work was available to them at home at the set prices. If any man refused to take the oath or violated the statute, he was to be put in the stocks for three days, or until he agreed to submit to the new law. For that purpose, the statute ordered that stocks be constructed in every single village in England.

Craftsmen were not overlooked. The statute set wages at three pence per day for a master carpenter, four pence for a master mason, three pence per day for roof tilers and thatchers. All producers of products—saddlers, goldsmiths, tanners, tailors, bootmakers, and so on—were to charge no more than their average price during the four years before the plague, and all were to take oaths that they would obey the law. Breaking the oath, and the law, carried an unusual punishment. For a first offense, the overcharger would be imprisoned for 40 days—with the prison term to be doubled for each subsequent offense. Thus a third offense would mean prison for 160 days (40, 80, 160). Under this provision, if a bootmaker could be convicted on nine counts of selling shoes at too high a price, the ninth offense alone would earn him 10,240 days in jail.

Attempts were made to enforce the Statute of Labourers, some vigorous, but essentially it just didn't work. It was trying to suppress a popular black market filled with eager buyers and eager sellers. Actually, the situation got worse. As farm workers and craftsmen left the market place because of death or old age, a smaller pool of new young workers took their places because of the disproportionate rate of infant and child deaths during the Black Death. Inflation continued to climb. Villeins and serfs with no claim to freedom, or who were too closely watched to be able to move elsewhere, could only go about their daily tasks in ever-reduced circumstances because of higher prices for everything they bought. Just as much victims, because they had no bargaining power, were the lower orders of the clergy. The bishops, in order to maintain themselves in a proper state of luxury and to meet the demands of a papal court whose income had been shattered by a rival claimant to the Throne of Peter, refused to increase the stipends of their ordinary clergy. This left the village priests at near-starvation levels in times of incessant inflation and gave them common ground with their parishioners against great lords, whether temporal or spiritual.

To add to the demand for goods and services, the Hundred

Years' War had begun in 1337. This war saw the change from great mobs of people struggling in hand-to-hand combat, stabbing, cutting, and thrusting at each other, to the use of improved missiles—means by which men could kill each other from a distance. Bows and arrows had been around forever, but were comparatively weak and no threat to the armor-plated warrior, nor to his position as the invincible "tank" of the medieval battlefield. Before the improved missiles the most effective weapon on the field may not have been the knight, but rather his war-horse. What today is thought of only as a heavy work-horse was bred to carry a man and his weight of weapons and armor, as well as the weight of the horse's own armor and its massive horseshoes, which were terrible weapons in themselves. No mob of infantry could withstand that massive bulk crashing into it. For the melee following the charge, the war-horse was trained to bite and kick.

Then along came the crossbow, presenting the first material threat to the battlefield superiority of the armored knight. Its short compound bow, made of layered wood, bone, and horn, could propel a short thick arrow (or "quarrel") at a speed that would penetrate light armor. Thus the armored warrior, the aristocrat in war or peace, could be killed by an opponent he could not get his hands on—worse, an opponent from the lower classes. It wasn't fair, and if it wasn't fair to the lords, it probably was not in keeping with God's will. A pope went so far as to ban the use of the crossbow by Christians, but the ban had no noticeable effect. Bans on weapons never work because they are always accompanied by the unspoken caveat, "We won't use it unless we absolutely must in order to win."

The crossbow was not the ideal weapon, because it had two shortcomings. First, the range was short. More important, the crossbow was very difficult to draw. Some had a stirrup for the bowman's foot, to hold the bow to the ground, while the bowstring was attached to a hook fastened to a strap around the bowman's waist or shoulders. He would crouch down, hook the string, and then use the entire strength of his legs and back to draw the bow to a locked position for firing. This procedure was not only slow but required strength. It required training to draw and to aim. In addition, the crossbow was relatively expensive to manufacture: A peasant subject to feudal military service would not have one lying about the house. The crossbowman became a mercenary.

It took cash to employ the crossbowman's services, not feudal obligation. At the Battle of Crecy in 1346, the crossbowmen of the French army were a band of Genoese mercenaries. On the other side, the English were about to demonstrate a weapon that immediately overshadowed the crossbow, the so-called English longbow ("so-called" because it was actually the product of Welsh ingenuity). The demonstration, that day, of the superiority of the longbow rocked all of Europe. Forget the total death toll; the important item was that over fifteen hundred fully armored French dukes, counts, and knights had fallen in one battle. That single fact changed the course of European society. Previously, knights had expected to be killed, if at all, only by each other. They held the monopoly on warfare, and so on power. Now hundreds of invincible aristocrats had been done in by a handful of the lowest level of commoner with pieces of wood and string in their hands. It changed forever the way the two classes regarded each other. No longer was the feudal levy that called a mob of untrained peasants to war of any account. Archers became professional soldiers, well trained, well paid, and well treated. They became the heroes of the hour, and they were peasant heroes. It may be impossible for us to evaluate the class distinctions that had existed before that time. The armored knights were, to the peasant, invincible, and on such a lofty plane as to be superior creatures akin to gods from another planet. One did not even contemplate standing up to them, and now the gods had dropped a notch. The knight had reason to sit in his hall and stare at the fire with wrinkled brow, and the peasant had an entirely new feeling of his own worth and pride. He might still share that new worth with his fellows in whispers, but the thought once planted continued to grow.

With the changes in the conduct of war, the king more than ever needed feudal obligations to be fulfilled with money, rather than with service. The new professional soldier worked for pay and needed to be supplied with food, equipment, and baggage animals, as well as transportation to the continent. In spite of labor shortages, inflation, and disease, the monarchy would not relent in the pursuit of the Hundred Years' War, which had started in 1337. The only answer was—quite literally—taxes, taxes, and more taxes.

Out of that state of affairs grew a situation that had to cause trouble: The landowners called upon old rights under the law, propounded by lawyers that only they could afford to hire, to take away a man's freedom and that of his descendants. Men who called themselves free were ordered to prove it. Genealogies and parish records were searched to prove that a man's mother or grandmother had been a villein or serf and that he had irrevocably inherited that status. It was the one way to use the law to get cheap and legally bound labor that could not leave for better conditions elsewhere. The only beneficiaries were the landowners. The bigger the landowner, the greater the benefit from the enforcement of villeinage, and the church was the biggest landowner of them all. It had the largest number of serfs and villeins to be held, or forced back from their temporary freedom elsewhere. Bitterness against the church grew among the common people, and the flames of their resentment were frequently fanned by the discontented lower clergy.

An Oxford priest and scholar named John Wycliffe set in motion more, perhaps, than he had intended when he began to preach church reform. He was especially incensed by the corruption of the church and by what he saw as its constant struggle for more power and material trappings, at the expense of the traditional pastoral mission of the church. He saw a direct line of contact between men and God that did not require the services of a priest. He claimed that no one but God had control over men's souls. He said that the king was answerable directly to God and did not need a papal intermediary. One of his most shocking claims, for its day, was that sacraments served by priests who were themselves sinners, and not in a state of grace, were of no effect whatever, and that included the pope. He even went so far as to translate the Vulgate Bible into English, on the grounds that all Christian men and women should have direct access to holy scripture, for in scripture he found perfection and would not question a word of it. However, he pointed out, there is no scriptural mention of a pope.

Such attacks on the church could not go unanswered, and Wycliffe was arraigned on charges of heresy at St. Paul's. That he was not sentenced to death is probably attributable to the London mob that raged in protest. Wycliffe was merely removed from his post and sent down to live in his parish of Lutterworth. He did not curtail his criticism of the church but redirected that criticism from the audience of his fellow churchmen to the people, who were of a mind to listen. His followers became wandering preaching priests and took Wycliffe's message to the towns and villages.

More immediately effective on the home front was John Ball, whom the French chronicler Jean Froissart called "a mad priest of Kent." Ball preached against class and privilege, including in the church. He also demanded agrarian reform, insisting that the landholdings of the great barons and of the church be taken away from them and distributed among the people. Since 1360 Ball and his following of priests had roamed central and southeastern England, preaching doctrines of equality of rights and the redistribution or common ownership of property. He was arrested by church authorities a number of times and finally excommunicated. In 1381, at the outbreak of the Peasants' Rebellion, he was in the archbishop's prison at Maidstone in Kent.

There had been hope that the French influence on the papacy would end when Pope Gregory XI returned the Holy See to Rome in 1377. Unfortunately, a large segment of the church hierarchy had not agreed with the move. By that time many of the cardinals were French and much preferred the French base at Avignon. When Gregory XI died the following year, the people of Rome rioted to secure their demand that the new pope be an Italian, and so he was, taking the name of Urban VI. The French cardinals declared the election invalid. They elected their own French pope, who would rule as Clement VII, and returned to Avignon. This was the Great Schism in the church, which was not healed for many years. It became a political schism as well, with the anti-Roman Clement VII at Avignon supported by France, Scotland, Portugal, Spain, and several German principalities, while the Roman pope Urban VI was supported by the enemies of France: England, Hungary, Poland, and the German Holy Roman Emperor. Each pope excommunicated all of the adherents of his rival, barring them from the sacraments, so that all across Europe every single Christian soul of the time had been damned and placed outside God's protection by one pope or the other. This was not a circumstance to be taken lightly. In one instance pro-English forces, supporters of the Roman pope, captured a French convent whose members recognized the pope at Avignon. The soldiers and their clerics had no problem agreeing that these poor misguided sisters were totally outside the protection of either civil or ecclesiastic law. Accordingly, they saw no deterrent to looting all of the possessions of the convent and raping all of the nuns. By the rules of the day, they didn't even have to mention the event at their next confessions.

And all the time, the war between England and France went on, with both sides starved for the tax revenues needed to support the conflict.

In 1377 a poll tax of fourpence per head had been imposed on all the people in England. In 1379 Parliament came up with a graduated tax based on social status. Both taxes failed, and some of the crown jewels had to be sold to maintain the war with France. In November 1380 the tax was set at one shilling per head, with the extraordinary provision that the rich should help the poor to pay the tax. They did not, of course, and the tax failed.

The English Parliament of 1376 became known to the people as the Good Parliament, primarily because it condemned corruption in the king's government. Addressing bribery, it said that the king's counselors should take nothing from any party to business brought before them except presents of little value, such as small items of food and drink. On the subject of taxation, the members asserted that if the king had loyal officers and good counselors he would be rich in treasure without any need for taxation, especially considering the "king's ransoms" exacted for the release of King David II of Scotland after his capture at the Battle of Neville's Cross in 1346 and for King John II of France, captured at the Battle of Poitiers in 1356. They suggested that the men who had bled away those fortunes should be accused and punished.

The Good Parliament also impeached a merchant of London named Richard Lyons, finding him guilty of various crimes of extortion and corruption. It was charged that, as a royal tax collector, he had generously helped himself to funds intended for the royal treasury. It was adjudged that all of his lands, goods, and chattels should be seized by the crown and that he should be imprisoned for life. Instead, Lyons's wealth and his friends secured a royal pardon for him.

The name "Good Parliament" may have been descriptive, but equally so would have been the title, "The Ignored Parliament."

So here we have an England in an incessant state of war, with skyrocketing inflation, attempts to return free men to bondage, a

Great Schism in the church that found every man in England excommunicated by the Avignon pope, a growing segment of vocally angry priests, and the burden of the highest poll tax ever levied upon the people. The powder keg was filled to the brim. In the spring of 1381, the government accelerated its efforts to collect the tax and the fuse was lit. The explosion of rebellion was just a few days away.

CHAPTER 2

"FOR NOW IS TYME TO BE WAR"

The Encyclopaedia Britannica calls it a "curiously spontaneous" rebellion.

Barbara Tuchman, in her fourteenth-century history, A *Distant Mirror*, said that the rebellion spread "with some evidence of planning."

Winston Churchill went further. In *The Birth of Britain* he wrote, "Throughout the summer of 1381 there was a general ferment. Beneath it all lay organization. Agents moved round the villages of central England, in touch with a 'Great Society' which was said to meet in London."

The spark of rebellion was being fanned vigorously, and finally the signal was given. Even though he had been arrested, excommunicated, and even now was a prisoner in the ecclesiastic prison at Maidstone, in Kent, letters went out from priest John Ball and from other priests who followed him. Clerics were then the only literate class, so letters must have been received by local priests and were obviously intended to be shared with or read aloud to others. They all contained a signal to act now, which could put to rest the concept that the rebellion was simply a spontaneous convulsion of frustration that just happened to affect a hundred thousand Englishmen at the same time. This from a letter from John Ball: "John Balle gretyth yow wele alle and doth yowe to understande, he hath rungen youre belle. Nowe ryght and myght, wylle and skylle. God spede every ydele [ideal]. *Now is tyme.*" From priest Jakke Carter: "You have gret nede to take God with yowe in alle your dedes. *For now is tyme to be war.*" From priest Jakke Trewman: "Jakke Trewman doth you to understande that falsnes and gyle have reigned too long, and trewthe hat bene sette under a lokke, and falsnes regneth in everylk flokke. . . . God do bote, *for now is tyme.*"

One letter from John Ball, "Saint Mary Priest," is worth quoting in its entirety. Even with the medieval English spelling, the meaning will be clear. Lechery and gluttony were frequent points in his accusations of high church leaders. "John Balle seynte Marye prist gretes wele alle maner men byddes hem in the name of the Trinite, Fadur, and Sone and Holy Gost stonde manlyche togedyr in trewthe, and helpez trewthe, and trewthe schal helpe yowe. Now regneth pride in pris [prize] and covetys is hold wys, and leccherye withouten shame and glotonye withouten blame. Envye regnith with tresone, and slouthe is take in grete sesone. God do bote, *for nowe is tyme* amen.*"

In all the letters quoted, the emphasis has been added to identify the common signal "now is tyme." More evidence of planning and organization would come.

The violence erupted in Essex, prompted by new and more stringent efforts to collect a third poll tax. The idea of having special commissioners to enforce the tax collection had come from the king's sergeant-at-arms, a Franciscan friar named John Legge. That idea would cost him his head a few weeks later.

The commissioners in some instances attacked their duties overzealously. Some were reported to have examined young girls to see if they had engaged in sexual intercourse, as an aid to determining whether or not they were fifteen years of age and so taxable. One man, John of Deptford, was arrested after he struck the tax gatherer who had raised his daughter's dress to see if she had pubic hair, evidence of taxable age.

In some areas the tax collectors were either simply ignored or beaten up by the villagers. A great local lord, John de Bamptoun, set himself up in the town of Brentwood in Essex and demanded that the men of the neighboring towns come to him with complete lists of names and their tax money. Over a hundred men responded to his orders—not to pay the taxes, but to inform him that they had no intention of doing so. Optimistically, de Bamp-toun ordered his two sergeants-at-arms to arrest the hundred villagers and put them in prison. The crowd angrily attacked the royal officers, and de Bamptoun counted himself lucky to be allowed to flee back to London.

In response, the government sent back Sir Robert Bealknap, chief justice of common pleas. Sir Robert came armed with specific indictments and statements signed by jurors. (In those days, jurors were the opposite of independent. They were witnesses, literally those with "wit-ness" or "possession of knowledge" of the matter at hand, and frequently they were the accusers as well). In spite of Bealknap's ponderous authority, his reception was no better than that previously accorded de Bamptoun. The locals seized the royal party and forced Bealknap to reveal the names of the jurors who had named and sworn against de Bamptoun's assailants. With that information, parties set out to hunt them down. Jurors caught were beheaded and their heads mounted on poles, as examples to others, while those who couldn't be found had their houses burned or pulled down. As for the chief justice, he was berated as a traitor to the king and to the kingdom but in the end was permitted to return to London. Not allowed to go with him were his three clerks, who were recognized as the same clerks who had been with de Bamptoun. They were beheaded.

Meanwhile, in Kent, the county just south of Essex across the Thames, a knight of the king's household, Sir Simon Burley, had come to Gravesend and had leveled against a freeman named Robert Belling the charge that Belling was Burley's serf. He set a fine of three hundred pounds in silver as the price of Belling's liberty. The men of Gravesend were outraged at both the charge and the fine, a sum they declared would ruin Belling entirely. The royal officer responded by having Belling bound and thrown into the dungeon at nearby Rochester Castle. At the same time, a tax commission had arrived in Kent on a mission similar to that of Sir Robert Bealknap in Essex; the Franciscan sergeant-at-arms John Legge came armed with specific indictments against a number of people in the county. They had planned to establish the seat of the Kentish inquiry at Canterbury, but were driven off by the local citizenry.

As word of these events spread, the men of Kent began to gather, centered on the town of Dartford. A group of Essex men

crossed the Thames in boats to join them. Showing not just organization but perhaps discipline as well, the leaders decreed that
no men who lived within twelve leagues (about thirty-six miles) of
the sea would be allowed to join their march, because those men
might be needed at home to help fight off any surprise French
attack on the English coast.

The Kentish mob moved not toward London but away from it,
heading east to lay siege to Rochester Castle, where they
demanded the release of Robert Belling. After just half a day, and
no recorded defense, the constable of the castle opened the gates
to the rebels. They released Belling and every other prisoner,
then turned south to Maidstone, where they arrived on June 7.
There they were joined by more men, including one known as
Walter the Tyler. Remarkably, he was immediately acknowledged
by thousands of men as their supreme commander and gave his
name to the rising: "Wat Tyler's Revolt." Nothing is known of
Wat Tyler's prior life, nor of the means by which a supposedly dis-
organized mob acknowledged his leadership on the very day he
arrived.

One of Tyler's first acts was to free John Ball, the "Saint Mary
Priest" of York, from the church prison at Maidstone, and Ball
became the unofficial chaplain of the expedition from that point
forward.

Still moving away from London, Tyler took his force farther
east to Canterbury, the seat of the leading churchman in
England. That Tyler planned all along for his rude army to march
on London is indicated by the rebels' first act upon their arrival
at Canterbury on Monday, June 10. Thousands of rebels crowded
into the church during high mass. After kneeling, they shouted to
the monks to elect one of their number to be the new archbishop
of Canterbury, because the present archbishop (who was off in
London with the king, who had recently appointed him chancellor of the realm) "is a traitor and will be beheaded for his iniquity,"
as indeed he was before the week was over. The rebel leaders then
asked for the names of any "traitors" in the town. Three names
were provided, and the three men were sought out and beheaded.
Then the rebels left the town, allowing just five hundred Canterbury men to join them because Canterbury was near to the coast
and the balance of the men would be needed in the event of an
attack by the French.

On the same day (June 10) that Tyler took over Canterbury in Kent, the gathering Essex mob sacked and burned a major commandery of the Knights Hospitallers called Cressing Temple. This wealthy manor had been given to the Knights Templar in 1138 by Matilda, the wife of King Stephen. When the Templars were suppressed by Pope Clement V, all of their property in Britain, including this manor of Cressing, was given to the Hospitallers. The church owned one-third of the land surface of England at that time and suffered greatly at the hands of the rebels, but no single group suffered losses comparable to those inflicted over the next few days on the Knights Hospitallers, who seemed to be on an especially aggressive hit list of the rebel leaders.

The following day, June 11, the rebels in both Essex and Kent turned toward London. Even with the burning, beheading, and destruction of records along the way, their purpose and discipline were such that both groups, upwards of a hundred thousand men, made the seventy-mile journey in two days, reaching the city at almost the same time.

Warned of the rebels' approach, the fourteen-year-old King Richard II moved from Windsor to the Tower of London, the strongest fortress in the kingdom. He was joined there by an entourage that included Sir Simon Sudbury, who was both archbishop of Canterbury and chancellor; Sir Robert Hales, who was both the king's treasurer and the prior of the order of the Knights of the Hospital of St. John of Jerusalem (the Hospitallers); Henry Bolingbroke, who would one day depose Richard and take the throne himself as Henry IV; the earls of Oxford, Kent, Arundel, Warwick, Suffolk, and Salisbury; and other peers and lesser officials, including the chief justice Sir Robert Bealknap, the unsuccessful tax collector John de Bamptoun, and the hated Franciscan sergeant-at-arms, John Legge. They all had reason to fear for their lives at the hands of the rebel horde advancing on the city.

On June 12 the Essex men began arriving at Mile End, near Aldgate. Across the river, the Kentish rebels gathered at Southwark, at the south end of London Bridge. Confederates and sympathizers streamed out of London to join them. One Kentish group came through nearby Lambeth, on the south side of the Thames, and sacked the archbishop's palace there, burning the furnishings and all the records they could find. (On that same day, across the river in the Tower, from where he could see the smoke rising from his palace, the archbishop returned the Great Seal to the king and asked to be relieved of his public duties as chancellor.) Other rebel groups broke open the prisons on the south side of the river, including the ecclesiastic prison of the bishops of Winchester on Clink Street, a location that gave the name "the clink" to prisons everywhere. On smashing open the Marshalsea prison in Southwark, the mob searched for its commander, Richard Imworth, famous for his cruelty. Unable to locate Imworth, they contented themselves, for the moment, with the destruction of his house.

Messengers went out to the rebels from the king, asking the reason for this disturbance of the peace of the land. The answer came back that the uprising was dedicated to saving the king and to destroying traitors to king and country. The king's reply to this was to ask the rebels to cease their depredations and wait until he could meet with them to resolve all injustices against them. The rebels agreed and asked the king to meet with them early in the morning of June 13 at Blackheath on the Thames, a few miles from London. The men of Kent gathered at the meeting place on the south bank of the river and the men of Essex on the north. The king and his party left the Tower in four barges but only got as far as the royal manor at Rotherhithe, near Greenwich, where Archbishop Sudbury and Sir Robert Hales persuaded the party to get no closer to the rebels. Upon learning that the king was not coming to them as promised, the Kentish leaders sent the king a petition asking him for the heads of fifteen men. Their list included the archbishop of Canterbury, the prior of the Hospitallers, Chief Justice Bealknap, and the tax collectors John Legge and John de Bamptoun. Not surprisingly, the royal council would not agree to these demands, and the barges returned to the Tower. Each on their own side of the river, the Essex men moved toward Aldgate and the Kentish faction marched back toward Southwark and London Bridge. For reasons we shall probably never know, Aldgate was undefended, and the Essex rebels simply walked into the city. As much mystery attaches to the approach of the Kentish mob to London Bridge. No attempt was made to man the fortified gatehouse, and the drawbridge was lowered for them to cross.

Moving through the city, the rebels touched nothing until they reached Fleet Street. There they attacked the Fleet prison and released all the inmates. They destroyed two forges that the Hospitallers had taken over from the Templars. Some joined a London mob and went to the Savoy Palace of the hated royal uncle, John of Gaunt, pausing on the way only to destroy any houses they could identify as belonging to the Hospitallers. The Savoy Palace itself was destroyed in a mood of rage. Furniture and art objects were smashed, linens and tapestries were burned. Jewels were hammered to powder. Finally the building was set aflame, boosted by the addition of several kegs of gunpowder.

From the Savoy the rebels returned to the Hospitaller property between Fleet Street and the Thames, to buildings leased by that order to lawyers who practiced before the king's court in the adjoining royal city of Westminster. They vandalized and burnt the lawyers' buildings, burnt their records, and killed anyone who registered an objection. They destroyed the other Hospitaller buildings on the property, with one exception. Instead of burning the rolls and records stored in the church where they found them, they went to the trouble of carrying them out into the high road for burning, avoiding any damage to the church itself. One historian goes so far as to say that certain of the mob "protected" the church from damage. This attitude was an anomaly in the midst of an orgy of destruction of church property and church leaders. This property, too, had been taken from the Templars and given to the Hospitallers, and even today that portion of the City of London is known simply as "The Temple." The church that was left unscathed by the rebels had been the principal church of the Knights Templar in England. This attitude toward the old Templar church stands out in marked contrast to the mob's feeling for the grand priory of the Hospitallers at Clerkenwell, where they turned next. Still seeking out Hospitaller property for destruction along the way, they arrived at Clerkenwell and embarked upon an effort of total destruction. While the Templar church still stands today, all that remains of the principal Hospitaller church at Clerkenwell is the underground crypt.

Some of the mob went from London into the City of Westminster, where they released all of the prisoners in Westminster prison. Moving back into London, they did the same at the famous Newgate prison, taking chains and shackles to place on the altar of a nearby church.

One group went to the Tower to seek an audience with the

king. When they were unsuccessful, they laid siege to the Tower. Word was sent out by the rebel leaders to the bands still roving the city that every member of the Chancery and Exchequer, every lawyer, and anyone who could write a writ or letter should be beheaded. Ink-stained fingers were enough to condemn a man to death on the spot. The church at that time had a virtual monopoly on literacy, so the victims were most likely to be administrative clerics, who also held a near monopoly on what we might now think of as the "civil service" of the king's government.

So far, the king's council had appeared numbed into inactivity, but something had to be done, and finally a plan was agreed upon. It could not be based on force, because they had no force. The weapons they did have were trickery and deceit. Word was cried out in every ward of the City that on the following morning of Friday, June 14, the king and his council would meet with the rebels and that all of their demands would be satisfied. The promise was easily made because there was no intention to keep it. The place selected was the open fields at Mile End, outside the City beyond the Aldgate. It was expected that this move would achieve the initial goal of pulling the rebels out of the City. In fact, most of them did go, but Wat Tyler and his chief lieutenant, Jack Strawe, stayed behind with several hundred men. Their "chaplain," the priest John Ball, stayed with them. The rebel leadership had something more important to do than meet with the king to discuss manumission of villeinage and serfdom.

In those days, the Thames came right up to and inside the south wall of the Tower, so there was direct access by means of a water gate. As the king's party made ready to go to Mile End on Friday morning, the archbishop of Canterbury tried to escape by boat. He was recognized, and the ensuing hue and cry caused his crew to beat its way back through the water gate to the safety of the Tower.

As promised, the king's party left the Tower to meet the rebels at Mile End. Chroniclers tell us that he was accompanied by such dignitaries as the earls of Kent, Warwick, and Oxford, as well as by the mayor of London and "many knights and squires." What they do not tell us is why he was *not* accompanied by two of his very highest officials, Sir Simon Sudbury, who was the archbishop of Canterbury and chancellor of the realm, and Sir Robert Hales, who was prior of the order of the Knights Hospitaller and the king's treasurer. We shall never know whether they chose to stay behind or were ordered to do so. There is also no record of who spoke for the rebels at Mile End while Tyler, Strawe, and Ball were on a mission more important to them back in London.

At the meeting place all seemed to go well. The rebels asked two things: first, that they should have the right to hunt down and execute all traitors to the king and common people, and second, that no man should be bound to another in serfdom or villeinage. Every Englishman should be a free man. As to the first request, the king agreed that all "traitors" should be put to death, provided that they were proven guilty under the law. He asked that all such accused be brought to him for trial. As to the request for universal freedom, he had brought about thirty clerks with him, who began speedily grinding out writs of manumission.

As soon as the king was safely out of the City, Tyler, Strawe, and Ball made their move. Incredibly, their plan was to take the Tower of London with a few hundred ill-armed men. The Tower had been built to be the most secure fortress in Britain, so secure that it housed the royal mint. It was equipped with a heavy gate, an iron portcullis, and a drawbridge. At the time of Tyler's approach, the Tower was manned by professional soldiers, including hundreds of experienced archers. It had leadership and authority in the person of Archbishop Sudbury and, even more so, in the person of Sir Robert Hales, commander of a military order.

Here again, there had to have been collusion and friends on the inside. Tyler and his small band found the drawbridge down, the portcullis up, the gate open. They simply walked into the Tower. No contemporary chronicler refers to so much as a scuffle.

Inside, the archbishop had sung a mass and had confessed the prior of the Hospitallers and others. The rebels found him at prayer in the chapel of the Tower. A priest tried to hold them back by holding the consecrated host in front of them, a practice known to turn aside all manner of demons and evil spirits, but the rebels simply brushed him aside. The archbishop was beaten to the floor and dragged out of the chapel and out of the Tower by his arms and hood. Others dragged out the prior of the Hospitallers, while still others searched the rooms for their proscribed victims. Among these were the Franciscan sergeant-at-arms and tax collector John Legge and another Franciscan friar, William Appleton, physician and counselor to John of Gaunt. The captured men were all led out to Tower Hill, where a great crowd had gathered. With background roars of approval, the rebels struck off the heads of their special prisoners, which were put on poles and taken to be mounted on London Bridge. As an aid to identifying the archbishop of Canterbury, they took his miter along and nailed it to his head.

After the execution, the rebels and the London mob broke out through the City, looking for additional victims. One man was beheaded simply because he spoke well of Friar William Appleton, whom the rebels had executed at Tower Hill. By the time their fury had abated, the rebels had beheaded about 160 of their enemies. An especially noteworthy target was Richard Lyons, the wealthy London burgess who had been impeached and found guilty of many acts of corruption by the Parliament of 1376. He had been sentenced to life imprisonment, but his influence was such that appeals to the king by his friends had resulted in his being restored to freedom. There was no appeal from the judgment of the rebel mob that pulled him from his house and summarily chopped off his head.

While the rebels roamed the City with their hit list, the rebel leadership mounted another unexplained project of its own. A group was organized and sent out from London by Wat Tyler, commanded by his lieutenant Jack Strawe and apparently guided by Londoner Thomas Farndon. They marched about six miles out of London for the very specific purpose of destroying the Hospitaller manor at Highbury, which a contemporary chronicler said had been "recently and skillfully rebuilt like another paradise."

Word of the rebel violence at the Tower and in the City reached Mile End, and the royal party came back to London. They did not return to the fortress of the Tower but went directly to the king's wardrobe near Castle Baynard, where his clerks continued to execute writs of manumission. Many of the rebels took those writs for themselves or their villages and headed back to their homes.

History gives us no clue as to how or why it was arranged, but agreement was somehow reached that the king would meet again with the rebels at Smithfield on the following day, Saturday, June 15. In the early morning of that day, the king and his party were met by the prior and canons of Westminster Abbey, all barefoot, who led them to the abbey cathedral for services, accompanied by a number of curious rebels. The king heard mass at the high altar and left a gift for the abbey. Rebels behind the altar recognized Richard Imworth, the hated tormentor and marshal of the Marshalsea prison, hiding in the shrine of St. Edward the Confessor. When Imworth saw that he had been spotted, he clamped his arms around one of the marble columns of the shrine and cried for mercy. The unmoved rebels pried his arms loose from the column and carried him out to Cheapside, where he was publicly beheaded.

Gradually the rebels gathered to await the king at Smithfield. They lined up on one side of the great open field, while the king's party and its excort lined up on the opposite side, in front of St. Bartholemew's Hospital.

What happened next is usually cited as the result of the insulting behavior of Wat Tyler, but was more likely the result of a plan. Any force grossly outnumbered is likely to give thought to a victory by means of the death of the opposing leader. In any case, Mayor William Walworth was sent over to the rebel side to invite Wat Tyler to meet with the king. Tyler would be far from his men, and he recognized the danger. As a safety measure he demonstrated a hand signal, upon which the rebels should charge forward and kill everyone except the king. Accompanied by just one man carrying a banner, Tyler rode across the broad field.

All of the accounts of what happened during the next few minutes were written from the viewpoint of the government, not the rebels, and most of those accounts were recorded by people who weren't there. It appears that Tyler recited a list of demands to the king that included the repeal of laws of serfdom and of the game laws, the end of men being declared out-law (outside the protection of the law), the seizure of church property and its division among the people who worked it, and the appointment of just one bishop of the church for all of England.

Putting aside all of the versions of the cause, what happened was that at one point Mayor Walworth drew his baselard (a double-edged dagger) and struck at Tyler, cutting his neck. Ralph Standish, one of the king's squires, drew his sword and stabbed Tyler twice. Tyler tried to turn his horse back to his own men, but dropped to the ground, mortally wounded.

The confused mob on the other side of the field could not clearly see what had happened. The young king was said to have cantered over to the rebel side, whether alone or with escorts we don't know, and to have held up his hand. He told the rebels that he would personally be their "chief and captain" and that they could look to him for the accomplishment of all their goals. He told them to meet with him at the fields by Clerkenwell, where the Hospitaller priory was still burning. At this, he rejoined his own group, which quickly moved off toward Clerkenwell, leaving the confused rebels discussing what they should do next. Some went out to pick up their dying leader and take him into St. Bartholemew's Hospital.

It took the rebels about an hour to reach a common decision and to set off for Clerkenwell. During that time, and probably earlier, Sir Robert Knolles, starting with about two hundred retainers of his own, was gathering forces in London to oppose the rebels, their courage undoubtedly strengthened by the news that Wat Tyler had fallen. Mayor Walworth, too, sent out word for every able-bodied man to grab such weapons as he could and make all speed to Clerkenwell to support the king.

At Clerkenwell the rebels demanded the heads of those who had struck down Wat Tyler. As they argued and demanded, the armed Londoners gathered around and behind them. Finally Sir Robert Knolles could inform the king that six thousand men had gathered to protect him. The rebels at Clerkenwell were outnumbered. The king now demanded that they disperse to avoid punishment for their actions. Seeing their predicament, the rebel band began to break up. The only organized group was made up of men of Kent, led by Jack Strawe and John Ball. They were led out of the City, back over London Bridge, which they had crossed in triumph just three days earlier.

Upon the breakup of the rebels, William Walworth went looking for Wat Tyler. He found him having his grave wounds tended at St. Bartholemew's Hospital and ordered that he be dragged outside, where his head was struck off. Mounted on a pole, it was sent to relace the heads of Archbishop Sudbury and Sir Robert Hales on London Bridge.

There in the field, King Richard knighted William Walworth, Ralph Standish, and other burgesses of the City. For London the rebellion was over, but not so outside the city, where the rebellion had its expression in dozens of towns, manors, and priories at locations hundreds of miles apart.

While the revolt in London has received most of the attention of history, our quest for evidence of organization requires that we take a brief look at events in other parts of England, where the rebellion went on even after Tyler's death.

On Wednesday, June 12, when the rebels were gathered outside the walls of London, sacking Lambeth Palace and breaking open the Marshalsea prison, a priest named John Wrawe appeared at Liston in Suffolk with a band of rebels, sending out messages of recruitment to nearby towns. His first move was to destroy the manor at Liston belonging to that same Richard Lyons who had been impeached for fraud and corruption by the Good Parliament of 1376 and then pardoned by the crown. (Lyons himself was taken from his townhouse and beheaded by the rebels in London. The attack on Lyons's estate was certainly not mere happenstance.)

Wrawe's next target was Bury St. Edmunds, the largest town in Suffolk. It was totally ruled by the local monastery, which had consistently refused to grant any municipal rights to the craftsmen and traders of the town. The rebels were permitted to enter, after threatening to kill anyone who opposed them. Townsmen were ready to guide the mob to their immediate sack of the homes of officials of the order, including that of the prior, who fled at their approach to the monastery at Mildenhall, about twelve miles away. The next day the prior decided to try to get farther away by boat but found rebels on the riverbank, blocking his escape. He managed to elude his pursuers and make for the woods, accompanied by a local guide. The guide went back to the rebels and informed them that the prior was in the woods, so they circled the area, then gradually closed the ring and found the prior. Taking their prisoner at dawn to Mildenhall, they cut off his head and mounted it on a pole. It became their banner as they marched back to Bury, where they placed the head in the public pillory.

Next came news of the escape route of Sir John Cavendish, chief justice of the realm and chancellor of Cambridge University. His flight was thwarted at the ferry at Brandon, near Mildenhall, when a woman cut loose and pushed off the only available boat before Cavendish could get to it. He was seized and beheaded on the spot and his head sent back to Bury to join the head of the prior, already in the pillory. The mob found ghoulish amusement in putting Cavendish's lips to the prior's ear as if in confession, and pushing their lips together to kiss.

Wrawe stayed a week in Bury, forcing the monks to give up records and taking their silver and jewels as bond for a charter of freedom drawn up for the town. During that week he also sent out messengers and envoys to spread the rebellion, who in some cases demanded gold and silver as ransom to save private and church property from destruction. In addition, he dispatched a force of about five hundred men to take nearby Nottingham Castle. Although it was well fortified with high walls and a series of draw-bridged moats, there appears to have been no resistance to the rebels, who looted the castle of its portable valuables.

To the north of Suffolk, in the county of Norfolk, the principal leader was Geoffrey Litster, not a "peasant" but a prosperous wool dyer. His second-in-command was Sir Roger Bacon of Baconthorpe.

Their first objective was the capture of Norwich, where Litster made the castle his headquarters. Several houses of prominent citizens were sacked and a justice of the peace named Reginald Eccles was dragged to the public pillory, where he was stabbed in the stomach and then beheaded. Sir Roger Bacon took a contingent out of Norwich to the port town of Great Yarmouth, which had angered its neighbors with a charter that required all living within seven miles of Great Yarmouth to do all of their trading in the town, regardless of the opportunities to buy for less or sell at a higher price elsewhere. This must have been a very specific target, because Bacon did not burn the charter. Instead, he tore it in two and sent one half to Litster and one half to Wrawe.

To the west, a band of rebels attacked the property of the Hospitallers at the market town of Watton. From the preceptor they extracted a written forgiveness of all debts to the order, plus a promise of a subsequent money payment in compensation for past transgressions.

While all this was happening, messengers came into Cambridgeshire from London and from John Wrawe in Suffolk, both reporting high levels of success and urging the locals to rise. On June 14 the first rebel attack in Cambridgeshire singled out a manor of the Knights Hospitaller at Chippenham. The next day the revolt exploded at a dozen different places throughout the county. Men rode through the county announcing that serfdom had ended. One man, Adam Clymme, ordered that no man, whether bound or free, should obey any lord or perform any services for him, upon pain of beheading, unless otherwise ordered by the Great Society (*magna societas*). All-out rage was directed at tax collectors, justices of the peace, and religious landowners. Attacks were made on the religious orders at Icklington, Ely, and Thorney, and on the Hospitallers' manor at Duxford.

On Saturday, June 15, the day Wat Tyler was struck down in London, certain prominent citizens of the city of Cambridge, burgesses and bailiffs among them, rode out with the full approval of their mayor to meet the rebels and plan their common attack on the University. They met the rebels in two groups, the first about fifteen miles from the city, attacking the Knights Hospitallers' manor at Shingay, and the other a couple of miles farther on, destroying the house of Thomas Haseldon, controller to the duke of Lancaster.

The combined forces returned to the city, where a signal for the rising of the town was given by tolling the bells of Great St. Mary's Church. The first religious target was the University, where the mob went to the house of the chancellor, Sir John Cavendish. They had not yet learned of his execution by the rebels at Bury St. Edmunds, so upon finding him not at home they smashed the furniture and anything else breakable.

Next on the list was wealthy Corpus Christi College, to which as many as one out of six townspeople paid rent. Everyone had vacated the college premises in fear of the rebels, who gave themselves over to an evening frenzy of smashing, burning, and stealing.

The next day was Sunday, and some churches tried to have business as usual. A mob broke into Great St. Mary's Church while mass was in progress and carried off records and anything they could find in the way of jewels and silver. They broke into the House of the Carmelites (on the site later occupied by Queen's College) and carried off records and books, which they burned in the marketplace.

A group of about a thousand rebels left the city to attack the priory at nearby Barnwell. There they pulled down walls and vandalized the buildings. Giving vent to specific grievances, they chopped down trees that they had been forbidden to use for firewood or lumber and drained ponds in which they were not allowed to fish.

The rising in Yorkshire requires special consideration, not only because it took place so far from London, but because of the primary involvement of craftsmen and others of the towns. The absence of any material participation of the rural population has even led some historians to the conclusion that the rising in Yorkshire was not really part of the Peasants' Rebellion, even though it occurred at the same time. If there were no peasants, how could it have been part of a peasant rebellion? The truth is that the major impacts of the revolt had come from substantial cooperation between rural and town dwellers, as we have seen at Cambridge, Bury St. Edmunds, St. Albans, and nowhere more than in London itself. That being the case, it appears foolish to say that events involving farmers only were part of the rebellion, but events involving townspeople only were not. Certainly there was communication with the other rebels, and, even more certainly, a high degree of organization in the risings at York, Scarborough, and Beverly.

These three Yorkshire towns are situated like points of an equilateral triangle about forty to fifty miles apart, a great traveling distance in those times. Scarborough is on the sea, and was reputed to be the only safe harbor between the Humber and the Tyne. Beverly, due south of Scarborough, boasted a thriving industry in woolen yarns and textiles. York, to the west, laterally about midway between Scarborough and Beverly, was the largest city in the north and the second largest city in England.

On June 22, 1381, one week after the death of Wat Tyler, royal letters patent were sent to just five towns in the north. These letters called for public mourning for the deaths of Archbishop Sudbury, Sir Robert Hales, and Chief Justice Sir John Cavendish. More important, the letters decreed that the local authorities were to permit no illegal assemblies whatsoever. Three of the five letters went to York, Scarborough, and Beverly. The royal court's fears were totally justified, but the letters arrived too late to prompt any preventive measures—the riots had begun five days before they were written. By Monday, June 17, the rebels in York had news of the revolt in London that had started just four days earlier on June 13. On that one day of June 17, 1381, the mob in York attacked the headquarters of the Dominican order, the friary of the Franciscans, St. Leonard's Hospital, and the Chapel of St. George.

A few days later, a former mayor of York named John de Gisburne appeared at Bootham Bar, one of the gates of York, with an armed party on horseback. They forced their way in and joined other rebels in the city. Most interestingly, de Gisburne's men were wearing a "livery" (a uniform item of decoration or clothing common to a group). In this case, it appears to have been a white woolen hood. Similar livery showed up in Beverly and Scarborough, where the records have left us a better description. The livery there was described as a white capuchon with a red liripipe. The capuchon was a common item of medieval clothing, a hood attached to enough cloth to cover the shoulders like a shawl. The point at the back of the hood was often drawn out to a long exaggerated taper, much as the toes of shoes were exaggerated. This long point was the liripipe, which could also end in a tasseled decoration. The livery, then, was a white hood with a red tail or tassel.

It would take about six square feet of woolen cloth to make one hooded shawl. In all three cities we are told that about fifteen hundred of these liveries were used by the rebels. That would require about one thousand square yards of white woolen cloth, plus the decorative red tails. Such material involved a great deal of cost and a great deal of work, more work than could have been executed in a few days in total secrecy. John de Gisburne had brought a supply of liveries with him from outside York to distribute to the rebels in the city, and most likely they came from Beverly, where the principal industry was the manufacture of woolen textile products. We have no idea how they got to Scarborough, where over five hundred men were reported to be wearing them. The presence of this common uniform not only speaks to preparation, but to the involvement of all three towns in some kind of common effort.

Common to all three towns, too, was the swearing of oaths of the "all for one and one for all" type used to seal a fraternal bond.

Another distinctive feature of the Yorkshire risings is the principal target of the violence. Although church property was attacked, the antireligious activities were a sideshow to the attacks on the ruling families, the wealthy merchants who comprised oligarchies in each town to the exclusion of the lesser merchants and craftsmen. We read in later indictments that the Scarborough leaders included William de la Marche, draper; John Cant, shoemaker; Thomas Symson, basket maker. In Beverly we find rebel leaders Thomas Whyte, tiler; and Thomas Preston, skinner. In York, Robert de Harom, mercer, was accused as one passing out "liveries of one color to various members of their confederacy."

In his very authoritative *Oriental Despotism*, Karl A. Wittfogel wrote: "The rise of private property and enterprise in handicraft and commerce created conditions that resulted in social conflicts, of many kinds, among urban commoners. In medieval Europe such conflicts were fought out with great vigor. Not infrequently the social movements assumed the proportions of a mass (and class) struggle which in some towns compelled the merchants to share political leadership with the artisans."

Mr. Wittfogel would have understood exactly what the rebels of York, Beverly, and Scarborough were about. And if the concept of a ruling oligarchy of certain families is a confusing one, one might shed light on it by studying the power structure of county government today in much of the American Southeast.

Although there were dozens of other incidents in England, we shall look at just one more, the revolt against the Benedictines of St. Albans, the largest landowners in Hertfordshire.

Back on June 14, the day the rebels broke into the Tower of London, men arrived at St. Albans saying that they had been commanded to collect all of the able-bodied men of St. Albans and Barnet. These men were to arm themselves with any available weapons and follow the messengers to London, and they were quickly assembled because the abbot gave his approval as a means to divert the mob away from his own domains. As the men of St. Albans approached London, they came upon Jack Strawe and his band destroying the Hospitaller manor at Highbury. They enthusiastically joined in the fun and then followed Strawe back to London. In the City their leaders met with Wat Tyler to discuss their desire to take the rebellion home to St. Albans. He instructed them as to the manner in which they should seek their freedom from the abbey. They swore to obey his commands explicitly, and

Tyler in turn told them that if they had any trouble with the abbot, the prior, or the monks, he would march on St. Albans with twenty thousand men to "shave their beards" (cut off their heads).

The Benedictines of St. Albans had held autocratic sway over the town and the countryside for over two hundred years. They were well known for scrupulously guarding every prerogative of the abbey and for zealously collecting every fee and every service due them under the ancient manorial contracts. They could not be expected to voluntarily yield a single point of freedom from manorial obligation to town or tenants, especially under their current abbot, Thomas de la Mare.

The St. Albans mob returned from London to great rejoicing, as they spread the word that the king had freed all serfs and villeins. Messengers went out in all directions, issuing orders from the rebel leader, William Grindcobbe, that all men must arm themselves and gather the next day, Saturday, June 15. Those who refused would suffer death and the destruction of their houses.

On the Saturday, a mob of several thousand men assembled and were administered an oath to be faithful and true to their brothers-in-arms. Marching to the abbey, they demanded and gained entrance. Next they demanded the release of all the men being held in the church prison. In freeing the prisoners, they agreed that one was guilty and not worthy of freedom, so they took him out to the mob in front of the abbey gates, where he was beheaded.

About 9:00 A.M. a rider galloped up to the rebels. He was Richard of Wallingford, a substantial tenant farmer on abbey land. He had stayed behind in London to get a letter from the king that would reestablish ancient peasant claims relating to rights of grazing, hunting, fishing, and other freedoms.

Armed with the king's letter, written just that morning, the leaders demanded to meet with the abbott. Reading their letter, the abbott responded that the rights spoken of were very ancient and had been terminated generations ago. He shrewdly maneuvered the leaders into a negotiating posture, while outside the impatient rebels broke fences and gates, tore down walls, and generally vandalized the monastic property. They drained the fish ponds and hung a dead rabbit on a pole as a banner to proclaim the end of the strict game laws. Hours went by in debate, until word arrived of the death of Wat Tyler. The attitude of the rebels changed instantly, as did that of the abbot. He pressed his advantage, and with the sure knowledge that Tyler's support column would not be coming, while the royal troops most assuredly would, the rebels caved in, even agreeing to put up two hundred pounds to compensate for damaged property.

The rebels were right. The royal troops were on the way, accompanied by a new chief justice, Robert Tresilian. The new chief justice was out for blood. The announcement came that all writs issued by the king to the rebels were null and void. On June 18 royal letters went out charging all sheriffs to put down the rebels in their districts and charging all knights and nobles to assist in the effort. The government's numbness and shock having now apparently worn off, the counter-rebel forces, far better armed for battle than their adversaries, set about the task of dispersing the rebels and arresting their leaders. Now was the time for judicial vengeance.

CHAPTER 3

"WHETHER JUSTLY OR OUT OF HATE"

"The time came for the King to punish the delinquents," wrote the monk Henry Knighton. "Lord Robert Tresilian, justice, [who had been appointed to replace the murdered chief justice, Sir John Cavendish] was therefore sent by the King's command to investigate and punish those who had risen against the peace. He was active everywhere, and spared no one, causing a great slaughter. And because the malefactors had attacked and put to death all the justices they could find, including John de Cavendish, and had spared the lives of none of the lawyers of the realm whom they could apprehend, so Tresilian now spared no one but repaid like for like. For whoever was accused before him on the grounds of rebellion, whether justly or out of hate, immediately suffered the sentence of death. He condemned (according to their crimes) some to beheading, some to hanging, some to drawing through the cities and then hanging in four parts of the cities and some to disembowelling, followed by the burning of their entrails before them while the victims were still alive, and then their execution and the division of their corpses into quarters to be hanged in four parts of the cities."

The priest John Ball was captured in Coventry and brought to St. Albans on July 12 to be tried before Chief Justice Tresilian. The trial took place the next day. Ball made no attempt to recant, expressed no regrets, and admitted to authorship of the letters that had gone out over his name. Tresilian drew upon the whole catalog of execution techniques and sentenced Ball to be hanged, drawn, disemboweled, beheaded, and quartered.

William Grindcobbe, the principal rebel leader at St. Albans, was released on bail with the provision that he use his influence to calm the people. He did the opposite. One speech attributed to him was, "Friends, who after so long an age of repression have at last won yourselves a short breath of freedom, hold firm while you can, and have no thought of me or what I may suffer, for if I die for the cause of the liberty we have won, I shall think myself happy to end my life as a martyr." Which is exactly what he did, as he was summarily recaptured and executed.

Men of St. Albans whose bodies had been left intact, including Grindcobbe, were taken down from the gallows and buried by their friends. A couple of weeks later an angry order came from the king's court, demanding that the bodies be dug up and hanged on public display until they rotted apart.

Off in Norwich, the rebel leader Geoffrey Litster learned of the death of Wat Tyler and the collapse of the revolt in London. In response, he decided to send a delegation to the king, requesting a charter of manumission and pardon for all Norfolk. The mission was ostensibly headed by two hostage knights, Sir William de Morley and Sir John de Brewe, but with them went three of Litster's closest followers, to make certain that the two knights followed Litster's orders. As an extra incentive for the king to look with favor upon their requests, the mission leaders took with them as a royal gift all of the money that they had collected as fines on the citizens of Norwich. On the way, near the town of Newmarket, the delegation had the great misfortune to cross the path of the warlike Lord Henry le Despenser, bishop of Norwich. The young Bishop le Despenser had been at his manor of Burleigh, near Stamford, when he got word of the uprisings in Norfolk. He decided to return to his diocese of Norwich, taking with him eight mounted knights and a small company of archers. As evidence of some military background, he wore a metal helmet, a hauberk, and a fighting sword. He recruited from the local gentry, adding to his force as he advanced. At Peterborough the rebels had demanded charters and writs of manumission and were just starting to ransack the monastery when le Despenser hit them with a surprise attack. He ordered a number of rebels killed on the spot and the rest imprisoned. At Ramsey in Huntingdonshire, the bishop's force easily defeated a small group of rebels at the monastery. They were taken prisoner and turned over to the abbot as the bishop pressed on to Cambridge. By now his group had grown to a small army, including many experienced military men, and the Cambridge rebels were quickly brought under control. Unlike the secular reprisals by law, the bishop acted as accuser, judge, and jury. He designated the rebels to be executed and those to be imprisoned.

Leaving Cambridge, le Despenser continued toward his own diocese at Norwich. It was on that leg of his journey that he met the mission to the king that had been dispatched by the rebel leader Geoffrey Litster. The two hostage knights told him of their forced mission under the control of the three rebel leaders, two of whom were in the camp, while the third had gone off to forage for their supper. The bishop ordered the immediate beheading of the two rebel leaders present and sent a detachment to find the third. Once the three heads were mounted on the pillory in nearby Newmarket, le Despenser moved on, his army steadily increasing in size as it was joined by now-eager recruits.

At Norwich the bishop found that Litster had flown at his approach. Le Despenser went after him and Litster's band made a stand near North Walsham. They were easily overwhelmed by the bishop's army, and among the prisoners taken was Geoffrey Litster himself. The bishop immediately ordered that he be executed by hanging, drawing, and beheading, then personally heard Litster's confession and granted absolution. The bishop then gained the accolades of his fellow ecclesiastics for his mercy and piety as he walked beside the prisoner being dragged by his feet to the gallows, holding up the rebel leader's head so that it wouldn't hit the rocks in the road. (Litster himself, in view of what was about to be done to him, might have considered it more merciful to be allowed to be knocked unconscious by the rocks.)

The rebellion in Norfolk had been put down swiftly and totally, albeit ruthlessly, by the efforts of one angry man, a service that would seem to merit the gratitude of the king's court even though the law of the land had been ignored for a few days. To the contrary, someone (because the king was still not of age) arranged that Bishop le Despenser be impeached two years later, in 1383,

for his conduct in putting down the rebellion in Norfolk in contravention of the law.

On July 16 writs went out calling for a parliament to convene
on September 16, but the meeting was postponed until November 4, 1381. If the Parliament of 1376 deserves to be remembered
as the "Good Parliament," the 1381 session could well be memorialized as the "I-Told-You-So Parliament."

The 1376 Parliament had cited corruption in the king's court,
bribery, diversion of tax monies, and inept management. The
members had warned the royal council that these things must be
corrected. They had impeached the London merchant and finan-
cier Richard Lyons on a variety of charges of corruption, only to
have the sentence of life imprisonment set aside. All of their
fears, advice, and actions had been ignored, but now the rebellion
had proven their points.

It can only have been with a deep feeling of smug satisfaction
that the members of the November 1381 Parliament listened to
the charge given to them by the king and his council, as read to
them by the speaker, Sir Hugh Seagrave:

> "Our lord the King, here present, whom God save, has com-
> manded me to make the following declaration to you. First our
> lord the King, desiring above all that the liberty of Holy Church
> should be entirely preserved without blemish, and that the estate,
> peace and good government of his kingdom should be maintained
> and preserved as best it was in the time of any of his noble progen-
> itors, the kings of England, wills that if any default can be found
> anywhere, this should be amended by the advice of the prelates
> and lords in this parliament." (We can hear a slouched back-
> bencher muttering under his breath, "If you'd kept your bloody
> ear-holes open five years ago, you'd know the answers already.")

The parliamentary roll leaves no doubt as to where that parliament laid the blame for the revolt (the word *commons* refers to
the common people, not to a House of Parliament that did not yet
exist):

> "If the government of the realm was not shortly to be amended,
> the very kingdom itself would be completely lost and destroyed for
> all time and, as a result, the lord our King and all the lords and
> commons, which God, in his mercy, forfend. For it is true that

there are many faults in said government, about the King's person, and in his household and because of the outrageous number of servants in the latter, as well as in the King's courts, that is to say in the Chancery, King's Bench, Common Bench and the Exchequer. And there are grievous oppressions throughout the country because of the outrageous multitude of embracers of quarrels and maintainers, who act like kings in the country, so that justice and law are scarce administered to anybody. And the poor commons are from time to time despoiled and destroyed in these ways, both by the purveyors of the said royal household and others who pay nothing to the commons for the victuals and carriage taken from them, and by the subsidies and tallages [literally, "cuts," taxes] levied upon them to their great distress, and by other grievous and outrageous oppressions done to them by various servants of our lord the King and other lords of the realm—and especially by the said maintainers. For these reasons the said commons are brought to great wretchedness and misery, more than they ever were before."

Having had its say on the subjects of burdensome taxes and of corruption in the royal court and the legal system, Parliament next turned to the national defense, a major reason given for that taxation:

"One might add that although great treasure is continually granted and levied from the commons for the defense of the realm, they are nevertheless no better defended and succoured against the King's enemies, as far as they know. For, from year to year, the said enemies burn, rob and pillage by land and sea with their barges, galleys and other vessels; for which no remedy has been, nor is yet, provided. Which mischiefs the said poor commons, who once used to live in all honour and prosperity, can no longer endure in any way."

All of which, in the self-serving opinion of Parliament, was the clear-cut cause of the rebellion: "And to speak the truth, the said outrages as well as others which have lately been done to the poor commons, more generally than ever before, made the said poor commons feel so hardly oppressed that they caused the said mean commons to rise and commit the mischief they did in the said riot." Then a warning to the king and his council: "And greater mischiefs are to be feared if good and proper remedy is not provided in time for the above mentioned outrageous oppression and mischiefs."

Parliament had a suggested solution, of course, which reflected its principal objective over the past years: a stronger voice in the central government and greater influence on the selection of men to serve in that government:

> "It suggested that the commons can be restored to quiet and peace by removing whenever they are known evil officers and counsellors and putting better and more virtuous and more suffi- cient ones in their place, as well as removing all the evil circum- stances from which the late disturbance and the other mischiefs befell the realm, as said above. Otherwise, all men think that this realm cannot survive for long without greater mischief than has ever befallen it before, which God forbid."

This time Parliament was listened to, and changes were made in key positions. The poll tax was abandoned, and there were no more attempts to create ingenious new taxes. We can find no rec- ord of an attack on the person or property of a rank-and-file mem- ber of Parliament; thus it would appear that to that group, at least, the rebellion was a rip-roaring success. It got what it had wanted. In fact, it is difficult to dismiss the temptation to conclude that the shadowy Great Society inciting and directing facets of the revolt included members of Parliament.

Its own goals furthered by the revolt, Parliament did not act to satisfy the desires of others. When asked by the king's council if it wanted to abolish villeinage and serfdom, the answer was a vehement no. The same negative response went to William Cour- tenay, the new archbishop of Canterbury, who asked Parliament for stronger laws for the definition and punishment of heresy.

What the Parliament did do for the rebels in general was to rec- ommend amnesty for all, except for those on a special list and the citizens of the towns of Canterbury, Bury St. Edmunds, Bridgewater, Cambridge, Beverly, and Scarborough. This exclu- sion of towns was soon reduced to Bury St. Edmunds alone, whose citizens took five years to pay the fine of two thousand marks levied against them. As to individuals, there was a general exclusion from amnesty of those directly involved in the deaths of the archbishop of Canterbury, the prior of the Hospitallers, and Chief Justice Cavendish. A more interesting exclusion was of all those who had escaped from prison, none of whom is recorded as being recaptured. The list of names of specific rebels not included in the general pardon totaled 287, of whom 151 were citizens of London. Those not already in prison simply disappeared.

The general amnesty put a stop to the judicial vengeance, so that even with the "bloody assizes" of Chief Justice Tresilian, fewer than 120 rebels were actually executed—fewer than those beheaded by the rebels in London alone on a single day. Except for a few rebels who were summarily executed by avenging swords, such as that of Bishop le Despenser, all were accorded some sort of trial and defense.

Rebel leaders taken now, or already in prison, did not automatically go to the block or the gallows if they had friends to intercede for them. Litster's chief deputy, Sir Roger Bacon, was on the list of those excluded from amnesty but won a pardon, some say at the request of Richard's future queen, Anne of Bohemia. Thomas Sampson, rebel leader at Ipswich, was held in prison for eighteen months, then pardoned. The Somerset leader, Thomas Engilby, was taken and put in chains, only to be pardoned a few months later. Thomas Farndon, whose guilt was unquestioned, had acted as a leader and guide to the rebels in London and had directed them out to the Hospitaller manor at Highbury. Although on the list, Farndon was pardoned in March 1382.

One of the most interesting cases was that of John Awedyn of Essex. He was indicted and found guilty of being "one of the rebels against the lord King in the City of London" and "a captain of the said rebellious malefactors." He, too, was on the list of those excluded from the general amnesty, but on March 16, 1383, he received a full pardon from the king *at the request of the earl of Oxford.* How much it would help our understanding of the rebellion and the organization behind it if someone had recorded just a bit about who was pressing the buttons of influence, and why.

While Parliament was in session, inquiries and inquisitions were going forward simultaneously. The London sheriffs' inquisitions of November 4 and November 20, 1381, speak strongly to the point of view that the rebels didn't march on London in some sort of instinctive lemming-march to the capital but were incited, encouraged, and invited to come by residents of London. The records of the inquisition of November 4 state: "Item, the jurors declare under their oath that a certain Adam atte Welle, then a butcher . . . and now a provider of victuals to the lord duke of Lancaster, travelled into Essex fourteen days before the arrival of the rebels from that county in the city of London: there Adam incited and encouraged the rebels of Essex to come to London, and promised them many things if they did so."

The same inquisitions make charges against a London alderman, John Horn, fishmonger. Horn was one of a three-man delegation sent out by the mayor of London to meet with the leaders of the Kentish rebels, both to ascertain their strength and to try to dissuade them from approaching the city. Horn did the opposite. He met privately with the Kentish leaders, apparently to advise them to come ahead. It was after this meeting that the Kentish rebels moved to Southwark at the south end of London Bridge and broke open the Marshalsea prison. Horn also gave the rebels a royal standard he had taken from the guildhall. Somehow he got three of the rebel leaders into London in advance of the mob and entertained them all night in his house, presumably to discuss plans and objectives for the next few days.

Another London alderman and fishmonger, Walter Sybyle, was indicted as Horn's co-conspirator. Sybyle's ward included London Bridge. He was accused of countermanding the mayor's orders to close the gates and raise the drawbridge, as well as dispersing a crowd that had gathered at the north end of the bridge to prevent the rebels from crossing into the city.

A third alderman, William Tonge, was accused of opening the gate at Aldgate to permit the entry of the Essex rebels. In the indictment, the jurors do admit that they "do not at present know whether William Tonge had Aldgate opened because of his own malice, because he was in league with John Horn and Walter Sybyle, or because he was frightened by the threats of the malefactors of Kent who were already in the city."

Historians have warned us that we should be skeptical of the London inquisitions because they may have been politically motivated. That is a sensible precaution, because every chronicle of the rebellion was politically motivated, if only to the extent of currying favor with the king or the church. The rebels had no diarist or historian to memorialize their side of the story.

Other aspects of the inquisitions, however—not involving highly placed persons like aldermen, and so perhaps less prone to political distortion—are equally revealing. Some indictments speak of craftsmen of London going back from London to the towns of their birth to incite their friends and relatives to rebellion. Other men were accused of, and confessed to, being agents or messengers of a Great Society and giving orders in the name of that society. Unfortunately, there is no recorded indication that the inquisitioners, sheriffs, or justices expressed any desire for additional information about this Great Society, which has led some historians to conclude that such a society never existed. Many more historians assert that there certainly was organization behind the rebellion of 1381, but conclude that we shall probably never know the nature of that organization. There are just too many unsolved mysteries. A closer look at some of those mysteries, however, led to the conclusion that the organization behind the rebellion need not remain a total mystery forever.

CHAPTER 4

"FIRST, AND ABOVE ALL . . . THE DESTRUCTION OF THE HOSPITALLERS"

The first distortion to be dealt with is the role attributed by the chroniclers to King Richard II. When his father, the legendary Black Prince, died in 1376, Richard was declared heir to the throne by his grandfather, Edward III. The following year Edward died, and England had a ten-year-old king. A council of two bishops, two earls, two barons, two bannerets, two knights bachelor, and a civil lawyer was appointed to govern the country and to govern the boy king. So long as Richard remained a minor, a new council was to be elected each year. No mention of this all-powerful council is made in any of the accounts of the rebellion of 1381. Instead, the young king himself is made to appear as the major and unilateral force acting for the royal government. None of this rings true, not only because Richard had no royal authority of his own, but also because he just wasn't the Victorian-stories-for-boys hero that we are asked to accept.

A contemporary chronicler, remembered only as the monk of Evesham, has left us a description of Richard that includes the words ". . . arrogant . . . rapacious . . . timid and unsuccessful in Foreign war . . . remaining sometimes till morning in drinking and other excesses that are not to be named" and, perhaps most important to our evaluation, "abrupt and stammering in his speech." Richard was so afraid of the council of regents that not until he was twenty-three years old did he muster up the necessary spirit to make the simple assertion that, as he had long since come of age, he should rule as king. This is the man we are asked to believe acted with such astonishing courage and charisma at age fourteen. We are told that he cantered up to the rebel mob that had just seen its leader struck down and with a clear voice took control of the situation by volunteering to be the rebels' chief and champion. He gave the orders to arrange the meeting at Mile End to get the rebels out of London. He personally commanded the army of retribution in Essex. He decided to pardon the rebels. The ruling council apparently played no role, exercised no authority, made no decisions.

Not likely. What has been saved for us as "history" is the chronicle of events by writers opposed to the rebels, writers whose careers would be enhanced (or at least secured) by currying favor with the monarchy. Anyone actually working behind the scenes would have been pleased to let the boy have the credit.

Behind the scenes? Consider the meeting at Mile End. Was it really set up to get the rebels out of London? If so, it didn't succeed, because a substantial organized band stayed in the City, as did the principal leaders Tyler, Ball, and Strawe. They had something to do that was obviously more important to them than a meeting with the king to discuss grievances. They stayed away from that meeting to take the Tower. It is entirely reasonable to speculate that the meeting at Mile End was arranged not to get the rebels out of the City, but to get the king out of the Tower. A key to the arrangements was to have the archbishop of Canterbury and the prior of the Hospitallers not go with the king, but stay behind in what they would have believed was total security. Somehow they were influenced to decline to go, or were ordered to stay. The archbishop may have been relieved of his duties as chancellor, because he had been allowed to attempt his escape by river that morning, but what of Sir Robert Hales?

He was not just the chief administrator of a military monastic order, but a famous battlefield leader and personal fighter. In 1365, as bailiff of Egle, he had led a Hospitaller force in a great Crusader battle at which he became known as "the hero of Alexandria" for his feats of valor in a great victory that left twenty thousand Moslems dead. Sir Robert was the most experienced fighting man in the king's entourage. He should not only have been part of the king's bodyguard, he should have commanded it. So why did he let his youthful king ride out to meet thousands of bloodthirsty rebels, choosing rather to stay safely behind the massive walls of the Tower? It all smacks of stagecraft, and at the highest levels.

If that conclusion appears too speculative, consider Tyler's entrance into the Tower. A few hundred men could have held the Tower for weeks, even months, against a mob with no missile-throwers or siege engines, especially if those few hundred were led by an experienced military man like Hales. Tyler knew that he didn't have time to build a siege tower or a "cat" housing a battering ram. There was a much easier way: make arrangements guaranteeing that the drawbridge would be down and the portcullis up. Have control of the gates so that the rebels could walk right in. No chronicler tells us of any fight at the gate, or of resistance of any kind. No one has even tried to speculate as to how such a remarkable feat of arms could be.

There is also the mystery of why Tyler wanted to take the Tower in the first place. In any ordinary revolt, the seizure of the most powerful fortress in the area would have been the high point, militarily. The leader would have immediately made it his headquarters, his base of operations from which he could threaten all the surrounding area. That was clearly not Tyler's objective. When the executions were over, he had no more use for the place. As he left, he told the garrison that they could now close the gates and raise the drawbridge. The objective was not the Tower, but the deaths of a few men in it.

When the meeting was over at Mile End, the king did not come back to the Tower but was escorted to the building that housed his wardrobe (his personal staff, not his clothing). It was a substantial building but not a fortress. Richard had been neatly removed from the firing line to assure his personal safety. In fact, since his counselors ruled him, and not the other way round, Richard's itinerary and escort would have been chosen for him. Considering the number of times he was exposed to the rebels—at Mile End, at Westminster Abbey, at Smithfield, parading through the streets—it may have been well known to certain members of the court that the king's person would be protected not only by his personal escort but by the rebel leadership as well.

All in all, the king seems to have been handled adroitly. Quotations attributed to him undoubtedly stemmed from others speaking on his behalf. The chroniclers totally ignored the fact that in 1381 the king was not yet the reigning monarch. He was guided, ordered, and manipulated over the years even beyond the age that the law said he must attain in order to rule. The accounts of his heroic direct command of the situation during the rebellion can only be sycophantic fiction, but they do point to cooperation between the rebel leadership and one or more of the members of the court.

That cooperation didn't seem to stop with the suppression of the rebellion. When the Parliament of November and December, 1381, was sold on the concept of a general amnesty, it moved to exclude from that grace all of the citizens of Cambridge, Canterbury, Bridgewater, Beverly, Scarborough, and Bury St. Edmunds. The church would have been especially eager to have retribution for the attacks on its English headquarters at Canterbury and on its religious and scholastic property at Cambridge. Notwithstanding, an order came "from the king" overriding the Parliament and extending the royal pardon to all of the towns except Bury St. Edmunds.

As to the individuals excluded from the general amnesty, we have already seen that a number of the rebel leaders got their pardons in spite of being specifically excluded, by means of help from men in high position, including the earl of Oxford.

As for the 287 men listed by name as being outside the amnesty, they constitute a separate mystery. Except for those already in prison, they simply disappeared. Typical were the cases of Richard de Midelton, Thomas White, and Henry de Newark of Beverly. A royal writ went out from Westminster on December 10, 1381, demanding the arrest and questioning of these three men relating to their part in the Beverly riots. The reply to the royal court from the officials of the town concluded: "Moreover, they declare that Richard de Midelton, late alderman, Thomas

White, tiler, and Henry de Newark, late chamberlain were not to be found within the liberty of Beverly after the receipt of this writ: on account of which we cannot execute the intentions of this writ in the said matters." They were gone, but to where? Was each of these hundreds of fugitives completely on his own, or was there help available to him? An intriguing aspect of this mass disappearance is that it was not unlike the mass disappearance of the Knights Templar seventy years before. Both were groups already condemned, wanted by church as well as by lay authorities, and in immediate need of clandestine sources of food, lodging, new identities, and safe houses. It would be remarkable indeed if unassisted they found dozens of separate, unrelated pockets of safe help, among men willing to risk life and limb (literally) to provide for them. On the other hand, if there was a Great Society of men sworn to mutual support, one of its functions would have been to provide all the help required to brothers on the run or in hiding. The fact is that there is no record that any one of the condemned men was ever captured, so it is reasonable to assume that protection was available to them from someone, somewhere, somehow.

While all this was happening, the church seemed to turn its back on the whole concept of the rebellion, as though to pretend that it hadn't happened. The new archbishop of Canterbury, William Courtenay, did not go after the rebels. He went instead for the Oxford don and priest John Wycliffe and his followers. Courtenay did not ask Parliament for stronger efforts to find and punish the rebel leaders who had vandalized church property and murdered his predecessor. What he did demand was stronger laws to seek out and punish *heresy*. Recent historians have postulated that John Wycliffe and his criticisms of the church had little to do with the outbreak of the rebellion. Archbishop Courtenay would have disagreed with them. Harassed to the end by the church he wanted to purify through the elimination of nonscriptural sacraments and doctrine, John Wycliffe died in 1382. His ideas, however, lived on, so that at the Council of Constance, thirty-five years after his death, it was ordered that Wycliffe's remains be dug up and burned for heresy.

We have already seen the effects of the agitation and leadership provided the rebels by the lower orders of the clergy, especially parish priests like John Ball, John Wrawe, and their followers, as they moved against wealthy monasteries and church-approved serfdom. What Archbishop Courtenay may have seen or sensed was that something much bigger than a riot of rustics and tradesmen had happened in England. It was not the throne of England that concerned him, but the Throne of Peter, and that throne had felt the first tremor of an antichurch attitude that would smolder underground in England until it erupted as the Protestant Reformation.

The overriding mystery of the Peasants' Revolt of 1381, of course, is the organization that lay behind it. Most historians now agree that there was indeed organization and planning over a wide area of England, but none has cared to speculate on just what the source of that organization could have been. Was it marshaled just for the rebellion, or had it existed for some time before 1381? Did it stop at the end of the rebellion, or was there some residual or ongoing association that might have had a bearing on religious and political disturbances in Britain over the years ahead? Was it one organization or simply an informal once-in-a-lifetime communication among hastily assembled groups?

Consider this item from a royal letter of July 23, 1381, to the sheriffs and bailiffs of an administrative unit of the county of Cheshire called "the hundred of Wirral," over 150 miles from London: "From the evidence of trustworthy men we have learnt that several of the villeins of our beloved in Christ the abbot of Chester have made certain assemblies within the area of your jurisdiction; and they have gathered in secret confederacies within the woods and other hidden places in the said hundred. They have held secret counsels there contrary to our recent proclamation on the subject." Even in such a relatively remote local area such "secret confederacies" would require planning. Someone has to select a meeting place. Word must go out, in total secrecy, notifying those attending of time and place of the meeting. Screening must be carried out to determine who may be trusted, because anyone attending could inform on the whole group: Each man is trusting the others with his life and property. Care must be taken for the participants to approach the meeting by various routes to avoid suspicion. Cover stories must be invented to be employed by families and neighbors in the event that suspicion is aroused by a number of absences at one time. Sentries or guards must be posted to alert the group to the approach not only of authorities but of anyone who might subsequently yield to the innocent temptation to tell others of the odd circumstance of coming upon an assembly of men in the deep woods. Someone must set the agenda for the meeting and decide, alone or with one or two other leaders, that the matter at hand is important enough to run the risk of a meeting.

It is obvious that to organize and operate a secret society in just one section of a remote rural area would require organization, planning, and discipline. Now expand those requirements to a national or regional level and one can begin to appreciate the vast amount of planning and ingenuity necessary to implement even a working system of communication. Who initiates the communication? Who delivers it? If all delivery was made on foot it would take forever. On the other hand, if on horseback, we are not looking at a "peasant" society.

Another problem with messengers is recognition. How does one know that a messenger is not a spy? The usual method is with body signals, items of clothing or decoration, and catechism. "Have you traveled far?" "Not as far as I must, but far enough for one day." "A long journey brings a fierce hunger." "Yes, and of more than one kind. My stomach hungers for food, but my tired bones hunger for a soft bed." In the Chinese secret societies, such a catechism of identification might, in certain dangerous circumstances, wind its way through fifty different questions and answers. Signals can pass by how the hands are used to hold a cup or how the fingers are held when a kerchief is used to wipe one's brow. (As we shall see later, Scotland's heroic Sir William Wallace was identified for arrest by an informer's reversing a loaf of bread on the tavern table.) The important point about all such means of identification and communication is that they must be understood by both parties. To have them known in a number of geographic locations takes something far more complex: It takes standardization, which in turn requires an autocratic leadership to dictate the standards or, in the case of a more democratic form, a meeting of the minds of a group of leaders, a ruling body empowered to set standards of passwords, signals, recognition, and so on. Especially is this true if a member is frequently expected to meet and help, or meet and obey, a total stranger. Practicalities point to the probablity of a ruling council or committee, which in the case of the Great Society seems most certainly to have been based in London.

Does this mean that the society had widespread individual membership with just one chapter or base in London? That's hardly likely, in view of those times of very difficult travel. Its contacts in the towns would more likely have been cells or chapters made up of residents of those towns. Even more important, those contacts or members would have to have included persons of some influence in their respective areas. To have a mass rebellion and to be able to order all those within thirty-six miles of the sea to remain at home meant more than mere organization: It meant orders given by people who expected to be obeyed. In a time of miserable communications, the march on London took advance planning, leadership, and a superior clandestine system of message generation, both to set a day to move and then to actually motivate one hundred thousand men to rise in contravention of the law. That kind of action would have required what cultural anthropologists call a "war dance" phase. That's the time and energy needed to coordinate and spread the information (or disinformation) and propaganda necessary to work a group into a frenzy—to get a large group into the mood to act, even to kill. In our time the "war dance" that marshals a people to start a revolution, or to back a national war effort, is a fast multimedia exercise drawing on newspapers, radio, television, and public-relations consultants. In the fourteenth century none of those things existed: Virtually all communication was local and, in an illiterate society, by word of mouth. The pulpit was one source of group communication, and certainly the disgruntled lower orders of the clergy, including John Ball and his followers, did their part to stir unrest in the three medieval gathering places: the church, the tavern, and the market.

All this is not to say that the Great Society "created" the Peasants' Rebellion. The Great Society, whatever it was, did not bring on the Black Death. It could not have been responsible for the attitude of the church toward the freedom of the people on its lands, nor for the war that brought the need for extra taxation. Revolutionary leaders rarely create the ills that cause revolution; rather, they opportunistically use them, articulating the issues for the distressed people (and not always accurately), focusing blame, painting pictures of the better life possible, stirring the pot to the boiling point. Their hope is to turn distress and frustration into anger, to turn anger into action, then to provide the plans and leadership to divert and direct that angry action, with a view to taking ultimate control. We have seen this pattern used effectively and often in recent history. Unfortunately, Wat Tyler was cut down before his demands were made clear, so we may never be able to clearly pinpoint the goals of the Great Society, or its true leadership.

Before moving on, one point should be made for the sake of clarity. There is no indication that there was ever an organization called *the* Great Society. It was simply referred to as *a* great society, and no one has ever put a name to it. However, it is extremely difficult to discuss or even think about a group with no label. We've seen that in our own time as the press finally realized that the Italianate branch of organized crime in America, which includes more than a fair share of Calabrians and Neapolitans, could not truthfully be called "Mafia" because the Mafia is a purely Sicilian phenomenon. For a while they tried "the Syndicate" and even "the Combination," but those terms didn't work. Then a wiretap picked up a conversation in Italian that referred to the criminal society as "our thing" (in Italian, *la cosa nostra*). The press pounced on a term that would finally fill the label vacuum, and they still won't let go. Of course, they keep the term in Italian, because it would look a bit silly to report that "the FBI has just arrested Angelo Pigliacelli of Jersey City, a reputed boss of Our Thing." Similarly, we are required by both convenience and necessity to use the term "Great Society," knowing that it did not bear that name, until someone tells us what the real name was.

In searching for the true nature of the Great Society, there was not much to go on. There is no official record of any secret society in medieval England, with the exception of the Lollards, the adherents to the teachings of the heresiarch priest John Wycliffe, who expounded his criticisms of the church both before and after the rebellion. John Ball was said by some to be a follower of Wycliffe, but Ball's preaching predated Lollard activity. However, in a published confession of John Ball the statement is made that there was a "secret fraternity" of the followers of Wycliffe traveling throughout England, spreading his beliefs. Historians agree that this "confession" is a later product and not the scaffold confession of Ball. It is interesting, however, in that Lollardy indeed was subsequently driven underground and did exist for a couple of centuries in secret cells all over England, which have never clearly been identified or described.

There has been another well-known secret society in Britain, the Ancient Order of Free and Accepted Masons. However, no documentation exists to suggest that Freemasonry was active at the time of the rebellion (as none exists to indicate that it wasn't). The Masonic writers who began extolling the virtues of their fraternity after it came out of the world of secrecy into public view in 1717 frequently took jet flights into fantasy land. They variously claimed as Masonic members and Grand Masters such noteworthies as Adam, Noah, Pythagoras, Achilles, and Julius Caesar, claiming existence from "time immemorial." More sober heads backed off the Creation and the Flood and asserted that King Solomon had actually been the first Masonic Grand Master and his Temple the first Masonic edifice. In the mellowing of time Masonic historians tended to bring their founding forward, to cite their beginnings in medieval guilds of stonemasons, currently the most widely accepted theory of the origins of the fraternity.

The first indication that Freemasonry might have been related to the rebellion was the name of the leader, Walter the Tyler. He exploded into English history with his mysterious uncontested appointment as the supreme commander of the Peasants' Rebellion on Friday, June 7, 1381, and left it as abruptly when his head was struck off eight days later on Saturday, June 15. Absolutely nothing is known of him before those eight days. That alone suggests that he was not using his real name. Historians have suggested that his name probably indicates that he was a roof tiler by trade, which, based on his obvious military experience and leadership abilities, is not very probable. But if he had indeed adopted a pseudonym, why would he call himself a "Tyler"? Freemasons reading this will already see the point. The Tyler is the sentry, sergeant-at-arms, and enforcer of the Masonic lodge. He screens visitors for credentials, secures the meeting place, and then stands guard outside the door with a drawn sword in his hand. If the Great Society was in any way connected with Freemasonry, "Tyler" would have been the only proper Masonic title for the military leader who would wield a sword and enforce discipline. It was, admittedly, a tenuous connection.

Another possible but equally tenuous Masonic connection was

the highly organized liveried risings in Yorkshire, especially in the city of York. When four London Masonic lodges decided to go public in 1717, they met on June 24, the day dedicated to their patron saint, John the Baptist, and elected a Grand Master for their new Grand Lodge. The Masons at York were incensed at this unilateral decision on the part of London Masons to throw off their ancient veil of secrecy and at the Londoners' presumption that they could set themselves above all the Masonic lodges in England. The lodge at York considered itself to be the oldest lodge in the country, dating back to the seventh century and the building of York Cathedral. In 1725, the York lodge decided to assert itself and formed its own "Grand Lodge of All England." Much later, in 1767, the York Grand Secretary wrote that "this Lodge acknowledges no Superior, that it pays homage to none, that it exists in its Own Right, that it grants Constitutions, and Certificates in the same Manner, as is done by the Grand Lodge in London, and as it has from Time Immemorial had a Right and use to do."

York occupies a very special place in Freemasonry, especially in the United States, where many Masons believe that York Masonry is the purest and most ancient form of Masonry.

Another cloudy Masonic relationship found in the rebellion was the rage to be free, to end all serfdom and villeinage. One of the ancient Landmarks of Freemasonry is that a Mason must be a "free man born of a free mother." If a lawyer proved that a free man who was a Mason was no longer free that man might have had to relinquish his Masonic membership. It was noted with interest that by the late fifteenth century virtually every man in England was free. The existence of free status as a requirement for Masonic membership indicated that Freemasonry was already an ancient organization when it revealed itself in 1717. As interesting as all this was, however, it did not present any strong evidence that the Great Society was Freemasonry or a precursor of it. More direct and dramatic evidence lay in another direction, with an organization well documented as having existed before the Peasants' Rebellion, but believed to have completely passed away.

The first glimmer of that evidence was the especially vicious rebel attacks on the Knights Hospitallers, including the murder of their prior, Sir Robert Hales. Consider the case of George de Donnesby (Dunsby) from Lincolnshire. He was arrested over two hundred miles from home, and confessed to being a messenger of the Great Society. Is it simply coincidence that at his hometown of Dunsby, back in Lincolnshire, the tenants went on strike and refused to pay their tithes to the local Hospitaller manors? Or take the case of the destruction of the recently rebuilt Hospitaller manor at Highbury. Right in the middle of dramatic events in London, in the midst of all of the church property they could ever hope to wreak vengeance upon, Wat Tyler chose to send his principal lieutenant and a band of rebels on a mission outside the city. They had to walk six miles just to deliberately destroy that one Hospitaller property at Highbury, then march back to rejoin Tyler. At Cambridge, officials of the city, with the approval of the mayor, rode out to join a rebel band at Shingay, a Hospitaller manor that they were burning, and then all went back to Cambridge together to attack the University. Why should the city men ride ten miles out into the countryside to watch rebels burn a Hospitaller manor? Why didn't they just wait for the rebels at home? Or did they meet by arrangement to plan their unified attack, in circumstances under which a meeting concurrent with the destruction of a Hospitaller property would be of some significance to them?

All of the religious orders owned properties in London, but only the Hospitaller property was deliberately sought out for destruction, and not just the major establishments at St. John's Clerkenwell, and the "Temple" area between Fleet Street and the Thames. The chroniclers state that the rebels sought out every Hospitaller house and rental property to smash or burn it. For that purpose native Londoners had to have been involved, not just to identify such property but to lead the rebels to it; at that time London streets were not marked by sign posts, and not until hundreds of years later would London have a system of numbered buildings. The rebels even smashed two forges in Fleet Street that the Hospitallers had taken over from the suppressed Templars. Perhaps indicating the intensity of the bond between the rebel leadership and leading citizens of London, records indicate that twenty years later the Hospitaller order was still trying unsuccessfully to rebuild those two forges in the face of opposition from certain citizens of London.

In all of the destruction in London, why did the rebels not burn the records stored in the Hospitaller church off Fleet Street right where they found them? Why go to all the trouble of carrying boxes and bundles out of the church to the high road, away from the building, unless it was to avoid the risk of damage to the structure? How was this church different from any other property? Only in that it had been the principal church in Britain of the Knights Templar, consecrated almost three hundred years earlier, in 1185, by Heraclius, the patriarch of Jerusalem. The manner of its consecration alone didn't set it apart, however, because the patriarch had also consecrated the Hospitaller church at Clerkenwell in 1185, during the same month that he had dedicated the Templar church; yet no consideration was given by the rebels to protecting the church at Clerkenwell.

The highly organized rebels at York, Scarborough, and Beverly, who were townsmen, not "peasants," had displayed a common livery. This was a white hooded shawl with a red decoration, reportedly worn by about five hundred men at Beverly alone. Certainly these were not run off the night before on the neighborhood Singer; their existence bespeaks formal, organized leadership and decision making, not to mention the availability of funds. It may be pure coincidence that red and white were also the Templar colors: a red cross on a white mantle.

Most haunting of all was a single sentence from the deathbed confession of Wat Tyler's principal lieutenant, Jack Strawe. According to the account of Thomas Walsingham, a monk of St. Albans, Strawe was captured and taken to London, where he was sentenced to death by the mayor. Before the sentence was carried out, the mayor promised Strawe a Christian burial and three years of masses to be said for his soul if Strawe would confess the true purpose of the rebellion. In that confession, it is reported that Strawe said, in part, "When we had assembled an enormous crowd of common people throughout the country, we would suddenly have murdered all those lords who could have opposed or resisted us. *First, and above all, we would have proceeded to the destruction of the Hospitallers.*" (Emphasis added.) Strawe did not explain this special hatred for the Hospitallers, and there is no record that anyone ever asked. If there was an organization stirring up rebellion, at least one purpose was made clear, "the destruction of the Hospitallers." What organization, or even what segment of society, could have sought such total annihilation of that highly respected order of military monks? There was only one.

The Knights Templar had been officially abolished by Pope Clement V in 1312, after the knights had suffered almost five years of imprisonment, torture, and death at the stake. Almost all of their property in Britain had been given to their great rivals, the Knights Hospitaller. The Templars certainly had reason to hate both the Holy See and the Hospitaller order. They would have completely approved the destruction of the Hospitaller property, would have approved the execution of Sir Robert Hales, grand prior of the Hospitallers in England, and would have approved as well the sparing of their own central church. As to the Holy See, which had whipped and racked and burned their brothers, they would probably have agreed with the rebels as they ignored the rights of sanctuary, brushed aside the Holy Sacrament, and cut the head off the archbishop of Canterbury.

One notable exception to the apparent concentration on the properties of the Hospitallers was the especially vicious attack on the Benedictine monastery of Bury St. Edmunds, led by the rebel priest John Wrawe. Here the head of Chief Justice Cavendish was taken to be played with as a puppet with the head of the prior, John de Cambridge. Those two were joined by the head of another monk, John de Lakenheath, who had been in charge of the monastery's properties. The rebels also searched for another monk, Walter Todington, hoping to put his head with the others, but couldn't discover his hiding place.

As the general amnesty was ultimately defined, it excluded only the citizens of Bury St. Edmunds, because of the particularly bloody events there. At first there appears to be no connection between those events and any possible secret society. There seems to be no possible connection with the Templars, either, until the chronicles of the abbey are consulted. They document a firm base for violent Templar anger, quite apart from any reference to the Hospitallers.

A translation of the original chronicle, with its accusations against the Templars, is provided by Antonia Gransden, who edited *The Chronicle of Bury St. Edmunds 1212–1301*. The words speak well enough for themselves: "On the vigil and on the day of Palm Sunday the Christians and the infidels met in battle between Acre and Safed. First eight emirs and eighteen columns of infidels were killed, then eventually the infidels were victorious, but not without very great loss of men. *The Christian army was very nearly wiped out by the sedition of the Templars."* (Emphasis added.)

This report, written in 1270, was based on the attack of the Egyptian army on the Templar castle of Safed four years before. The new sultan was a brutal and treacherous Kipchak warrior named Baibars Rukd ad-Din, who had taken the throne by murdering the former sultan. When his attacks on the castle failed, he offered free escape and pardon for all Turcopoles, the native-born troops who comprised the major part of the garrison, and they began to desert in numbers. Stripped of their support, the Templars sent one of their Syrian-born sergeants, Brother Leo, to negotiate with Baibars. Leo returned with the good news that all of the Templars were free to leave, with a guarantee of safe-conduct through the Egyptian lines. The Templars had not yet learned the character of their enemy, and accepted.

As soon as Baibars had taken control of the castle and the Templars, he gave them that night to decide whether they would choose conversion to the Islamic faith, or death. In the morning they were lined up outside the castle gate to announce their decisions. Before they could speak, the Templar commander of the castle called out to them to choose death rather than abandon their Christian faith. He was promptly seized, stripped, and skinned alive in front of his brother Templars. Unshaken by the screaming and the blood of their leader, the Templars to a man chose death rather than give up the cross. They got their choice, as Baibars ordered their immediate beheadings.

That is the story of the loss of the castle of Safed and the martyrdom of the Templars as it actually occurred, and as it must have been recounted to every new Templar as an example of the piety and sacrifice of his predecessors. Somehow the story was turned and twisted by the time it was accepted and recorded by the Benedictines at Bury St. Edmunds. Accusing the martyred brothers of Safed of treason would have boiled the blood of any Templar who learned of it. Nor was it the only accusation against the Templars in the chronicles of Bury St. Edmunds.

The other anti-Templar item in the chronicles appears to be not so much an accusation as a final judgment: "Hugh of

Lusignan, King of Cyprus, his son and others of his household were killed by poison by the knights of the Temple."

There is no doubt that for the greater part of his reign, Hugh III of Cyprus was at odds with the Templars, seizing their property and at one point even accusing them of arranging a Moslem raid on his troops. Hugh wanted to establish supremacy over the mainland by asserting his controversial claim to the kingdom of Jerusalem, and it was public knowledge that the Templars were opposed to his ambitions. However, there is no historical basis for the accusation that they poisoned King Hugh and his sons. Hugh died on March 4, 1284, and his eldest son, Bohemond, had died the previous November. His frail second son, John, inherited his crown and, upon John's death, the crown passed to Hugh's third son, Henry. But back in England, at the Benedictine abbey of Bury St. Edmunds, the scribes wrote that the Templars were guilty of the mass murder of the king, his heir, and members of his household.

There was indeed a Templar connection, and should there have been an unleashing of Templar vengeance under cover of the Peasants' Revolt, Bury St. Edmunds would have been a primary target.

If the leadership and its "bending" of the angry mob in the direction of certain goals was inspired by a desire for Templar revenge, the rebellion may not have been the failure that history has labeled it. Certainly, if the goal was to wreak vengeance on the three great enemies of the Templars—the Hospitallers, the church, and the monarchy—a degree of success is obvious. Yet as Templar-oriented as the rebel targets might appear, it just did not seem practical that the Great Society that steered parts of the rebellion could be based on an order abolished sixty-nine years earlier. A Knight Templar twenty-one years old at the time of the supression would have been ninety years old at the time of the rebellion. The Templar connection would have to have reached down into the second and third generation. A Templar connection would mean that the Great Society was not just an underground group organized to foment or cash in on this rebellion of 1381, but rather was a secret society that had been in existence for almost seventy years. Was such a thing possible?

It was apparent that some kind of loose organization or group of sympathizers must have been working for the Templars at the time of their arrest in England by Edward II because so many had escaped arrest and had disappeared so effectively. A royal dragnet assisted by the religious orders had turned up just two fugitive Templars in England and one in Scotland. In addition, a number of them escaped from their imprisonment, which undoubtedly had required help from inside or outside, or both. Then, too, the arrests in England had come three months after the arrests in France, providing ample time to make preparations. Some kind of loose mutual assistance organization might have been hastily thrown together at the time, but for it to have stayed alive and functioning for seventy years would have required that the usefulness, or need, for that underground mutual protection society extend beyond the life span of the original fugitive members. There would have had to be a common goal, a common fear, or a common enemy to motivate such longevity. If indeed the Great Society had Templar origins, perhaps clues to that common bond could be found in the organized activities associated with the Peasants' Rebellion. To seriously pursue the prospect of a Templar connection, it would be necessary to take a fresh look at the history and workings of this militant order of monks that had been born in the First Crusade.

This meant turning away from any further speculation of the involvement of Freemasonry but, as it turned out, not for long.

CHAPTER 5

THE KNIGHTS OF
THE TEMPLE

After a year of battling their way south through Nicaea and Antioch, the Christian warriors of the First Crusade found themselves before the great walls of Jerusalem on June 7, 1099.

Upon the approach of the Crusaders, the Egyptian governor of Jerusalem destroyed or poisoned the water wells around the city and drove away the flocks surplus to his own needs. All of the Christians in the city were told to leave, not just as an act of mercy but to place the additional burden of their needs for food and water on the invaders. One of the ejected Christians was Gerard, master of the Amalfi hostel in the city. He immediately approached the Christian leaders to share all he knew of the layout and the defenses of Jerusalem. His intelligence was most welcome.

No one had warned the Crusaders about the heat, particularly unbearable to men who had to wear clothing under armor, with no shade to keep the sun from beating down on that armor all day long. No one had told these men, used to the heavily forested areas of Europe, that there was no timber around Jerusalem for the construction of siege engines. The material had to be brought from the coast or from the forests of Samaria, requiring as many as sixty Moslem prisoners to carry a single beam. They had not expected a twelve-mile round trip for water for themselves and their animals. Then, after six weeks of agonizing physical discomforts, magnified by deficiencies in food and water, word came from Cairo that the Egyptians were marshaling a large army to relieve the city. Despair and panic ran through the Christian army.

As if in answer to their prayers, a priest in the Christian camp reported that he had a vision that had revealed the conditions under which the Crusaders would be granted the victory. First, they were to put aside all sinning, all selfish ambitions, and all quarrels among themselves. Next, they were to fast and pray for three days. On the third day they were to process in humility with bare feet around the walls of God's holy city. With all of these conditions met, God would grant them the victory within nine days. The vision was accepted as valid, and the leaders ordered the entire army to comply. After two days of fasting the entire army shed their footwear and began the two-mile walk around the city. Up on the walls, the Egyptian defenders looked down on the Crusaders with shouted taunts and laughter, urinating on crosses held up in view of the penitent marchers.

Fortunately, the prophecy was helped along by a surge of activity to complete three siege towers. To roll them up to the walls at the selected positions, it was first necessary to fill in portions of the great ditch or dry moat in front of the wall. This was done, but at great cost from the constant barrage of stones and sulfurous Greek fire dropped on them by the defenders on the wall. By the evening of July 14, the army was ready and began to roll the giant siege towers into position. Raymond of Toulouse positioned his tower at the wall first but could not get his men across the bridge from the tower to the wall. Godfrey de Bouillon had his tower against the north wall by morning and dropped the bridge to the top of the wall. Hand to hand combat went on for hours, but by noon Godfrey had men on the city wall. Other men beat their way over the bridge to support them, and soon Godfrey commanded enough of the wall to permit the safe use of scaling ladders to bring more and more men to him. When he had a large enough party, he sent them to open the Gate of the Column, and the main Crusader force poured into the city. Jerusalem had been taken on the ninth day, as the prophecy had promised.

Seized by a frenzy of vengeful blood lust after weeks of suffering outside the walls, the victorious Crusaders poured through the streets, breaking open houses, shops, and mosques to butcher every man, woman, and child they could find.

One of the reports to the pope read, "If you would hear how we treated our enemies at Jerusalem, know that in the portico of Solomon and in the Temple our men rode through the unclean blood of the Saracens, which came up to the knees of their horses."

Word spread that the local Moslems sometimes swallowed their gold as the surest way to hide it, and disemboweling thereafter became a common practice in the search for plunder.

Hoping to avoid the maniacal slaughter, Jews crowded into their principal synagogue to give notice that they were not Moslems. The Crusaders burnt down the synagogue, killing them all.

Raymond of Aguilers, writing about the mutilated corpses that covered the temple area, quoted Psalm 118: "This is the day the Lord has made. Let us rejoice and be glad in it."

And so the stage was set for that strange blend of piety, self-sacrifice, blood lust, and greed that marked the history of the Christian kingdom of the East for two centuries to come.

An interesting aftermath of the First Crusade lay in the treatment of the little order that had run the Amalfi hostelry for pilgrims. In gratitude for their information and assistance, and in the flush of victory, the monks were rewarded with gifts of treasure and grants of land. They were able to expand their operations under the enthusiastic sponsorship of the new Christian rulers. By about 1118, their new prior, a French nobleman, decided that they should do more than just provide lodging and care for pilgrims; they should accept knights into their order and have a military arm that would fight for the Holy Land. They changed their name to the Hospital of St. John of Jerusalem and applied to the pope for a constitution or *Rule* of their own, which was granted. With their new wealth and importance, they felt that they had outgrown their patron saint, St. John the Compassionate. They declared that their patron saint would now be St. John the Baptist.

In that same year, another order was founded in Jerusalem that would rival the Hospitallers in numbers, in wealth, and in power.

The support given by Baldwin I to the newly reorganized order of the Hospitallers of St. John may have inspired one Hugh de Payens, a vassal of the count of Champagne. In 1118, de Payens petitioned King Baldwin II, on behalf of himself and eight other knights, for permission to establish themselves as a new religious order. To the patriarch of Jerusalem they had made vows of poverty, chastity, and obedience. Unlike the Hospitallers, who operated hostels and hospitals in the Holy Land, this new order would devote itself totally to the military protection of pilgrims to the holy places. They sought permission for, and were granted, quarters for their new order in a wing of the royal palace in the temple area. This was the former mosque al-Aqsa, said to have been built on the site of the original Temple of Solomon. From this location the group took its name: The Poor Fellow-Soldiers of Christ and the Temple of Solomon. Over the centuries to come they would be referred to as the Order of the Temple, the Knights of the Temple of Solomon in Jerusalem, and a number of other variations. Two things remained standard, however: Whatever the form of their name, it was always based on the Temple of Solomon, and it always took second place to the popular name they bear still, the Knights Templar.

The new order apparently did very little in the first nine years of its existence, and there is no record that it even took in new members. Then in 1127 it seems to have decided to break out. In that year, King Baldwin II wrote a letter to Bernard (later St. Bernard), abbot of Clairvaux and the most influential churchman of his day, sometimes referred to as "the Second Pope." Baldwin asked that Bernard use his considerable influence with Pope Honarius II to obtain papal sanction for the new order of Knights Templar and asked him to establish a Rule for the life and conduct of its members. Bernard responded favorably.

The order, in the beginning, seems to have been little more than a private club formed around the count of Champagne. All of the founding Templar Knights were vassals of Champagne. Hugh de Payens was his cousin. Andre de Montbard, who was to become the fifth grand master, was an uncle of Bernard, who was himself from Champagne, while Pope Honarius had been a Cistercian follower of Bernard. The pope selected the capital of Champagne, the city of Troyes, as the meeting place for a council to review the Templar requests. The first gift of land granted to the Templars was at Troyes, and it was there that they established their first preceptory in Europe.

Bernard did contact the pope with Baldwin's request, backing it with all the approval and encouragement he could bring to bear. When Hugh de Payens and five other Templars arrived in Rome, they were made welcome by the pontiff. The pope did call for a council to be held the following year at Troyes, in Champagne, and instructed the Templars to be present there. Bernard could not attend in person, but he wrote setting forth his excitement about the prospects for the new order. He gave his reasons for asking the council to grant the order official recognition, calling for the establishment of a Rule, for which he would offer his personal assistance. Bernard's fame was based upon his great success as a reformer and propagator of the monastic life, and his position was so well established that any project approved by him could hardly be rejected by the church or the laity. Bernard helped to devise a Templar Rule based upon that of his own Cistercian order, which in turn had been based on the much older Benedictine Rule.

To understand the nature of the Templar order, it is important to see it as a monastic order of monks and not as an order of chivalry. Templars were religious at a time when monks were generally regarded as better than the secular priests and much closer to God. St. Bernard himself said, "The people cannot look up to the priests, because the people are better than the priests." Today the Roman Catholic church has well-organized lines from the Holy See through the bishops to the secular clergy, and contemporary monastic orders may appear somewhat less than absolutely necessary to the structure, except when they perform certain specialized tasks such as teaching or healing. It is difficult, then, for us to comprehend how central the monastic orders were to the church; they even supplied it with popes, particularly in the eleventh and twelfth centuries.

The monastic life had begun early in Christianity as an individual effort. The man frustrated with the worldliness about him, consumed with the desire to live the life that he believed God expected of him, would simply wander off by himself. This was the age of the ascetic hermit, a movement that seems to have taken hold first in Egypt. A preoccupation was to fight off all desires of the flesh and all impulses to materialism. Through the biography written by Bishop Athanasius we know most about a monk named Anthony, who opted for the life of a religious hermit late in the third century. Although he lived in the hot Egyptian desert, Anthony wore a hair shirt for the rest of his life, under leather clothing. He never bathed, and he fasted to the brink of death. His greatest temptations arose not from abstinence from creature comforts, but from sexual desire. He reported that the Devil appeared to him at night in the form of sensuous women, tormenting him until he screamed out loud. He sought ever more painful ways to torture his body to purge it of sinful thoughts. This all-out effort to please God made Anthony a near-saint during his lifetime, and pilgrims flocked to see him and to seek his advice. The most famous hermit of all, of course, was the Syrian ascetic Simeon Stylites, who built a pillar sixty feet tall and lived on top of the column for thirty years until his death, fed by followers and pilgrims, who presumably also made some contribution to rudimentary sanitation.

The church did not stop such extremists but did not encourage them, either. Rather, the church's influence was directed toward community living, with the solitary hermitlike existence partially preserved through having the monks occupy private cells for personal devotions, meditation, and rest. This was combined with some communal activities, however, such as celebrating mass, reading of offices, group prayer, eating, and working. Citizens who admired the monks and even envied them, but who could not bring themselves to their level of personal sacrifice, could share in their sanctity by founding and supporting a monastery or by giving gifts of land and other valuables to existing houses. Most of the early houses were totally independent units, comprised of an abbot and twelve monks, emulating the twelve disciples of scripture.

Perhaps the most influential man in this early monastic era was Benedict of Nicosia. Unable to tolerate the vice and corruption of Roman life, Benedict fled to the hills nearby and commenced a life of abject poverty and fierce self-punishment. Gradually his fame spread, and young men came to him both as pilgrims and as volunteers to share his faith and conduct. He began to organize communities for these disciples, which culminated in his founding of the monastery at Monte Cassino about A.D. 530. Its bombing and restoration during and after World War II have been well documented, and it still sits perched on a commanding hilltop south of Rome.

More important than the monastery itself was the Rule that Benedict created for the monks who followed him. This Benedictine Rule became the foundation model for a number of monastic orders that followed, such as the Cistercians, whose Rule in turn became the basis of the Rule created for the Knights Templar. The Benedictine Rule's central theme was embodied in the three vows of poverty, chastity, and obedience, all rigorously enforced. For first offenses, the Rule called for verbal rebuke and solitary confinement, heavily supported by prayer. If this did not cause the monk to abandon his willful ways, his abbot was authorized to use the whip. If his errors could not be beaten out of him, the monk could then be expelled from the order. Although the monks worked to be as self-sufficient as possible, their primary obligation was service to God through devotions and charity. The monks, because they lived according to a Rule (*regula*), became known as the "regular" clergy. Priests, who were free to move about in society (*saeculum*), became known as the "secular" clergy. As the church became increasingly worldly and materialistic, the monastic "regular" clergy appeared far holier to the general population, which contributed to the monks' influence and position of trust. The soft braided belt worn by monks and friars now appears to be just an item of their habit, but in the early days of the monastic orders everyone knew that the coarse rope around a monk's waist was for self-flagellation, to drive out sinful thoughts and urges.

Of course, worldliness crept into the monasteries as well, as the gifts of land and gold enabled them to have tenants and serfs on their property, and eventually the monastic system itself called out for reform. The call was answered most dramatically by Bernard of Clairvaux. In 1112, Bernard joined the relatively new Cistercian order at the age of twenty-one. He soon became the abbot of Clairvaux and founded no fewer than sixty-five daughter houses. He was a brilliant speaker, a persuasive writer, and was said to have lived a blameless life according to the strict Cistercian Rule.

Bernard was just twenty-eight years old when the Council of Troyes asked him to help create a Rule for the Templars. He did more than that. He became their most vocal champion, urging that they be supported with gifts of land and money and exhorting men of good family to cast off their sinful lives and take

up the sword and the cross as Templar Knights. Bernard also succeeded in establishing a form of recruitment that may have
infused the Templars with freethinkers throughout their entire
existence. Service in the order, which coupled adherence to strict
monastic vows with the constant threat of mutilation or death on
the holy battlefield, was enough penance to compensate for any
sin. Murderers, thieves, fornicators, and even heretics were welcomed, provided they renounced their former sinful ways and
embraced the order's sacred vows. During the years of the Albigensian Crusade in southern France, a number of self-avowed
penitent Cathar heretics were taken into the order. It is impossible
to evaluate the influence such men had in the secret enclaves of
the order, but it would be foolish to think that they had none.

Bernard exhorted all young men of noble birth to join the Templars and called upon all Christians to support the order with generous gifts. The king of France responded with grants of land, as
did a number of his nobles. Traveling on to Normandy, Hugh de
Payens met there with King Stephen of England. As the son of
Stephen of Blois, a hero of the First Crusade, the English king
quickly avowed his support. He gave the Templars substantial
gifts of money and made arrangements for them to carry their
recruiting efforts to England and Scotland. There they not only
received gifts of gold and silver but also were presented with pro-
ductive manors, which were to provide a continuing stream of
income. Stephen's wife, Matilda, contributed the valuable manor
of Cressing in Essex (the same manor of Cressing Temple that was
transferred to the Hospitallers and later smashed by the English
rebels in the Peasants' Revolt).

Hugh de Payens had departed Jerusalem as one of a group of
just nine knights bound together in an obscure, unofficial order.
He returned two years later as grand master of an order responsible
only to the pope and possessed of gold, silver, and landed wealth,
with three hundred knights sworn to stand and die if their master
so ordered.

All the time, the work on their Rule was moving forward. It
could not be just like any other monastic Rule because the Templar life would require travel, military training, and participation
in battle, activities little known to the other monastic communities. First came the three basic monastic vows of chastity, poverty, and obedience. Chastity took count of both sexes. No Tem-

plar was to kiss or touch any woman, not even his mother or sister. Even conversation with any woman was discouraged, and often forbidden. Templars wore sheepskin drawers that were never to be removed. (The Rule ordered that Templars should never bathe, so the ban on the removal of drawers was seen as support for the prohibition of sexual activity.) No Templar was to allow anyone, especially another Templar, to see his naked body. In their dormitories, lamps burned all night to keep away the darkness that might permit or encourage homosexual practices, a constant concern in all-male societies, including monasteries.

In keeping with his vow of poverty, Hugh de Payens gave all of his property to the order, and the other founding Templars soon followed suit. If a new Templar recruit did not have property to contribute, he was expected to come with a money "dowry." Once a Templar, he was permitted to keep no money or other valuables, not even books, in his personal possession. If loot was taken, it went to the order. This Rule was so important that if, upon his death, it was learned that a Templar had money or property of his own, he was declared outside the order, which precluded Christian burial.

Instant obedience to his superiors was required of every Templar, and since the order was responsible to no one but the pope, it essentially created its own system of punishments, up to the death penalty, for disobedience. For example, a penitential cell only four and a half feet long was built into the Templar church in London, and in that cell the brother marshal (military commander) for Ireland was confined for disobedience to the orders of the master. Unable to stand up, unable to stretch out, he was kept in the cramped stone cell until he starved to death. In no way were the Templars to be bound by the laws of the countries in which they might reside from time to time. Only their own Rule governed their conduct, and only their own superiors could discipline them.

Templars were allowed no privacy, and if a Templar received a letter it had to be read out loud in the presence of a master or chaplain.

On the battlefield the Templars were not permitted to retreat unless the odds against them were at least three to one, and even then they had no right to retreat unless ordered to do so. If it happened that under oppressive odds, with the right to retreat according to their Rule, the field commander told them to stand and fight until the last Templar was dead, that order was to be obeyed. Men who joined the Templar order fully expected to die in battle, and most of them did. There was little point to individual surrender in the field because the Templars were forbidden to use the funds of the order to ransom any Templar taken prisoner. As a result, Templars taken in battle were often summarily executed by the enemy.

The order was divided into three classes. The first class was the full brothers (the "knights"), who had to be free and nobly born. Their distinctive garb was a white mantle, to which was added later a red eight-pointed cross; the mantle signified the new white life of purity entered into by each knight. The second class, generally called sergeants, was drawn from the free bourgeoisie. The sergeants acted as men-at-arms, sentries, grooms, stewards, and so forth. They wore the red Templar cross on a black or dark-brown mantle. Third came the clerics, priests who acted as chaplains to the order and, because they were the only group of the three with any claim to literacy, frequently acted as scribes and record keepers and were responsible for other duties of a nonmilitary character. The clerics also wore the Templar cross, on a green mantle. The clerics wore gloves at all times, to keep their hands clean for "when they touch God" in serving mass. The clerics were clean-shaven, according to the custom of the time, while the knights were required to keep their hair cut short but to let their beards grow.

As outward evidence of their vows of poverty, the knights were limited in adornment of their clothing or equipment. The only decoration permitted in their dress was sheepskin. In keeping with the regulation, the girdle they were required to wear at all times as a symbol of chastity was also made of sheepskin.

The Templar Rule further provided for just two meals per day but permitted meat where forbidden by other monastic Rules, because of the strenuous nature of Templar duties. The Templars were allowed no talking during mealtime. They were absolutely required to participate in daily religious devotions, like any other monastic group.

The Templar banner was vertical, divided into two bars or blocks; one was solid black, to symbolize the dark world of sin that the Templars had left behind, and one was pure white, to reflect the pure life of the order. The banner was called the "Beau Séant," which was also a battle cry. The word *beau* is now generally conceived to mean "beautiful," but it means much more than that. In medieval French it meant a lofty state, for which translators have offered such terms as "noble," "glorious," and even "magnificent." As a battle cry, then, "Beau Séant" was a charge to "Be noble!" or "Be glorious!"

Templar initiations and chapter meetings were conducted in total secrecy. Any Templar revealing any proceeding, even to another Templar of lower rank than himself, was subject to punishment, including expulsion from the order. To preserve secrecy, the meetings were guarded by knights who stood outside the door with their swords already drawn. Although there is no documentation, legend has it that several times spies, or perhaps the merely curious, met death the moment they were caught.

The total contents of the Rule, which could be altered, added to, or even ignored from time to time by each grand master, were highly confidential. The beginner was told just enough of the Rule to permit him to take his place at the bottom of the order. As he rose in the Templar hierarchy, further sections of the Rule were revealed and explained to him. Knowledge of the contents of the complete Rule was confined to the very highest ranks of the order. To everyone else it was doled out on a "need to know" basis. One of the most serious offenses in the order was for a knight of any rank to reveal any part of the Rule.

A meeting of the Templar Knights in one of their churches could well call to mind the legend of King Arthur and his Round Table, because most of the Templar churches were circular, to emulate the Church of the Holy Sepulcher in Jerusalem. The circular Templar church in London, for example, has a stone bench around the entire perimeter so that seated knights would all be looking toward the center. There is no "throne" or special decoration to indicate that any seat is more important than any other.

Ultimately, according to Matthew of Paris, the Templars held over nine thousand manors all over Europe, plus mills and markets. In addition to these income-producing properties, the Templars had other sources of revenue. Loot taken or shared in by any brother went to the order. During its two hundred years of existence, over twenty thousand initiates brought land or money dowries to the order. As they bought and eventually built their own ships to transport men and supplies to the East, as well as fighting ships to guard the others, the Templars earned revenues by transporting materiel, secular Crusaders, and pilgrims to the Holy Land. They were often given memorial gifts or remembered in wills. The church in Rome contributed regularly and urged others to do so as well. Part of the penance of the English King Henry II for his role, direct or indirect, in the murder of Thomas à Becket, archbishop of Canterbury, was his well-known public flogging. Not so well known is that another part of the penance required that Henry make a substantial money payment to the Knights Templar for use in a subsequent crusade. The result of all this was a surplus of funds, and as the surplus was put to work, the Templars entered a relatively new business: the money business.

Many references have been made to Templar financial activities under the term "banking," which doesn't quite fit. *Fortune* magazine uses a term for a category of business that is much more apt: "diversified financial services." The easiest financial service for the Templars was safe deposit. Since they had to maintain continuous guard on their own treasure, it took no extra effort or manpower to perform the same service for others. So secure were their facilities supposed to be that even governments took advantage of them; England, at one point, stored part of the crown jewels with the Templars. There are records of theft from Templar commanderies, but they were still a favored source in a day when the only protection for valuables was armed manpower or a secure hiding place. If a rich man traveled he could take his treasure with him, and risk its loss to bandits or a rival lord, or leave it at home, at the risk of having it stolen by relatives or retainers or by an attack on his home during his absence. Now an effective alternative was a service offered by militant monks who had a reputation for safeguarding the treasure of others as vigilantly as they did their own.

Another important Templar service was acting as agents for collection. They took contracts for the collection of taxes and sometimes acted as agents to negotiate the ransom and return of important prisoners, even to the point of participating in arrangements for funding the ransom payments. They performed these services for either side, if both parties were Christian.

The Templars maintained trusts, in the sense that they collected income or managed income properties. They dispensed payments to heirs on the basis of a specified agreement, ensuring proper management of the income for beneficiaries. A fee was exacted in return for the service.

As mortgage bankers, the Templars loaned money on income property, often avoiding the ban on usury by taking the revenues of the property until it was redeemed. In this case, they acted as property managers as well, which they were able to do by relying upon the personnel they employed to manage their own properties. Perhaps their most famous financial service was the issuance of paper for money. The documents were honored at any Templar commandery and as such might be considered forerunners of checks or sight drafts. It was an important service. If a nobleman in Provence wanted to send funds to his son and retainers off on a crusade, he had to find a trustworthy messenger, hire guards to accompany him, and then carry the expense of a thousand-mile journey, with the danger of bandits on land and of pirates or shipwreck at sea. It was much easier and less expensive to turn the money over to the local Templar master, then have the funds dispersed in, say, Jerusalem, with absolutely no danger of loss. A fee for "expenses" was paid gladly.

It is impossible to say which, if any, of these financial services were actually invented by the Templars. Italian banking families were beginning to offer similar services, and the Venetians had long since perfected techniques of international money transfer and certain aspects of risk sharing and merchant banking, if only among themselves. The Jews of Europe, forbidden by law in most countries to own agricultural land or other means of production, had been forced to turn to trade and related financial transactions, although, once again, largely among their own. They did make loans to rulers, but usually as a communal activity, not as a "bank." The Templar financial services were conducted on a broader scale and were much more public in nature, which may have resulted in overenthusiastic accreditation by historians for Templar financial inventiveness.

One thing the militant monks would have to have invented, however, was their own means of identification for the completion of financial transactions. Today we have ID cards with photographs, Social Security numbers, driver's licenses, bank account numbers, holograms, invisible fluorescent inks, fingerprints, and an entire industry devoted to security and identification. Even with all that technology available, money and valuables are still occasionally passed to the wrong people, and stolen checks still get cashed. We can only speculate on the problems of a man in Jerusalem asked to turn over a large sum of cash to a stranger who walked in the door with just a piece of paper issued three months earlier in Paris. There was no telex, no telegraph, no radiophone, no way to determine that the document was not forged or that the man bearing it was indeed the man whose name appeared on it.

Novelists are fond of the broken coin or talisman, to be used years later to prove that the foundling is indeed the long-lost prince. Unfortunately, the use of the "matching pieces" means of identification requires that one half be sent on ahead to the other party, a not very practical solution, especially if the draft is to be good at *any* Templar commandery. What were absolutely necessary were standard identification techniques. One method was to require two or more "witnesses," persons who could affirm identity. Sometimes this went further, to the point of demanding a bond. The person affirming identity would sign a paper saying, in effect, "If, because of my witness, you give the money to the wrong man, I will make it good." Another method was to put one or more personal questions which, it was hoped, only the authorized recipient could answer. *Question*: As a boy you fell out of a tree and hurt yourself. How old were you then? *Answer*: Nine years old. *Question*: What kind of tree was it? *Answer*: An oak. *Question*: Who picked you up and carried you into the house? *Answer*: My uncle Thomas. That ancient system is still in use today, as I found recently when wiring money from America to a friend in England. I was asked for a question which only the recipient would be likely to answer correctly. The question was "What was your mother's maiden name?" Upon the revelation of the secret word *Jamieson*, the money was delivered.

Letters also required verification, since most were written by scribes and copyists. False letters could carry dangerously misleading instructions as to military moves or ship movements. Built-in codes, however, could be used to assure authenticity. In a buried-letter code, the second letter of the third word in each sentence might spell out a message. Codes were used to hide information in the text of seemingly innocuous correspondence.

The hidden message could be anything from "Send two ships to Messina" to "Kill the man who bears this letter."

The Templars were known to maintain intelligence agents in the principal cities of the Middle East and the Mediterranean coast, and they would necessarily have employed covert means of communication. International financial dealings required total secrecy, naval operations required it to hide shipping information from Moslem or pirate forces, and military administration over two continents would certainly require it. As a matter of record, the Templars gained a reputation, and not a good one, for their dedication to secrecy, even in the meetings and councils of the order.

Taken all together, the intelligence network of codes, signals, identification techniques, and surreptitious dealings associated with continuous military and financial operations, coupled with a fierce dedication to secrecy in initiations and meetings, provided an ideal base from which to construct a secret society. Perhaps no other organization in fourteenth-century Europe had the need for and love for covert activities that characterized the Knights of the Temple. It is certain that if the Templars resident in Britain had felt the need to hastily construct an underground organization after learning of the arrest of their French brothers on October 13, and before their own arrest almost three months later on January 10, they had the perfect background from which to do so.

In all this administrative activity, it should not be imagined that armored warriors, largely illiterate, spent their odd hours decoding messages or in the countinghouse maintaining ledgers and checking inventory or out in the barn supervising the annual sheepshearings. Although they did not call themselves, or each other, "knights," or employ the honorific "Sir," observing rather their ecclesiastical standing with the simple title of "brother" (*frater* or *frère*), the Templars were required to be of knightly rank and lineage. They were warriors, not scriveners. In the Order of the Temple, they were the officer class, and they had as their principal training and occupation direct participation on the battlefield; the army of administrators, native troops, and employees behind them outnumbered them by as much as fifty to one. The order could not be composed of 100 percent "knights" any more than a modern air force could be made up of 100 percent pilots. The sergeants were more diversified and could be mounted or foot soldiers in battle, personal attendants to knights, or stewards of one or more agricultural manors. The Templar clerics were the literate faction, and far more likely to be assigned duties of a managerial or accounting nature, including the drafting of letters in code. Other administrators, supervisors, and scribes were simply employees, and in later years a number were Arabic-speaking. As the Holy Land became populated with mixed European and local blood over succeeding generations, young men were recruited locally and trained by the Templars to be "Turcopoles," members of a light cavalry unit in the Holy Land commanded by a special Templar officer called the brother Turcopoler (*frère Turcopolier*).

The grand master, who also ranked as an abbot, was the autocratic ruler of the order, although he received advice and counsel from his principal officers. Masters of preceptories or commanderies were similarly autocratic, unless the grand master was present. The headquarters of the order and the residence of the grand master were at the temple in Jerusalem. He was not just an administrator but a front-line military leader, which is evident from the fact that of twenty-one grand masters, ten died either in battle or from the wounds they suffered in combat.

As the order matured, growing in wealth and numbers, the cowl of humility fell away. Although a monastic brotherhood, the Templars inevitably became involved in politics, especially in the kingdom of Jerusalem. Their role in political machinations made it inevitable that they develop an intense rivalry with the Order of the Hospital of St. John in Jerusalem. That rivalry grew so heated that at times there was actual fighting in the streets between Templars and Hospitallers.

As a background to understanding how the Templars changed from pious and humble monks, devoted to the service of pilgrims, to a haughty power center, asserting themselves as secular lords and kingmakers, one must examine the activities of the Order of the Temple in the final years before the loss of the Holy Land and the brutal suppression of the order.

CHAPTER 6

THE LAST
GRAND MASTER

Tedaldo Visconti, archbishop of Liège, was in the Holy Land in 1271 when word came to him that he had been elected pope. As Gregory X, he finally had the influence to stir up the new Crusade that he felt was so desperately needed. Jerusalem had fallen years before, and the Christian territories now occupied just a narrow strip centered on fortified port cities that lay like loosely strung beads along the coast of what is now Lebanon and Israel, with each city the center of a separate feudal fiefdom.

Wealthy Christian potentates, living (and even dressing) like Oriental potentates, wanted to preserve their wealth and their incomes, which now depended upon trade with their Moslem neighbors and upon the merchant skills, fleets, and financing of arch-rivals Genoa and Venice. They did not share the pope's enthusiasm for a new Crusade to recapture the holy places of Christendom with a war that might shatter their own fortunes.

Following the usual course to get a Crusade under way, Gregory X called for a council at Lyons, which opened in May 1274. The ruling princes who alone could order out the fresh supply of military Crusaders declined to attend. The elderly King James I of Aragon was the only reigning monarch to put in an appearance, but he saw no benefit to himself and soon went home. Maria of Antioch was permitted to address the council, to complain to the members that although she was one generation closer in line, her cousin, King Hugh of Cyprus, had usurped the throne of Jerusalem. Most dramatic, delegates were there from Michael of Byzantium to give that emperor's pledge that, after eight hundred years of dispute, he would cause the Eastern Orthodox church to recognize the supremacy of the Roman church. Theology had nothing to do with the concession; the emperor was expecting that his recognition of the overlordship of Rome would cause the Holy See to dissuade the pope's closest ally, Charles of Anjou, from his avowed intention to conquer Byzantium. The Byzantines were not alone in their fears, for the entire council was under the shadow of this one man.

Charles, brother of Louis IX of France and uncle of the present king, was count of Anjou and Provence. The Holy See, in order to unseat the antipapal house of Hohenstaufen from its Italian possessions, had acted quickly upon the death of the leader of that house, the German emperor Frederick II. The church made a deal with Charles of Anjou and loaned him the money to mount a military campaign against Frederick's heir. Charles was victorious, and the pope declared him to be the king of Sicily and the king of Naples. Charles became the strong man of the Mediterranean, with papal backing for everything he did. He also had the unswerving support of his cousin, Guillaume de Beaujeu, who had just been elected grand master of the Knights Templar.

As for the petition of Maria of Antioch, Pope Gregory X encouraged her to sell her claim to the throne of Jerusalem to Charles, and helped negotiate the terms. Charles agreed to pay Maria ten thousand gold pounds, with a promise of four thousand pounds a year for life, for the right to assert himself as king of Jerusalem. His cousin the grand master, in attendance at the council, assured him of Templar support of the royal claim he had just agreed to purchase.

As to a new Crusade, it was not to be. Bishops reported to the council that they could find no crusading zeal in their home territories. Knights and barons no longer believed in the spiritual benefits promised by the church. They knew that the crusading concept had been born of reverence for the Holy Land of Jesus Christ, but now they felt that its spiritual rewards had been denigrated, bartered by the popes for military support in Prussia, in Lithuania, and against the Albigensians in France. They felt that the idea of the Crusade had degenerated into a means of getting military backing for the schemes of the church at the cost of heavy tax burdens on all the people, and they knew that much of that tax money had never been spent for the purpose for which it had been raised; far too much of it went to support the luxurious life-styles of the higher clergy. The people, too, were disillusioned. There was a growing feeling that if God directed the arms of single combatants in the trial by combat, it could be reasoned that He did the same with whole armies. Since Jerusalem, Bethlehem, Nazareth, and most of the Holy Land had been lost, perhaps that was the way God wanted it to be. There would be no Crusade.

The only one who appears to have taken any benefit from the Council of Lyons was Charles of Anjou. His plans were not thwarted by the submission of the emperor Michael, because when the people of Byzantium learned that their emperor planned to subject their church to the authority of the Roman church the result was near revolt, and Michael had to back down.

When the bishop of Tripoli took his delegation back to the Holy Land to report the failure of the council to stir up a new Crusade, the political maneuvering accelerated. The resident Crusaders, who did not want to fight the infidel, fought each other incessantly. King Hugh of Cyprus, who had commandeered the throne of Jerusalem over the superior claims of his cousin Maria of Antioch, tried to impose his lordship over Beirut. The husband of the heiress of Beirut, an Englishman called Hamo L'Estrange ("Hamo the Foreigner"), was suspicious of Hugh's intentions, so before he died Hamo made an agreement to put his wife and her lands under of the protection of the Egyptian sultan Baibars. After Hamo's death King Hugh kidnapped the widow, intending to force her to marry a man under his control. True to his agreement, Baibars, with local support, forced Hugh to return her to Beirut. To make certain that no similar attempts would be made, Baibars provided a permanent bodyguard for the widow. An armed force of the infidel was guarding a Christian noblewoman against the designs of the king of Cyprus and Jerusalem.

King Hugh's next move was to try to get direct control over the county of Tripoli. When Prince Bohemond VI of Antioch had died in 1275, the title, and Tripoli, passed to his fourteen-year-old son. Hugh declared that he would act as regent until the boy came of age, but upon his arrival in Tripoli he found that the boy's mother had declared herself to be regent and had taken the boy into the care of her brother, King Leo III of Armenia, beyond Hugh's reach. Hugh found no local support for his claim and withdrew from Tripoli, back to Cyprus. The regent placed Tripoli under the administration of the bishop of Tortosa, who used the position to attack his personal enemy, the bishop of Tripoli, attempting to unseat him and exiling and even executing some of his followers in the process. Fortunately for the bishop of Tripoli, he had made friends with the Templar grand master when they had spent months together at the Council of Lyons, so he had an armed protector. Two years later, when Bohemond VII came of age and returned to Tripoli, he found that he had to deal with two strong enemies, King Hugh of Cyprus and the Order of the Temple.

Hugh was not having much success asserting himself as king of Jerusalem, but he hoped for better things as he proceeded to the port of Acre, a walled seacoast city larger than London, with a population of almost forty thousand. Located about midway between Tyre and Haifa, it was the principal port for trade with the Syrian capital of Damascus. Since the loss of Jerusalem, Acre had also become the major base of the Templars, who were opposed to the claims of King Hugh and whose grand master Beaujeu was totally dedicated to furthering the ambitions of his very ambitious cousin, Charles of Anjou. The Hospitallers, having lost their massive inland citadel, Krak des Chevaliers, were reduced to just about three hundred knights in the Holy Land, down from their peak of several thousand, and so were not a strong political factor. The Venetians, however, with their troops and ships and trading houses, were a very strong political factor, and they sided with the Templars against King Hugh. Aware of the alliance between the pope and Charles of Anjou, the patriarch of Acre remained neutral, as did the Teutonic Knights, a military religious order that had been organized earlier by German crusaders.

With no strong support anywhere, Hugh pulled back to his island kingdom of Cyprus in 1276 but left as his *bailli*, or deputy, for Acre his loyal vassal Balian of Ibelin. The following year Charles of Anjou completed his agreements to purchase her claim to the throne of Jerusalem from Maria of Antioch and made his move. He sent an armed force to Acre with his own *bailli*, Roger de San Severino. Notified in advance, the Templars and Venetians arranged for Roger to disembark and enter the city. Faced with documents signed by Maria of Antioch and by the pope, backed by the troops of Venice and the Knights Templar, Balian had little choice but to step aside, and Charles of Anjou was declared king of Jerusalem.

In that same year, young Prince Bohemond VII broke his word to his cousin and vassal, Guy of Jebail. Guy had been assured that his brother John would have the hand of a certain wealthy heiress, but the bishop of Tortosa interfered. He wanted that wealth in his own family and got Bohemond VII to disavow the arrangement with Guy of Jebail in favor of a marriage to the bishop's own nephew. Guy's response was to kidnap the young heiress and to marry her to his brother. Knowing that Bohemond would come after him, Guy sought refuge with Bohemond's enemies, the Knights of the Temple. To punish the Templars, Bohemond tore down the Templar buildings in Tripoli, and in response Grand Master Beaujeu took his Templars from Acre on a raid of revenge against Tripoli and burned Bohemond's castle at Botrun. Leaving a small Templar force to support Guy at Jebail, Beaujeu retired to his headquarters at Acre, but as soon as the grand master was back at his base, Bohemond moved on Jebail. Guy and his troops, along with the Templars left with him, went out to intercept Bohemond and defeated him soundly.

In January of 1282 Guy decided to try for the capture of Tripoli. With his brothers and a small group of close followers, he surreptitiously entered the city and went first to the reestablished Templar commandery. The group then moved on to hide in the quarters of the Hospitallers, but someone sent word of their presence to Bohemond. The prince trapped them in a tower, but the Hospitallers negotiated terms with Bohemond under which the lives of Guy, his brothers, and his friends would be spared if they would peaceably surrender. Once he had his hands on the group, Bohemond disregarded his promise. He ordered that all of Guy's followers be blinded. As for Guy and his brothers, they were buried with only their heads exposed above the ground, for a lingering public death from thirst and starvation.

In 1279 King Hugh, still seething over the deal made between his cousin Maria and Charles of Anjou, decided to have another try at asserting his authority over Acre as the true king of Jerusalem. Accompanied by his armed vassals he put ashore at Acre and called for the local nobility to rally to him. None did. The primary force working against Hugh was the Knights Templar, with their grand master still dedicated to the support of King Charles and with Charles's Venetian allies ready to lend their political and military support. The feudal contract between King Hugh and his Cypriot vassals required them to spend no more than four months of military service off the island, and as the time ran out they returned to Cyprus. King Hugh felt that he had no alternative but to leave with them, but he took vengeance upon the Templars by confiscating all of their valuable properties on Cyprus. Not even the intercession of the pope could cause him to give them back.

By this time the Mongol hordes, under descendants of Genghis Khan, had penetrated the Middle East, and the Mongols now ruled over Persia (Iran) and the land between the Tigris and Euphrates rivers (Iraq). Their major enemy was Baibars's successor, the Mameluke sultan Kala'un, who now ruled Egypt, Syria, and Palestine. In 1280 the Mongol ilkhan sent an ambassador to Acre, reporting that he was going to throw an army of one hundred thousand men into Syria the following spring and asking for an alliance that would bring Christian men and armaments to bear on their common enemy. The Christians did not respond, but the Egyptian sultan did. Anxious to limit his military campaigns to just one enemy at a time, Sultan Kala'un proposed a ten-year peace treaty with the Christians. The treaty was signed, and included the signatures of the grand masters of the Hospitallers, the Teutonic Knights, and the Knights Templar. As the viceroy of Charles of Anjou, Roger de San Severino signed for Acre, following his orders to maintain favor and alliance with the Egyptians, who would be at Charles's back when he launched his campaign against Byzantium.

In spite of the indifference of the Crusaders, the ilkhan took the field with his Mongol horsemen in September 1281, and the Egyptian sultan Kala'un, who had massed his armies around Damascus, went out to meet him. There were several violent clashes, with tens of thousands of men slain and mutilated on the field, but no decisive victory on either side. Then in a great battle the ilkhan's brother, Mangu Timur, was seriously wounded and ordered his Mongols to pull back. Kala'un had suffered too much in losses of men and supplies to mount a pursuit and let them go. The war was a draw.

Then, within six months, an event occurred that changed the power and the politics in the entire Mediterranean basin, from Spain to the Holy Land. Some Italian historians have said that the criminal society now known as the Mafia evolved from a secret society formed by the lower nobility and peasant leaders of Sicily, as an underground resistance to their French conquerors. If they are correct, the Mafia or its predecessor may have had a dramatic role in the final loss of the Holy Land. On one evening, March 30, 1282, in an operation that would have required many weeks of most secret preparation, the Sicilians rose and murdered every one of the hated Frenchmen on their island, a shocking bloodbath remembered in history as the Sicilian Vespers. That night rocked the empire of Charles of Anjou and the papacy that supported him.

King Charles had been assembling an army in southern Italy for his conquest of Constantinople. Now he had to use that army for the conquest of his totally lost Sicilian kingdom. King Pedro III of Aragon had the same idea and began pouring troops into Sicily, so that when Charles arrived he found that he had a war on his hands. Then the naval forces of Aragon defeated Charles's fleet at the Straits of Messina and a few months later trounced his Neapolitan fleet in the Bay of Naples. The papacy came to his aid with men and money and almost drained the treasury of the church as the conflict spread. Genoa, engaged in a war with Charles's strong ally, the Venetian republic, came out with renewed vigor. Philip III of France supported his uncle Charles with a direct invasion of Aragon, but his troops were decisively beaten by Pedro III, who by now had been excommunicated by the pope. Charles of Anjou was no longer the strong man of the Mediterranean, or of any place else, for that matter.

Off in the East, the emperor Michael could relax. There would be no invasion of Constantinople and no need for submission of the Eastern Orthodox church to the supremacy of Rome. The Egyptian sultan saw his Christian ally drop in power and prestige and knew that Charles would not be able to defend his claim to the throne of Jerusalem, much less rid the Mamelukes of their Byzantine enemies. Nor was there now any strong power to protect the Crusader bases in the Holy Land, nor any likelihood of a new Crusade while almost all the princes of Europe were at each other's throats.

King Hugh of Cyprus was especially pleased to hear that Charles needed his vassal Roger de San Severino and had ordered him back to Italy, leaving Roger's confused seneschal, Odo Poilechien, as *bailli* of Acre. In July 1283 Hugh set sail from Cyprus, determined this time to be recognized as king of Jerusalem. His fleet steered a course for Tyre, but the winds blew the ships off course to Beirut. Hugh decided to move south to Tyre by ship, while his troops would make the journey by land. On the march, they were attacked and cut up by Moslem raiders, an attack that Hugh was convinced had been instigated by the Knights Templar.

Hugh was well enough received at Tyre, but he waited in vain for word to come that he would be welcome at Acre. The Templars there, as well as the local nobility and the Venetian traders, much preferred the laissez-faire government of Odo Poilechien, who in his confusion about his authority and that of his master, King Charles, was leaving them alone to do as they pleased without government interference. Once again Hugh was sweating out the four-month feudal military contract of his vassals. As before, they returned to Cyprus when their time was up, but this time King Hugh decided to stay on the mainland to pursue his claims. Then, on March 4, 1284, he died, and the crown of Cyprus and the claim to Jerusalem passed to his frail seventeen-year-old son John, who had not much more than a year to live.

While the Christians were maneuvering for position among themselves, Sultan Kala'un was preparing his final campaign. He began by leaping over all of the Crusader port cities to besiege the great coastal castle of Marqab, a Hospitaller base about twenty-five miles north of Tripoli. He arrived there with a great army of soldiers, engineers, and miners on April 17, 1285.

Unable to bring the walls down with stone-throwing mangonels, the sultan's engineers undermined a tower on the north side of the castle, which came tumbling down as its wooden underpinning was burned away. The Hospitallers surrendered on terms that allowed the garrison to leave the castle unharmed.

Five days before Marqab fell, King John died, and the crown of Cyprus and the claim to Jerusalem passed to his fourteen-year-old brother Henry.

During the siege of Marqab, Charles of Anjou also died, an event much more important to young King Henry than the loss of a Hospitaller castle. On June 4, 1286, Henry landed at Acre, and now no one opposed him but the *bailli*, Odo Poilechien. The grand masters of the Templars, the Hospitallers, and the Teutonic Knights got together and among them convinced Odo that with Charles of Anjou dead and his son Charles II totally occupied with the Sicilian war there was no point in believing that anyone was going to defend any Angevin claim in the Holy Land. King Henry of Cyprus was declared the undisputed king of Jerusalem.

There was still one chance that there would actually be a kingdom of Jerusalem for Henry to rule, and that chance lay in an alliance with the Mongols against the Egyptian sultan. It was not an alliance that the Christians had to seek out, but rather one to which they simply had to agree. The Mongol Ikhan Ahmed had assumed the Persian throne in 1282 but had been murdered in a palace conspiracy in 1284, opening the throne to his son Argun. In the first year of his reign Argun wrote to Pope Honorius IV, urging a combined Mongol-Christian effort against the Mameluke sultan, a letter the pope didn't even bother to answer. In 1287 Argun sent his personal ambassador, a Nestorian Christian named Raban Sauma, but by the time he got to Rome the pope was dead. Raban Sauma traveled Europe looking for an alliance. He called on the doge in Genoa, on Philip IV in Paris, on Edward I of England in Bordeaux. Then in February 1288 Raban Sauma learned that a new pope had been elected as Nicholas IV, and he hurried to Rome. Everywhere he proclaimed that the Mamelukes were even now making preparations for the final destruction of all of the Christian cities in the Holy Land, but he could find no one who cared, not even the pope. The papacy, in league with France and King Charles II, was embroiled in the Sicilian war with Aragon and Genoa, which was also at war with Venice. Philip IV of France wanted to push Edward I of England off the continent, while Edward was dedicated to holding his French possessions in one hand while scooping up Scotland with the other. Raban Sauma went home in the spring of 1288 to report to Argun that he could hold out no hope of Christian cooperation with the Mongols.

Argun tried one more time, sending letters in 1289 to Philip IV,

Edward I, and the pope. He proposed to mount a campaign against the Mamelukes in January 1291 and assured them that, in exchange for Christian support with men and materiel, the Christians would have Jerusalem and the Holy Land for their own. Unfortunately for Argun, the ambitions of Philip and Edward were centered much closer to home, and no longer could masses of men be motivated to foreign wars by religious zeal and promises of the great spiritual benefits to be bestowed upon them by Christ's Vicar on Earth. Even the pope had other problems, being totally involved in the European wars. The Christian nobles in the Holy Land were on their own.

As for those nobles, they no longer dreamed of Christian ownership of the roads and towns where Jesus Christ had walked and taught. They had learned what all occupants of that land eventually learn, from the Phoenicians long before them to the Israelis long after: The land yielded little in the way of natural resources or raw material for production, but had natural advantages for trade. The descendants of the original Crusaders had turned into merchants and traders, their attention directed to tolls, taxes, and harbor fees. They didn't want to fight the infidel but to trade with him, and Moslem merchants operated freely in every Christian port city. They felt that to a great extent the Moslems needed them and their ports, and they seemed no more aware of their imminent danger than their counterparts in Europe.

The Knights Templar had a comprehensive intelligence network that extended even to the court at Cairo, where one of the Moslem officials, the emir al-Fakhri, was on the Templar payroll. He got word to the grand master that the Sultan Kala'un was massing a huge army in Syria for an attack on Tripoli. The grand master immediately warned that city to gather supplies and men and strengthen its defenses, but no one in authority in Tripoli believed his story: After all, he was the bitter enemy of their liege lord, King Henry. Nevertheless, the grand master sent a contingent of Templars to help the city in what he alone believed was an impending attack.

The leaders of Tripoli became believers when Kala'un showed up outside their walls in March 1289 and began to put his huge stone-throwing catapults in place. When two towers and a large section of wall crumbled under the incessant daily bombardment, the residents knew that their city was lost. The Venetians had ships in the harbor, which they loaded with all their portable possessions and sailed away. The Genoese loaded their ships during the night and made off early the next morning. As they sailed out of the harbor, Kala'un ordered a general assault, and his troops poured through the wide breach into the city. The harbor provided the only escape route, but there were few ships left. The marshals of the Templars and the Hospitallers got away with Prince Amalric of Cyprus and the countess Lucia of Tripoli, while the Templar commander left behind was killed trying to hold back the Mamelukes, who soon engulfed the local population. Every adult male was killed where he stood, and the women and children were bound together to be marched off to the slave markets. After Tripoli was emptied of people and loot, Kala'un had the city dismantled, stone by stone.

The Christians at Acre were in shock. They had believed that their trading activities were a benefit that the Moslems would not want to lose. It was true that the military orders were there, who were certainly not merchants, but wasn't it also true that the Templars extended their banking services to the Moslems and Christians alike? They grasped at the antidote to their trauma when Kala'un offered the kingdoms of Cyprus and Jerusalem a hollow truce of ten years, ten months, and ten days.

To his credit, King Henry was suspicious of the truce and sent his own ambassador to the pope and to the courts of Europe to seek help, with the hope that he might succeed in conveying the desperation of his plight now that Marqab and Tripoli had fallen.

Henry's ambassador got the usual round of warm welcomes and regretful excuses, but he did have one success that Henry would have been better off without. In the summer of 1290 a mob of near-rabble arrived at Acre from northern Italy, saying that they were ready to fight the infidel. They were loud, drunken, and offensive to the local population. Then one day a drunken gathering turned into a riot that overflowed into the streets, where the Italians began butchering the Moslem merchants of the city. Finally the local barons and the military orders were able to bring the mob under control and to arrest a number of the leaders, but the dead Moslems in the streets gave Kala'un an excuse he was not going to pass up.

When envoys arrived from the sultan demanding that the guilty prisoners be turned over to him for punishment, a council was called of the leaders of Acre. Beaujeu of the Templars advised the council that for its own protection it should turn the Christian criminals over to Kala'un. He got no backing for his proposal and the consensus was that, criminals or not, no Christians were going to be sent to certain death at the hands of the Mamelukes. Kala'un couldn't have been happier with the decision, for he now had all the reason he needed to break the truce. He called for the mobilization of the Egyptian army and ordered his Syrian army to move to the Palestinian coast. He publicly announced that he was preparing a campaign into Africa, but the emir al-Fakhri earned his pay again by getting word to the Templar grand master that Kala'un's real target was Acre. Once again the grand master passed on a warning derived from his own spy system, and once again he could find no one in authority who would believe him.

Frustrated in his attempts to arouse the leaders of Acre to their danger, Grand Master Beaujeu sent his own envoy to the court of Kala'un. The sultan pointed out that he wanted the place, not the people, and agreed that all of the inhabitants could leave the city unharmed in exchange for a number of Venetian gold *zecchine* (ducats) equal to the total population. When the grand master announced this offer to the high court of Acre, the response was shouted insults and accusations of treason, which did not let up as Beaujeu stomped from the hall.

It seemed that the Templar grand master was wrong and the leaders of Acre were right when word arrived at the city that Kala'un was dead. He had moved out of Cairo at the head of his army on November 4, 1290, and had died within the week. His son, al-Ashraf, however, had sworn to his dying father that he would take up the sword and carry out his father's plans against the Christians, and it didn't take long for the people of Acre to learn that the son was going to be as relentless as the father. Hoping to fend off the invasion, the Christians sent an embassy, comprised of a leading noble, a Templar, and a Hospitaller to the new sultan. Upon their arrival the young sultan had them taken to a dungeon before they could even state the purpose of their mission. The people of Acre did not learn by what means their envoys died, just that they were all dead.

True to his filial vow, al-Ashraf arrived before the walls of Acre in April 1291. The city could boast a defensive force of fifteen thousand men, while the sultan had ten times that many, plus siege engines, catapults, and engineers.

The defense of Acre consisted of a double wall to the north and east, with the sea to the south and west. Both inner and outer walls were strengthened by towers, but those inside did not take total comfort from those high, thick walls because it was said that al-Ashraf had brought enough engineers to provide a thousand miners for every tower.

The assault began with mangonels and catapults lofting great stones and pots of incendiaries over the walls, while archers darkened the sky with flights of arrows. After ten days of this battering, the Templar knights made a night raid on a Moslem camp, taking the enemy totally by surprise. Unfortunately, in the darkness many of the armored Templars tripped over tent ropes and were captured. The rest were beaten back into the town. The Moslems were ready for repeat raids, and when the Hospitallers came at them in the dark a few nights later, the sentries promptly lit fires and torches, and the Hospitallers were easily beaten off, with heavy losses.

The mining had already begun on May 4 when King Henry arrived to take command, with about two thousand additional men. By May 15 five towers had tumbled and the defense had to move back to the inner wall. On May 18 the sultan ordered a general assault on the entire length of the wall, with a heavy concentration on the Accursed Tower, a fortified corner where the northern inner wall and the eastern inner wall came together. The local knights of its garrison were pushed out of the tower, and a counterattack by the Templars and the Hospitallers, led by their grand masters, was no match for the hordes of Mamelukes pouring through the breaches. Guillaume de Beaujeu was mortally wounded in the counterattack and was carried away by his Templar knights to die in the Templar headquarters across the city. As the Accursed Tower fell, King Henry took ship and sailed back to Cyprus.

With the Accursed Tower secure, the Moslems fought their way south along the inner east wall and opened the St. Nicholas Gate. The Moslems poured into the city and the bloody street fighting began, but with no doubt as to the outcome. As at Tripoli, the only escape was by sea. Soldiers and civilians joined a crushing mob at the harbor seeking to escape in anything that would float. His servant found a small boat for the wounded Patri-arch Nicholas, but that good man invited so many others to share it with him that the boat sank, drowning all on board. A Templar named Roger Flor used a Templar galley to make a huge fortune for himself as he asked noblewomen on the pier to choose between their lives and the jewel cases they were clutching in their hands.

As the Mamelukes moved through the streets they took no pris-oners. Every Christian was killed, with no regard to age or sex. Those who cowered in their houses were gathered up later for the slave markets, where it is said that so many slaves from Acre went on the block that the price of a young girl fell to a single drachma.

By nightfall the Moslems had the entire city except for the for-tified Templar building at the extreme southwest corner of the city, which had two walls on the sea so that it had a means to receive additional supplies. The Templars had chosen to defend their temple rather than flee in their galleys and had taken in all of the women and children who had sought refuge with them. After five days Sultan al-Ashraf tired of this one building tying up his army, and he offered terms to Peter de Severy, the grand mar-shal of the order. If the Templars would surrender their fortress, all inside could leave for Cyprus with their arms and all of the per-sonal possessions they could carry. The grand marshal agreed, and a hundred Mamelukes led by an emir were admitted to the temple to monitor the withdrawal. Perhaps on the excuse that they had been too long in the field, the Mamelukes immediately began to sexually abuse the women and the young boys. This was more than the Templars were willing to tolerate, and they drew their weapons and fell on the Mamelukes, killing them all. They hauled down the sultan's flag and announced that they were pre-pared to fight to the death.

The sultan sent an envoy the next day to express his regrets over the misconduct of his men. He offered the same terms as before and asked that the Templar marshal and his officers be his guests so that he might offer his apology and discuss the surren-der terms in person. Peter de Severy selected a few men to accom-pany him, and as they approached the sultan's tent the sultan's bodyguard seized the Templars and beheaded them in full view of the Christians watching from the walls.

While all this was happening, the sultan's engineers were driving a tunnel to the temple foundations. They undermined the two landward sides of the building and set the supporting timbers ablaze. On May 28 the landward walls began to settle and tumble down. The sultan ordered two thousand men across the breach into the building, and their added weight completed the devastation as the entire stone structure collapsed, killing everyone inside. There was no Christian left in Acre.

Next on the sultan's list was Tyre, thought to be the strongest fortification on the coast, perhaps because it had twice successfully fended off the attacks of the legendary Saladin. This time there was no fight to record, because upon news of the approach of the Mamelukes the commander of Tyre promptly set sail for Cyprus. Al-Ashraf's men simply walked in and took over.

Tibald Gaudin, the treasurer of the Templar order, was at Sidon, where he learned that the surviving knights had elected him their new grand master. Inevitably, a Mameluke army appeared before Sidon a few weeks after the fall of Acre, and the knights fell back on the Castle of the Sea, built on projecting rock about a hundred yards offshore. The new grand master immediately sailed for Cyprus with the treasure of the order, ostensibly to return with help. None ever came. Now the Mameluke engineers could not turn to their favorite technique of mining because the sea would be above them, so they did the opposite. They began to construct a broad causeway out to the castle. The situation was hopeless, and the Templar garrison sailed off to its castle far up the coast at Tortosa. The Mamelukes, under the emir Shujai, entered the castle on July 14 and proceeded to take it down.

With Sidon out of the way, Shujai turned his army to Beirut. Perhaps taking a cue from the tactics of his sultan, Shujai invited the Christian leaders to visit with him to discuss the situation. Apparently having learned nothing from the events at Acre, the leaders of the garrison accepted Shujai's invitation and were made prisoners the moment they arrived at his tent. Without its leaders the garrison panicked and fled the city in any ships available. The Mamelukes walked in on July 31. All the Christian ornament and decoration was torn out of the cathedral and it was reconsecrated as a mosque.

A few days later another Egyptian army to the south took Haifa without a struggle. The monasteries on Mount Carmel were put to the torch and all the monks were slaughtered. The Templars had a castle a few miles south of Haifa at Athlit, but with a small garrison in no position to hold off the Egyptian army. They abandoned it two weeks later on August 14. Far to the north, on the other side of Tripoli, the same decision was reached at the Templar castle at Tortosa, which was abandoned that same month. As the Templars sailed away from their castles at Athlit and Tortosa, the Mamelukes were in total control of every square foot of the Holy Land. The defeat was total. The Knights of the Temple were without a base in the Holy Land for the first time since the day they were founded over 170 years before.

The Templars continued to maintain their castle on the tiny island of Ruad, two miles offshore from Tortosa, but it was of no strategic importance and more trouble than it was worth—even drinking water had to be brought in by ship—and after a few years they simply abandoned it. After the fall of Acre they set up their headquarters on the island of Cyprus, with the reluctant permission of King Henry. With no place else to go, the Hospitallers also moved their base to that same island kingdom.

During the following year Tibald Gaudin died and the Templars convened to elect a new grand master, not suspecting that he would be the last to hold that honor. He was Jacques de Molay, a knight of the lesser nobility of eastern France and a confirmed disciplinarian. He had spent his entire adult life in the Templar order since his initiation in 1265 at the age of twenty-one. Now, at forty-eight, he was grand master, having already served as master of the temple in England and most recently as grand marshal, the supreme military leader of the order. Although the Templar fortunes in the Holy Land had collapsed, de Molay still controlled the wealth of thousands of agricultural manors in Europe, plus mills, markets, and trade monopolies. He controlled a fleet of fighting ships and still maintained an international banking operation. From dozens of commanderies in Europe he could still call up the best-trained, best-equipped standing army in Christendom, and his fierce pride reflected that power.

As a military man, one of de Molay's first moves was to attempt to restore morale by enforcing strict discipline and returning to more orthodox behavior within the order. Possession of all books and other writings was forbidden the knights, without exception. As an illiterate soldier-monk, de Molay saw no purpose in the

Templars' being able to read: They would be told what they needed to know, and no good could come of their knowing more than they needed to know. He ordered a general increase in discipline throughout the order, demanding rigid enforcement of the Templar Rule as it related to diet, dress, personal possessions, and religious devotions.

A continuing problem for de Molay was the assertion by King Henry of Cyprus of his royal right to command all of the military forces in his island kingdom, including the Templars. This concept was totally and repeatedly rejected by de Molay, who recognized no authority higher than his own on the face of the earth, with the single exception of the pope himself. The king and the grand master quarreled so bitterly on this point that finally the only way to settle the matter was to put it to the pope. In August 1298 Boniface VIII ruled in favor of the grand master, pointing out that King Henry should be happy to have the courageous Templars based in his kingdom because of the added protection they afforded his crown in those times of total military uncertainty. The pope's ruling reinforced de Molay's already exaggerated appraisal of his own stature and power.

Encouraged by this expression of support from the pope, de Molay put forward arguments for a new Crusade to regain the Holy Land, but his pleadings came at an awkward time. Pope Boniface VIII was wallowing in the success of his jubilee year of 1299, a turn-of-the-century celebration in which it seemed that all the world wanted to come to Rome to bow to the supreme pontiff as the new Caesar and to seek his favor with gifts of silver and gold. Discussions of a new Crusade surely could wait until the following year.

The delay was frustrating to de Molay, who with his background of military planning and leadership felt he knew just how the next Crusade should be mounted, but it gradually became obvious that there would be no new Crusade as long as Boniface VIII sat on the Throne of Peter. Then in 1305 Bernard de Goth, archbishop of Bordeaux, ascended that throne as Pope Clement V. The orders of fighting monks anxiously waited to see what the new pope's attitude would be toward the reconquest of the Holy Land. They didn't have to wait long.

In 1306, during the first year of his reign, Pope Clement V sent instructions to the grand masters of the Templars and the Hospitallers ordering them to meet with him in person later that year in Poitiers. The purpose of the meeting was to plan the military and financial aspects of a new Crusade. So that the infidel would not know that the two principal Christian military leaders had absented their eastern bases, they were told to travel to Poitiers incognito. Their journeys were to be kept secret from everyone.

The Hospitallers were engaged in an attempt to conquer the island of Rhodes, and their grand master was not rebuked when he reported that he could not meet at the requested time.

Jacques de Molay had no such excuse, but he managed to put off answering the summons until the early part of the following year because he needed time. The new Crusade was vital to the Templar order, and the plans de Molay would put to the Holy See must be well thought out, highly credible, and demonstrative of the superior military skill and experience of his order. Everything must be done to assure that the new Crusade would go forward, because without it the Templar order would have no purpose. It had been founded to guard the pilgrim roads to Jerusalem, but now those roads were guarded by the Moslems who owned them. The order had been created to protect pilgrims, but now there were no pilgrims to protect. A new Crusade was vital, too, for renewed respect and support. As a mendicant order embracing vows of poverty, the Templars relied on support in the form of gifts from their fellow Christians, but that giving had fallen away. True, the order still possessed great wealth, but that wealth could be eroded quickly by the costs of the all-out invasion and war that the order needed now. De Molay felt that the whole world should respect the gallantry and selfless courage of his Templar brothers who had spilled their blood in the losing battles for the Holy Land, but he also knew that he was in a profession that was ultimately judged not on efforts but on victories.

The other military orders had benefited from accepting reality. The Teutonic Knights wrote off the Crusade against the Moslems and directed their total attention to a Crusade against the pagans in northeastern Europe. They conquered a territorial region that eventually became their state of Prussia; the knights themselves provided the core for what would become the Prussian Junkers, the officer class, who preserved the black eight-pointed cross of the Teutonic Knights as their military iron cross. The Hospitallers were not content to be resented guests on

Cyprus and looked about for a territorial base of their own. Expanding their fleet and seeking out allies, they gained a foothold on the island of Rhodes, the first good news from the East in fifteen years and a victory that earned them increased respect within the church and at the courts of Europe. Completing the conquest in 1308, they were content to become known as the Knights of Rhodes. Many years later they were pushed off Rhodes and backed off to the island of Malta, until unseated by Napoleon. The Hospitaller order still exists today in Rome, where it is recognized by the Vatican as a sovereign state under its current name, the Knights of Malta.

Of the grand masters, only Jacques de Molay refused to take off the blinders that directed his every vision of the future to a new Crusade to retake Jerusalem. He apparently had no idea how far his mind had strayed from the reality of European politics. Every prince in Europe would give lip service to a new Crusade, but not his sword arm, and not his purse. The church could not get Philip IV of France to do anything; reality was quite the other way round. Perhaps if de Molay had kept up with the twenty-year battle between Philip and the Holy See he would have been able to see through Philip's machinations and perceive how he used the false hope of a new Crusade to fill his own treasury with the gold of the church and of the Templar order. As for England, King Edward I had no real desire to fight the turbaned infidels across the Jordan: His concern was the kilted Christians across the Tweed. The Crusades were finished.

So was Jacques de Molay, but he didn't know it yet. No matter what rumors or reports he may have heard, he consistently refused to bow to reality, until at last he redeemed himself at the price of a slow, agonizing death over a charcoal fire.

To gain the understanding that de Molay lacked, to better comprehend how the Knights Templar could be so thoroughly suppressed and how England and Scotland could provide such a perfect haven for fugitive Templars, we will need to look briefly at what was happening in Europe between the fall of Acre and the arrest of the Templars. The significant conflicts were between Philip IV of France and the popes, and between Edward I of England and the uncontrollable Scots on his northern border. For a short space we shall leave Jacques de Molay on his way to Marseilles, standing in the bow of a Templar galley, looking over the horizon to the shores of France where he expects to rally a mighty army of God to retake the Holy Land, not dreaming for even a moment of the whips and chains being readied for him in Paris.

CHAPTER 7

"THE HAMMER OF THE SCOTS"

On a stormy night in 1286 King Alexander III of Scotland rode into Burntisland to change horses. He was riding to Kinghorn to be with his second wife. The storm was so fierce that Alexander was urged to spend the night at the changing post, but he insisted on riding off into the night, with fatal results. His horse galloped over a steep cliff and Alexander was killed.

Alexander's first wife had borne him a daughter who grew up to become the wife of Eric II of Norway but was fated to die after giving birth to a daughter named Margaret. This child, the great-granddaughter of Henry II of England and granddaughter of Alexander III of Scotland, was known as the Maid of Norway. Six years before Alexander's death the Treaty of Brigham had betrothed the then four-year-old princess to the first Prince of Wales, who would become Edward II of England. The great plan was to unite the crowns of England and Scotland in one dynasty, although the countries would be administered separately, but fate decreed otherwise. As the little queen, now ten years old, proceeded by ship to Scotland, a storm off the Orkney Islands sank the vessel and the Maid was lost. The Scottish succession was thrown into confusion.

No vacant throne waits long for claimants, and in Scotland there were no fewer than thirteen, although only four of them were considered to have any chance of success. They included two Comyns of Badenock, identified by the color of their beards as Comyn the Black and Comyn the Red, to avoid confusion between the branches of the family. The Black Comyn was favored by many, but he indicated that, if it should be deemed necessary to resolve any dispute, he would stand aside for the apparent favorite choice, John Baliol, a grandson of Margaret, the eldest daughter of King David I of Scotland. The fourth major claimant was Robert Bruce, a son of King David's second daughter, Isabel.

Legally, Baliol had the strongest claim, being descended from the elder daughter of the Scottish king, but he was not popular with the common people. His timid ways had earned him the popular nickname of "Toom Tabard," or Empty Coat, indicating that he had nothing inside.

Bruce was easily the most popular of the thirteen candidates, and his secondary position was offset by the fact that he already had a male line of succession in place. There was a son in his forties and a sixteen-year-old grandson, who would one day hide in a cave and watch a spider and go on to become king of Scotland.

If civil war was to be avoided, there must be negotiation. King Edward I of England, renowned as a lawmaker and arbitrator, arranged to have himself asked to arbitrate the succession. He summoned the Scottish lords to meet with him in May 1291 at Norham Castle, a border fortress just inside England across the Tweed. He shocked the assembled nobility with his opening announcement that a precondition for arbitration, whatever the outcome, must be that he himself should first be acknowledged as supreme lord of Scotland. Further, several border castles were to be ceded to the English crown to bind the arrangement. Fearing treachery, the Scottish lords immediately withdrew north across the river to Scottish soil to confer. A delegation returned to Edward and asked for thirty days to consult with those nobles and church leaders not in attendance.

When the delegation returned thirty days later, the number of claimants had dropped from thirteen to eight. Faced with the very real prospect of civil war among the adherents to the several claimants, the spokesmen agreed to Edward's overlordship, and each of the remaining claimants took an oath to that effect. Since the choice by now was obviously between Bruce and Baliol, it was decided that the decision would be made by a group consisting of forty men to be selected by Baliol, forty more to be selected by Bruce, and an additional twenty-four to be nominated by Edward. This group debated on and off for over a year and finally convened at the Dominican chapel near the castle of Berwick to announce their decision. The very weaknesses that caused the Scots to scoff at John Baliol made him attractive to Edward of England as a potential puppet, so Baliol was named king of Scotland. On November 30, 1292, he was crowned at Scone, the ancient capital of the Picts, seated on the sacred Stone of Scone, which legend said had served as a headrest for St. Columba. Later, the new Scottish king appeared south of the border at Newcastle to do homage to Edward as his liege lord. Edward provided the illustrious audience with a jolting sign of how he perceived the relationship between the crowns of England and Scotland. He sent for the Great Seal of Scotland and broke it into pieces, which were then placed in a bag for deposit in the English treasury in London. The significance was not lost on anyone present.

Legally the problem of the Scottish succession had been solved without the shedding of blood, but the manner of its accomplishment had set the stage for the spilling of rivers of blood on both sides in the years ahead. The deed was done, but the people didn't like the manner of its doing. Scottish nobles, who usually wanted no master, now had two.

It didn't take long for them to discover what kind of a master Edward was going to be. Within months after King John's coronation, Scots who could not get satisfaction in their own courts were encouraged to bring their suits in England. King John himself was summoned to appear in an English court in the matter of a disputed bill for wine sold to his predecessor. Then a Scottish earl whose brother had been killed by Lord Abernathy decided that he had a better chance against the murderer by taking the case to Westminster. The English Parliament agreed to hear the case and demanded that King John appear before them as a witness. When word of his refusal arrived, he was immediately found guilty of contumacy ("disobedience, especially to an order of a court") and, as punishment, orders were issued for the seizure of three of his castles. At this, King John's resolve collapsed and he agreed to come to London at the next convening of Parliament.

In London, King John got another shock. Edward was preparing for war with France and told John that he, as Edward's vassal, would of course be expected to provide Scottish troops and money. There were angry words on both sides, and John, deciding that he would be safer at home, left London secretly and made a dash north to the border.

He was no happier with what he found on his return. His people resented his caving in to the English king's demands to appear in London and felt that his humiliation was theirs as well. They were fed up with his weakness and appointed a board of four earls, four barons, and four bishops to advise their king and they made it clear that they expected that advice to be followed.

With the people on its side, the new board began to act in its own national interest. A parliament was convened at Scone, which instigated a series of moves that it knew involved the risk, if not the likelihood, of war. It formally rejected Edward's demands for Scottish troops to serve the English cause in France. All English officials in Scotland were deposed, and all lands held in Scotland by English subjects were declared forfeit. Then the parliament took an action that it must have known would leave Edward no choice but to declare war: It sent a parliamentary delegation to the court of Philip IV to seek an alliance between Scotland and France. The alliance was consummated with the agreement that should either country be invaded by England, the other would come to its aid. To bind the arrangement, it was agreed that Philip's niece Isabel, daughter of Charles of Anjou, would be married to the son and heir of King John of Scotland.

Upon learning of all this, Edward demanded instant possession of all border castles in order to protect his kingdom from Scottish raids while he was away at war in France. The demand was not only refused, but the Scots, their confidence bolstered by their new alliance with France, raided over the border into England. The Scottish nobles, however, as they had been before and would be again, were cursed by their unwillingness to sacrifice any of their fierce personal and clan pride in order to work together or obey any higher authority. Lacking discipline or direction, the raids were abortive and ended with a serious defeat at Carlisle. The Scots retreated to their own country to prepare their defenses against the vengeance of the English king and his army.

It was not long in coming, and the first battle of that war is still remembered for its butchery.

At the head of an army of thirty thousand foot and five thousand horse, Edward crossed the River Tweed, with the rich Scottish port of Berwick as his initial target. The city easily beat off the naval attack launched against it, but was ill-prepared for the land attack, although crude palisades had been hastily raised, protected by an ineffective ditch. Still, the garrison was commanded by the redoubtable Sir William Douglas, and the townspeople felt confident of their security. Edward led the attack himself on his great war-horse Bayard. Spotting a low point in the stockade, he leaped the ditch and then jumped over the palisade to enter the city, with his army right behind. There was brief but bitter fighting in the streets and a group of thirty Flemish merchants defended their Red Hall until it was burned around them, but it was not much of a battle. The castle garrison surrendered on terms that permitted it to march out of the city, leaving the citizenry to the sack. After binding and imprisoning the entire population, Edward ordered that every male citizen of Berwick be killed. The slaughter took days to accomplish, with the number of those executed estimated at between eight and ten thousand. The scale of the massacre was a shock to both countries, even in those bloody times.

Restoring the fortifications of Berwick, Edward moved his army north from the Tweed. He met the Scottish army, just back from its raids into northern England, and defeated it with ease at Spottswood. As he had anticipated, the lesson of the massacre at Berwick had not been lost on the towns and castles in his path. The castle at Dunbar surrendered with no fight worth the telling. One town after another capitulated, and by June Edward found himself before Edinburgh. The city put up no fight and its castle held out for just eight days. From there he advanced to Stirling, where the castle garrison fled upon news of his approach, then on to Perth, where he received the message that King John was prepared to surrender.

Edward met John at Montrose, where the latter knelt to present the white rod as a token of submission. The deposed Scottish king was taken to the Tower of London, where he languished until the pope interceded on his behalf and he was permitted to go into exile in France. To make clear forever to the Scots just

who it was who ruled their nation, Edward removed the holy coronation stone from Scone to Westminster. Perhaps no single act
aroused the national Scottish ire as did the theft of their holy symbol of kingship. (Over six hundred years later, in 1950, a group of
nationalistic young Scots stole back the stone from it resting place
in Westminster Abbey and restored it, temporarily, to Scotland.
While this effort was ultimately thwarted, rumors of more plans
to retrieve the stone continue to crop up to this day.)

Finally, at Berwick, Edward demanded and received the submission of almost every Scottish leader—earls, barons, bishops,
clan leaders, and major knights. He demanded their names in
writing, and the list required thirty-five sheepskin parchments.
This collection of parchments, sewed end to end, was derided by
the Scots as the "Ragman Roll." That name for tedious business
further degenerated into the term *rigamarole,* which has found a
permanent place in the language. Rigamarole or not, the English
defeat of Scotland was complete and, apparently, irrevocable.
Edward could turn his attention again to his war with France.

And so it might have been, except for that strange phenomenon that has occurred repeatedly throughout history, in many
times and in many places. A man rises to fit the occasion. Not a
ruler, but a man of the people who meets their yearnings and
then matches that empathy with unschooled military genius.
Such men often come to sad ends, without reward, but live on as
legends of their people. For Spain, it was Rodrigo Díaz de Bivar,
called El Cid. Mexico produced Emiliano Zapata. For the Cuban
revolutionaries it was Ché Guevara. Morocco had Abdel Krim,
who, when invited back from forced exile to a hero's place upon
the achievement of his country's independence, declined to
return to his homeland because his bitter enemy, France, had
been diplomatically recognized. Such a man rose in the time of
Scotland's greatest need. His name was William Wallace.

Wallace was the second son of an obscure knight of Renfrew
and was in his early twenties when he decided to take up his
sword against the hated invader from the south. Wallace's country, in southwest Scotland, did not have the Highlands' topo-
graphical advantages but consisted of low hills and rolling plains
intersected by many streams, and it was well spotted with
English-garrisoned fortifications. Under these disadvantages Wallace assembled a small group of followers and embarked upon a

course of guerrilla attacks. He attracted national attention when he attacked Lanark, the headquarters of the English sheriff, William de Hessilrig, with a small band of just thirty clansmen. They took Lanark and killed the sheriff. The feat also took the attention of Sir William Douglas, whose estates were in Lanarkshire and who was burning for revenge for his defeat by Edward at Berwick. When Douglas and a few others of the Scottish nobility decided that, with Edward pinned down by his wars in France, now would be a good time to strike back, they sent for William Wallace.

Wallace and Douglas quickly agreed upon an operation that would please themselves and all of Scotland as well. They would attack William de Ormesby, the English justiciar of Scotland, who had calculatingly established the seat of his courts at Scone. It was a place steeped in Scottish tradition and regarded with reverence. In the dim past it had been the Pictish capital. Its abbey had been the home of the sacred coronation stone until Edward had stolen it away, and from time immemorial, issues important to the people had been decided in meetings held on Scone's Moot Hill.

Ormesby apparently felt that having his seat at Scone would lend validity to his rulings, and any Scot who refused Ormesby's summons to Scone was heavily fined. If the fine was not paid the Scot was "out-lawed," placed outside the protection of the law, and was thus fair game for anyone to rob or kill. It was a temporal equivalent of excommunication. Arrogant in victory, Ormesby proved prudent in the face of danger, as he gathered up his gold and his records and hastily departed Scone upon hearing of the approach of the Scottish army.

Wallace was a poor man, with nothing to lose, but Douglas was not. Upon learning of the seizure of Scone, Edward ordered the confiscation of the extensive Douglas landholdings in England. Later, Douglas himself was captured and sent back to Berwick, where he died in less than a year, loaded down with fetters and heavy chains in a deliberately miserable prison.

After Scone, Wallace swept north, with no shortage of recruits. Even some of the Scottish nobility joined him, but often with their maddening insistence upon their individual prerogatives, fighting when and where and how they chose, reluctant to totally acknowledge a supreme military leader in the field. To offset this, Wallace became a stern disciplinarian to the troops under his direct command. One man in each five was appointed a leader, as was one man in each twenty, each hundred, and each thousand. Thus his orders could be passed quickly to every single man in his army, and disobedience of those orders, or disobedience to any leader on any level, meant just one punishment: death. Those Scottish leaders who fought apart from Wallace with their traditional clannishness were no match for the English, who mauled them with ease. Wallace was of another breed. He commanded the best-organized, most disciplined army on either side with a fanatic's will and with awesome military skill, facts not yet known to the English. They thought that they were going to once more chastise a disintegrating mob of clansmen.

In preparation for his most famous battle, Wallace laid seige to Dundee and sent a large force to Cambuskenneth Abbey. These moves threatened Stirling Castle, and the English had to respond. An experienced English army of fifty thousand foot and a thousand cavalry moved to meet Wallace's army of less than forty thousand foot and a mere one hundred and eighty horse. Wallace was a guerrilla who had never before commanded such a large military force. The English leader was John de Warenne, earl of Surrey and governor of Scotland, drawing upon a lifetime of practical experience in military leadership. The English were professionally armed, while Wallace's men, many of whom had lost their clan leaders in previous battles, were armed primarily with long spears or axes. For armor, they had only double tunics stuffed with rags or tow to ward off sword-cuts. They were almost all barefoot. They were also largely without supplies. They were, however, fully equipped with a high degree of hatred for the invaders and a high regard for their leader.

Wallace knew that the English would march toward him from Stirling Castle, to the south. To reach him, they would have to cross the tide-swept River Forth over Stirling Bridge, a wood structure that would pass no more than two horsemen abreast. He placed his men north of the bridge, concealed in dense thickets, with strict orders to stay hidden until ordered to advance. It is a tribute to Wallace's discipline that this order was obeyed implicitly by thousands of men eager for the fight. The English knew that the clansmen were out there somewhere, but not exactly where, nor exactly how many. Why hadn't the Scots destroyed the bridge? Should a larger bridge farther up the tide-fed river be used to flank the Scots? Finally, Bishop Cressingham, the king's treasurer and tax collector for Scotland, had his way, demanding that the king's limited revenues not be wasted by prolonging the issue. The English army started across the narrow bridge.

Wallace needed all his self-discipline to wait for the optimum split of the English army on the two sides of the river. It had been calculated that it would take a minimum of eleven hours to get the whole English army across. First came horsemen, to test the strength of the bridge. Once over the bridge, they fanned out on the Scottish side as a semicircular picket to guard the crossing. Then came the foot soldiers and the Welsh archers. Hour after hour the clansmen crouched uncomfortably in the thickets they had occupied the night before. Finally, at eleven o'clock in the morning, Wallace decided that the force on his side of the river was big enough to have its defeat be a crushing blow, but small enough to be beaten swiftly and decisively by what would be his superior numbers. The signal was given.

Out from the thickets poured tens of thousands of wild, screaming Scots. To the English, there seemed to be no end to them, leaping across the open ground with bare feet and bare legs, brandishing twelve-foot spears and long hooked axes, with an occasional claymore, the deadly two-handed Scottish broadsword. Every throat was filled with bloodcurdling screams and battle cries. Wallace had his best men on his right, and these charged into the left flank of the English army, swiftly cutting and slashing their way to the control of the north end of the bridge so that no reinforcements could get across. The English on the Scottish side were now trapped in a bend of the river. Those toward the advancing Scots were cut down and those to the rear were pushed into the river, now swollen with the incoming tide. Laden with armor and chain mail, they quickly drowned.

The helpless de Warenne watched his cavalry and archers being cut to pieces and pushed off the bridge, or off the bank, to drown in the rushing tidewater. He gave the order to retreat, but it was not to be a retreat that the Scots would permit to be orderly. As soon as the bridge was cleared, Wallace sent his men off in a wild chase to cut up the stragglers. When news of the rout reached the Scottish nobles who had declined to fight under the commoner Wallace, many of them decided to take a hand in the chase. Thousands of English soldiers ran for safety, with no time to stop to eat or sleep. They were driven off the roads, hunted down in the forests and in the hills. The hunted shrank in number daily, while the pack of hunters grew as more and more joined in the chase. Prisoners were not the objective. The Scots wanted only to kill and then to continue the chase to kill again. Back at the bridge, the body of Bishop Cressingham was flayed and a portion of the skin presented to Wallace as a covering for his sword belt.

Wallace gathered what he could of his scattered army and recruited more. In a few months he had retaken Stirling, Berwick, Dundee, and Edinburgh. With Scotland secure, he engaged in a punitive expedition to burn English towns across the border, raiding into Cumberland and Westmoreland.

At home again in Scotland, Wallace, who would have had little opposition in claiming the throne had that been his goal, was knighted, and he selected the title "Guardian of the Kingdom." He had brought some organization and national union to his country, but he was a fighting man, not a politician, and the Scottish nobles still plotted to keep their precious independence from higher authority.

Scotland was free, but it had regained that freedom from an England operating without its redoubtable King Edward I, who was away almost continuously attending to his war with France. How would he react to the loss of Scotland?

His reaction was to enter into prolonged negotiations with France, to free himself to deal with the threat on his own doorstep. In 1294 it was agreed that King Edward would marry King Philip's sister, Princess Margaret, while Edward's son and heir, Prince Edward, would marry Philip's daughter, Isabella. This double marital alliance made further negotiation a mere matter of course, and by 1297 Edward was able to turn his attention, and the bulk of his military strength, to the problem of Scotland.

Back in England, Edward's first official act was to call a Parliament at York, commanding the Scottish nobles to appear as well, with the admonition that any noble who did not appear would automatically be judged a traitor. None came, not necessarily because they followed Wallace, but because some simply recognized no higher authority than themselves. More were afraid of treachery.

Edward led his army north into a wasteland. All crops had been burned and all livestock moved away from the war zone. English ships were waiting at the Firth of Forth with provisions, but Wallace blocked the way. The English had expected to be able to forage along the way and then pick up fresh supplies at the Firth, but now they could do neither. Wallace had based his strategy on the fact that, sooner or later, the starving English army would have to retreat to find food, and then he would attack and harry. Unfortunately, two Scottish earls decided to use the English to get rid of Wallace the commoner and sent informants to Edward. They told him that Wallace's army was hiding near Falkirk, just a few miles away, waiting for the English retreat. That was all Edward wanted to hear. "They need not follow me! I will go to meet them this very day!"

By nightfall of that same day the English army had moved up to within striking distance of Falkirk. After a few hours rest, Edward led his army through the remaining hours of darkness, and as the sun rose the English could see the Scottish army stationed halfway up the slope of a ridge in front of them. Wallace had just a few hundred cavalry under the command of John Comyn the Red and a few archers armed with the crude, short Highland bow, which was no match for the range or power of the longbow of Edward's Welsh archers. Most of the Scotsmen carried the twelve-foot spear, and they were formed up in three schiltrons, hollow circles of spearmen who created a bristling hedge of spear points, with reserves in the center of the hollow to replace the fallen. The long spear was effective against cavalry but almost useless in close hand-to-hand fighting, and it was no defense at all against the long-range English archers. Wallace placed his own archers between the schiltrons, with the small cavalry unit held in reserve to be used as the course of the battle dictated, primarily to break up formations of archers, against whom there was no other defense.

Both Comyn the Red and Sir John Stewart, who commanded the Scottish archers, argued before the battle that, because of lineage and titles superior to those of Wallace, they should be in supreme command. Wallace prevailed, but to his cost. At the first attack by the English, Comyn the Red and his cavalry abandoned the battlefield, leaving Wallace without screen or reserves. Sir John Stewart fell with his troops early in the combat.

For a while the schiltrons stood against the English attacks and it seemed that the Scots would again be the victors. Edward, however, decided to try a different approach, and the Scots in their wool-rag armor experienced a weapon totally new to them in the field, one against which they now had no defense. Edward had his troops fall back and lined up his archers. Arrows that flew at speeds fast enough to pierce light metal armor and chain mail had no problem with the crude cloth armor of the Scots. Flight after flight of arrows struck the massed schiltrons of spearmen, who dropped where they stood with no chance to strike back. The proper countermove would have been a cavalry sweep through the bowmen, as Wallace well knew, but the cavalry had gone. With nothing to do but stand and die, the schiltrons began to break up. When Edward saw this, he sent his own cavalry in a wide sweep to the rear, and the Scots broke into a rout. Fortunately, Wallace had placed them close to the woods, and those who fled there were more difficult prey for the pursuing heavy cavalry. Wallace himself was chased into a thicket by Sir Brian de Jay, master of the English Templars. Wallace killed him.

By the time the battle and the rout were over, ten thousand Scottish dead lay on the field. The nobles of Scotland now overlooked no opportunity to denigrate Wallace, and all of them refused to follow him. Calling on the alliance with France, Wallace went to King Philip to seek aid for his country. By way of response, Philip put Wallace in chains and wrote to Edward, offering to deliver the prisoner to him. Edward expressed his gratitude and asked that Wallace be held in France for the time being. Subsequently, Philip changed his mind and released Wallace. Instead of the military aid that Wallace had come for, Philip gave him a letter to take to the pope, soliciting the pontiff's help. There is no record that Wallace ever used it.

By 1304 John Stewart of Menteith, an early supporter and friend of Wallace, had gone over to the English and had been rewarded with the post of sheriff of Dumbarton. Later that year, Menteith was approached by a man named Jack Short, a servant of Wallace. Short wanted to collect a reward, now that his master was a fugitive with no future, and reported to Menteith that Wallace was at Robroyston, near Glasgow. Menteith arranged that he himself would go to the inn to seek Wallace and, if he found him there, he would signal soldiers in the tavern that this was their man by turning around the loaf of bread on the table. Menteith did, indeed, find his old friend Wallace and sat at the table with him. As the soldiers entered, Menteith picked up the loaf, turned it around, and put it back on the table, whereupon Wallace was seized.

No time was lost in loading Wallace down with chains and parading him to London. On August 22, 1305, only one day after his arrival, Wallace was placed on trial in the Great Hall at Westminster. A platform had been erected for his display at one end of the hall and a laurel wreath was placed on his head—a mockery, some Scots will tell you, not much different from the mockery of the Roman soldiers in placing a crown of thorns on the head of Jesus Christ. Wallace was charged with a long list of crimes against the crown, including treason, sedition, murder, and arson. Having been declared outlaw, he was not permitted to say one word in his own defense. He was found guilty by a panel of five judges and sentenced to be hanged, drawn, and quartered.

Less than an hour after the sentence was passed it was put in motion. Wallace was taken from Westminster to the Tower. There, a waiting cortege took him in hand to deliver him to the execution ground at Tyburn, to which he was dragged behind horses along streets crowded with spectators. In anticipation of his sentence, the gallows at Tyburn had been raised higher to permit good viewing for the entire crowd. Wallace had a noose placed around his neck and was raised slowly, choking and twisting, then taken down before he was dead. Somewhat revived, he was castrated, then a small cut made in his stomach through which his visceral organs were slowly pulled from his body, finally bringing death. His head was cut off to be placed on a pike above London Bridge. His body was cut into four pieces and salted. The quarters were sent north for display in Newcastle, Perth, Berwick, and Stirling as proof of Wallace's death and as examples to others who might think to emulate their leader. Scotland's greatest patriot had died the most revolting death that gory imaginations could dream up for him. His legacy was a deep smoldering hatred.

On February 10, 1306, after the butchering of Wallace, Robert Bruce met John Comyn the Red at the Franciscan monastery at Dumfries. His grandfather and father now dead, Bruce was a direct claimant to the throne of Scotland. Comyn the Red, the same who had run off with Wallace's cavalry at the Battle of Falkirk, had assumed the Baliol claim to the throne, based on a distant kinship. Bruce and Comyn argued in front of the high altar and grew so heated that Bruce drew his dagger and plunged it to the hilt into the side of his rival. Bruce came out of the church and said to his followers, "I doubt me I have killed the Red Comyn." One of his followers drew his own long Highland dirk and cried in answer, "I'se mak' siccar!" ("I'll make sure!"), then entered the church to deliver the deathblow.

Moving swiftly to give no enemy time to react, Bruce went directly to Scone. In response to his summons, Bishop Wishart of Glasgow met him there with the robes for the coronation. He was joined by a group of bishops and nobles who well knew that their very presence at this ceremony would earn them the undying enmity of Edward I, off in England where he did not even suspect that the Scottish peace was about to be broken.

The heroine of the day was Isabella, countess of Buchan. She was the wife of a Comyn, now blood-feud enemies of Bruce. More important to Isabella, she was also the daughter of the earl of Fife, a fast supporter of Bruce's claim to the throne. Hearing of the impending coronation, she demanded that her saddle be placed on the fastest horse in the stables, and without her husband's knowledge she made for Scone as fast as her horse could travel. Arriving just before the ceremony, she asserted that since her brother, the present earl of Fife, was too far away to be present in person, she would be the one to exercise the hereditary right of her house to place the crown of Scotland on the head of its rightful king. As impressed by Isabella's spirit as by any legal right, her countrymen accorded her the honor, and Bruce became King Robert of Scotland.

When Edward I received news of the coronation of the new Scottish king, he exploded. Orders were dispatched to his lieutenant for Scotland, Aymer de Valence, that all who followed Bruce were to be killed. There were to be no prisoners taken by the army that was assembled in England for the fresh invasion of Scotland. Largely because of his own failing health, but also in an attempt to get his effete son, Prince Edward, to assume some manly responsibility, Edward placed the army nominally under the command of the young man, who was the first heir to the English throne to carry the title of Prince of Wales.

To lend ceremony to the new stature of Prince Edward, he was knighted at Westminster. Two hundred and seventy young men who were to accompany him to war were also knighted in one great chivalric event. The formal ceremonial procedure at that time called for the young man who was to be knighted to be prepared for the ceremony the night before, by shaving him and fixing a scented bath (this in marked contrast to the Knights Templar, who took vows not to bathe and not to shave). After his bath, the candidate spent the night in a chapel in prayer and meditation, while watching over his armor and weapons. On this occasion, no available facility was large enough for all of the candidates, and many were housed at the Templar compound in London. Some of the trees in the Temple orchard had to be cut down to provide room for the tents of the candidates, with their servants and attendants. Most made their all-night vigil in Westminster Abbey, but many stood watch over their knightly gear in the Templar church. (It is interesting to note the high standing of the Templars with the English royal family on this special occasion, just a few months before their arrest in France.)

The ceremony itself crowded Westminster Abbey as never before. In the crushing pressure of the throng gathered to watch the historic spectacle, two men died of suffocation before the high altar. After the prince and each of his new companions had achieved their knighthood with a sword tap on the shoulder, the whole entourage retired to a great feast. There, the king swore an oath to seek vengeance for the murder of the Red Comyn and to take no rest until he had killed Robert Bruce. The young prince followed with his own oath not to sleep more than one night in the same place until Scotland had been conquered. Joining in the festivities were two new young knights who were to play destructive roles in the future of the English prince: Roger de Mortimer, who would become the lover of Isabella of France after she had married the future king, and Hugh le Despenser the younger, who would years later become the lover of that future king with whom he had just been knighted.

Meanwhile, in Scotland, Aymer de Valence was mindful of the orders of Edward I. When he advanced toward Perth he found Bruce, with his newly formed army, eager to lock in battle with the English. The Scots were pleased with themselves when the English refused to close with them, and they finally retired from the field to relax and gloat over the reluctance of their cowardly enemy. Completely off guard, they were totally surprised by the sudden attack of the English army and in their confusion were easily defeated.

Bruce retreated to the hills and finally fell back with a remnant of his army to a refuge in the Western Isles. The dispersed Scots, assembled just days before and now with no leader, had nothing to do but try to return to their homes, and along the way they were easy prey for the still organized English. Every follower of Bruce who fell into their hands was executed in accordance with the orders of the English king. Bruce's brother Nigel was captured and taken to Berwick Castle to be publicly hanged. His brothers Thomas and Alexander were taken together and dragged through the streets tied to horses' tails, to the gallows awaiting them.

Aymer de Valence knew his king. When the countess of Buchan was taken he did not execute her but sent to Edward for instructions. They were not long in coming. Still furious that she had left her loyal (to Edward) husband to personally place the Scottish crown on the head of Robert Bruce, Edward decided to give the countess a crown of her own. He ordered a cage, built in the shape of a crown, placed in one of the high turrets of Berwick Castle. Here the unrepentant countess was placed, and in good weather the cage was swung outside on a beam for all the world to see the price of offending Edward of England. Two English women, questioned to make certain that they entertained no sympathies, were assigned to provide for her needs for food and sanitation, to keep her alive as long as possible. Isabella's husband, Comyn the Black, was totally in agreement with her punishment and made no attempt to even have her imprisonment made more tolerable. Finally, after four years in her crown-shaped cage, the countess was transferred to confinement in a monastery. It was not until after her husband's death several years later that friends were able to intercede and secure her freedom.

King Robert had been guilty of committing his people to battle before they were ready. It was while he pondered his mistakes that winter, planning how he would again take up the sword against England, that he is supposed to have watched the spider try and try again until it succeeded in connecting its web. Whatever the source of his inspiration, the Scottish king returned to mainland Scotland in the spring of the following year ready for war. Edward I once again marshaled an English army and this time decided to lead it himself. By now too weak to ride, he accompanied the army on a litter. He did not complete the journey, dying along the way in July 1307, just three months before the mass arrests of the Templars in France.

Had Edward I lived, it is doubtful that Philip of France would, or even could, have made his move against the Templars. In concert with the Order of the Temple, Edward would have been too powerful an opposing force, for he was one of the strongest kings England would ever have. Fortunately for Philip, the young Prince of Wales who now became King Edward II was perhaps the worst and weakest monarch ever to sit on the English throne.

Throughout his reign, Edward I had made consistent attempts to bring Scotland under his control, and in so doing he had set in motion a bitter enmity toward the English that was to last for generations among the Scots and of which traces linger today. His tomb in Westminster Abbey reads "Here lies Edward the Hammer of the Scots," but his legacy to his son was a Scotland blazing with renewed patriotic fervor under a king determined to do some hammering of his own on the English enemy. He also left a Scotland ready to welcome and shelter any fighting man fleeing English authority. The Knights Templar would flee that authority because of a brutal suppression born in the conflict that had been growing between Philip IV of France and the popes of the Holy Roman Church.

CHAPTER 8

FOUR VICARS OF CHRIST

Upon the death of Pope Nicholas IV in 1292, the cardinals were divided into two principal factions led, as they were upon several such occasions, by the two principal families of Rome, the Colonna and the Orsini. Neither could achieve the election, so they did what the cardinals have often done. They selected an old man with not much time to live and with no allegiance to either side. In this case, they chose Pietro Morrone, a peasant priest who had never occupied high office in the church hierarchy. His followers, called Celestines, led an austere existence of fasting and self-flagellation. They were not permitted to laugh, because although scriptures said that "Jesus wept," nowhere did they say that Jesus laughed. The life suited Morrone, who did not want to be pope, but his objections were ignored and he was taken from his cave in the mountains to Naples, where he became Pope Celestine V. Charles II, the French king of Naples and son of Charles of Anjou, easily dominated the new pope, who was already experiencing the difficulties of senility. He was confused and vague but tractable enough to name thirteen new cardinals, of whom three were Neapolitan and seven French.

The cardinals soon saw that they had made a mistake. What they had thought would be a neutral papacy turned out to be under the influence of a growing third faction, the French monarchies of France and Naples. Their answer was to suggest that Celestine V abdicate. The most ambitious of the cardinals, Benedetto Gaetani, went beyond mere suggestion to pressure and persecution. There is a legend that Gaetani had a hole made in the wall of the pope's chamber behind a hanging. He is said to have spoken through the hole during the night, telling Celestine that his voice was that of a messenger from God, relaying the Almighty's command that Celestine quit the Throne of Peter. Finally the pope announced that he must resign because his age and failing health had rendered him unable to rule the Church properly. His resignation was summarily accepted.

Once again the cardinals were back to the problem of choosing between the candidate of the Colonna and the candidate of the Orsini. When Gaetani put himself forward as the candidate of neither, he did not seem to have much of a chance. However, he had ingratiated himself with Charles of Naples and the French interests, which as a result of the recent appointments of new cardinals by Celestine now constituted the swing vote. The French group, backing Gaetani, sought alliance with the Orsini. They, in turn, were determined to block any candidate of the Colonna, and Benedetto Gaetani became Pope Boniface VIII.

An annoyance to the reign of Boniface VIII was that many people would not accept that a divinely chosen pope could resign the divine plan and therefore contended that Celestine was still the true pope and Boniface simply an imposter. Pilgrims started to visit the former pope, bowing down to him and receiving his blessing. This was more than Boniface VIII was prepared to tolerate, so he had Celestine seized and imprisoned in a tiny cell in which the bewildered old man could hardly stretch out. In the spring of 1296 Celestine died in his cell.

Depending upon the point of view, Boniface VIII was the grandest champion of the papacy or the most egomaniacal of all the popes. He maintained that he had authority over every kingdom and principality in Christendom and over every human being on the face of the earth. He also had time to deal with his enemies. The house of Colonna had not only opposed his election as pope but continued to assert that, since he had been elected while Celestine was still alive, his election was invalid. They demanded that he vacate the Throne of Peter. Boniface's reaction was to determine to wipe out the Colonna family once and for all.

The two Colonna cardinals were stripped of their privileges as princes of the church. Boniface condemned all the Colonna, past and present, and suggested that their lands should be forfeit to the church. He further delivered a public warning that, in this downfall of the Colonna cardinals, the whole world should recognize that the Holy See knew how to deal with its enemies. The Colonna replied with the accusation that Boniface had not been validly elected and therefore was not the true pope. In addition, they recited a catalog of crimes and irregularities of which they alleged he was guilty. Boniface's response to the accusations was to declare that the Colonna properties were forfeit to the papacy and to declare that no member of the Colonna family could enter the priesthood for the next four generations. He characterized his battle against the Colonna family as a holy war and promised all participants on the papal side the same indulgences and privileges as had been given to the Crusaders. The Orsini leaped at the chance to finally eliminate their bitter rival, and they were joined by thousands of others seeking the papal rewards. Every castle, town, and fortified house of the Colonna fell before the papal army until only Palestrina, their strongest fortress, remained to them. In this almost impregnable position the two Colonna cardinals had taken refuge. After some time, Boniface broke the siege by promising full pardon, the personal safety of the occupants, and the sparing of their property. He had no problem breaking all three promises, and the Colonna family was broken as a power—or, at least, appeared to be.

Boniface VIII proceeded to impose his authority on all the states of Europe, with mixed success. He met resistance from Edward I of England, which several times led to compromise, but the greatest stumbling block to the pope's ambitions was Philip IV of France. In 1296 Philip had imposed a tax on church property and income in France to help finance his constant war with England. The pope denounced this tax as a misuse of the secular power, asserting that neither church property nor revenues could be taxed without the specific permission of Rome, and he demanded the withdrawal of the tax. Philip responded with a new law prohibiting the export of gold and silver from France without his express permission, which effectively blocked the substantial

French church revenues being sent to Rome. The blockage hurt, and in 1297 a compromise beneficial to Philip was reached.

However, within two years Boniface had found a way to advance his fortunes and his power without the need for the cooperation of secular princes. The turn of a century had long been a time of religious celebration, but Boniface turned 1299 into a great jubilee. He promised absolution to all pilgrims who would come to Rome for fifteen days that year, and they came in a flood that some historians have claimed saw as many as 2 million visitors. The people of Rome had never experienced so much business from pilgrims nor seen so much money pour into the city. Gifts to the church were expected as part of the pilgrimage, and they came in such a stream that at the Church of St. Paul priests stood behind the altar pulling off the gold and silver with wooden rakes as fast as it was deposited by gift-laden pilgrims who had fought their way up to the altar. Boniface was elated. He is said to have put on the insignia of the old Roman Empire and to have styled himself as Caesar, going out with two swords held upright before him, symbolic of his dual authority over the spiritual and secular worlds, with heralds going before him crying, "Behold! I am Caesar!" Intoxicated and emboldened by his new wealth, Boniface returned to his battle with Philip of France.

Philip had done much to defy and anger Boniface. Among other things, he had seized church lands for himself and had provided sanctuary to Boniface's bitter personal enemies, the Colonna. Boniface summoned the clergy to a council in Rome, to convene at the end of the year, to discuss the problems between the church and France. He warned Philip not to interfere, but Philip did interfere by calling a great council himself. This was the first time that the third estate, the commoners of France, had been called. The first two estates, the clergy and the nobility, had always sufficed, but now the commoners must be rallied in case the king should have an outright confrontation with the pope. The nobles and commoners quickly rallied to the king and supported the view that Philip held his throne directly from God, not from the pope. They called upon the cardinals to rebuke and discipline the pope. The French clergy reaffirmed their loyalty to Philip but pleaded that they also owed loyalty to Rome and therefore must answer the pope's summons to the council in November. The king flatly refused to permit any of the clergy of France to attend a council called to criticize their king.

Faced with this latest defiance, and against the advice of several cardinals, Boniface issued his historic bull, *Unam Sanctam*, which asserted the superiority of the papacy over all secular rulers and stated that, furthermore, "it is a condition of salvation that all human beings should be subject to the Pontiff of Rome." This bull was and is the strongest statement of papal supremacy ever put forward by any pope.

Boniface warned the French clergy that if they did not attend the council in Rome they would be subject to his anger and discipline. Philip warned them that if any of them *did* attend, he would be stripped of all his property in France. A few of the French clergy did run the risk, but the council fell flat from want of attendance.

As he would several times in the future, King Philip called upon the special talents of Guillaume de Nogaret, whom various historians describe as a "lawyer," a "minister," and an "agent" of Philip. In April 1303 de Nogaret proposed to a council in France that Boniface should be proclaimed unfit to sit on the Throne of Peter. His reasoning was that the church had been married to Pope Celestine V and that Boniface had committed adultery in stealing away the bride of the former pope while he still lived. Three months later de Nogaret appeared again, this time with a list of twenty-nine charges against the pope. He accused Boniface of heresy, sodomy, blasphemy, stealing from the church to enrich his family, revealing secrets of the confessional, murder, and so on, including the extraordinary charge of secret sexual relations with a pet demon that lived in the pope's ring. This document was circulated throughout France to gain popular support for the king. Meanwhile, Philip appealed to all the princes of Christendom to impeach Boniface, with little result. In France, however, he had full support. Almost all of the nobility backed the call for impeachment, as did over twenty bishops, a host of lesser clergy, and French representatives of the Knights Templar and the Hospitallers.

Boniface had one final card to play. He had already, in April of 1303, proclaimed the anathema, the most extreme form of excommunication, against Philip personally. To the pope's annoyance, his proclamation had the undesired effect of arousing the sympathy and anger of the French people. Now he announced that on September 8, 1303, he intended to put the entire kingdom of France under interdict. The interdict was not excommunication, but rather an ecclesiastical censure. Under this censure, the pope could preclude every Christian in France from baptism, holy communion, absolution, even ecclesiastic burial. This was the ultimate threat to Philip, because it could lead to outbreaks of rebellion or even full-scale revolution. The decision was made to stop the interdict by any means possible, and the task was given to Philip's trusted agent, Guillaume de Nogaret. He was enthusiastically joined by Sciarra Colonna, eager to get at his family's most hated enemy.

Boniface was scheduled to issue the proclamation of interdiction from his own ancestral palace at Anagni, in Italy. On the night before the announcement was to be made, de Nogaret and Colonna, who had recruited a small local force, invaded Anagni, many of whose inhabitants fled at their approach. They found the palace almost deserted and easily took the eighty-six-year-old pope as their prisoner. For three days they heaped verbal and even physical abuse on the old man. Colonna was for killing Boniface on the spot, but de Nogaret restrained him. Finally, on the fourth day, the people of Anagni returned to effect the pope's rescue and drove off the invaders. The pope returned to Rome badly shaken in mind and body, where he died a few weeks later. There is a legend that he killed himself by beating his head against the stone wall of his room. There is another legend that someone else's hands were guiding his head toward the wall.

There were no repercussions, no condemnation by other princes of Philip's rough handling of the supreme pontiff. Perhaps they saw in Philip a champion in their own struggles to maintain freedom from papal control. Without fuss or argument, the successor to Boniface VIII was elected within ten days, and the new pope selected the name Benedict XI. He began his papal reign with a conciliatory attitude toward Philip IV of France. He made concessions. Philip took those concessions but demanded more, and their relationship deteriorated. Philip, still consumed with hatred for the dead pope, demanded that Benedict XI call a council to follow through on the accusations that had been made against his predecessor. Benedict was incensed, and in July 1304 he issued a severe rebuke against all participants in the attack on

Boniface at Anagni and ordered the excommunication of the participants. Philip braced himself for another papal battle, but a few weeks after his condemnation of the "Crime of Anagni" Pope Benedict XI was dead. There were those who claimed that he had been the victim of poisoning at Philip's direction.

Next Philip turned his attention to the man who would become the principal actor in the drama of the brutal suppression of the Knights of the Temple, Bernard de Goth, archbishop of Bordeaux. The relationship between de Goth and Philip was not based on any prior cooperation, and they disliked each other intensely. It was not born of a desire to resolve the differences between church and state; de Goth had sided consistently with Boniface against Philip. It was simply that Philip wanted a pope he could control and Bernard de Goth wanted more than anything else in the world to be pope. They made a deal.

Burning with ambition, the archbishop wanted—at any cost—the honors, the wealth, and the power that would be his as the vicar of Christ. Philip held the appointment in his hands, because after almost a year of negotiating, arguing, and politicking, the cardinals had still not agreed upon the successor to Benedict XI. There were now three solid factions. To the ancient Roman houses of Orsini and Colonna (the latter now restored to influence) had been added the French cardinals. To break the deadlock, a decision was reached to seek a candidate outside the cardinals, and the French faction sold the conclave on a unique concept: Within forty days the French cardinals would elect one of three candidates nominated by their opponents.

The archbishop of Bordeaux was fully expected to be one of the three nominated because of his history of opposition to Philip and his support of Boniface. He owed no fealty to Philip, because at that time Bordeaux was in English territory. Checking the list, Philip felt that he had his man, that Bernard de Goth would overlook any enmity and disavow any previous stand in order to be elected pope. In complete control of the French cardinals, Philip could personally designate which of the three candidates would become the next supreme pontiff.

There remained only the matter of making the deal with de Goth. Philip kept faith with the Colonna for their support and demanded the reinstatement of their two cardinals. Everyone who had fought against Boniface and been punished with excommunication or censure was to be completely absolved. The bulls of Boniface were to be erased and the deceased pope was to be officially condemned. Philip was to have the right to tax the French clergy to the extent of 10 percent of their gross revenues for a period of five years. (There is said to have been one more covenant, kept secret, that de Goth would cooperate in the suppression of the Knights Templar.) The archbishop agreed and took a most solemn oath on the host to keep his part of the bargain. As an indication of the true state of feelings between the two men, Philip was not assured by the sacred oath alone and required that the archbishop deliver up his brothers and two nephews as hostages to guarantee the arrangement. On November 14, 1305, Philip kept his part of the bargain as Bernard de Goth was unanimously elected to the Throne of Peter. Thus began the reign of Pope Clement V.

During his reign, Clement V set the stage for the "Babylonish Captivity" of the papacy outside Rome by appointing twenty-four cardinals, of whom twenty-three were French. A number of them were his relatives. Philip managed to play a strong hand in the appointment of cardinals, for although consumed with ambition, Clement V was a physical coward. As he proceeded with his retinue from his home toward Italy, he was never long without some evidence of Philip's intention to keep him under guard and under control. He wandered through southern France, ostensibly headed for Rome, but never reached his destination. Instead, in 1309 he took up residence in Avignon. It was then not part of France but of Provence, which was owned by Jane of Naples. She was in need of funds, so she sold Avignon to the papacy for eighty thousand gold florins. The Avignon popes built a palace and fortress and the papal court settled down for a stay of seventy-five years, during which time only one pope even made a visit to Rome.

Clement kept most of his part of the bargain with Philip but constantly balked at a formal condemnation of his fellow pope, Boniface VIII, a stand for which Philip would berate and threaten him regularly.

The Colonna family emerged stronger than ever. Their lands were restored and the courts of Rome required that the sum of one hundred thousand gold florins be paid to them by the Orsini and other supporters of Boniface VIII.

It should not be thought that the struggle for power between secular and spiritual authorities was limited to the battle between the Holy See and the kingdom of France. Medieval kings were autocrats. They believed that all persons and properties in their domains were subject to them and that the complex upward interlocking of feudal fealties stopped at the throne, which ultimately had power over all of them. In contrast, the church felt above and apart from secular authority. The Holy See assumed the right to criticize, judge, and chastise all secular authority and would admit of no circumstances in which it might be the other way round. In *Unam Sanctam* Boniface VIII had finally summed it up: Every human being on the face of the earth was subject to the Roman pontiff. The spiritual power, being held direct from God, was in all ways superior to the secular, which had been born in original sin.

The secular princes did not agree. No absolute monarch could possibly be comfortable with a host of clerics in his kingdom holding vast properties and with sympathies and loyalties binding them to an alien power. It was like (and often was) playing host to an army of spies for a foreign enemy. Compromises were worked out and they were constantly shifting. Princes needed money and frequently looked with envy and anger at the never-ending stream of wealth flowing from their lands to the Holy See. In compromise, they were sometimes permitted to tax that revenue, but only upon very special occasions and only with permission. Within the secular domain, the church not only owned over 30 percent of the land surface of Europe, but maintained separate and independent ecclesiastic courts and prisons.

Often an agreement was reached that gave a prince the right to approve, or even to designate, the holders of important church offices in his dominions. It was a right jealously guarded. A shocking example of just how jealously is cited by Edward Gibbon in his *Decline and Fall of the Roman Empire*. Relating an incident in the life of Geoffrey, son of the king of Jerusalem and father of Henry II of England, Gibbon writes, "When he was master of Normandy, the Chapter of Seez, without his consent, proceeded to elect a bishop: upon which he ordered all of them, with the bishop elect, to be castrated, and made all of their testicles to be brought to him on a platter." (Gibbon's comment on this act of cruelty is in itself incredible. He states, "Of the pain and danger they might justly complain; yet, since they had vowed chastity, he deprived them of a superfluous treasure"!)

With the pope entrenched in Avignon, under the strong influence, if not the domination, of the French monarch, the question of temporal power was somewhat abated and church energies turned toward the acquisition of wealth, luxury, and personal aggrandizement. Gold was poured into furnishings, sumptuous clothing, hundreds of liveried servants, and elaborate ceremonial. Money was all that mattered, and everything was for sale. The profits were almost 100 percent, because what were sold were rights, not material goods. Indulgences, exemptions, honors, all went on the block. Clement V invented "annates," fees based on percentages (up to 100 percent) of the first year's revenue from benefices. Faced with this liability, appointees to these bishoprics and other benefices passed the problem to those below, milking every property for every penny it could or could not spare, often leaving a destitute clergy at the bottom of the heap.

Prestige and personal stature became all-important to the higher clergy. Endless meetings were held to define the exact relationship of the hierarchy of the church to the secular nobility. Protocol was established regarding positions in processions and at the table. Ego defined honor and the church demanded for itself every conceivable right, privilege, and gesture of respect. Not even idle-hour games were exempt. The Crusaders had brought home the Persian game of chess, a board game which was a battle between two kingdoms, leading to the capture or death of one or the other king. (The modern chess player's cry of "Checkmate!" is a corruption of the Persian "Shakh Mat!" which translates, "The king is dead!") Each piece in chess moves according to its ability. The eight pawns protect the whole array. As foot spearmen, they move one step at a time, except in the opening move when they can move two squares, in keeping with a common Persian military tactic in which the spearmen ran out to make a bristling picket in front of the host. The rook or castle was originally an elephant, with a fortified chamber or "castle" on its back. The elephant moved inexorably, but only in a straight line. Next came the cavalryman, whom the Crusaders dubbed the knight. He galloped, moving two squares in one direction and one to the side. Next came the navy, represented by a ship, which could only advance by tacking, so the ship moved only on the diagonal. In the center was the king, burdened with his household, his administrative staff, and most of all his treasure, which he had to take to the battlefield with him as its only means of protection. So laden the king moved heavily, just one square at a time. The queen, on the other hand, was guarded by swift light cavalry and could move in any direction as far and as fast as was necessary. So what did all of this have to do with the Holy Roman church? Simply that it was intolerable that there could be a popular game that pitted nation against nation with no role for the church. Further, only the position next to the royal family would do, so the ships became bishops, and to this day every chess player moves his bishop diagonally across the board, tacking like a ship to catch the wind. In summary, the medieval church perceived itself as the ultimate power center. Secular kingdoms, duchies, and counties were power centers. Holy orders like the Knights Templar were power centers. Real life was a game of chess, but the real name of the game was power.

Philip IV of France had played the power game very well, but it was far from over. With Boniface out of the way and Clement V substantially under his control, he could get on with the larger issue that had caused most of his rift with the church: the need for more money to conduct his territorial war with England. He was heavily in debt, largely to the Knights Templar, who were the major bankers in Europe. They were incredibly wealthy, with manors and mills and monopolies on which they paid little or no tax. Here was Philip's chance at a double reward, the cancellation of his debts and the plundering of the Templar treasury. Even with the new pope under this influence, even with the timely death in July 1307 of the English king Edward I, the one European monarch who could have thwarted his ambition, the suppression of the Templars would take careful planning, skilled propaganda, and bold action. It was a great risk, and Philip was probably the only man in Christendom with the ambition and the nerve to try it. He began to make his plans.

CHAPTER 9

"SPARE NO KNOWN MEANS OF TORTURE"

Arriving in Marseilles, Jacques de Molay decided not to proceed to Poitiers, as the pope had instructed, but to go directly to his temple-fortress in Paris. Also ignoring the pope's orders to travel incognito, he decided to remind the world of his wealth and power and paraded to Paris like an eastern pasha. His escort consisted of sixty Templar Knights with their servants and attendants, plus twelve packhorses burdened down with a treasure of 150,000 gold florins.

De Molay was convinced that he would be made most welcome in Paris by King Philip, who owed the Templars for many favors. They had supported the king in his confrontations with Pope Boniface VIII. They had loaned him the money he required for the dowry of his daughter, Princess Isabella, who had been betrothed to the future King Edward II of England. They had allowed him the use of the Paris temple for the treasury of France. During the Paris riots the year before, they had sheltered Philip in the Paris temple for three days, keeping him safe from the angry mob. Philip had even asked Grand Master de Molay to be godfather to his son Robert. Surely no one merited more of the gratitude and respect of King Philip the Fair than the Order of the Temple and its venerable leader, and surely de Molay could count on Philip's support in the one matter that troubled the grand master.

As part of the planning of a new Crusade, the pope had indicated that he wanted to discuss the proposal that the Templars and Hospitallers be merged into one order, an idea that had been coming up more and more frequently in recent years. Just two years earlier a Dominican friar, Ramon Lull, had written a merger plan that had aroused much interest. He proposed that the Knights of the Hospital of St. John of Jerusalem and the Knights of the Temple of Solomon be combined into a single order to be called The Knights of Jerusalem, and that all of the rulers of Europe combine their Crusading forces under a single commander to be known as the *Rex Bellator*, the "War King." A few years earlier a French priest, Pierre de Bois, had submitted a written plan for the recuperation of the Holy Places called *De Recuperatione Sanctae*, in which he cited the efficiencies to be achieved by combining the military orders.

The pope had responded favorably to the merger concept. The Hospitallers had brought new hope for a Crusade and new respect to themselves by their recent invasion of the island of Rhodes, and the pope leaned toward the appointment of Foulques de Villaret, grand master of the Hospitallers, as grand master of the proposed combination.

Philip, too, looked upon these merger proposals with favor, but from a totally different point of view. He proposed to the pope that the kings of France be named the hereditary grand masters of the combined orders and that he himself be appointed *Rex Bellator*, with full access to the surplus wealth of the united orders. The only person who seemed disposed to favor that plan was Philip himself, so, as an alternative, Philip developed a plan to bring down the Templar order. Their most valuable properties and their largest treasure were in France, and he intended to expropriate it all for himself. As an added bonus he should thus be rid of his substantial debts to the Templars, which was important to him because his personal crusade to acquire the continental possessions of the English kings had drained his treasury. Edward I had been a formidable enemy, but his effete son was quite another matter. Philip was certain that his time had come, and he just could not pass up this opportunity.

Jacques de Molay did not know of Philip's personal ambitions and so must have expected Philip's support for the document the grand master had prepared for the pope, in which he set forth all of the reasons why the Templars were opposed to any concept of a merger with the Hospitallers. His stubborn refusal even to consider such a move undoubtedly had a great deal to do with the events of the weeks that lay ahead, and played into Philip's hands.

Certainly de Molay got no clue of the impending disaster from Philip, who in true mafia fashion feted and praised the man he planned to destroy. That plan had been put together by Guillaume de Nogaret, the same man who had engineered the kidnapping of Pope Boniface VIII. De Nogaret's mother and father had been burned at the stake as Albigensian heretics and he overlooked no opportunity to get back at the Roman church. In preparation for his attack on the Templars, de Nogaret had planted twelve of his own men as spies in various commanderies of the order.

Unaware of the plots against him, de Molay made a call at the papal palace and submitted to the papal planners the Templar suggestions for the conduct of a new Crusade. He recommended that the definitive plans for the invasion of Palestine be kept totally secret and not even committed to writing. As for his personal advice, he indicated that his secret suggestions were so germane to a successful war plan that he would only reveal them to the pope in person. When the expected subject of a merger of the Templars and Hospitallers came up, de Molay was ready. He presented a formal document entitled *De Unione Templi et Hospitalis Ordinum ad Clementum Papam Jacobi de Molayo relatio,* a work he could discuss only in general terms because he himself was totally illiterate. He couldn't even read the text of his own arguments.

De Molay also used that meeting to deal with rumors he had heard since returning to Paris, rumors that there were serious improprieties within the Order of the Temple. He suggested that a formal papal inquiry be implemented, which would most assuredly put to rest any criticisms against his holy fraternity.

All the while the grand master was asserting his confidence in himself and the Templar order, the plan to bring them down was in work. As part of that plan a former Templar knight, who had risen to the post of prior of a Templar preceptory in France before being expelled from the order, had been recruited for an ingenious bit of playacting. He was put in prison in Toulouse with a man under the death sentence. In keeping with the ecclesiastic provision that members of the Catholic laity may confess each other in the absence of a priest, the two prisoners heard each other's confessions. The former Templar confessed to blasphemous and repugnant practices he claimed to have witnessed within the Templar order. The shocking confession was used to prepare the list of items on which the Templar prisoners were subsequently "put to the question" by the torturers of the Inquisition. New members, he said, as a part of the initiation rituals, were required to spit or trample upon the cross. Templars were required to put their order and its wealth ahead of any other principle, temporal or religious. Any member suspected of revealing the secrets of the order was secretly murdered. The Templars scoffed at the sacraments of the church and absolved each other of sins. They kept secret contact with Moslems. They permitted and encouraged homosexual activity among members. They had lost the Holy Land to Christianity through their insatiable greed. They worshiped idols, usually in the form of a head or a cat.

The other prisoner (who was also a plant) demanded of his jailers that he be allowed to pass on this vital information. It was duly delivered to the king, who passed it to the pope with the suggestion that a formal inquiry be implemented. Both prisoners were then rewarded and sent on their way.

De Nogaret had much to do. The logistics of obtaining chains for fifteen thousand men and arranging for their imprisonment would be difficult enough in public view, but the problems were multiplied by the need for total secrecy. That secrecy was important because the plan was to arrest every Templar in France at the very same time.

As a covert operation, the concept of simultaneous apprehension was not totally new to de Nogaret. In a similar plan the year before he had effected the arrest and imprisonment of every Jew in France on one day, July 22, 1306. A few weeks later, in accordance with the master plan, the Jews were all exiled from France, but without their property. Their cash was taken directly into Philip's treasury and arrangements were made for auctions of their chattels. Then it was announced that the crown of France had also taken possession of their accounts receivable, and the state became a very efficient collection agency, demanding that all sums due to the Jews of France be paid to the lawful holder of those accounts, the Exchequer of France. Correspondingly, of course, all debts owed to the Jews by the state were cancelled, just as Philip expected that in a suppression of the Temple all debts owed by the state to the Templars would also be cancelled. The simultaneous arrest of every Templar would take a similar operation, but one made more complex because the group to be arrested contained many experienced fighting men. It was decided to move while they were asleep. Sealed orders went out to the seneschals of France, with instructions not to open those orders until October 12.

There is ample evidence that de Molay and his principal officers had to have been aware that something was stirring. A knight who applied to leave the order was commended on his decision by the treasurer of the Paris temple, who told him to act with dispatch because a catastrophe for the order was imminent. The Templar master for Paris issued an order to every Templar commandery in France to tighten security and under no circumstance to reveal anything to anyone regarding the secret rituals and meetings of the order. Several former Templars were placed under protective arrest by the state for fear that they would be killed if it was suspected that they might reveal secrets of the order. Unfortunately for the order, Jacques de Molay took no action at all, blindly serene in the confidence engendered by his wealth and power. After all, he was responsible to only one man on the face of the earth, and only that man could bring harm to the order. Of that there seemed no danger whatsoever. The Templars were not subject to the laws of any land, could not be punished by any secular ruler for any offense, and, as a holy order, were exempt from torture. Add enormous wealth and a standing army, and what danger could there possibly be?

Upon de Molay's return to Paris from his papal visit, he was further lulled into complacency by a great honor bestowed upon him by the king. On October 12, 1307, the grand master was among the highest nobility of Europe who acted as pallbearers at the funeral of Princess Catherine, the deceased wife of King Philip's brother, Charles of Valois. As de Molay performed this somber service in the company of the mighty, seneschals all over France were opening their sealed orders.

When de Molay retired that night, there was no way he could have known that just before the dawn of the next day an event would occur of such shattering dimensions that the date, Friday the Thirteenth, would live for centuries in the minds of millions as the unluckiest day of the year. And indeed it was for the Order of the Temple as Philip's troops descended on every Templar commandery over an area of one hundred and fifty thousand square miles to put fifteen thousand men into the chains that had been made ready for them.

The following day de Nogaret launched the second part of his plan. Announcements were read to local citizens all over France setting forth shocking charges against the Templars; the chief was heresy and the rejection of Christ, as exemplified in spitting and trampling on the cross. Sodomy, that faithful companion to almost all medieval charges of heresy, was alleged, along with "obscene kisses" required of each new Templar at his initiation. The charges were elaborated upon from the pulpits of France on the following day, all calculated to first shock and then win the support of the general population for the Templar arrests.

When the news of the arrests came to him, Pope Clement V was furious, not because of any sympathy for the Templars but at the usurpation of papal authority, the only power that could legally make such arrests. Philip justified his actions by claiming to have received the authority of the pope to investigate the accusations against the Templars. Clement V had apparently approved such an investigation but had meant investigation by an appointed council, not through mass arrests and torture. Philip also fell back on a papal directive that ordered all Christian princes to give all possible assistance to the Holy Office of the Inquisition, arguing that as king of France he had simply rendered the required assistance to the grand inquisitor of France (who was also Philip's personal confessor).

The pope responded with a formal protest to King Philip. As pope, he had sole authority over the Templars and had not been consulted in the matter of their arrest and imprisonment. The Templar wealth seized by Philip had been intended to help finance a new Crusade (which probably means that the proposed merger with the Hospitallers had already been decided upon). For flouting the papal authority, the Dominican grand inquisitor of France, Guillaume Imbert, was removed from office. Finally, the pope demanded an immediate cessation of the proceedings against the Templars.

Philip's reaction to the papal directive was to launch a propaganda campaign against Clement V to the people of France, followed by a visit to the pope with a small army at his back. Philip denounced the pope with charges of lenience toward heretics, a desire to have the Templar wealth for himself and his family, and befriending the enemies of Holy Mother Church. The harangue continued day after day, with Philip's army camped about the city. What agreements they reached we shall never know, but within a few weeks pope and king were in complete accord, and the grand inquisitor was restored to his grisly office. On November 22 Clement V promulgated the bull *Pastoralis Preeminentae*, in which he praised King Philip, stating the official papal position that the charges against the Templars appeared to be true and calling upon all the monarchs of Christendom to arrest and torture all of the Templars in their domains. From that day forward, the pope pursued the Templars with enthusiasm.

All the while this political maneuvering was in progress, from the arrests at dawn on October 13 to the issuance of the papal bull on November 22, the imprisoned Templars in France were being tortured to obtain confessions of heresy. Torture for confession involved the fine art of inflicting all of the pain possible short of death, only because death precluded the possibility of confession, which was the object of the exercise. As an indication of the brinksmanship practiced by the good friars of the Inquisition in stopping short of the agony-death borderline, thirty-six Templars died in the first few days after the tortures began. Of course, there were great differences in the men being tortured. Physically, some were young men in their prime and others were quite elderly. Culturally, some were warrior knights, some were priests, and many more were men-at-arms or employees. All had been suddenly wrenched away from one of the most powerful organizations in the world and rendered helpless. The only legal authority over them was the pope himself, yet here they were as prisoners of the king of France and the grand inquisitor, who had no legal right to hold them without the direct authority of the pope. As members of a holy order, they were exempt from torture, but here were the priests of the Inquisition with their racks and red-hot irons. Add to all of this the deliberately repugnant nature of medieval confinement, and they could be expected to confess anything, for the conditions of confinement could well be considered part of the torture process, with abject, revolting misery acting on both mind and body.

Unlike the modern jail, with its divisions into series of cells, the medieval dungeon generally consisted of a large room with very small windows, or even no windows, to ensure maximum security. Prisoners were usually chained to rings in the wall or in the stone floor. If the punishment decreed was lenient, chains might be light and loose enough to permit a man to move his limbs and to lie down. A ring higher up the wall, with a chain fastened to an iron collar, might force him to sit or kneel. As a temporary punishment, the neck ring might be fastened higher for some hours to force the prisoner to remain standing or risk being choked to death. Heavier chains and weights could be added to make it difficult to stand at all, or even to move. Variations could find the prisoner on his back with his ankles fastened several feet up the wall, or hanging by his wrists or ankles, or both.

With few or no sanitary provisions, and no air circulation, the stench would be almost three-dimensional. In purpose-built dungeons, a drain was provided for the urine, excrement, vomit, and blood. This gave the French the opportunity to develop a Gallic refinement called the "oubliette." The oubliette was a small pit or chamber just beneath the heavy iron sewer-drain cover in the floor. Into this chamber was put any prisoner who was unusually unruly, incorrigible, or destined for particular degradation. With a cell too small (and too deep) to lie in, the wretched man had to sit or kneel in the half-full drain pit, which was constantly replenished by the filth of his fellow prisoners.

Confinement usually meant little or no clothing. If sanitation and comfort were thought of, it was generally in the negative sense—to enhance the atmosphere of sickening misery calculated to induce confessions that would lead to freedom from such conditions, if only through death. In the summer, the prisoner roasted. In the winter, he froze. The water was foul and the food often deliberately revolting, designed to maintain life at the barest subsistence level for as long as the jailer chose. (At one castle in that era, it was ordered that prisoners must not drink the clean well water but were to be given only water from the moat into which all of the castle latrines were emptied.)

Certain instruments of torture were cumbersome and not easily moved, such as the rack and the wheel, but others were easily carried to any chamber, so that the agony inflicted upon the sufferer being questioned would not be lost to the audience of his fellow prisoners. Frequently, witnessing the suffering and screams of others while awaiting his own turn was sufficient to induce a strong man to break down and confess to anything his tormentors chose to suggest.

So many members and servants of the Templars were arrested in France that they had to be distributed to dozens of locations, many of which had not been designed as prisons. This must have placed a strain on the number of complex instruments of torture available, so that some improvisations were called for, the simplest of which were charcoal fires and hot irons. Since friars and priests were generally forbidden to spill blood, a number of devices had been developed to enable them to convey exquisite agony without breaking the skin. One of these was a device with two iron bands, widely spaced behind the calf, and a screw that was turned to apply pressure at the front between the braces, breaking the shinbone. A common and easily rigged device was a box frame around the leg. Boards were placed between the frame and the leg and wedges driven between them with mallets. By this means, deliberate local pressure could be applied to break the bones of the foot, the ankle, the knee, and the legbones between.

The hot iron might be applied anywhere on the body, including the genitals, and sometimes was used in the form of pincers, to nip away pieces of flesh with the red-hot jaws automatically sealing and cauterizing the wounds. Cold pincers were used to pull out the fingernails and teeth of some of the Templars, with tooth sockets probed to add to the pain.

A number of Templars were bound horizontally with their lower legs fastened to an iron frame and their feet well oiled. Then a charcoal fire was brought to bear. Some had their feet burned totally off in this manner and, understandably, a number are reported to have gone mad from the pain. One Templar was helped to a council of inquiry later, carrying with him the blackened bones that had dropped out of his feet as they were burned off. He had been permitted by his torturers to keep the bones as sickening souvenirs.

Why all the grisly details? Because to understand the elaborate steps that were taken in Britain for men to run and hide, to form new opinions and beliefs about God and about the papacy that had unleashed upon them the hatred and persecution of the Church, requires a thorough understanding of the level of terror and anger that drove the fugitives. Even to this day there is little proof that fear of punishment actually prevents crime, but it is quite certain that fear of punishment motivates men to take almost any action to avoid being caught. It had been ordered by the pope that no known means of torture was to be spared in questioning the Templars. Arguably, it could be stated that at no time before or since has any group been subjected, by direct order, to the entire range of the known means of inflicting intolerable pain.

The charges to which the Templars were asked to confess were profuse and included several that frequently showed up in allegations of heresy and witchcraft and would for centuries to come. The Templars were asked to admit that initiates were required to deny God, Christ, and the Virgin Mary; that they were required to bestow the *Osculum Infame,* the "kiss of shame," on the prior by kissing him on the mouth, navel, penis, and buttocks; that they worshiped idols; that in their secret ceremonies they were required to urinate and trample on the cross; that they did not consecrate the host; that the order not only permitted but encouraged homosexual practices among its members. The all-encompassing charge, proof of which would permit confiscation of property and total suppression, was heresy, defined as denial or doubt by a baptized person of any "revealed truth" of the Roman Catholic faith.

The primary responsibility for the "discovery, punishment and prevention of heresy" had been bestowed on what by now was known as the Congregation of the Holy Office but was still referred to as the Inquisition. Its functions were largely in the hands of the Order of Preachers, the Dominicans, founded by the Spanish priest Dominic Guzman (later St. Dominic), who had made his name by his extraordinary zeal against the Albigensian heretics in southern France. Unfortunately for the accused, it had been decided that confession under torture was valid and irrevocable. A convicted heretic, once having confessed his doubts and denials and then admitting the whole truth of the teachings of the church, would suffer a light penance, a fine, imprisonment, death, or such other punishment as the tribunal might fix according to the seriousness of the heresy. On the other hand, any person who confessed, even under horrible torture, and later retracted that confession was beyond hope. He was known as a "relapsed heretic" and was turned over to the secular authority, which had no choice but to burn alive all such persons delivered to them for that purpose. That was the trap that caught dozens of Templars who confessed under torture to one or more of the allegations against the order and then retracted those confessions when the torture stopped. Fifty-six of them were publicly burned alive as relapsed heretics on a single day in Paris.

In the meantime, the pope was not getting the results he had hoped for outside of France. On the Iberian Peninsula the Templar fighting forces were too important to lose, for to the Christian monarchs of Spain and Portugal the Moslems were not enemies across the sea, but enemies across the next range of hills. The bishops of Aragon announced that their inquiries had found the Templars innocent of the charges against them. In Castile the archbishop of Compostela announced the same finding. In Portugal the king went further. Not only were the Templars found to be free of guilt, but they and their property were converted into a new order called the Knights of Christ, reporting to the king, rather than the pope, as their supreme head. In Germany the local Templars managed on their own. The Templar preceptor Hugo of Gumbach clanked into the council of the archbishop of Metz, arrayed in full battle armor and accompanied by twenty of his brother knights. Hugo proclaimed to all present that the Templar order was innocent of all charges and that Grand Master de Molay was a man of religion and honor. Pope Clement V, on the other hand, was a totally evil man, illegally elected to the Throne of Peter, from which Hugo now declared him deposed. As for the Templars present, they all stood ready to risk their bodies in the ordeal of trial by combat against their accusers. Suddenly there were no accusers, and the archbishop's council adjourned.

The situation at Cyprus, home of the Templar headquarters, was especially frustrating to the pope. Prince Amalric did not even acknowledge receipt of the pope's bull of November 22 until the following May, and when the Templars were subsequently tried they were found to be completely innocent. In anger, the pope dispatched two inquisitors to Cyprus to stage a retrial, but only after his orders to torture the Templars for confessions of heresy had been carried out. If necessary, because of the numbers involved, the inquisitors were given authority to call on the Dominicans and Franciscans on the island to help with that torture. Strangely, no documentation exists to tell us the outcome of the second trial, or if it even took place.

In Britain, resistance to the papal orders was strong. That situation is so important, however, that it will be dealt with separately and in detail.

As to treasure, Philip was again frustrated, as much of the wealth he expected to take from the Templar commanderies was gone. Gone, too, was the entire Templar fleet from its naval base at La Rochelle, and no historical record exists of the fate of even one of the eighteen ships that were supposed to be there.

As could be expected, the Templar reactions to the tortures inflicted on them varied widely. Some went insane from the agony. Some died rather than confess to anything. Most confessed to two or three of the charges, probably in the hope that their inquisitors told the truth when they said that upon their confessions the pain would stop. Two Templars confessed to worshiping a bearded idol, apparently a head, which they called "Baphomet." The treasurer of the order collapsed completely, avowing that under such torture he would freely admit to killing God. Jacques de Molay was approaching seventy years of age and apparently could not face up to the prospect of torture. He confessed to a number of charges against the order and against himself but balked at the personal allegation of homosexual practices, which he furiously denied.

As the confessions were collected and passed on to the Holy See, Clement V was able to promulgate a formal, public list of charges against the Templars on August 12, 1308, ten months after their arrest in Paris. He also called the fifteenth ecumenical council of the church to convene in Vienne two years later to deal with a number of matters, including plans for a new Crusade and the fate of the Templar order.

Records of Templar trials and inquisitions held throughout Christendom were sent to the Holy See, and finally the Council of Vienne convened a year late on October 16, 1311, by which time the arrested Templars had been agonizing in their miserable prisons for four years. Jacques Duese, cardinal-bishop of Porto, who was to follow Clement V to the papal throne as the controversial Pope John XXII, gave advance notice of his attitude toward papal power by advising Clement V to ignore the council and condemn the Templars on his own authority, but the pope wanted the legitimacy and support of an ecumenical council. He had even formally invited any members of the Templar order to appear in their own defense, apparently on the assumption that none would dare to be present. When nine Templars did show up just before the opening of the council, saying that they had come to present a defense, the pope promptly had them arrested.

As for the members of the council, many expressed their feelings that the Templars should be permitted to present their case. The French prelates, knowing that their every word would be reported to Philip, took the opposite view. So vacillating were the members, and so reluctant was the pope to take a firm stand, that five months later the whole matter of the Templars' fate was still up in the air. The ultimate decision might fall either way, a situation which Philip of France would not tolerate. In March 1312 the king wrote to the council demanding that the Templar order be suppressed and that all of its rights, privileges, and wealth be transferred to a new military order. He hammered home his suggestion by showing up in Vienne a few days later, on March 20, with a strong military escort.

Contrary to the opinions of church historians, Clement V demonstrated over the following weeks that he was not under the total domination of Philip of France. The pope's goal was the merger of the Templars and the Hospitallers into a single order, and he was not eager to brand a holy order responsible only to him as heretical. Philip's ambition, as expressed to the council, was a new military order to be headed up by himself or one of his sons, with complete access to the wealth and property of the present orders. The pope prevailed, in his own way. On April 3, 1312, he promulgated the papal bull *Vox in Excelso*, which disbanded the Templar order without actually proclaiming it guilty of the charges brought against it. The order was simply dissolved in the parliamentary sense, and not as punishment for proven crimes against the church.

Achieving, in a sense, his desire to make one order out of two, the pope promulgated yet another bull, *Ad Providum*, about a month later, on May 2. This decree ordered that all of the property of the Templars be transferred to the Hospitallers, excepting only on the Iberian Peninsula, where the Spanish and Portuguese monarchs had exerted adverse pressure on the basis of their continuing struggle against the infidel on their home grounds. Perhaps as a concession to Philip, it was agreed that the Christian monarchs could recoup from Templar property their own expenses for the arrest, imprisonment, and feeding of the Templar prisoners, as well as for the custodial care and management of that property since the day of the Templar arrests. Suddenly, to the distress of the Hospitallers, those expenses became very high indeed.

Another problem was that quite a few of the Templar properties had been donated to the order with various bonds and agreements under the prevailing feudal system. Many of the original owners simply seized back the properties on the basis that their gifts were not transferable. This meant many a legal battle for the Hospitallers, but they did succeed over the next decade in enforcing the pope's desire by acquiring the bulk of the Templar holdings. Templars subsequently released were free to seek membership in the Hospitallers, and a few of them did. As it turned out, however, the whole business was basically meaningless; its purpose from the standpoint of the church was to create a combined order that could more effectively support the next Crusade, but that Crusade, although authorized and encouraged by the Council of Vienne, just never got off the ground. The Crusades were finished. The notion of a combined order was finished as well; although the Hospitallers did gain new wealth, they gained very few new members from the Templar suppression.

There remained the business of the Templars still in prison, which was settled a few days later by the papal decree, *Considerantes Dudum*. It set forth that the high Templar officers would be judged by the Holy See, while the fates of the rank and file would be determined by provincial councils of church leaders. The latter generally determined that those Templars who had not confessed their guilt, or those attempting to change their statements made under torture, would be sentenced to life imprisonment. Those who had confessed and made no effort to change or retract those confessions were released from prison, but not from their vows, and were put on very small pensions. No provisions were made for those Templars who had not been caught. They were still subject to arrest if found, a necessary precaution because word had reached the council that as many as fifteen hundred Templars and sympathizers were hiding in the area around Lyons, planning some sort of revenge. The manhunt launched to round them up was totally unsuccessful.

As for the high officers, it was almost two years after the Council of Vienne before they were brought before a panel of three cardinals. Since all of them had confessed to a number of charges either under torture or, as in the case of de Molay, under the threat of torture, the review was cursory, leading to sentences of life imprisonment. To put to rest all thoughts or rumors that the Templars were not actually guilty but rather had been the victims of greed-oriented persecution, it was decided to have the order's grand master make his confession before the world. The nobility, prelates of the church, and influential commoners were invited to witness the historic event on March 14, 1314. A high platform was erected in front of the great cathedral of Notre Dame from which de Molay would confess his shame, so that all the world would know that the Templars were indeed guilty of gross obscenities and heresies.

The grand master was escorted up the steps to the platform, accompanied by the Templar preceptor of Normandy, Geoffroi de Charney, and two other officers. De Molay must have thought and prayed long about this moment, which would be his very last chance to vindicate his order. To do that, to retract his confessions of guilt to defend the honor of the Order of the Temple, would be a form of suicide. Yet all those men who had followed him, who had looked to him in vain for leadership in their blackest hour, who had suffered humiliation, inconceivable agonies, and the most painful deaths known to the medieval mind, would all have suffered and died to no purpose if their grand master pronounced them all guilty out of his own mouth. It was the most important moment in Templar history, and the aging grand master found the courage to use it. Stepping forward on the platform to address the crowd, most of whom had been told what he was going to say, de Molay condemned himself to martyrdom:

"I think it only right that at so solemn a moment when my life has so little time to run I should reveal the deception which has been practiced and speak up for the truth. Before heaven and earth and all of you here as my witnesses, I admit that I am guilty of the grossest iniquity. But the iniquity is that I have lied in admitting the disgusting charges laid against the Order. I declare, and I must declare, that the Order is innocent. Its purity and saintliness are beyond question. I have indeed confessed that the Order is guilty, but I have done so only to save myself from terrible tortures by saying what my enemies wished me to say. Other knights who have retracted their confessions have been led to the stake, yet the thought of dying is not so awful that I shall confess to foul crimes which have never been committed. Life is offered to me, but at the price of infamy. At such a price, life is not worth having. I do not grieve that I must die if life can be bought only by piling one lie upon another."

In the tumult that followed, Brother de Charney shouted out his own retraction and assertion of the innocence of the order, as he and de Molay were hustled off the platform. The monumental embarrassment they had brought to both king and church assured that there would be no backing off from the rule that relapsed heretics would be burned alive, and the prospect of their causing additional embarrassment assured that their deaths would not be put off one hour longer than necessary. The burning was announced for that same evening.

There were variations in the practice of death at the stake, and even the possibility of small mercies. The victim might be given a brain-numbing potion to dull the awareness of pain. For a fee, the executioner might add green wood and even boughs of evergreen to produce a dense smoke that the victim would suck in frantically, to produce unconsciousness or death from smoke inhalation before the pain grew too great. A roaring fire could assure the fastest possible death. None of these reliefs was to be available to the recanting Templar leaders.

The executions were held on a small island in the River Seine, but a crowd still managed to gather by boat to witness the end of the drama that had exploded that morning. The fires were carefully prepared of dry, seasoned wood and charcoal, to make a low smokeless pyre of intense heat, calculated first to blister the legs and to drag out the final relief of death by slow roasting from the ground up. De Molay and de Charney, as long as they could, continued to shout out the innocence of their order. Legend says that as Jacques de Molay's flesh was being burned away he called down a curse on Philip of France and upon all of his family for thirteen generations. He called upon both king and pope to meet with him within the year for judgment at the throne of God. Clement V died in the following month of April, followed by Philip's unexplained death in November of that same year. As we shall see, the death of Clement V was an almost insignificant revenge compared to the continuing impact of the Templar suppression on the Roman church over the centuries ahead.

After the execution of de Molay, King Philip received a formal complaint from the Augustinian monks who owned the island on which the executions had been carried out. They expressed no objection or outrage over the burning of the abbot and master of a holy monastic order. Their complaint was trespassing.

This background of six and a half years of the Templar suppression in France in the shadow of king and pope will help us to better understand the very different circumstances surrounding the Templar suppression in England and Scotland, where conditions, including a substantial advance warning, were much more conducive to the formation of a secret society for mutual protection.

CHAPTER 10

"NO VIOLENT EFFUSIONS OF BLOOD"

In July 1307, three months before the arrest of the Templars in France, the twenty-four-year-old first Prince of Wales became King Edward II of England. Thus the crown passed from one of England's strongest kings to its weakest and most deplorable.

For his part, Edward II was happy to have his stern old father out of his life because the young king was in love; not with the Princess Isabella of France, to whom his father had arranged his betrothal, but with a handsome young man named Piers Gaveston, a poor knight from Gascony. They had been friends since childhood, and Edward's father had encouraged the friendship in the belief that the courtly young Gascon, so skilled in arms and apparently possessed of all of the knightly virtues, would be an effective role model for his weak son.

The old king was preoccupied with his wars against Scotland and France and had not noticed the development of the relationship between the two young men. Then, in the last year of his reign, he summoned the young prince to join him in his campaign against the Scots. Gaveston, of course, accompanied the Prince of Wales, and watching them the king could see that this was an unnatural relationship. The real blowup came when the prince asked his father to give Gaveston the French province of Ponthieu. This royal territory was located on the Channel and vital to the defense of the king's French possessions. It is said that the king flew into such a rage at the extraordinary request that he struck the prince in the face and dragged him around the room by his hair, screaming at him for his stupidity. Piers Gaveston did not get Ponthieu. Instead, he got banished from England.

Now, as king, young Edward II could do as he liked. His first official act as monarch was to call his lover back to the English court, where he was compensated for the discomfort of his brief exile by being made earl of Cornwall.

As Edward II was using the first few months of his reign to exercise his royal powers for the benefit of his favorite, his barons used the time to reduce that power. They gained control of the Curia Regis, the king's council, and created within it a governing committee of what they called the "lords ordainers." Gaveston seemed to divide his time between making incessant demands on the king for wealth and power and using his wit and facility with words to mock the nobles at court, even making up insulting nicknames for each of them. That antagonism set the tone of the English court for the next five years. Whereas the suppression of the Templars was a grim dedication at the court of France, to the English court it was more of a distraction. Other major events had to be addressed: Robert Bruce had left his sanctuary in the Western Isles and was back on the mainland of Scotland rallying his people. The king's wedding with Isabella of France had been scheduled to take place in Boulogne during the following January, and the preparations would take months.

Philip sent an envoy, Bernard Pelletin, to his future son-in-law, urging that he arrest the Templars in his realm, and the pope transmitted his written instructions for those arrests. The reaction of Edward II to the charges against the Templars was one of disbelief. He had grown up with the Templars all about him. The London temple had acted as host to many of the young men who had been knighted with him, even willingly chopping down part of their temple orchard to accommodate tents for the newly made knights who would fight for their king against Scotland. An English master of the temple, Brian de Jay, had died fighting for England against William Wallace. The order didn't appear guilty of anything to the young king, and he said so as he dispatched letters to other Christian monarchs, asking that they support him in defending the Templars against the false charges. On December 4 Edward wrote to the pope, declining to arrest the Templars in England on grounds of their innocence. In transit, his letter crossed the path of the bull *Pastoralis Preeminentae*, the official papal condemnation of the Templars that had been published on November 22, 1307. Edward II received his copy on December 15. His personal feelings no longer mattered, and he now had no choice but to order the Templar arrests. But he didn't have to do it right away.

We do not know if the delay was born of the king's own personal feelings, his propensity to procrastinate, or the influence of the Templars and their friends at court, but the arrests in England did not begin until January 7 in London, and stretched out from there with the passage of additional days as orders were disseminated throughout the kingdom and to the English provinces on the continent. Whatever arrangements had been made for the Templars' flight during the two months between news of the Templar arrests in France and the receipt in England of the papal bull on December 15 would have been greatly accelerated by the alarming news that the arrests were imminent. We can only imagine the stir when the English master, William de la More, returned from the court to the Temple at London to report the arrival of the papal bull. Riders undoubtedly went galloping out from London in all directions to warn their brothers in the shires.

That there was effective planning in those twenty-three days between the arrival of the bull on December 15 and the start of the arrests on January 7, 1308, is beyond question. When the royal troops came for them they were able to arrest a few, but most of the Templar knights, sergeants, and clerics were not to be found. Records were missing or destroyed. At the London temple the soldiers of the king, expecting to seize the greatest treasure they would ever see, actually found less than two hundred pounds. The gold and silver plate, the jewelled reliquaries, all were gone.

Also gone was the king. He and many of the lords of the household had embarked for France and the king's wedding to the twelve-year-old Princess Isabella of France (her preteen innocence giving no clue that she would one day be known to Englishmen as the "She-Wolf of France"). To the fury of his nobles, Edward II named Piers Gaveston the regent of the realm, to govern in the king's absence. Gaveston would see no personal gain in the matter of the Templars, and the nobles left behind had no heart for the task of arresting their brothers-in-arms, among whom many friendships existed. A royal dragnet, assisted by the religious orders, turned up only two fugitive Templars in all of England. Some Templar preceptors were permitted house arrest and stayed in their quarters. English master de la More, who probably had to stay behind because his flight would have given away all the careful preparations, was taken to prison in Canterbury, but lodged in relatively comfortable quarters with a royal allowance to permit him to purchase additional comforts from his jailers. Several of the captive Templars escaped from their prisons, which had to have involved help from inside or outside, or both. Perhaps the assistance they received was efficiently organized, or perhaps their pursuers had something less than an intense desire to recapture them, but for whatever reason not one of the escaped Templars was ever found.

As for those few Templars remaining in prison, they benefited from the fact that the Channel was not just a water barrier between Britain and the continent but was in many ways a philosophical barrier as well. Since the days of the old Celtic church, which had never been subject to the authority of Rome, leaders of the church in England and of the secular government had struggled against papal authority in the island kingdom, and one of the institutions they had resisted was the Inquisition, which did not exist in Britain. The Dominicans had been permitted to come in, but they had had to leave their charcoal fires and red-hot pincers at home. The Templar prisoners were incarcerated but not tortured, a situation that was taken by Pope Clement V as a personal affront to his authority. He demanded that the Templars be tortured for confessions of heresy as he had originally instructed. The pope also decreed that any person giving aid and assistance to a fugitive Templar, anyone even giving *advice* to a fugitive Templar, would be punished and excommunicated. Remarkably, the threat of torture and excommunication for those aiding the fugitives did not result in the reporting of even one missing Templar. While the pope was struggling to get Edward II to bend to his will, his fellow Gascon, Piers Gaveston, was enjoying huge success in that same endeavor. Upon his return from his wedding, Edward had given Gaveston some of the most valuable jewelled wedding gifts. At the king's coronation the following month, Gaveston was given a position above all the peers of the kingdom.

Two years went by, and the Templars being questioned without torture confessed nothing, constantly reaffirming their innocence, perhaps heartened by the occasional escape of one of their brothers. In response to a papal demand that torture be applied, Edward replied that torture had never played a role in either ecclesiastic or secular jurisprudence in England, so that he didn't even have anyone in the kingdom who knew how to do it. Exasperated, Clement V wrote warning Edward that he must look to the fate of his own soul in thus flouting the direct orders of the vicar of Christ on earth, and saying that he would try just one more time, giving King Edward the benefit of the doubt. The pope was dispatching ten skilled torturers to England in the charge of two experienced Dominicans; now Edward should be out of excuses. Further, when the torturers reached their destination, Clement expected that they would be put to work promptly. It says something for the pope's resolve that he took time out from the important religious duties of his holy office on Christmas Eve, December 24, 1310, to deal with the problem of ensuring the infliction of agonizing physical abuse on the captive Templars. His Christmas gift to the people of England was the introduction into their legal system of interrogation by torture.

Edward did receive the papal torture team, but ordered that their ministrations must exclude mutilation and that there must be no permanent wounds and "no violent effusions of blood." There is very little that history can report to Edward's credit; however, these restrictions on the torturing of the English Templars may be the first recorded effort to place some kind of check on the runaway madness that peaked in the fourteenth century and made the application of maximum pain on another human being a vital part in deposition and interrogation. As with the pain inflicted by angry parents or schoolmasters, it was probably born of frustration, but it grew in frequency of application and in ingenuity until it tipped over the edge of sanity when someone decided that this would be an effective tool in protecting and furthering the teachings of Jesus Christ. The church did ultimately put curbs on the use of torture by the Inquisition, but not without strong objection being registered by leading Dominican friars, who felt that their effectiveness was being curtailed. It remained for secular authority to provide the most dramatic limitations to legal torture in what is probably the most misunderstood term in its long history, the "third degree." Somehow this term has been taken by some to have a relationship to Freemasonry, probably because of the bloody oath of the Master Mason in the "third degree" of Masonry.

The phrase actually originated in what was at the time considered an extremely humane decree. Up to the time of the Austrian Empress Maria Theresa, individual authorities were very much on their own in setting limits on the types and intensity of torture used to question "witnesses" or to extract confessions. Innocent people often died as a result of the questioning, and many more were crippled for life. Under Maria Theresa in the eighteenth century, the tortures to be used for questioning were standardized throughout her domain. The First Degree of the Question was the thumbscrew. This little machine was tightened by two threaded bolts until pressure by a bar or blunt point was brought to the base of the thumbnail. Then the questions began, with subsequent turns of the screw until the thumb joint was crushed.

In the Second Degree of the Question, the victim was stripped to the waist and tied, with arms stretched upward, to a crude ladder placed at an angle against a table or wall. The torturer held a candle flame in position to burn the sensitive skin of the side, at locations from the waist to the armpit. With so large an area to work in, on two sides of the body, and with wide latitude as to the time the flame could be held to the flesh, the torturer had considerable discretion as to the amount of pain inflicted, according to his appraisal of the importance of the witness or his own mental set.

The Third Degree of the Question was the strappado. The victim first had his hands tied behind his back; then a rope was tied to his wrists and passed through a pulley attached to the ceiling. By pulling on the rope, the torturer and his assistants would pull the victim's arms straight up behind him, causing excruciating shoulder pain, until the victim's feet actually left the floor. Now, two variations might be introduced. With the victim's feet several feet off the floor, the torturer could release the rope and grab it again, causing the victim to drop and be jerked to a stop, a procedure that frequently led to the dislocation of one or both shoulders. In the other variation, once the victim was suspended in the air, the assistant would tackle his legs and pull with all his weight toward the floor, thus intensifying the pain and perhaps tearing the victim's arms out of their sockets.

Anyone who passed through the third degree without confessing was to be judged innocent and released. It is important to understand that the foregoing, however brutal it may appear, was hailed by secular and religious leaders alike as an example of Christian mercy, and indicative of the humanitarian qualities of the empress.

Edward's orders had not been as restrictive as the three degrees of the question of Maria Theresa, but perhaps his expressed sympathy for the victims had some bearing on the fact that even under torture no material confessions were extracted from the English Templars. They may have benefited as well from being in confinement for three years before the torture began, during which time they could talk among themselves and steel their resolve, in contrast to their French brothers, who had been taken completely by surprise and subjected to the agonies of the Inquisition immediately after their arrests.

One effect of the commencement of the torture of the Templars in England would most certainly have been to increase the determination of the fugitives not to be caught. For three years capture had meant only imprisonment with their fellow Templars, but to be taken now would mean to share their suffering at the hands of the ten papal specialists in human agony.

While all this was happening in England, the pope's efforts to have the Templars in Scotland arrested and questioned got nowhere. There were a few Templar arrests in January 1308, but Robert Bruce was busy with problems of his own and was more likely to recruit warrior knights in his kingdom than to arrest and torture them. Bruce knew that the death of Edward I had bought him additional time but that sooner or later an invading English army would cross the Tweed to bring him down. He had no interest in the military orders, no interest in a Crusade to the Holy Land, no interest in the ambitions of Philip of France or Pope Clement V. Bruce's interest was totally dedicated to the security of an independent Scottish nation. As a Christian monarch, he had received a copy of the papal bull of condemnation, with instructions to carry out the decree it embodied, but he apparently just cast it aside. The papal bull was never published, announced, or acknowledged in Scotland, thereby giving that country the aspect of a legal haven for fugitive Templars from England or the continent. Not only would a fugitive Templar knight have felt safe, but if he had no compunction about fighting against the English king he would have been a welcome addition to Bruce's pitifully small force of armored cavalry. How important that small force was to Bruce would be amply demonstrated when the English finally launched their invasion of Scotland just a few years later.

As the persecution of the Templars in England moved into the stage of formal inquiries in November 1309, the tribunals had little in the way of confessions to help them, and little in the way of witnesses. Most of those who came forward to testify against the Templars were members of other religious orders and had little to offer except rumor and hearsay. As to the rulers of the country, they were not all that interested: Their attentions were focused elsewhere. The ten professional torturers provided by the pope knew their business—there was a variety of ways in which they could inflict excruciating pain while still staying within the king's guidelines—but in spite of that revolting expertise they extracted no material confessions. They were only able to get admissions that to preserve their secrets Templars were told to go only to their own priests for confession, that they might have occasionally absolved each other of sin in special situations, and that they wore a cord next to their skin, although they didn't know why. It was conceded that this cord might have been a dividing line defining the "zones of chastity," a device invented by St. Bernard of Clairvaux for holy orders. There were no confessions of heresy, blasphemy, obscene kisses, or homosexual practices.

In 1311, the year that the Templar torture began in England, the lords ordainers had had enough of the king's homosexual favorite, not so much because of his and the king's sexual proclivities as because Piers Gaveston had used his hold over the king to secure almost total control over the monarchy. Much to the anger of the king, the barons, aided by the fact that Gaveston had been excommunicated by the archbishop of Canterbury, exiled Gaveston to Flanders. Within the year, however, he was back, and while the Council of Vienne was sitting to talk a new Crusade and the fate of the Templar order, the lords ordainers were busy chasing Gaveston around the north of England. They finally trapped him in Scarborough Castle where, characteristically, he talked them into sparing his life. As he was being taken under guard to London, Gaveston's escort was surrounded by the troops of the earl of Warwick. Although a lord ordainer himself, Warwick maintained that since he had not been at Scarborough, he had not been a party to the agreement reached there with Gaveston and so was not bound by it. Gaveston was taken back to Warwick Castle, but knowing that the king would exert any pressure to save his favorite, Warwick had his men take the prisoner outside the castle to Blacklow Hill, where they struck off his head on July 1, 1312.

Edward II evidently learned nothing from this incident, apart from new levels of rage, and before long he was under the influence of yet another homosexual lover. For the moment, however, his fortunes seemed at their lowest ebb and the monarchy itself in great danger, as the lords ordainers could reflect on their victory over their defenseless king. Edward decided to take the advice given to disturbed rulers for centuries before and after him, that the way to pull the nation together again and regain his own authority was to take his country to war. In 1313, at the urging of his father-in-law, Philip of France, Edward took the cross and swore to lead his people on the great new Crusade that had been declared by the same Council of Vienne that had abolished the Templar order the year before. However, neither Edward nor his people had any desire to travel to the Holy Land. Politically and militarily, it would be disastrous for English fighting men to absent themselves at the very time that the energetic King Robert in Scotland was inexorably evicting the English from one Scottish stronghold after another, until in all of Scotland only the castles of Dunbar, Berwick, and Stirling remained in English hands. No, it was not a costly Crusade under the domination of the French king that would establish Edward's supremacy over his warrior barons, but rather a great victory over the threatening enemy at England's back door. The promises to his father would be kept. Edward II would be the king who would finally bring the Scottish nation to heel and make it a part of the English realm.

In 1314, while the hot coals were roasting the flesh from the blackening bones of Jacques de Molay, Edward II was marshaling a great force for the final invasion and conquest of Scotland. Bruce was able to assemble ten thousand men to defend their homeland, while England drew on all its resources and territories to amass an army of over twenty-five thousand, including five thousand heavily armored cavalry and about ten thousand archers.

The lords ordainers, the chief barons of the realm, had no desire to risk their lives to make a national hero of the despised king, and a number of them simply declined to go. That was apparently all right with Edward, who made no moves to force them, probably because he had no desire to share the anticipated glory with the men he was striving to dominate.

As the strung-out army advanced through the north of England, foraging for many miles on either side of its route, Robert Bruce had ample warning of its approach. The English were looking for him, which gave Bruce the advantage of selecting his ground, a field where his men could relax and refresh themselves while the weary English troops tramped mile after mile to meet him. Bruce chose ground that placed his men between the approaching English and Stirling Castle with its small English garrison, a few miles to the north.

Having learned well from the campaigns of Wallace, Bruce set his schiltrons, those circles of men with twelve-foot spears, along the top of a slope, between dense patches of woods. In anticipation of the charge of the vastly superior English cavalry, he had hundreds of potholes dug at random in front of his spearmen and covered with grass and brush like animal traps. His horde of camp followers, carters, cooks, and families was ordered to safety behind a nearby hill. Finally, remembering that Wallace's cavalry, his only defense against the English archers, had abandoned him on the field of Falkirk under their disgruntled commander, Bruce himself assumed direct command of his few hundred mounted knights. It was into this crucial force that legend says Bruce welcomed a group of fugitive Knights of the Temple.

At the bottom of the slope was the valley floor of marshy land, with just one hard road. The valley and its boggy bottom were intersected by a small stream, or "burn" in the Scottish dialect, called Bannock Burn. It was about to assume the highest place in Scottish military history.

Learning of Bruce's position, the English army turned toward him, and finally the vanguard arrived on the opposite side of the burn. The huge force was so strung out that it took three days for the rear echelon to close up. While they were gathering, a small force was sent to relieve Stirling Castle, which would give the English a fortified position at Bruce's back. Scouts reported the move, and Bruce acted quickly to intercept the English relief force. Its leader, Sir Henry de Bohun, rode out in front of his men to challenge Bruce to single combat. Bruce accepted the challenge and galloped out to take his stand in front of his men. Sir Henry lowered his lance to its rest and spurred his heavy warhorse toward the waiting Scottish king. Bruce had selected his light mount that day for swift pursuit and was armed with a battle ax having nowhere near the reach of de Bohun's lance. As the lance point reached him, Bruce deflected it with a back-stroke of his ax and followed with a swift forward stroke of the broad blade, killing the English knight with a single blow. The raid to relieve Stirling was over, and as the news spread the Scots swelled with renewed pride in their warrior king.

On the English side the king, who was anything but a warrior, ordered the attack and unleashed his heavy horse. They slogged through soft ground on both sides of the stream, then spurred their mounts up the slope to the waiting spearmen. Horses tripped in the potholes, horses tripped over other horses, but at last they reached the bristling picket of spears. English and Scots locked into a mass from which neither side would back off. English reinforcements were poured in but couldn't get to the enemy on the limited six-thousand-foot front. The archers were ineffective because their massed flights of arrows had more chance of hitting their comrades than of striking the outnumbered Scots. The answer was to move the archers to the Scottish flank where they could pick their targets.

As the English archers moved across the field, Bruce readied his mounted knights, holding them in tight control. To get the maximum impact from the charge of the huge war-horses, he needed the archers to be massed together to begin their arrow flights, not strung out and moving. Finally the archers were in place, prepared to decimate the Scottish spearmen, and Bruce gave the command his knights had awaited so eagerly. The English archers were bowled over by armored war-horses trained to kick, bite, and trample, ridden by armored men who laid on the armorless archers with ax and mace. The bowmen broke and fled scrambling down the hill.

Perhaps the observers from Bruce's camp followers thought that the retreating archers meant a Scottish victory, or they may have been stirred to action by some patriotic zealot, but for whatever reason the Scottish noncombatants decided to change their status. Waving homemade flags, shouting and blowing horns, the unarmed men, women, and boys came pouring over their hill and into the woods on the English left. The English troops were threatened by what they took to be fresh Scottish reinforcements. Their left began to falter, and Edward II decided to leave the field. His household and bodyguard went with him, soon joined by other confused and poorly led units, until the entire invading army was in full flight. The jubilant Scots came bounding down the slope after them, plunging their spears into one back after another. It was the worst military disaster in English history, with an estimated fifteen thousand Englishmen lost, as compared to about four thousand Scots. The Battle of Bannock Burn ended the hopes for English dominion over Scotland, which maintained its status as an independent nation until the union of the two countries under one king almost four centuries later, in 1707.

As the survivors of Bannock Burn, including King Edward, made their way back to their homes, they traveled through a land in a state of near anarchy. The weakness of the king had permitted the erosion of central power by a group of ambitious barons, eager for their own personal gain but having not the slightest interest in engendering any increase in the voice in government for the common people. Their leader, Thomas of Lancaster, had managed to usurp for himself the great holdings of the earldoms of Lancaster, Lincoln, Leicester, Derby, and Salisbury.

The central government, almost microscopic in the terms by which we think of government personnel today, depended upon the nobles and knights to maintain law and order in the realm, but beyond protecting their own personal interests they were both indifferent and not up to the demands of the job. Outlaw bands proliferated. In some areas they comprised the only law and order available, and on several occasions they were hired as mercenaries by both ecclesiastic and secular lords to defend their properties. Outlaws so dominated some territories that local lords were ordered to have all trees and bushes cut back on either side of well-traveled stretches of road to prevent ambush and surprise attacks. This was the age that made folk heroes of outlaws and furthered legends like those of Robin Hood. No one condemned these heroes for pouncing on wealthy abbots and bishops to relieve them of the pounds and pennies that had been extracted from their parishoners. No sin was here, because the legendary robbers did not enter churches to steal golden crosses and silver candelabra but only took what was perceived to be the personal wealth of greedy prelates. Bold robbers broke all the game laws, too, to take fresh meat whenever they liked, the dream of every peasant. It doesn't matter that the outlaws were not really like the fabled Robin Hood, but it does matter that it is in that context that they lived in folk memory. The peasant could act out his fantasies vicariously—thrash an arrogant baron, take the gold away from a greedy bishop, treat his family and friends to a great feast of illegal venison. The popularity of Robin Hood and his like tells us much of how the common people felt about their lives and about those that man and God had set above them.

As to the outlaw bands, they were made up of men who were "out-law," outside the protection of the laws of the land, which allowed anyone to beat, rob, or even kill them with no fear of legal punishment. Their only hope of protection from law-abiding citizens was to band together with others of their kind. Templar knights and men-at-arms with no trade other than fighting, already condemned by both king and church, would have been ideal recruits. We do not know that any fugitive Templars did join the outlaws or form bands of their own, but we do know that such bands operated all around the areas of the Templar manors and commanderies.

Edward looked for allies and found two in the earl of Winchester, Hugh le Despenser, a lord of the Welsh marches (borderlands), and his handsome son, also named Hugh. Once again Edward was totally captivated by a homosexual lover, the younger Despenser, and permitted the older man to manage much of the affairs of the kingdom. The Despensers used that power to encroach upon the other lords of the Welsh marches to the extent that those lords allied themselves with Thomas, duke of Lancaster, and the other lords ordainers who followed him. Despenser organized a campaign against Lancaster and defeated the march lords, taking as prisoner one of their leaders, Roger de Mortimer. In the following year, 1322, Despenser organized a campaign against Lancaster and defeated him at the Battle of

Boroughbridge in Yorkshire. Lancaster was taken back to his own castle at Pontefract and beheaded there. Roger de Mortimer managed to avoid the similar fate planned for him by escaping from his prison and fleeing to France, where he would soon be joined by a royal co-conspirator.

Charles IV, king of France and brother of Queen Isabella of England, took advantage of the troubles in England to seize the duchy of Gascony. This was a great blow to Edward's purse, because the wine trade that operated through Bordeaux earned him more income than all of his English holdings. Isabella offered to go to Paris to negotiate with her brother for the return of the rich province, and Edward agreed.

In France, Isabella met and fell in love with Roger de Mortimer. Mortimer wanted revenge and the return of his lands. Isabella was totally disgusted with her husband's relationship with the younger Despenser and thoroughly detested both the young man and his father. Together, Isabella and Mortimer hatched a plan to seize the English throne for the underage Prince of Wales, with themselves as regents and rulers of England. Isabella sent for the prince on the excuse that he should do homage to her brother for the Gascon province. As soon as the boy was with them, Isabella and Mortimer put together an army of mercenaries and invaded England in September 1326. They were made welcome by a people angry at the arrogance of the Despensers and the king's neglect of almost every royal duty in his consuming preoccupation with his lover. The Despensers, father and son, were quickly taken and met death by strangulation in the hangman's noose. The king himself was imprisoned and forced to abdicate in favor of his fourteen-year-old son. After a year in various prisons, Edward II was finally murdered at Berkeley Castle in Gloucestershire on September 22, 1327. The rough knights who did the job apparently decided that since he had chosen the way he wanted to live, he could bloody well die the same way, as they held him down and pushed a red-hot iron spit up his rectum.

The reign of Edward II was perhaps the most dismal and deplorable period to be found in English history, but as such was a blessing for men on the run and in hiding. We have seen that the fugitive Templars, who may well have been joined by fugitive brothers from the continent, had ample motivation to run to escape the chains and tortures waiting for them. We have also seen that the shambles that was the government of Edward II was ideal for fugitives who could only benefit from the demise of law and order. Scotland would welcome them, but only in a clandestine sense, in that their presence would have to be kept secret from the religious orders, who would most certainly have followed the pope's orders and turned them in. But what about the fugitives themselves? What were their needs and fears as they sought refuge, new identities, new homes? Under the circumstances, would those needs be better served by a secret society than by the security of individual effort? In the search for the Great Society, there was a need to look at the problems of the man on the run from the point of view of the man doing the running.

CHAPTER 11

MEN ON THE RUN

The one common characteristic of fugitives on the run is their mental state, which is one of unrelenting stress, never knowing when to expect the hand on the shoulder or the door crashing in. The outward manifestation of that stress is panic, a state that interferes with thinking and acting in a rational, constructive manner. The most effective antidotes for that panic are a plan and some assistance from fellow human beings. The fugitive with no plan and no objective, all alone, is in constant danger of betraying himself. The most successful escaped convicts or prisoners of war have always been those who spent as much time planning what they would do after the escape as they spent on planning the escape itself. Those who have escaped by grasping a sudden opportunity, finding themselves outside with no idea of what to do or where to go, have almost always been recaptured quickly.

The Templars were fortunate in having almost three months' warning of their impending arrests, which gave them time to plan both individually and in concert with their comrades. They also had funds and means of transportation. They had friends and connections in all parts of Britain, which was, as we have seen, by no means a single political unit. Their biggest problem would be one of discovery by the other religious orders, whose holdings constituted fully one-third of the land surface of Britain. It was not that all of the other orders bore them any special animosity so much as that the Templars were living proof that the pope could and would punish a religious order with imprisonment, pain, death, and loss of property. This was no time for any order to overlook any opportunity to demonstrate loyalty and obedience to the Holy See. No fugitive Templar could expect another religious to look the other way.

Another problem that must have arisen was the diversity of the men involved. The order to arrest the Templars and their associates included representatives of almost every free stratum of medieval society. Members of the order included the full brothers, the knights who, as a condition of their membership, had to prove their lineage as members of the knightly class; the sergeants, drawn from the bourgeoisie; and the clerics, the Templar priests who could come from any of several classes so long as they were freeborn. Beyond these, the arrest orders included other Templar associates who might give information about their activities, such as their servants, the stewards and tenants of Templar manors, the craftsmen who operated the Templars' forges, saddleries, mills, and so forth, and the mercantile employees who supervised buying, selling, and shipping, and who operated their franchised markets.

The Templar officers alone could draw on the central Templar treasury, although local preceptors and stewards might have some funds available. Many of the others might have nothing and have to be assisted in some way. As to transportation, each knight had at least three horses. He had his powerful trained war-horse, his hack or other light, swift horse for travel, and a packhorse to carry his armor and weapons, with other supplies. The fleeing knight had more than enough ready transportation. That was not true of the bulk of the other Templar fugitives, who would have had to move on foot or by boat.

In spite of his obvious advantages, the knight also had his own special problems. His hair was close-cropped at a time when long hair was the fashion, but he could at least contrive to wear some kind of head covering until it grew out. His beard was a different matter. The fashion was to be clean-shaven, so the Templar's full, untrimmed beard would mark him in a crowd. He could shave it off, but if he had recently reached Britain after spending years in the Middle East he would have looked just as strange beardless, with a face the color of mahogany above, and a snow-white chin and cheeks below. Applying dirt or stain, or staying out of sight until his tan skin paled, would have been absolutely necessary, because there was no way that his pale cheeks and chin would tan to match the rest of his face under a British winter sun.

Clothing was a concern, too. The normal dress of all three degrees of the Templar order was a cowled robe, as was appropriate to an order of monks. They did, of course, have battle dress, but they wore that hot, heavy garb only when necessary. A look into a Templar dining hall would have revealed a gathering of silent, robed monks, not a vociferous gustatory gathering of armored knights like that in the great hall of King Arthur's court. To flee the papal arrests, the fugitive members would need complete new wardrobes suitable to the roles they would be assuming.

An even more challenging consideration would have been that of language. The Templars were essentially a French-speaking order, and French was the language of the British nobility and monarchy. It would be another fifty years before legal trials in England would be conducted in English rather than French. Some of the knights and Templar priests must have possessed a working knowledge of English in order to supervise their properties and employees, but any one of them would have revealed his social stratum with the first sentence or two spoken in his French-accented English. Undoubtedly the Templar knight who knew no trade but fighting would find his safest home among his own kind. He might pledge himself in feudal contract under a different name to one of the barons of the realm, who would welcome an experienced fighter and probably not be concerned that the recruit was being sought by the church and the English crown. There were plenty in England who might welcome him, and there were also Norman-French barons in Wales and Scotland and even in Ireland, where, for example, the great landholding Norman family of de Burghe had not yet had its name evolve into what now appears to be the purely Irish name of Burke.

To the man on the run, safety frequently is represented by geography. He must get out of enemy territory or beyond the reach of the law. For a fugitive from the church, however, there was no completely safe haven in all of Christendom. His safety would have to come from secrecy, from a new name, a new home, a new means of livelihood. This would be extremely difficult in a world of small communities (London itself, the largest city in Britain, had a population of just about twenty-five thousand).

The fourteenth-century fugitive would have needed help, including assistance from friends who would support him and swear to his new identity. That particular sort of problem is dealt with by one of the Old Charges of Freemasonry, which says that a visiting brother is not to go "into the town" unless accompanied by a local brother who can "witness" for him (i.e., vouch for him to the local authorities, who had the right to arrest strangers of unknown business in the town).

On the run, the fugitive would have one overriding concern, which was to not be caught. That meant traveling off the main tracks, preferably with a guide or with directions provided by a friend. In a village or smaller town he would be most vulnerable, because a stranger would be easily spotted. His next major concerns were something to eat and a safe place to sleep, with the latter far more stressful to him. Eating can be done at odd times, on the move, and even postponed for long periods. Sleeping cannot be put off beyond the point at which the human body absolutely demands it, and then the fugitive is at gravest risk. The toughest, strongest, most experienced fighting man alive is as defenseless as any child when sound asleep. Safe lodging would have been an imperative.

At the hundreds of Templar properties throughout Britain, the local employees would certainly have been aided by their own families and friends in order to remain in hiding in nearby areas. Those families and friends would also be vital contacts for fugitives on the move through those areas, contacts who could provide bread and meat and lodging for the night in a barn, a croft, a gamekeeper's hut. Such safe lodging would provide the things a fugitive hungers for: food, news, a chance to rest, directions to the next stop, a bit of food or money to take with him on the next leg of the journey, a sympathetic ear.

At the next stop, he would need a device or signal by which he could locate the man who was to befriend him there and by which he could safely identify himself. Later in that century, Lollards hiding from the church would use the line, "Let's all drink from the same cup," as a means of establishing their identities. The Freemasons were to develop a much more elaborate system in which a Mason had a sign by which to identify himself (his "dueguard"), a sign to appeal for help to any brother who might be present (the Grand Hailing Sign of Distress), words to use in darkness or to direct to others who might be out of sight or looking in another direction ("O, Lord my God, is there no help for a Son of the Widow?"), and even a confirmatory catechism ("Are you a traveling man?" "Yes, I am." "Where are you traveling?" "From west to east"). Exactly such a system of covert identification and acknowledgment would have been necessary—or at least very beneficial—to men on the move, hopefully going from one safe lodging to another, looking ultimately not for a safe house but for a safe harbor, a place at which to stop running and settle down to get on with the business of living. Included in the system would have to be totally trustworthy friends and sympathizers outside the order willing to run the risk of participating in an underground network.

The Templars certainly had the background to create secret signs and signals and would have known that no such system could work without standardization. The signals had to be known and agreed to by all, which meant that they needed to be devised and promulgated by a small center of leaders and then simply revealed to the others; any democratic process of voting on possible choices would have been logistically impossible in those days of poor communication and poor travel conditions. With an illiterate populace as well, the system would have to be implemented verbally, to be learnt by rote and repetition.

Once the signs and signals were set, it would be of paramount concern that they be passed on only to those considered absolutely trustworthy. In the custom of the day, the assurance of that trust would probably have required a sacred oath, coupled with an earthly penalty to supplement God's displeasure at the breaking of an oath made in His name. We have seen this in the secret bargain made between Philip IV of France and the archbishop of Bordeaux that would designate the next leader of the Holy Roman Church. An archbishop of that church swore the most sacred oath on the host itself, but that was not enough security for Philip, who demanded the archbishop's brothers and nephews as hostages; the archbishop's penalty for breaking his oath was agreed to be the murder of his family. Nor was the oath-with-penalty limited to the highest lords of royal and spiritual authority. We see it passed on in folk memory to children throughout the English-speaking world in their childish assurance of secrecy as they make the sign of the cross over their left breasts and say,

"Cross my heart and hope to die." The sign of the cross makes it a religious oath. The penalty for breaking the oath is death. The key word is "hope," which means that the penalty is freely and voluntarily assumed: "If I break this oath, I *want* to die, as fitting punishment for my sin." The object of the oath is to instill total trust. Since, in the case of the fugitive Templars, betrayal would mean treatment much more horrible than a clean death, the penalty for breaking the oath would also have needed to be something horrible. This called to mind the much-condemned oath in the initiation of the Master Mason in the third degree, when he asks that his body be cut in two and his bowels burned to ashes should he break his oath of secrecy. Such a penalty would seem totally out of line for a broken oath taken by a stonecutting guild member, but would not have seemed too much to a man whose betrayal would mean days and weeks of torment with whips and chains and red-hot irons, with the ultimate risk of being burned alive at the stake.

The years that passed between the first Templar arrests in 1307 and the final dissolution of the order in 1312 would have provided ample time and opportunity for the underground system to mature into a clandestine organization that could admit other sympathizers and other fugitives, especially those who had escaped their prisons during those years. The organization may well have aided in those escapes and have been able to speed the journey of the escapees into the underground stream. Some Templar knights joined the Hospitallers, as the pope had suggested, and many Templar priests went into other religious orders, but that does not mean that they would not have willingly joined a newly formed secret society functioning to help their brothers— especially because of the mental state that takes over after panic dies down.

The man who experiences great fear; who must run and hide; who has lost his freedom, his standing in the community, even his own name; who has been reduced upon occasion to running like an animal, is of one dedicated frame of mind, thinking only of avoiding capture and prison. Once he feels safe, however, and the panic subsides, his mind moves to those who brought him to that condition. His mind moves from fear to hate and from panic to thoughts of revenge. It is that state of mind that can keep an underground group alive, even for generations. Some may be willing to forget, but many are not, and some among the Armenians, Kurds, Irish, Sioux, Sikhs, Jews, Palestinians, Basques, and Ukrainians make certain that their children and grandchildren don't forget, either. Hatred and the passion for revenge do not necessarily die with the original victims.

The fugitive Templars who sailed off with the order's ships would have been in a special situation. We do not know the fate of the Templar vessels that carried Jacques de Molay and his entourage to Marseilles. There is no record of the seizure of eighteen Templar ships from their naval base at La Rochelle on the French coast, or of any Templar ships anchored in the Thames or at other seaports in Britain. The Templars who fled with those ships got a double benefit: The ships provided a place to live and also the means to make a living. For pirates and corsairs in the Mediterranean it was open season on almost everyone, with hundreds of separate countries, provinces, city-states, and island communities. Since many of the Templar ships were galleys, they were ideally suited for piracy, because becalmed ships were always easy prey for those that did not depend upon the wind. If a corsair happened to have a religious orientation, there were plenty of targets of Moslem, Roman Christian, and Orthodox Christian allegiance from which to select, but even within the aggressor's own religious persuasion political differences usually provided substantial targets. Fighting ships were to be avoided as targets, because easy plunder was the objective. Fishing vessels and coastal luggers were fair game but had to be searched out. The most dependable point of attack was the coastal settlement, the size of the target being selected according to the size of the pirate force. After the harvests were in, the pirate season heated up. There was always a ready market for food and animals, and if a church happened to yield up a bejewelled reliquary or a silver communion cup, that was a bonus. People were prime targets, with the wealthy held for ransom and the rest sold in the slave markets. Great ports grew up where the freebooters could dispose of their cargoes, then recruit and restock for the next voyage out. Christian slaves were readily marketed in the ports of North Africa, such as Tunis and Mahdia.

The speculation about the disappearance of the Templar ships and the men who manned them calls to mind one of the most mysterious tenets of Freemasonry. In the lecture that sums up the initiation of a new Master Mason, the newly admitted candidate is told that this degree "will make you a brother to pirates and corsairs." That statement makes no sense whatever in the context of a society descended from medieval stonemasons. It really can't be explained, and I have never talked to a Mason who could offer any basis for this strange statement. There is a legend of Freemasonry, however, that is frequently recounted. The story is that in 1813 a Freemason was captain of the merchant ship *Oak*, which was taken by a pirate. In desperation, the captain gave the Grand Hailing Sign of Distress of a Master Mason. The sign was recognized by the pirate chief, who returned the Masonic captain's goods and sent him on his way. In addition, the pirate tied a ship's biscuit in a ribbon which he fastened around the neck of the Mason's dog. This ribbon and biscuit are reputedly still in the possession of Lodge of Amity (No. 137) in Poole, England. The pirate is remembered in Masonic history as "Jacques le Bon."

As intriguing as the anecdote may be, it offers nothing in the way of explanation of why a Master Mason could be considered "a brother to pirates and corsairs." If, on the other hand, some relationship had developed between the fugitive Templars and the Freemasons, the mysterious statement would make very good sense, in that the Templar fugitive on land was indeed a brother to any Templars who had taken the order's ships to sea as freebooters.

The possible relationship between the Templars and Freemasons was coming up more and more. Any fugitive Templar taken would be subjected to imprisonment and torture to extract confessions of heresy, and any person assisting him even with advice and counsel could be punished and excommunicated, risking the loss of any property he might have. Under those circumstances, the matter of who could be trusted was literally a matter of life and death. If to let a man know your name might put your life and property at stake, what kind of oath, or threat, would be sufficient to give a feeling of comfort? The fugitive Templar would have needed a rule such as that ancient Old Charge of Freemasonry, that a Mason tell no secret of any brother that might cause that brother to lose his life and property. To the fugitive Templar that charge would be absolutely necessary, while for the medieval stonemason it would make no sense. What secret could the stonemason possibly have that would threaten his life and property? An ingenious new way to hold a chisel? A formula to calculate the load-bearing ability of a foundation? What secret would he fear that a brother Mason could whisper to the authorities, who might then take his life and property as a result of learning that secret? Had the fugitive Templars somehow merged with the Freemasons and injected into their rituals these points, which would apply to all of the fugitive Templars but to no stonemason? That would mean that the Templars had not only found a haven in Masonry but had somehow come to dominate it.

There was another Masonic connection that was hard to let go. The Templars had three enemies: the monarchy, the Hospitallers, and the church. For a Templar, the idea of the church as his enemy would have been both depressing and confusing. Membership in the Templar order did not make a man a knight; he had to be of that class to be eligible to join. The great radical change in his life was that, by his own volition, his Templar initiation made the knight a monk whose entire life was thereafter pledged to the service of the church and its pope. That dedication caused him to abandon all thought of having a wife and children through his vow of chastity, led him to give up all his worldly possessions in the vow of poverty, and made him bend his own will to those placed above him in their service to God by his vow of obedience. He was a member of a religious community of men who had on many occasions elected to die rather than save their lives by denying or compromising their Roman Catholic faith. The Templar monk lived according to a strict monastic Rule and rigidly adhered to a daily program of adoration and prayer, as his church had decreed that he should do. How could he suddenly adjust to having that same church revile him, accuse him of blasphemies and obscenities, arrest him, chain him, burn him at the stake?

One would expect that various Templars would have had different reactions to their rejection by God's appointed representatives on earth. Some would have rejected the entire church hierarchy. Others might well have differed in such matters as the sacraments, the Christ who through Peter had let the popes rule his church on earth, or the Virgin Mary who was revered by that church. However, they clearly would have needed one focal point of agreement, that there indeed was a God, for how else could one have effective oaths? Let those who had been shocked or angered into a total disbelief in God stand aside; no man wanted his security in any way dependent upon the oath of an atheist, for with no belief, there could be no trustworthy oath. As for differences of opinion among the brotherhood of the Temple as to which parts of the church and its teachings they would retain or reject, let them keep those to themselves. This was to be a secret brotherhood of mutual protection. Lives were at stake, so the religious differences didn't matter. Arguing about personal beliefs could only drive them apart, so let them not argue.

Given that set of thoughts and conclusions, the rejected military monk found himself in a weird, totally new condition. The pope had rejected him, so he had no choice but to reject the pope. Hitherto, during his entire life in the Templar order, his link with God had been through his grand master, who was responsible only to the pope, who claimed to be God's sole viceroy on earth. Now his religious order had been dissolved, his grand master had been burned at the stake, and Christ's vicar on earth had cast him aside. He still believed in God, but his chain of intercession with God had been ripped away. Now, for the first time in his life, no one stood between God and himself. His prayers of solicitation and thanksgiving, his acts of adoration, his hopes for salvation could no longer be through the pope, so were now on a purely personal basis. With such thinking and such conclusions, the seeds of the Reformation and even Protestantism may well have been germinating fully sixty years and more before John Wycliffe and the Lollards. Those seeds were free to germinate and propagate because they were nurtured in complete secrecy, perhaps nourished by beliefs held by others religiously disillusioned or persecuted, who would have been welcomed into the brotherhood.

All this is speculative, no matter how much sense it may make, because there is absolutely no historical evidence of the existence of a secret society specifically based on fugitive Templars. The search could be reasonably abandoned, except for one point that locks into the mind and won't let go. All of the foregoing could be the first logical explanation of the very heart of Freemasonry. The single point that most characterizes that fraternity, and which has been without explanation for hundreds of years, is the central tenet of Freemasonry that each member must assert his belief in a Supreme Being, but that how he worships that Supreme Being may not be questioned. He is not permitted to discuss his religious beliefs in the lodge, nor may he try to persuade any other Mason to his point of view or creed.

Most Masons today believe that their fraternity was born in medieval guilds of stonemasons. Traced from such beginnings, the Masonic attitude toward religion is extremely difficult to comprehend. The guilds were very religious, had patron saints, owned holy relics, staged religious plays, contributed to pilgrimages. They usually venerated the Virgin Mary. They made extra gifts to the Holy See. How could guilds of stonemasons ever have acquired an attitude toward religion and the church that said, "If they matter to you, it's perfectly all right with us, but to our protective secular brotherhood the sacraments don't matter, Christ doesn't matter, His Holy Mother doesn't matter, and the pope in Rome doesn't matter. All that matters is that you agree that there is indeed a Supreme Being over all of us." That doesn't mean that Freemasons cannot be Christians, because most of them certainly are. However, it does mean that the basic fraternity of Freemasonry is not structured on the Christian ethic, per se, but welcomes any man who believes in any perception of a monotheistic Supreme Being. It welcomes any believer and rejects only the atheist. The Christian initiate takes his oath on the Holy Bible, the Jewish initiate uses the Torah, and the Sikh may place his hand on the Khalsa of the Guru Gobind Singh. To ask us to believe that such a central theme could have evolved from a medieval guild is too much. On the other hand, as we have seen, it could easily have been born in the circumstances of a brotherhood condemned by the church and driven into hiding by the threat of papal imprisonment and torture.

On the one hand there is a group of men in hiding, with all the motivation and the skills necessary to form a secret society and with good reason for adopting a radical attitude toward the prevailing religion, but no specific evidence of an ex-Templar organization. On the other hand, there is burdensome evidence of a secret society that actually existed and flourished in the late Middle Ages, with the common belief that since its members at some point came to be called "Masons" it must have sprung literally from that craft guild, but with no documentary evidence to support that theory. Moreover, we have men in hiding who could have benefited from all of the protective Old Charges of Freemasonry, while a guild of stonemasons would have had a practical need for almost none of them.

Finally, was it just pure coincidence that the Knights Templar and the Freemasons were the only organizations in all of history that found their principal identification in the Temple of Solomon, or was that history trying to tell us something?

One could grow weary, and wary, of trying to shrug off too many Templar/Masonic similarities as coincidence. It would be necessary to dig much deeper before coming to any conclusion, but enough had already presented itself to warrant a much more intense look at the rituals, legends, and history of Freemasonry, in order to reject or reinforce what now appeared to be a very definite relationship. Several times in the past 270 years there had been claims of a connection between the Templars and the Masonic order but those claims had all been dismissed for want of any real facts and were ultimately regarded as spurious. Still, almost every probe of the origins of Freemasonry had been from the inside out, trying to build a case on legend and symbol, somewhat like an investigator using the swastika to prove that the Nazi party originated in ancient India and Greece, with connections to the Hopi Indians. This time the investigation would be from the outside in, trying to trace the reasons for the Masonic secret society existing in Britain alone, along with the factors that could keep it alive, and secret, for centuries.

The answers were there waiting.

PART 2

THE FREEMASONS

Prologue

The Victorian Embankment along the Thames River in London is one of the most impressive promenades in the world. Its most notable feature is an ancient Egyptian obelisk called Cleopatra's Needle, dating from the reign of Thothmes III, about 1500 B.C. It had been offered to the British people several times, beginning in the time of George IV, but it was 1877 before it began its sea voyage to London. On the way, a storm sank the ship in the Bay of Biscay, but in shallow enough water that the obelisk was raised and brought to its new home.

The unveiling of Cleopatra's Needle on the Embankment in 1878 was a great occasion, and someone had an interesting idea to make the celebration, and the obelisk, even more memorable. Since the hieroglyphics gave clues of a culture three thousand years old, the favor would be returned by providing clues of contemporary British society for future archaeologists. To that end, two earthenware jars were sealed in the base of the obelisk, and in those jars were placed objects indicating the greatest achievements of the British Empire—for example, a complete set of newly minted coins, for surely the British monetary system, preeminent in the world, was among the greatest British achievements.

The complete list of objects placed in the jars was carried in the London *Times* on the day of the unveiling. No one seems to have noticed, or commented upon, a very ordinary object placed in one of the sealed jars. It was a twenty-four-inch metal ruler. What was the achievement symbolized by this ruler? The invention of the inch? Freemasons reading this will already have guessed. The ruler, called by Masons a "twenty-four-inch gauge," is a very important symbol in the legend and ceremonial of Freemasonry. The twenty-four-inch gauge is the first working tool presented to a new Mason as part of his initiation as an Entered Apprentice. The moral lesson it illustrates is the proper use of the Mason's twenty-four-hour day, dividing it into periods for work, rest, and charity. It also appears in Masonic ritual as one of the tools used to assault the Master Mason at the building of the Temple of Solomon, in the initiation rites for the degree of Master Mason.

Apparently the Metropolitan Works Board, or their superiors, or all of them, decided to quietly place the twenty-four-inch gauge inside the base of the obelisk to tell archaeologists a thousand years later that to be counted among the greatest achievements of the British Empire is that quasi-secret organization known as the Ancient Order of Free and Accepted Masons.

CHAPTER 12

THE BIRTH OF GRAND LODGE

The task of describing Freemasonry is formidable. It is the largest fraternal organization in the world, with almost three million members in the United States, over seven hundred thousand members in Britain, and a million more around the world. It has been the subject of over fifty thousand books, pamphlets, and articles since it revealed itself to the world in 1717.

Although based on the primary membership requirement of firm belief in a Supreme Being, admitting men of all religions, and having a central theme of moral behavior, constant self-improvement, and a dedication to acts of charity, Freemasonry probably has aroused more enmity than any secular organization in the history of the world. It has been consistently attacked by the Roman Catholic church, its membership forbidden to men of the Mormon faith, and even the Salvation Army and the Methodist church in England have advised their members against Masonic membership. It has been, and is today, outlawed in a number of countries, although Masons certainly do not mind their order having been declared illegal by Adolf Hitler, Benito Mussolini, and Francisco Franco. They do mind having been branded an alternate religion, the Antichrist, and the force behind subversive plots to overthrow governments. Most recently, they have had to contend with the involvement of a

175

clandestine, disavowed Masonic lodge in the Vatican banking scandals and allegations of unwarranted preferment and coverups in the British police and civil service.

Many anti-Masonic allegations are difficult to address because of the traditional policy of Freemasonry to decline to respond to attacks. Critics of Freemasonry benefit from the concept of "confession by silence," their accusations usually standing unanswered by a quasi-secret society that apparently feels, even in our media-burdened society, that deeds will outweigh press releases. Because of that policy, the Freemasons may be destined to remain controversial, although their legions of critics are easily matched by the legions of notables who have chosen to embrace Masonic membership.

Freemasonry was there in the American Revolution, with members such as George Washington, Benjamin Franklin, James Monroe, Alexander Hamilton, Paul Revere, John Paul Jones, and even the Marquis de Lafayette and Benedict Arnold. Other revolutions, against both church and state, were led by Freemasons Benito Juárez, Simón Bolívar, Giuseppe Garibaldi, and Sam Houston (aided in some cases by the products of their fellow Mason, Samuel Colt).

Kings and emperors who took the Masonic oaths include Edward VII, Edward VIII, and George VI in England, Frederick the Great of Prussia, George I of Greece, Haakon VII of Norway, Stanislaus II of Poland, and even King Kamehameha V of Hawaii. In addition to Washington and Monroe, the Masonic roll of presidents of the United States includes Andrew Jackson, James K. Polk, James Buchanan, Andrew Johnson, James A. Garfield, Theodore Roosevelt, William Howard Taft, Warren G. Harding, Franklin D. Roosevelt, Harry S. Truman, Lyndon Johnson, Gerald Ford, and honorary brother Ronald Reagan.

World War II was fought by British Masonic leaders Sir Winston S. Churchill, Field Marshal Earl Alexander of Tunis, Field Marshal Sir Claude Auchinlech, Marshal Lord Newhall (Royal Air Force), and General Sir Francis Wingate. American Masonry was well represented by Generals Mark Clark, Omar Bradley, George Marshall, Joseph Stillwell, and Douglas MacArthur.

Nor were Freemasons always on the same side. Napoleon threw his Masonic marshals Messena, Murat, Soult, MacDonald, and Ney against Freemasons Kutuzov of Russia, Blucher of Prussia, and their ultimate nemesis, the duke of Wellington.

One hardly knows where to stop in recounting Masonic influence on all aspects of western life in the past 270 years, whether that influence be political, military, or cultural. In music Freemasons ascend the entire scale from William C. Handy, composer of "The St. Louis Blues," to John Philip Sousa, and from both Gilbert and Sullivan through Sibelius and Haydn to Wolfgang Amadeus Mozart, whom some say was murdered for revealing Masonic secrets in his opera *The Magic Flute*.

Masonic members of the literary world include Sir Walter Scott, Robert Burns, Rudyard Kipling, Jonathan Swift, Oscar Wilde, Oliver Goldsmith, Mark Twain, and Sir Arthur Conan Doyle (who would never have permitted Stephen Knight's anti-Masonic book, *Jack the Ripper: The Final Solution*, to be rewritten, as it was, into a fictionalized motion picture version pitting Sir Arthur's creation, Sherlock Holmes, against Sir Arthur's own Masonic brothers in London).

As impressive, even legendary, as some of these actual Freemasons may be, they pale against the revelations of early Masonic historians, who claimed the Masonic membership for Adam, Abraham, Noah, Moses, Solomon, Ptolemy, Julius Caesar, and Pythagoras (remembered in Masonic verbal tradition by the delightfully anglicized name of "Peter Gower"). One Masonic writer was incensed that some of his contemporaries expressed doubt about the claim of Masonic membership for Achilles. Nor did the fantasy stop there. Claims were made to establish the origins of Masonry in ancient Egypt, and some traced Masonic sources to the Essenes, Zoroastrians, Chaldeans, and especially the Phoenicians, since they had been kind enough to sail to Britain to share their Mysteries with the Druids, also claimed as predecessors of Freemasonry.

Gradually the competition among Masonic historians to outdo each other in such fantasies died down, and more sober voices were given a chance to be heard. The first great retreat was to the establishment of Freemasonry at the building of the Temple of Solomon, based upon a literal interpretation of an allegory which, as we shall see, is central to the initiation ritual of a Master Mason. This theory was embellished to establish three original Grand Masters: King Solomon; Hiram, king of Tyre; and a mythi-

ical Hiram called "Hiram Abiff." Masonic writers have tried to
identify Hiram Abiff as the biblical Hiram, "son of a widow of
Naphtali," who was a master worker in bronze, a skill he used to
cast the great pillars, Jachin and Boaz, that flanked the entrance
on the outer porch of the temple. Their problem is that in
Masonic ritual the master builder, Hiram Abiff, is murdered and
the Temple of Solomon is never finished, while the biblical
account says that the temple was indeed finished and, as far as we
can tell, Hiram the metalworker went home, alive and well. The
biblical account in fact provides no clue to the real origins of Freemasonry. If there was to be any valid revelation of Masonic origins in the building of King Solomon's temple, it would have to
be drawn from the allegorical drama locked within the Masonic
ritual.

The next generation of Masonic historians, now striving for
truth rather than romance, finally admitted that there was absolutely no evidence of Masonic beginnings in the building of the
Temple of Solomon, but they thought that they had found those
origins in the medieval British guilds of stonemasons. This theory
has led to the trotting out of all the working tools of the stonemason, making them the symbols of moral lessons which the Mason
is to follow as he constantly strives for self-improvement. There
is absolutely nothing wrong with lessons of morality and charity,
in whatever form they are taught, just as there can be no objection to an incessant striving for self-improvement. The problem
is one of credible history, a believable basis for thinking that an
organization of dusty stonecutters with scraped hands and knees,
backs aching from struggling with heavy blocks of stone in all
weather conditions, somehow turned into a noble company led
by kings and princes, dukes and earls—not to mention that the
entire process was accomplished in total secrecy.

The basic problem, of course, is that prior to the year 1717 the
Masonic order was a true secret society; not just an organization
with secret signs and secret handgrips, but a widespread society
whose very *existence* was a secret. No Masonic historian claims to
fully understand why that secrecy existed, or even why the group
existed. When Masonry finally revealed itself, it gradually became
known that this secret society had cells, or "lodges" as they called
them, all over England, Ireland, Scotland, and Wales, but
nowhere else. What was it that had held them together, sworn to

preserving this tradition of total secrecy for generation after generation with oaths so sacred that the breaking of them could earn extraordinarily brutal punishments? Whatever the mortar of motivation was that had held the stones of the Masonic lodges together, giving purpose to the members' lives and demanding total secrecy, it had disappeared by the time that the first Hanoverian king, George I, ascended the throne of England, a throne by then legally forbidden to any Roman Catholic or spouse of a Roman Catholic.

It was an event of little importance at the time: Four lodges of Freemasons met at the Apple-Tree Tavern in Covent Garden in London in 1717 and declared that they were banding together to form an official association to be called a "Grand Lodge." There is no evidence that they had in mind at the time any confederation extending beyond London and Westminster. The news itself was not earthshaking to the people of London, whose first impression, if any, would have been that four eating and drinking clubs were combining to eat and drink together once a year. That impression would have been justified by the fact that these "Masons" held their "lodge" meetings with food and drink and tobacco at the Apple-Tree Tavern, the Crown Ale-House near Drury Lane, the Goose and Gridiron in St. Paul's Churchyard, and the Rummer and Grapes Tavern in Westminster. It turned out that the group claimed John the Baptist as one of its patron saints, and on St. John Baptist's day, June 24, 1717, the Grand Lodge was officially instituted with the election of a Grand Master and other officers.

The real shock would have occurred underground and been felt by all of the other Masons in Britain. The four London lodges, simply by revealing themselves and the existence of their order, had violated their sacred oaths of secrecy. They had unilaterally decided that total secrecy was no longer necessary, or even desirable. Every other Mason in Britain would have been in a quandary, and one can only imagine the concerned and heated discussions that took place in the secret lodge meetings throughout Britain during the months following the London disclosure.

Slowly other Masonic lodges, most of them in the areas around London, revealed themselves and asked to join with the new Grand Lodge. Others, however, were angry with the "oath-breakers" and would have nothing to do with them. Their ire may have been occasioned by the fact that the members of the newly formed Grand Lodge made no attempt to justify their actions, or even to explain why they had decided that the time had come to shrug off what they apparently felt was needless and even inconvenient secrecy. That there was resistance on the part of lodges still clinging to their original charges is shown by their reaction to a formal request made by the Master of the Grand Lodge at the second Grand Festival in 1718. All of the Masonic lodges in England were asked to turn over to the Grand Lodge any ancient records or other documents relating to Freemasonry so that they might be considered in drafting a constitution for the Grand Lodge. The reaction of many lodges was to burn all written references to their regulations or history, to prevent their being used to break the oath of secrecy. Historians may lament this destruction of valuable documents, but in a way their destruction does credit to those who were not quick to throw away their traditions or their vows.

The first formal objection to the concept of the Grand Lodge came eight years later, in 1725, from the Masonic lodge at York. York Masons based their complaint not upon the violations of the ancient secrecy of the order but upon the assumed superiority and antiquity of the Londoners. York Masonry, they asserted, was as old as the setting of the foundation of York Cathedral in the seventh century; Edwin, king of Northumbria, had been their first Grand Master. In the spirit of brotherhood, they said, they would not argue with the London group calling itself the Grand Lodge of England, but the whole world should know that York Masonry had an "undoubted right" to style itself as the "Grand Lodge of *All* England" (italics mine).

During that same year of 1725, Irish Freemasonry came out of its misty bog of secrecy and declared a Grand Lodge of Ireland, based in Dublin. The first Irish Grand Master was the twenty-nine-year-old earl of Rosse, probably a wise choice to get things moving, since he had inherited a vast fortune of a million pounds from his loving grandmother, the duchess of Tyrconnel.

Scotland was the longest holdout in bringing its Masonry into public view. (It has been said that if Freemasonry was to be classified like Judaism, America would be styled as Reformed, England as Conservative, and Scotland as Orthodox.) Finally, however, nineteen years after the launching of the Grand Lodge of England, the Scottish lodges began to meet to discuss their own situation. The year 1737 saw the first formal meeting of the new Grand Lodge of Scotland.

That same year also saw the beginning of an explosion of Freemasonry in France. It set off the proliferation of hundreds upon hundreds of new Masonic orders and degrees and sparked the creation of new legends and new fantasies that confuse any serious attempt to comprehend modern Masonry, even in the United States. It was all triggered by one man, a well-placed Scot whose motivations are as mysterious now as they were then.

Andrew Michael Ramsay was born at Ayr in Scotland in about 1681 and was educated at the University of Edinburgh. In 1709 Ramsay was appointed tutor to the children of the earl of Wemyss, but he soon became embroiled in the religious turmoil rending Scotland at that time and went to France. There, under the patronage of Archbishop Fénelon, Ramsay converted to Roman Catholicism. Some time later he was appointed preceptor to the Duc de Château-Thierry, and subsequently to the Prince de Turrenne. For his services he was rewarded with a French knighthood, being made a chevalier (knight) of the Order of St. Lazarus, for which he is remembered in Masonic history as the Chevalier Ramsay.

Perhaps Ramsay's most significant service was to a king, but a king without a country. He was called to Rome by the man who would have been King James III of England had his father, James II, not been deposed. James was dedicated to returning the Scottish and English crowns to his family and to returning the British people to the authority of the Roman church. If he could not get those crowns for himself, he could work to secure them for his son, Charles Edward Stuart, great-grandson of that monarch who had reigned both as James VI of Scotland and as James I of England and was therefore, in the eyes of Catholic Europe, heir to both the English and Scottish thrones. Searching for a tutor to the heir-in-exile, James sent for the Scottish chevalier Andrew Ramsay, who undertook the education of the tragic young man who would live in history as Bonnie Prince Charlie.

After a time in Rome, Ramsay returned to France, where he took an active role in Freemasonry. It was basic three-degree British Craft Masonry, which had been brought across the Channel by British Masons who had taken up residence in Paris and other major cities of France. They established lodges and took in a number of their French friends. The French seemed mildly interested but were not terribly impressed by a semisecret society that had grown out of an association of grubby stonecutters. Ramsay changed all that. Ramsay proclaimed an entirely new origin for Freemasonry; not in medieval stonecutters, but in the kings, princes, barons, and knights of the Crusades. He had not a shred of documentation nor even any reasonable basis to support his claim, but he was believed. After all, he was a tutor to royalty, a member of the Royal Society, a chevalier of the Order of St. Lazarus, and grand chancellor of the Grand Paris Lodge of Freemasonry. Ramsay's Oration, as it became known, was delivered for the first time at the Masonic Lodge of St. Thomas in Paris on March 21, 1737.

"Our ancestors, the Crusaders, gathered together from all parts of Christendom in the Holy Land, desired thus to reunite into one sole Fraternity the individuals of all nations," said Ramsay. He explained some of the secret words as protective, "words of war which the Crusaders gave each other in order to guarantee them from the surprises of the Saracens, who often crept in amongst them to kill them." He claimed that the ancient mysteries of Ceres, Isis, Minerva, and Diana became connected with the order. As to being "masons," Ramsay explained that the original Crusader-Masons were not themselves workers in stone, but rather men who had taken vows to restore the Temple of Christians in the Holy Land. He claimed that the fraternity had formed an "intimate union with the Knights of St. John of Jerusalem."

(Reflecting upon the major motivations of the Crusader nobles, one quickly concludes that they did not include a dedication to the Brotherhood of Man. Perhaps Ramsay can be credited with helping to start the wave of chivalric fantasy that swept over Europe in the eighteenth and nineteenth centuries, which held up as the ideal for all gentlemen the good, pious, compassionate knight, generous and honorable with his fellow man and superrespectful to all women, who is almost impossible to find in the pages of history.)

Ramsay further stated that lodges of Freemasons were established by returning Crusaders in Germany, Italy, Spain, France, and especially Scotland, where the lord steward of Scotland was Grand Master of a lodge at Kilwinning in 1286. (Perhaps he presumed that his audience already knew that the hereditary lord stewards of Scotland, with the title "steward" having evolved into the family name "Stewart" or "Stuart," had become the royal family of Scotland and England, whose scion, Ramsay's former pupil, was even then in Rome plotting to regain the lost throne.) The lodges, he went on, were neglected in every country except Scotland, and although Prince Edward had brought Freemasonry back to England, Scotland clearly had the earliest Masonry in Britain and was the fountainhead of the Masonic spirit. He appealed urgently to France to take up the cause and "become the centre of the Order."

France responded. Stonemasons were one thing, but kings, dukes, and barons were quite another. New Masonic degrees and rites exploded in France like the grand finale of a fireworks display. These new rites were exported to other countries, which, in turn, added embellishments of their own, until the day came when one Masonic historian claimed to be able to document fourteen hundred different degrees. Their ceremonies and rituals, even their names, strained the available nomenclature of the Old Testament and of all of the orders of chivalry.

One French system evolving from Ramsay's Oration— *Écossaise*, or Scottish Masonry—graduated up to a thirty-third degree and was exported to the United States, where it is still exercised, with modifications, as the Ancient and Accepted Scottish Rite of Freemasonry. It includes a relationship with the Ancient Arabic Order of the Nobles of the Mystic Shrine (the "Shriners"), for which Ramsay's claims of origins in the Holy Land provided a base for ritual and costumes in a polyglot Arab/ Turkish/Egyptian theme. In fact, of all the so-called "Scottish" Masonry in existence, only the Royal Order of Scotland has any direct connection with that country.

There is probably no direct connection, but in 1738, the year after Ramsay's Oration, Pope Clement XII issued the bull *In Eminenti Apostolatus Specula,* the first of a long series of papal bulls and encyclicals against Freemasonry, which provided a new area of interest and zeal for the Holy Roman Inquisition. Where the Inquisition had power to do so, Freemasons in Catholic countries were imprisoned, deported, and even tortured. In Portugal, one man was tortured and then sentenced to four years chained to the bench of a galley for the crime of being a Mason.

Another event in continental Masonic history may well have involved Ramsay. A German nobleman, with the ponderous name of Karl Gotthelf, Baron von Hund und Alten-Grotkau, believed that he had been commissioned to promulgate the true Freemasonry under a system known as "Strict Observance" because the oath of the Apprentice Mason included a vow of absolute obedience to "unknown superiors." Von Hund's diary indicates that while in Paris in 1743 he was received into a Masonic Order of the Temple by an unknown official he knew only as the Knight of the Red Feather. In attendance were Lord Kilmarnock (a Jacobite who was beheaded for high treason on August 18, 1746) and Lord Clifford. Later, von Hund claimed to have been presented to Prince Charles Edward Stuart as a distinguished brother. The "true history" of Freemasonry told to von Hund was that at the time of the suppression of the Templars a group of the knights had fled to Scotland, keeping their condemned order alive by joining a guild of working masons. They had chosen a grand master to succeed de Molay, and since then there had been an unbroken succession of Templar masters. For security purposes, the identity of the grand master was kept secret during his lifetime, his role known only to those few who had elected him. This made it necessary to swear to obey an "unknown superior." Von Hund was to start setting up lodges of Strict Observance in Germany and to await further instructions. He did as he was told, but lived in frustration, because he was never contacted again.

The concept of a chivalric order, strict obedience, and a secret grand master apparently had great appeal to von Hund's countrymen, because the new order spread like a grass fire in Germany over a twenty-year period and extended from there to almost every country of continental Europe. Then it began to wane and virtually died out within the next decade, because it appeared that the grand master was not only unknown but was also nonexistent. Von Hund went to his grave convinced that the "unknown superior" was Bonnie Prince Charlie himself. Those who feel that the whole concept of promulgating Strict Observance Masonry was to recruit men and money for the Jacobite cause are inclined to agree with him. If indeed von Hund was correct that Prince Charles Edward Stuart was the "unknown superior," his reasons for not contacting von Hund again would be very clear. The Jacobite cause was crippled forever by the bloody massacre of the Battle of Culloden Moor and the just as bloody aftermath as the English commander, William, duke of Cumberland—"the Butcher"—hunted and slaughtered Catholic Scots up and down the Highland glens. (As the English hero, the duke was honored by having his name given to a fragrant rockery flower, Sweet William, which understandably is known in Scotland as "Stinkin' Billie.")

While continental Masonry was occupied with weaving more and more complex patterns of rite and ritual, original three-degree British Craft Masonry was having problems of its own. With all knowledge of any prior purpose gone, Freemasonry was emerging as an eating and drinking society with perhaps a shade too much emphasis on the latter. All English Masons must regret that their moralizing brother, William Hogarth, memorialized the state of eighteenth-century London Masonry in his painting entitled *Night*, which depicts a stumbling-drunk Master Mason being helped home by his lodge Tyler, both in their Masonic regalia. The early frivolity was probably the result of the fraternity having no purpose other than the fellowship of the tavern, to the point that lodges were commonly named for the taverns that were their usual meeting places. With the original purposes of Masonry having been lost a generation or more before, the leadership realized that new purposes had to be found. The first of these was Masonic charity, beginning with needy brothers, then gradually extending to the widows and children of brother Masons and to the current inclusion of non-Masonic beneficiaries as well.

The other purpose layered onto Masonry to lure it away from its posture as a tavern-oriented eating and drinking society was the concept of constant self-improvement through the practice of moral behavior, as taught in the lodge. The lessons were taught by using the symbolism of the tools of the stonemason's trade, and Masonic expressions such as "on the square" became part of the common language. These mason's-tool symbols of morality were no part of Masonry before it came public in 1717, but they quickly took hold. The summation was reached in the symbol of the "ashlar," the building stone. The newly accepted Mason represented the just-quarried "rough ashlar" and was to use the symbolic tools of morality to cut and shape and polish himself into the "perfect ashlar," ready to take its place in the building of God's temple, for the most important tenet in Masonry was and still is the avowed belief in a Supreme Being.

These two new Masonic elements, charity and morality, constantly asserted and monitored, brought British Masonry out of those taverns and into purpose-built rooms and buildings, which, in turn, brought Masonry into a quasi-religious posture. Instead of having their supper, their wine, and their long "church warden" pipes all through the lodge meeting, those pleasures were banned and replaced by Masonic hymns, Masonic prayers, and organ music in the Masonic temple, all to enhance ever more formal ritual and atmosphere.

Based on little more than the fact that they knew they were called "masons" and that the central ritual involved the construction of King Solomon's temple, everything about the fraternity was bent in the direction of the stonemason's trade, and not only through the use of the simple tools as moralistic symbols. Anything that could be learned about medieval stonemasons, or about the construction of ancient buildings, was assumed to be significant to the history of Freemasonry. The lofty Gothic cathedrals especially attracted the attention of Masonic romanticists, who were busy creating a past for Freemasonry in medieval guilds. Descriptions of the better-known cathedrals filled Masonic books and were included in lectures in the lodges, complete with details of arches, buttresses, spires, and variations in the design of columns and capitals. It is now being recognized that there is not a shred of evidence to link Freemasonry to a single notable building, and most serious Masonic writers have now abandoned their once-trumpeted claim of Masonic Grand Mastership for Sir Christopher Wren.

Based on the inability to uncover even one piece of hard evidence, the British Masonic preoccupation with the building trades, like the French Masonic preoccupation with the Crusades and the Holy Land, could offer nothing constructive in the search for Masonic beginnings. The principal point was to determine whether one could establish any connection with the suppressed order of the Knights Templar, and nothing could be expected from words and symbols that were simply made up after Freemasonry came public in 1717. Those signs, symbols, words, and rituals most likely to yield clues regarding Masonic origins would be those preserved in purely verbal transmission, passed on by rote but *not* understood, thus making them less prone to additions and elaborations in the transmitting.

The best course, then, would be to concentrate on those aspects of Masonry known at the point at which the four London lodges revealed themselves in 1717, when all knowledge was from the past. This would be classified as "Secret" Masonry, as opposed to Freemasonry after 1717, which would be thought of as "Public" Masonry. That also meant that one could ignore the interpretations of secret Masonic facts made by early Masonic historians looking back, not to ascertain the truth, but to force every item of Secret Masonry to fit the preconceived dedication to establishing Masonic origins within medieval guilds of craftsmen.

As an example, there is the "clothing" of Masonry, the gloves and sheepskin apron, said by Masonic writers to be the working clothing of the medieval stonemason. Examining hundreds of drawings, paintings, and woodcuts showing medieval stonemasons at work there was no evidence of work gloves or a sheepskin apron. Another example is the guard who stands outside the door of the meeting with a sword in his hand, the Tyler. It was decided by Masonic writers that the guard might have been borrowed from the guild of roof tilers, or perhaps the secret meeting room at one time had a door covered with tile. Masonic writers are full of such strained notions as they cling tenaciously to the medieval guild theory of origin. By now, we felt that there was sufficient evidence to abandon that theory, but its acceptance was so widespread that perhaps something had been missed. To give the theory the benefit of the doubt, it was necessary to take a good, hard look at the medieval guilds of stonemasons in Britain. The conclusion of that inquiry was something of a shock to me and may be even more so to Freemasons.

CHAPTER 13

IN SEARCH OF THE MEDIEVAL GUILDS

The one aspect of Freemasonry that is not supposed to be a mystery turns out to be the biggest mystery of all, and that is how Freemasonry came to be, and why. The origin and purpose of Freemasonry is not supposed to be a mystery because Masons, anti-Masons, and the general press almost universally agree that Freemasonry originated in the medieval guilds of stonemasons in Britain. The research behind this book led to the conclusion that this theory, no matter how widely accepted, is wrong. To disagree with authorities, both Masonic and non-Masonic, who have expounded the belief in guild origins generated a great measure of self-doubt, which in turn provided the incentive for many months of research involving thousands of miles of travel. At the end of the search the conviction that the guild theory was erroneous was stronger than ever, and the doubt was gone.

It must be admitted that modern Masonic writers do allow more room for new speculations and new research than their non-Masonic counterparts. Freemasons F. L. Pick and G. N. Knight, in their authoritative handbook *The Pocket History of Freemasonry*, state: "Up to the present time, no even plausible theory of the 'origin' of the Freemasons has been put forward. The reason for this is probably that the Craft, as we know it, originated among the operative masons of Britain." The late Stephen

Knight, the most outspoken critic of Freemasonry in recent years, expressed no doubt as to Masonic origins in his book *The Brotherhood*, in which the title he gave to Part One is "Worker's Guild to Secret Society." He stated that the history of Freemasonry "is the story of how a Roman Catholic trade guild for a few thousand building workers in Britain came to be taken over by the aristocracy, the gentry, and members of mainly nonproductive professions, and how it was turned into a non-Christian secret society." That characterization didn't deter us, for several reasons. First, all trade guilds in medieval Europe might well be styled "Roman Catholic," because Roman Catholic was the only thing to be (unless one cared to risk loss of property, physical torture, and a premature end in the midst of a pile of burning faggots). Second, craft guilds were strictly local in nature and there was never a medieval craft guild that operated over the length and breadth of Britain. Third, the fact that Freemasonry does not require that a member be a Christian, but only that he believe in God and the immortality of the soul, suggests that such a group could not have originated in a craft guild, particularly one whose principal customer would have had to be the major customer for stone structures, the church.

On the other hand, one must take pause at the matter-of-fact declaration of the *Encyclopaedia Britannica*: "Freemasonry evolved from the guilds of stonemasons and cathedral builders of the middle ages."

It would be necessary to examine the guild connection carefully, but early research indicated the high probability that the Masonic role as card-carrying members of a guild of stonemasons was a cover story, a not uncommon feature of secret societies. During World War II the Japanese operated a secret society, known as the Shindo Rommei, in the Amazon Basin. Its objective was the preparation for the exploitation of the natural resources of the area after the expected Japanese victory. Its cover operation was fishing; its secret vocabulary was made up of fishing terms. When the society was finally exposed and its members arrested, it turned out that its supreme commander was a Japanese colonel disguised as the female cook on a fishing vessel. In India, members of a secret society known as Thuggee (which gave us our word "thug") traveled the roads disguised as itinerant traders and used the terminology of trading with secret meaning.

They easily mixed with other traveling traders whom they marked as victims, murdering them with strangling cloths and dedicating the deaths to the bloody goddess Kali. In Elizabethan England, the prohibited Jesuits and their followers used trading language as a cover. If one Catholic told another that "two new *merchants* from Italy have landed at Plymouth and are seeking connections in Sussex," the word had been passed that two new Jesuit priests had arrived and were seeking a safe house in Sussex. It would not be at all unusual for a secret society whose central ritual involved the allegorical building of the Temple of Solomon to gradually assume the cover story of being actual builders. On the other hand, a concept accepted as history for over two centuries could not be lightly shrugged aside, requiring that more be learned about the medieval guilds of craftsmen, especially those based on stonemasonry.

A guild was not an association of workers, but rather an association of entrepreneurial owners. It operated under a charter, which granted the association a franchise, a monopoly on a craft or service for a specified area, usually a town. The guild benefited by gaining the rights to shut out all competition, to set prices at levels guaranteed to turn a profit, to adjust the level of production to the current demand, and to control the number of new practitioners permitted to enter that trade or service. The benefit to the lord granting the charter was an orderly means of collecting tolls and taxes on raw material coming in and on the sale of the finished product. It could also mean the absence of petty problems or unrest by guaranteeing a level of product quality. Without a bakers' guild setting and enforcing standards, for example, some bakers might short-weight loaves, underbake, or even throw a little sawdust in the recipe. Under the guild system, as it developed, the guild not only set the quality levels of finished products but also decreed the type and source of raw materials, the tools to be used, and even the methods of using them.

The guild motivation was profit, and the recognized way to maximize profit was through a monopoly that could adjust the supply to the demand. No guild member would want to adjust supply by producing less than his own capacity, so the accepted method of holding down supply became regulations regarding how many could enter the trade, and especially how many could become master craftsmen, which meant that they could own tools and turn out finished products for sale. The masters ran the guild, so were reluctant to permit new masters if there was not a ready market for their proposed output.

The master was the only full member of the trade or craft guild and was an owner-operator. His shop and home were generally combined, and he owned the tools. He purchased the required raw materials, supervised the work, and looked to the marketing of the product. He frequently obtained an extra source of both income and free labor by taking on one or more apprentices. These were usually boys, who would be young men by the time they finished their term of apprenticeship, usually seven years. The boys worked and learned under a legally binding contract that gave them a status akin to that of a bond servant. If they tried to run away they could be arrested, brought back, and punished. In the contract of apprenticeship, the master agreed to provide training in every facet of the craft to the level of skill at which the apprentice could be accredited by the guild by means of an examination, which often included the presentation of a finished product from the candidate, his "master-piece."

The master also acted somewhat in the role of a foster father. He agreed to provide the apprentice with room and board and to raise him in the path of godliness. He set forth the rules of conduct and was legally entitled to punish the delinquent apprentice, even by beating. For all of these services the master was entitled to a fee plus all of the work he could get from his trainee.

Unfortunately, the completion of the apprenticeship, and even glowing praise accompanying the approval of his master-piece, did not mean that the newly accepted craftsman could automatically set himself up as a master. Only the guild could give approval of that status, which might not come for years, if ever. In the meantime, he drifted in limbo between the apprenticeship behind him and the master status ahead, which he might never achieve. All he could do was to offer himself as an employee to a master, who usually paid him on a daily basis for the days he worked. On that basis he became known as a "journeyman" (from the Middle English and Norman French word *journée*: "a day"). A journeyman who was particularly good might husband his pennies for the purchase of tools and look for a situation just outside the guild franchise area, perhaps just a mile or two from town, and risk the anger of the guild fathers by competing with their monopoly. For that reason the guilds were constantly striving to extend their franchised territories (as we saw during the Peasants' Rebellion, when the rebels attacked Great Yarmouth with enthusiasm because the monopoly of the guilds there had been extended to seven miles around the town.).

As labor began to be divided into specialties, guilds found their profits influenced by other guilds, and conflicts arose. The saddlers needed to buy leather from the tanners and iron and brass findings from the metalworkers, then have the saddle decorated by the painters and stainers. The interrelationships were most complex in the woolen industry, which in the Middle Ages was Britain's most important export. Profitability was influenced by the prices charged by the spinners, the dyers, the weavers, and the fullers. And by far the greatest influences on profitability were the great merchant guilds, which controlled the sources of raw materials, the shipping, and the export markets for the end products. Theirs was the greatest certainty of profit and they became wealthy enough to earn the envy of the landed aristocracy. Some of the merchant guilds were able to get permission to set up trading offices and warehouses in other countries, and foreign guilds, made up mostly of Flemings and Lombards, got the same privileges in Britain. The rebels in London, in their fury against the merchants, had dragged foreign merchants from their church to butcher them in the road. At Berwick, England's Edward I revealed his attitude toward a charter granted by that Scottish town as he attacked the foreign merchants and burned their guildhall down around them.

Among other things, the great merchants used their wealth to change the course of municipal government. Forming associations that could legally be regarded as individuals (*corpus*: corporation), they leased entire towns from their lords and, in the case of London, from the crown itself. Giving up entry tolls, market fees, and other sources of income was palatable to the ruling lord in exchange for a dependable annual fee, which only the wealthier guilds could afford. This was clear in the Peasants' Rebellion, as the craftsmen of York, Beverly, and Scarborough revolted to force the great merchant families to share the town government with them.

Eventually the craft guilds did achieve a voice in their own towns, and to this very day the ancient guilds of London, now

called the Livery Companies (because of their common ceremonial costumes), elect the lord mayor of London from among themselves. Sir William Walworth, the mayor of London who struck
down Wat Tyler, was a member of the Honourable Company of
Fishmongers.

Within the frameworks of their charters, the guilds enjoyed a
high degree of self-government, and they, not the courts, usually
heard grievances against the products or services of the guild
members, holding the power to discipline those found breaking
the guild rules. This is not as unusual as it sounds, and one might
gain a somewhat better understanding of the guild system by
examining the practice of law in the United States. Attorneys
have charters that grant them a monopoly on the practice of law,
and those charters are issued by states as well as by agencies of the
federal government. After a period of training, the student is
given an examination to prove that he or she has achieved sufficient knowledge to be worthy of admission. Although that training is now received by means of law schools, there are still attorneys alive who did not attend law school but learned by
apprenticeship to other lawyers, a practice known as "reading to
the law." The attorneys' associations have a strong influence on
schools of law and even assist in the establishment of curricula.

Internally, the attorneys have standards of conduct and service
called Canons of Ethics. Censure and discipline can be levied
upon members who transgress those rules. Attorneys also maintain grievance committees to hear complaints against members
and these may rule on such matters as the fees charged for services. In all of these things, the monopolistic associations of attorneys are much like guilds. Also like guilds, membership can
bestow privileges. One of those privileges, granted centuries ago,
is still treasured in remembrance by attorneys throughout the
English-speaking world.

It may be recalled that during the Peasant's Rebellion the rebels attacked the rooms of lawyers in the Temple area of London
between Fleet Street and the Thames River. That property had
been taken from the Templars and given to the Hospitallers, who
in turn leased part of it for inns and rooms for lawyers who came
to London to appear before the king's court in the adjoining
Royal City of Westminster. The location was perfect because it
was adjacent to a gate to Westminster called the Barrière du Tem-

ple. The *barrière* (from which we get our word "barrier") was a
checkpoint for the paying of tolls to pass through. Lawyers going
back and forth several times daily could not be expected to pay a
toll every time, so were granted the valuable privilege of passing
through the Barrière du Temple, eventually anglicized to the
"Temple Bar," without paying the toll. The young man who
finally qualified to appear before the court earned the right to
"pass the bar." Those entitled to pass the *Barrière* became known
as "barristers," and to this day the remembrance of that privilege
is preserved as young people take bar examinations to pass the bar
and join the attorneys' "guilds," now called bar associations.

Medieval guilds were also a strong support to the established
religion. They made gifts to the Church of money and of valuable
religious objects. Many owned relics of saints and had patron
saints whose feast days they celebrated publicly. Most had spe-
cially designated churches in which they performed their own
special observances and devotions. The practice lives on, and
today the lovely little Wren church of St. James Garlickhythe
(*hythe* means "dock") is the official church of eight London Livery
Companies: the Vintners, the Dyers, the Painter-Stainers, the
Joiners and Ceilers, the Horners (lantern makers), the
Needlemakers, the Glass Sellers, and the Gold and Silver Wyre
Drawers.

In their religious activities the craft guilds provided an earthy
experience the people could appreciate because the guild members were of the common people, not the aristocracy. They staged
religious miracle plays, many of which required months for the
preparation of costumes and scenery, and the dialogue was not in
Latin, but in the vernacular of the common people. They helped
in the transition into Christianity of the very ancient celebrations
occasioned by weather and the phases of agriculture, which could
not be totally stamped out by the Church and so were finally
taken over as Christian festivals. The winter solstice festival, celebrating the victory of the sun over the powers of darkness (as the
days grew longer), was celebrated as Christmas; the vernal equi-
nox was covered by Easter; the summer solstice became the feast
of Corpus Christi; and the fall harvest festivals were celebrated as
All Saints' Day. As far back as the seventh century the church had
begun to bend, trying to pry the people loose from their old natural religion. The Venerable Bede told his missionary priests not

to deny the British goddess known variously as the "Earth Mother," "Corn Woman," or simply "The Lady," but to tell people that *The* Lady was the same as *Our* Lady, and that the priests had come to clarify Her heavenly role. No longer is anyone concerned that certain pagan symbols have proven to be unrootable, and very few people today mind the use of the heathen term *Yule*, or the use of those symbols of the strong spirits that kept life going through the death of almost everything else in winter, as we tack up holly and mistletoe and decorate Christmas trees. Nor is anyone offended at the continuing popularity of the fertility symbols of the rabbit and the egg at Easter. (There did come a time in England, however, when the maypole was condemned and banned as a beribboned phallic symbol, which it was).

What the guilds did was to stage miracle plays, some lasting for days, that took the Christian teaching to the people in language they could understand and gave them a visual presentation of the Bible, which they were forbidden to read. Touches of the old pre-Christian religious customs were occasionally and inadvertently blended into scriptural accounts, doing much more to weld the audiences to the church than any of the Latin services they could not comprehend and with which they could not empathize. The guilds were very proud of their miracle play productions and strove to outdo one another, becoming a very important part of the medieval Christian experience. These, then, were the people who are supposed to have been the predecessors of religiously tolerant Freemasonry, in a guild devoted to the craft of the stonemason.

The first major problem with the concept of a Masonic predecessor guild of stonemasons is the franchise territory. Craft guilds were almost always local, but Freemasonry was found in cells all over Britain. Even if one could contemplate some loose association of guilds in England, it would be difficult to maintain that the same organization existed in Scotland. A guild, after all, required a charter. We have seen how things stood between England and Scotland in the Middle Ages, and it is highly unlikely that a group chartered by one would be welcome to the other: Quite the opposite would have been true. There is simply no way that any one guild could have been acceptable to the governments of England, Scotland, Ireland, and Wales. As to their charters, in such broad territories those charters would have had to come from the central governments, and there is no record, nor even a hint, of such a thing ever happening. There are, however, numerous records citing the master builders of notable structures, and quite often these were members of the religious orders for whom the buildings were being built, monks who certainly were not members of any guild.

Masons and non-Masons alike have explained the need for secret grips and signals by stating that medieval stonemasons were itinerant workers, traveling from castle job to cathedral site as work was available. Because they had no permanent base like other guilds, they would need secret signs by which to identify each other to maintain their "closed shop" monopoly status. With no fixed home, they would meet in lodges to discuss their affairs. That theory would have us believe that constructing an abbey, a castle, or a cathedral was not unlike throwing up prefabricated tract housing with temporary workers. To build a castle, in fact, might take five to twenty years, and the great Gothic cathedrals were under construction for generations, with some taking as much as a century to complete. On such jobs, a man was not likely to live in temporary quarters with the wife and children off somewhere at home. The theory would also require that the structure was being built outside the jurisdiction of the authority of the guild charter, which would require permission for legal travel. Evidence of membership in that guild would not have to have been kept a secret, nor would the evidence of such membership have been limited to verbal communication. To the contrary, proof of membership in a legally chartered association and proof of a job waiting would have to have been produced on demand, especially in the Middle Ages in England, when for much of the period a pass was required for a man to travel outside his own town or hundred. To get such a pass, the reason for the travel had to be stated and believed.

As for guild meetings in "lodges," there certainly were barracks built for the hordes of workmen who were frequently drafted at those times when they were not desperately needed for plowing, planting, and harvesting. They worked in the quarries, transported stone, and provided an army of muscle for the stonemasons. They were very temporary, and were provided with a place to sleep and food to eat. Certainly the master builders did not eat and sleep in the labor barracks, which just as certainly were not "lodges."

Freemasons have a few ancient documents they call the "Old Charges of Masonry," the oldest of which appears to date from the fourteenth century. They set forth rules of conduct and responsibility that have been assumed to relate to the conduct of the medieval stonemasons' guild. One of these charges is that no member is to reveal any secret of any brother that might cost him his life and property. The only such secret, one that would cost a man his life and property, would have been that he was guilty of treason or heresy, or, as is often the case when there is a state religion, both. Another charge is that no visiting brother is to go into the town without a local brother to "witness" for him. If a stonemason had legitimate employment with the local lord or bishop, he would have had no need for anyone to witness for him (evidence knowledge of him). On the other hand, if he had no proof of employment, had no travel pass and no means to explain his business in the town, he could and would have been apprehended and thrown into jail straightaway and held there until the matter was settled. A known local witness could provide a believable cover story and verification of a real or assumed identity. Most important, the resident brother could steer the visitor away from the very people and places that might cause the questions to come up.

Still another Old Charge was that the visiting brother be given "employment" for two weeks, then given some money and put on the road to the next lodge. We should not be asked to believe that medieval guilds of master craftsmen made a practice of hiring men they didn't need and bestowing money on itinerant stonemasons passing through. That kind of treatment is much more likely to be extended to a man on the run, who would be given lodging for up to two weeks, not "employment." Another interesting Old Charge is that no Mason should engage in sexual congress with the wife, daughter, mother, or sister of a brother Mason. This charge has been used by anti-Masons to show that Masons had selective morality, because their moral code was limited to their own members, allowing the brothers to have sexual relations with the wife, daughter, mother, or sister of any non-Mason. The mistake of such critics lies in seeing that charge as part of any code of morality, which it is not. This brotherhood was a secret organization that somehow included men being, or aiding and abetting, heretics and traitors. It was vital that they stick together.

A man coming home to find a brother having at it with his wife or daughter might forget his sacred oath of brotherhood on the spot, so that the prohibition of such activity was not morality; it was wisdom.

A very major difference between medieval guilds and Freemasonry was the one cited by Stephen Knight. The guilds were very religious, and any guild counting on the Roman Catholic church as its major customer would have been especially and overtly devout. Freemasonry, however, admits any believer in a monotheistic God. The ritual makes no mention of Jesus Christ, or of His Mother, while many guilds were in the forefront of the growing special veneration of Mary. How could such a transition have taken place? It didn't.

Taken all together, what had been learned about Freemasonry indicated that it was essentially a mutual protection society of men at odds with church or state, or both, and not a building society. That opinion was so far from the view held by almost everyone else that the point seemed best put to rest by going to the source, to the original charters of the medieval stonemasons' guilds, to check their territorial limitations and the monopolistic aspects of their franchises.

London was the first stop, but most of the records we might like to have seen were destroyed in the Great Fire of 1666. There is a Company of Masons among the Livery Companies of London, but it was formed much too late to have had a role in Masonic origins. It ranks twenty-ninth in precedence among the Livery Companies, many of which have permanent Masonic lodge rooms in their own guildhalls. If the London masons' company had had a role in Secret Masonry, it would now be treated with reverential awe, but there is no indication that it receives any special treatment from Freemasons.

It was decided to turn to Oxford, that most monumental of British cities, which holds in addition to its ruined castle and lofty churches a collection of colleges, all of stone, each with its own chapel and halls. Building went on there for generation after generation, and if only one city in Britain could have supported a permanent local guild of stonemasons, Oxford was surely it. Weeks before my arrival I arranged for a seat in the search room of the Archives of Oxfordshire County, where documents go back to the twelfth century. I had told the staff in advance that I would want to look at charters or any other documentation relating to any guild of stonemasons. Upon my arrival, the staff seemed embarrassed to tell me that they had searched their files and could find not even a reference to a guild of masons in Oxfordshire. In an extra effort, they contacted the clerk to the Town Council at nearby Burford, where some of the beautiful Cotswold stone is still quarried. That gentleman also tried, but could find no reference to any guild of stonemasons. He suggested that if I was eager to find a medieval guild of masons, I should go to France.

The next try was at Lincoln, a city known for its medieval stone buildings, including its magnificent cathedral, its massive castle, and the best collection of medieval houses and guildhalls in England. The library staff there were helpful but could provide no evidence of a medieval guild of stonemasons in Lincoln. The same spirit of helpfulness and the same negative result was encountered at the Lincolnshire County Museum.

A final check at Oxford's Bodleian, one of the great libraries of the world, and I finally felt absolutely secure in stating that Freemasonry did not evolve from the medieval guilds of stonemasons in Britain because it would appear that there were no medieval guilds of stonemasons in Britain. Freemasons, anti-Masons, and interested historians will apparently have to live with the simple fact that constant repetition does not create truth.

If I felt lonely in that discovery, the feeling didn't last long. Before leaving England, browsing the bookshops on Charing Cross Road, I discovered that a serious book on Masonry had been published in 1986. It was *The Craft*, written by John Hamill, the librarian and curator of the United Grand Lodge Library and Museum in London. Mr. Hamill opens the first chapter of his book with these words: "When, Why and Where did Freemasonry originate? There is one answer to these questions: We do not know, despite all the paper and ink that has been expended in examining them." Toward the end of that chapter he states: "Whether we shall ever discover the true origins of Freemasonry is open to question." Although it is possible that Mr. Hamill may not agree in any way with the conclusions finally reached in this book, at least his reasonable open-mindedness and impeccable credentials established a common ground of wiping out all prior notions as unproven. It had become possible to begin at ground zero to examine the rites and rituals of Freemasonry, unencumbered by advocacy or preconceptions.

To get to the heart of Secret Masonry required a look at the initiation ceremonies and lectures for the three basic degrees of Craft Masonry: the Entered Apprentice, the Fellow Craft, and the Master Mason.

What would be being sought was any clue to the great Masonic mysteries:

1. When did Freemasonry come into existence? Did it evolve, or was it triggered by an event or set of circumstances?

2. What was the purpose of Freemasonry that kept it alive underground for centuries and that kept it constantly supplied with new recruits?

3. Why was that purpose totally lost by 1717?

4. What are the meanings of the Mason's symbols—the compass and square, the apron and gloves, the letter G, the circle on the floor, the black and white mosaic?

5. How did Masonry come to attract and ultimately be led by the upper reaches of the aristocracy and the royal family?

6. How and why did Freemasonry adopt a policy of total religious tolerance in an atmosphere in which Roman Catholicism was the only legal creed, thereby risking torture and death?

7. What was Freemasonry doing for all those years that required such incredible secrecy and such bloody penalties for revealing its secrets?

8. Was there any direct connection between Freemasonry and the suppressed order of the Knights of the Temple?

It took some digging, but the answers were all there.

CHAPTER 14

"TO HAVE MY THROAT CUT ACROSS"

The Old Charges of Masonry set forth several regulations relating to the qualifications for membership. The major qualification is the assertion of belief in a monotheistic Supreme Being, for no "stupid atheist" can become a Mason. The candidate must be a "free man born of a free mother," an interesting bit of phraseology since under ancient British law the conditions of serfdom and villeinage were inherited through the mother, which would peg the origins of Freemasonry to a time when those conditions were extant. Age was also a factor, as the Old Charges forbid the induction of a man in "his nonage or dotage," eliminating the unreliably immature and the man laboring under the impending threat of onrushing senility. The actual age requirement has varied from time to time and from one Grand Lodge to another. At one time in Britain the minimum age was twenty-five, although twenty-one is now the most common admission age throughout Freemasonry. A lower age requirement has often been available to the son of a Freemason, a special candidate known to Freemasons by the unexplained title of Lewis. (General Douglas MacArthur became a Mason by a special short form of initiation which constituted being made a "Mason-at-sight," largely based on the fact that he was a Lewis.)

The mentally deficient are prohibited Masonic membership by the Old Charges, which is understandable. Not so clear is the reason for the prohibition of membership to any man who is not in full possession of all of his limbs. This had long been a requirement of military organizations and was a common clause in the rules of the religious orders, but it seems out of place in a fraternal organization. In practice, of course, Freemasonry no longer clings to that ancient rule. It does, however, claim to cling to the rule that a candidate must be of good character and good repute in his community.

Masons proudly announce today that no one is ever invited to become a Freemason, but must ask for admission by means of a written petition to a lodge. Such a procedure would have been impossible in Secret Masonry, since a man could hardly have been expected to work up a heated desire to be a member of an organization of whose existence he was totally unaware. In Secret times he would have been watched, evaluated, discussed, perhaps surreptitiously interviewed, and then very carefully made aware of the existence of the secret fraternity a bit at a time, until it was deemed absolutely safe to invite him in. A residual of the practice of admission by invitation only is still adhered to by a few Grand Lodges, such as those of Australia.

The candidate's petition for membership must set forth that he has come to respect and admire the Masonic order and that he seeks membership for reasons other than personal material benefits. His petition is reviewed, as are his character and reputation, and a vote taken in the lodge. Although practices vary, traditionally one negative vote (one black bean or black ball) is enough to reject his petition.

Finally the day comes when the candidate is scheduled to be initiated as an Entered Apprentice Mason. Today, that initiation generally takes place in a permanent "lodge room" equipped with an altar and candlesticks and chairs for the various lodge officers. The Masonic symbols appropriate to the degree are prepainted on panels of oilcloth. All of these are later additions, for convenience and to enhance the feeling of the solemnity of the ceremony, since they would have been impossible in the hidden meetings of Secret Masonry. In those meetings, which Masonic legend tells us were held "on high hills and in deep valleys," no so-called "lodge furniture" would have been available, or even wise. In consideration of British weather, we must assume that even in Secret times some of those meetings were held indoors, if only in a barn or shed, especially in major cities such as London where high hills and deep valleys were in rather short supply.

The lodge symbol that would always have been available to those Secret meetings was the circle on the floor, the center of Masonic lodge room symbolism. This circle could easily have been scribed in the earth of a clearing or in the dirt floor of a barn. In the very earliest days of Public Masonry, when almost all lodge meetings took place in the private rooms of taverns, the symbols were marked on the floor with chalk. The custom developed that the newly admitted brother, regardless of rank or lineage, was presented with a mop and bucket at the end of the meeting, which he used to erase the Masonic symbols from the floor. Although in this "tavern" period lodge meetings were held on an upper floor as a deterrent to snooping, Masons refer to the Entered Apprentice lodge as the "ground floor of Solomon's temple."

Another important feature of today's initiation which may have been absent in ancient ritual is the Bible or other holy book on the altar, used always in combination with the symbolic compass and square in the administration of the controversial oaths. It is hardly likely that a Bible was readily available to every little group throughout Britain in the fourteenth and fifteenth centuries, so the oath may well have been administered with a symbol only.

The Entered Apprentice candidate is subject to a final interrogation before being prepared for his initiation. He is asked to confirm that he has been prompted to seek admission by a favorable opinion of Masonry already formed, that he has no personal mercenary motives, that he has a desire for knowledge and self-improvement and a sincere wish to be of service to his fellow man.

Passing satisfactorily through the interrogations, he is asked to strip half-naked. Originally this meant stripping to just trousers and shirt, then rolling the left trouser leg above the knee and unbuttoning the shirt to permit slipping it off the left arm, leaving shoulder and breast bare. The left shoe and stocking were also removed. Today, all this is usually made easier by the provision of a costume and a slipper for the right foot. All metal objects of any nature are taken from the candidate.

When stripped, he is blindfolded (Masons say "hoodwinked") and a rope is looped around his neck and left trailing on the floor. The rope, used in a slightly different manner in each of the three initiation ceremonies of basic three-degree Craft Masonry, is called a "cable-tow."

In preparation for the initiation ceremony, the lodge has been convened as a Lodge of Entered Apprentice Masons. Outside the door stands the officer known as Tyler, a combined sentry and sergeant-at-arms, who is charged with the security of the meeting, including the screening of visiting Masons. His title, the meaning of which was lost long ago, had been used to create the Masonic verb *to tyle*, as we see when the Worshipful Master of the lodge asks the Junior Deacon the first care of a Mason. The answer comes back, "To see the Lodge tyled, Worshipful," to which the Master responds, "Attend to that part of your duty, and inform the Tyler that we are about to open a Lodge of Entered Apprentice Masons, and direct him to tyle accordingly." After following these instructions, the Junior Deacon reports back, "The lodge [or door] is tyled."

"By Whom?"

"By a Master Mason outside the door, armed with the proper implement of his office [a sword]."

"His duty there?"

"To keep off all cowans and eavesdroppers, and to see that none pass or repass without permission from the Chair [or Worshipful Master]."

There follows a routine of identifying each officer, his place in the lodge, and his duties. The Master then gives the signs of the Entered Apprentice degree which will be revealed to the candidate in the initiation ceremony, which signs are repeated by all of the Masons present as an indication that all in attendance are qualified to be there, and the lodge is opened.

An officer of the lodge (the Junior Deacon) takes the blindfolded candidate by the arm to lead him into the lodge room for the ceremony. There will be no need to set forth that ceremony in detail because the primary interest is in identifying only those most significant items that may provide clues as to Masonic origins. Also, Masonic ceremonies tend to be inordinately repetitious, which can be very tedious to the reader, but which was probably absolutely necessary to preserve ritual that could never be written down but had to be committed to memory. The repetition served an important purpose for Masons but will do little for us. In addition, because of the purely verbal tradition, there is variance in the exact wording from one lodge or jurisdiction to another. What is remarkable is that in the absence of official written manuals the worldwide performance of the ritual is so much the same.

As the Junior Deacon escorts the blindfolded candidate into the lodge room, the Senior Deacon is waiting with a compass in his hand. As the candidate is stopped in front of him, the Senior Deacon presses one of the compass points to his chest and says, "Mr.———, upon your entering this lodge for the first time I receive you on the point of a sharp instrument pressing your naked left breast, which is to teach you that as it is a torture to your flesh, so should the recollection of it ever be to your mind and conscience, should you attempt to reveal the secrets of Masonry unlawfully."

The Senior Deacon now takes charge of the candidate and begins to lead him once around the room. Just as they begin, the Master stops them with a rap of his gavel, admonishing them that such an important journey should not be undertaken without invoking the blessings of God. All bow their heads for a short prayer that dedicates the candidate to the service of God and the brotherhood, after which the Master puts the question to the initiate, "In whom do you put your trust?," to which the only acceptable answer is, "In God."

As the Senior Deacon and the candidate proceed around the room, they pause at the station of the Junior Warden, who asks, "Who comes here?"

"Mr.———, who has long been in darkness and now seeks to be brought to Light and to receive the rights and benefits of this Worshipful Lodge, erected to God and dedicated to the holy Sts. John, as all brothers have done before."

After questions relating to his qualifications and intentions, the blindfolded candidate is led on to the station of the Senior Deacon, where essentially the same questions and answers are exchanged. Led on to the station of the Worshipful Master, the same exchange takes place, except that the Master demands,

"From whence come you, and whither are you traveling?" This time the Senior Deacon answers for the initiate, "From the west, and traveling toward the east."

"Why leave you the west and travel toward the east?"

"In search of Light."

The Master then orders the candidate to be taken to the Senior Warden in the west to be instructed as to the proper manner in which to approach the east. The Senior Warden conducts the candidate eastward to the altar, positioning the heel of his right foot in the hollow of his left foot, forming a right angle.

The Master leaves his station in the east and approaches the altar to inform the candidate that before he can proceed any further he must take upon himself a "solemn oath and obligation," which the Master assures him will not interfere with any duty that is owed to God, country, family, or friends. After expressing his willingness to take the oath, the candidate, still blindfolded, is guided into the proper position for an Entered Apprentice. He kneels on his bare left knee, with his right leg ahead of him in the angle of a square. In front of him on the altar is the holy book of his faith, open, with the compass and square on the open book. In the Entered Apprentice ceremony, the square is on top of the points of the compass.

The candidate places his left hand under the book, palm up, while his right hand is on top of the compass and square, palm downward. In this position, he takes the first of the oaths that have brought so much criticism down on the Masonic institution.

"I,———, of my own free will and accord, in the presence of Almighty God, and this Worshipful Lodge erected to Him and dedicated to the holy Saints John, do hereby and hereon most sincerely promise and swear that I will always *hail*, ever conceal and never reveal, any of the arts, parts, or points of the hidden mysteries of ancient Free Masonry which may have been, or hereafter shall be, at this time, or any future period, communicated to me as such, to any person or persons whomever, except it be to a true and lawful brother Mason, or in a regularly constituted lodge of Masons; nor unto him or them until by strict trial, due examination, or lawful information I shall have found him, or them, as lawfully entitled to the same as I am myself. I furthermore promise and swear that I will not print, paint, stamp, stain, cut, carve, mark, or engrave them, to cause the same to be done on anything movable or immovable, capable of receiving the least impression of a word, syllable, letter, or character, whereby the same may become legible or intelligible to any person under the canopy of heaven, and the secrets of Masonry thereby unlawfully obtained through my unworthiness.

"All this I most solemnly, sincerely promise and swear, with a firm and steadfast resolution to perform the same, without any mental reservation or secret evasion of mind whatever, binding myself under no less penalty than that of having my throat cut across, my tongue torn out by its roots, and my body buried in the rough sands of the sea, at low-water mark, where the tide ebbs and flows twice in twenty-four hours, should I ever knowingly violate this my Entered Apprentice obligation. So help me God, and keep me steadfast in the due performance of the same."

Upon the completion of the oath, the candidate is instructed to kiss the holy book, as a token of his sincerity. He is then asked what it is that he desires most, to which the proper answer is, "Light." At this response, the blindfold is removed and the secrets of the Entered Apprentice are revealed to him. Among these are the handgrip and two hand signs. One is the penal sign, which recalls the penalty "to have my throat cut across," as the hand, thumb inward, is drawn quickly across the throat, then dropped to the side. The other sign repeats the position in which the hands were placed under and on the holy book when taking the oath: left palm up, right palm down, hands about two inches apart. It is the more interesting sign of the two because it has a name with a lost meaning. The sign is called a "due-guard." Several attempts have been made to explain the term, but they come off as clumsy contrivances, as in the thought that "with this sign you *do guard* yourself as an Entered Apprentice Mason."

Then occurs an especially intriguing part of the ceremony, the presentation of the Masonic "apron." This is now frequently of white cloth, or felt, but old usage would require that the apron be of white lambskin. Tradition indicates that originally it was not cut and trimmed as a garment but was simply a whole lambskin tied about the waist. Today Masonic aprons are of cloth, lined, trimmed in color, and decorated with a variety of Masonic badges and symbols, but as a clue to the past, all that matters is that original lambskin.

The newly made Mason is told that this white apron is an emblem of innocence "more ancient than the Golden Fleece or the Roman Eagle," more honorable a badge than any that could ever be bestowed by any prince or potentate. He is told how to wear the apron so that it will conform to the way that the same apron was worn by Entered Apprentices at the building of Solomon's temple.

The new Mason is now asked by the Master to contribute to the lodge some item, any item, made of metal, if only a pin or a button. Since all metallic items were taken from him prior to his initiation, he is confused and frustrated by the repeated demand. Finally the Master ends the confusion by pointing out that at this moment the new Mason is destitute, with not a penny in his pocket. He is told that this part of the ceremony has been staged as a reminder to him that if he ever finds a friend, and especially a brother Mason, in a like condition, he is to contribute as liberally as he can according to the need, but only to the extent that his generosity will not bring any material injury to himself or to his family. This is his first lesson in Masonic charity.

In the final portion of the initiation, presentation is made of the "working tools of an Entered Apprentice." First, the twenty-four-inch gauge (ruler), to be used symbolically to divide the Mason's day into periods of work, of refreshment and sleep, and of service to God and distressed brothers. Next, the common gavel or maul used to dress stones, but to be used symbolically now to chip away vices and superfluities so that the Mason may shape himself into a stone suitable for the temple of God. However, the use of a working mason's tools to teach lessons of morality was definitely no part of Secret Masonry, so cannot contribute to the search for beginnings.

More important for clues to origins are the Masonic terms revealed in this degree, which remain mysteries to this day. The *Tyler* is the officer who guards the lodge against *cowans* and eavesdroppers. The Entered Apprentice identifies his status by giving the *due-guard* of that degree. He is led through the ceremony by means of a *cable-tow*. If his father was a Mason he is a *Lewis*.

The symbols to be considered carefully were the circle and the black and white mosaic pavement on the floor, plus the compass and square on the Bible. Other parts of the ceremony to be addressed were the half-naked state of the candidate, the removal from the initiate of all objects made of metal, the concept of the Mason as a man traveling from west to east, and the white lamb-skin apron.

The next sources of Masonic mysteries would be the initiation rites of the second degree, that of Fellow Craft.

CHAPTER 15

"MY BREAST TORN OPEN, MY HEART PLUCKED OUT"

The term *Fellow Craft* is so awkward a title for a level of membership that it almost certainly began in some more conventional form, only to be bent out of shape to force it into some new mold. One meaning of that strange term might be "another craft," which would make no sense as the title of a degree of membership, so it can be assumed that at some point the term had been "Fellow *of* the Craft," which may be revealing. "Fellow" means a peer, an equal, as in a fellow of the Royal Society. Used in the Masonic "guild" concept, it appears to be an attempt to position a level between Apprentice and Master, designating the Fellow Craft as the equivalent of the journeyman. However, we have already seen that the journeyman was not a "fellow" of the guild—only Masters enjoyed that status. This gives support to the point made by early Masonic writers that in Secret Masonry there were only two degrees, the Entered Apprentice (the Scots say *Intrant*) and the Fellow. The title of Master was not representative of a degree but rather indicated the master of a lodge. The original Master

Mason, then, was a master of men, not the master of a craft. The Fellow Craft was in every way the full member.

This point is supported by the diary of Elias Ashmole, the English antiquary whose collections provided the base for the Ashmolean Museum at Oxford. A diary entry indicates that he became a Freemason on October 16, 1646, about seventy years before Freemasonry revealed itself in 1717. To the point, a much later entry on March 11, 1682, records his attendance at a lodge meeting in London. He says, "I was the Senior Fellow among them (it being thirty-five years since I was admitted)." It seems safe to assume that someone of Ashmole's stature would not have spent thirty-five years in the second degree if the third degree had existed in his day.

As to the Fellow Craft initiation ceremony, it is primarily a series of variations on the Entered Apprentice degree, with none of the dramatic change that characterizes the Master's ritual, although the lecture following is most revealing. This time the right breast, leg, and foot are bare, rather than the left. The cable-tow rope is looped twice around the initiate's neck instead of once (in some jurisdictions the rope is looped around the shoulder). Again, the candidate is "hoodwinked," or blindfolded. That term may be another indication of age, and originally may have meant (remembering the livery worn by the rebels at Beverly, Scarborough, and York) that a hood was pulled down over his face, as the hawk is "hoodwinked" in falconry. This meaning certainly was in use before the term came to indicate trickery and deception. Some have suggested that the blindfold is used in the ceremony to add drama and instill an exciting note of fear. The real reason is much simpler than that: In secret societies, especially illicit secret societies, the blindfold is a necessary precaution, used to make certain that the candidate does not see the face of any other member until after he has passed through the initiation, assumed the obligations of his oath, and been admitted.

After being guided through the ceremony, passing around the lodge room from station to station, the candidate once again finds himself before the altar, still blindfolded, where he takes the oath of the second degree. He is guided into a position that has him kneeling on his bare right knee. His right hand is on the compass and square on the Bible, while his left hand is raised with his upper arm horizontal and his forearm vertical, thus forming a square. Once again, the Master of the lodge assures him that the oath will not interfere with his duty to God or country. The candidate then repeats after the Master:

"I,——, of my own free will and accord, in the presence of Almighty God and this Worshipful Lodge of Fellow Craft Masons, erected to God and dedicated to the holy Saints John, do hereby and hereon most solemnly promise and swear, in addition to my former obligation, that I will not give the secrets of the degree of a Fellow Craft Mason to anyone of an inferior degree, nor to any other being in the known world, except it be to a true and lawful brother, or brethren Fellow Craft Masons, or within the body of a just and lawfully constituted lodge of such; and not unto him nor unto them whom I only hear so to be, but only unto him or unto them whom I shall find so to be, after strict trial and due examination, or lawful information. Furthermore, I do promise and swear that I will not knowingly harm this lodge, nor a brother of this degree myself, nor suffer it to be done by others, if in my power to prevent it.

"Furthermore do I promise and swear that I will obey all regular signs and summonses given, handed, sent, or thrown to me by the hand of a brother Fellow Craft Mason, or from the body of a just and lawfully constituted lodge of such; provided it be within the length of my cable-tow, or a square and angle of my work. Furthermore do I promise and swear that I will aid and assist all poor and penniless brethren Fellow Crafts, their widows and orphans, wheresoever disposed around the globe, they applying to me as such, as far as in my power without injuring myself and family. To all of which I most solemnly and sincerely promise and swear without the least hesitation, mental reservation, or self-evasion of mind in me whatever, binding myself under no less penalty than to have my left breast torn open and my heart and vitals taken from thence and thrown over my left shoulder and carried into the valley of Jehosaphat, there to become a prey to the wild beasts of the field and the wild vultures of the air, if ever I should prove willfully guilty of violating any part of this my solemn oath or obligation of a Fellow Craft Mason, so help me God, and keep me steadfast in the performance of the same."

(In reciting the penalty of the oath, a variation says, ". . . no less penalty then having my breast torn open, my heart plucked out and placed on the highest pinnacle of the temple." Quite apart from the fact that there is no indication that the Temple of Solomon had any pinnacles, the version using these words, with vital organs thrown over the left shoulder, has been cited by one anti-Mason as evidence that the brutal mutilations inflicted on several women in London by the murderer known as Jack the Ripper were not mindless butchery, but mutilation administered in conformity with this penalty of the oath of the Fellow Craft Mason.)

After taking the oath, the blindfold is removed and the new Fellow Craft is taught the handgrip and password of this degree. He is also taught the penal sign, which calls to mind the penalty of having the heart plucked from his breast; he is shown how to move his flat right hand across his left breast, then let it drop to his side. As with the first degree, the due-guard of the Fellow Craft repeats the positions that his hands were in as he took the oath: the right hand in front of him waist high, palm down (as he held his hand on the Bible and compass and square), and his left arm raised, forming a square.

In the second part of his initiation, the newly made Fellow Craft Mason is directed to a symbolic (or real, if the lodge is sufficiently affluent) spiral staircase leading to the Middle Chamber of the Temple of Solomon, reached by passing between two columns. These columns, he is told, represent Jachin and Boaz, the great bronze columns that flanked the outer porch of the Temple of Solomon. On top of each is a globe, one representing a map of the world and the other a map of the heavens (although neither would have been available at Solomon's court). Contemplation of these two globes is meant to motivate all Masons to study astronomy, geography, and navigation. The initiate is told that the original columns were hollow and used to protect the secret documents of Masonry from flood and fire.

The initiate next learns that Freemasonry incorporates both Operative (working) and Speculative (allegorical) Masonry and is told that Freemasons built the biblical Temple of Solomon, in addition to many other notable stone structures.

The first three steps to the Middle Chamber represent youth, manhood, and old age, equated to the initiation as Entered Apprentice in his youth, maturation into knowledge and good works as a Fellow Craft, and living out his days as a Master Mason in confidence of immortal life, as he reflects on his honorable life as a Freemason. The three steps are also said to stand for wisdom, strength, and beauty.

The next five steps have two symbolic meanings. First, they represent the five orders of architecture: Tuscan, Doric, Ionic, Corinthian, and Composite. Second, they are said to represent the five senses: hearing, seeing, feeling, smelling, and tasting.

The next seven steps are linked symbolically with a whole catalog of sevens, including the seven years of famine, the seven years of construction of the temple, the seven wonders of the world, and the seven planets, but most significantly they are said to symbolize the seven liberal arts and sciences, which are grammar, rhetoric, logic, arithmetic, music, astronomy, and, most emphatically, geometry. The initiate is encouraged in the lecture of this degree to dedicate himself to the study of the liberal arts, to the extent that this degree takes on more of the flavor of a university fraternity than a mutually protective secret society.

The Worshipful Master calls the new Fellow Craft's attention to the large golden letter G usually suspended from the ceiling or mounted on the wall above the Master's chair. This is the G found in the current compass-and-square badge of Freemasonry, and it stands for Geometry. It is explained that the Fellow Craft degree is founded on the science of geometry, which is the central theme of the entire Masonic order. It is with this science that man comprehends the universe, the movements of the planets, and the cycle of the seasons. Especially is geometry of use to man in the Masonic science of architecture, and it is the basis for a Masonic designation of the Supreme Being as the Great Architect of the Universe. The initiate is told that geometry is so important to Masonry that the two terms were once synonymous.

In our search for origins, however, it should be borne in mind that the entire aura of learning, and the emphasis on geometry, are not part of the basic ritual. They are presented and extolled in the lecture following, an almost certain sign that they were added at a much later date. More of the clues being sought would be found in the initiation ceremony of the Master Mason, the most mystic ritual in all of Masonry, centered on the legend of the beating and murder of the master builder of the Temple of Solomon.

CHAPTER 16

THE MASTER
MASON

The rites of initiation for the Master Mason are much more complex and dramatic than those for the Entered Apprentice and the Fellow Craft, and they reveal the most enduring and most important mystery of all Masonic ritual: the legend of the murdered Master. Prepared in a manner similar to the first two degrees, the candidate is half-dressed, with both arms out of his shirtsleeves, leaving his chest bare; all metal is taken from him; a rope (the cable-tow) is looped about his body; and a blindfold, or hoodwink, is in place.

After brief ceremonies similar to those of the first two degrees, the candidate is ready for the administration of the oath of the Master Mason, which the Master of the lodge once again assures him will not interfere with any duty which he owes to his God, his country, or his family. The candidate is on his bare knees in front of the altar, with both palms down on the Holy Bible, on top of which the compass and square have been placed, with both legs of the compass above the square. The oath may vary considerably in precise wording from place to place because of its history of maintenance by verbal communication only, but everywhere the essential points are the same:

"I, ———, of my own free will and accord, in the presence of Almighty God, and this worshipful lodge of Master Masons, dedicated to God and the holy Saints John, do hereby and hereon most solemnly and sincerely promise and swear, in addition to my former obligations, that I will not reveal the secrets of the Master Mason's degree to anyone of inferior degree, nor to any other being in the known world, except it be to a true and lawful brother or brethren Master Masons, within a body of a just and lawfully constituted lodge of such, and not unto him or them whom I shall only hear so to be, but unto him and them only whom I shall prove so to be, after strict trial and due examination, or lawful information received.

"Furthermore do I promise and swear that I will not give the Master's word which I shall hereafter receive, neither in the lodge nor out of it, except it be on the five points of fellowship, and then not above my breath. Furthermore do I promise and swear that I will not give the Grand Hailing Sign of Distress except I am in real distress, or for the benefit of the Craft when at work, and should I ever see that sign given or the word accompanying it, and the person who gave it appearing to be in distress, I will fly to his relief at the risk of my life, should there be a greater probability of saving his life than losing my own.

"Furthermore do I promise and swear that I will not be at the initiating, passing, or raising of a candidate in a clandestine lodge, I knowing it to be such. Furthermore do I promise and swear that I will not be at the initiating of an old man in his dotage, a young man in his nonage, an atheist, an irreligious libertine, an idiot, madman, or woman. Furthermore do I promise and swear that I will not speak evil of a brother Master Mason, neither behind his back nor before his face, but will apprise him of all approaching danger, if in my power. Furthermore do I promise and swear that I will not have illegal carnal intercourse with a Master Mason's wife, mother, sister, or daughter, I knowing them to be such, nor suffer it to be done by others, if in my power to prevent it.

"Furthermore do I promise and swear that a Master Mason's secrets, given to me as such, and I knowing them to be such, shall remain as secure and inviolable in my breast as in his own, when communicated to me, murder and treason excepted, and then they left to my own election.

"Furthermore do I promise and swear that I will go on a Master Mason's errand whenever required, even should I have to go barefoot and bare-headed, if within the length of my cable-tow.

"Furthermore do I promise and swear that I will always remember a brother Master Mason when on my knees offering up my devotions to Almighty God.

"Furthermore do I promise and swear that I will aid and assist all poor, indigent Master Masons, their wives and orphans, wheresoever disposed around the globe, as far as is in my power, without materially injuring myself or my family.

"Furthermore do I promise and swear that if any part of my solemn oath of obligation be omitted at this time, I will hold myself amenable thereto whenever informed. To all of which I do most sincerely promise and swear, with a fixed and steady purpose of mind in me to keep and perform the same, binding myself under no less penalty than to have my body severed in twain and divided to the north and south, my bowels burnt to ashes in the center, and the ashes scattered before the four winds of heaven, that there might not the least track or trace of remembrance remain among men, or Masons, of so vile and perjured a wretch as I should be, were I ever to prove willfully guilty of violating any part of this my solemn oath and obligation of a Master Mason. So help me God, and keep me steadfast in the due performance of the same."

After brief ceremonies, the blindfold is removed, and the newly sworn Master Mason is taught several secrets of that degree. He learns the penal sign, the hand signal based on the penalty of the Master Mason's oath, which is to pass the hand in a slashing motion, palm downward and thumb toward the body, across his stomach. The due-guard of the Master Mason repeats the position of his hands on the Holy Bible and the compass and square as he took the oath: with his upper arms along his sides, forearms out straight, with palms down. To this point, the ceremony is much like that of the first two degrees, but now is added a third sign, the Grand Hailing Sign of Distress of the Master Mason, given with the upper arms parallel to the ground, forearms vertical with hands above the head, palms forward. For those times when the Master Mason is out of sight of possible help, or in the dark, he is taught to summon assistance with the words, "O Lord, my God, is there no help for a Son of the Widow?" a reference to Hiram, legendary master craftsman at the building of the Temple of Solomon, about whom the initiate has as yet been told nothing, and whom Masons identify with the metalworker that scripture describes as "a son of a widow of Naphtali."

To this point, the ritual of initiation appears familiar to the newly raised Master Mason because it is so like the ceremonies he has experienced in his initiations for the Entered Apprentice and Fellow Craft degrees. He is not surprised when the Worshipful Master calls for a break in the meeting for refreshments and he is conducted back to the anteroom so that he may get dressed to rejoin the meeting as a full-fledged Master Mason. He will be very surprised a few minutes later when he learns that the important part of his initiation has not yet begun, nor even been hinted at.

Upon his return to the lodge room, by now bedecked in his Master's apron, with the ribbon and jewel of a Senior Deacon around his neck, the candidate is surrounded by the lodge members, shaking his hand and congratulating him upon becoming a Master Mason. Fellowship abounds, until the Worshipful Master uses his gavel to call the meeting to order once again. Seeking out the initiate, the Master asks if he considers himself a Master Mason. Upon his affirmative reply the Master corrects him and tells him that he will not be one until he has traveled a road full of peril and danger, meeting with thieves, robbers, and murderers. Only after surviving this impending ordeal will he be able to consider himself a Master Mason. Blindfolded again, the Senior Deacon, as "Conductor," leads him in a circle around the lodge room as the Worshipful Master begins to tell him the story of the murder of Hiram Abiff, the master builder of Solomon's temple and who, along with King Solomon himself and Hiram the king of Tyre, was one of the three Grand Masters of the Masonic order.

He explains that during the construction of the Temple of Solomon it was the custom of Hiram Abiff to enter the unfinished Sanctum Sanctorum of the temple each day at "high twelve" (noon), for the purpose of drawing plans on the "trestle-board" for the next day's labors by the workmen, after which he would offer up his prayers to God and then go out through the south gate of the temple courtyard. The initiate does not know that the rest of the story of Hiram Abiff will be in the form of a play or drama in which he himself has been given the role of the Grand Master; he discovers this with a shock as the party escorting him reaches the mythical south gate. There, he is grabbed and shaken by an unseen assailant. His attacker states that Abiff had promised the Fellow Crafts that when the temple was completed they would all be told the secrets of a Master Mason (some lodges say "the Master's Word"), so that they might travel to foreign lands to find work and to receive the rewards of a Master Mason. Not content to wait for the completion of the temple, the attacker demands those secrets now.

His Conductor answers for the startled, blindfolded initiate, telling his assailant that he must wait until the temple is completed, and then if found worthy he will be given the secrets of a Master Mason. Not satisfied, the attacker, whose name is Jubela, threatens to take the life of Hiram Abiff if he will not divulge the secrets, and when he is denied, he passes the twenty-four-inch gauge across the throat of the candidate, whereupon the Conductor moves him on to the "west gate of the temple." At this gate, he is seized by the second assailant, whose name is Jubelo. Once again the Master Mason's secrets are demanded, and when they are not forthcoming, Jubelo threatens him and strikes the candidate on the chest with a square. Conducted on to "the east gate," the initiate is accosted by the third assailant, whose name is Jubelum. After the candidate, still in the role of Hiram Abiff, refuses to divulge the Master Mason's secrets, even upon pain of death, he is struck on the head by Jubelum's setting-maul and falls "dead" (pulled to the floor by his Conductor and others).

Blindfolded on the ground, the initiate hears the three murderers decide to bury him in a pile of rubble until "low twelve" (midnight), when they will carry the body away from the temple. To symbolize the burial of Hiram Abiff, the candidate is wrapped in a blanket and carried to the side of the room. Soon he hears a bell struck twelve times and is carried from the "rubble" grave to a grave dug on the brow of a hill "west of Mount Moriah" (the Temple Mount). He hears the murderers agree to mark his grave with a sprig of acacia, then set out to escape to Ethiopia across the Red Sea.

Moments later, as the drama continues, King Solomon (played by the Worshipful Master of the lodge) arrives to determine the reason for all the confusion and is told that the Grand Master has disappeared, and that with no plans laid out on the trestle-board the workmen do not know what to do. Solomon orders that all the workmen search for the missing Grand Master, and the candidate in his blanket "grave" hears scuffling and shuffling noises throughout the room. Finally it is reported to King Solomon that Hiram Abiff is not to be found, so a roll call is ordered, which reveals the absence of Jubela, Jubelo, and Jubelum, collectively known to Masons as the Juwe. Solomon orders that twelve Fellow Crafts be dispatched, three each to the east, west, north, and south, to look for the fugitives. Those sent to the east and south return to report no sighting and no news. The three from the west report that they have news of the Juwe attempting to ship out of the port of Joppa (the ancient name for Jaffa), but prevented by the embargo placed on all shipping by Solomon as part of the manhunt. The three fugitives were reported to have turned back inland toward Jerusalem and the temple.

All are ordered to continue the search and, about fifteen (symbolic) days later, one stops to rest by the sprig of acacia, which comes out of the earth easily. He calls to his companions as another search group joins them to report that, while resting near some rocks, they had heard voices. The first voice, that of Jubela, had said, "Oh, that my throat had been cut across, my tongue torn out by its roots, and my body buried in the rough sands of the sea at low-water mark, where the tide ebbs and flows twice in twenty-four hours, ere I had been accessory to the death of so good a man as our Grand Master, Hiram Abiff." The second voice, the report goes on, was that of Jubelo, who had cried, "Oh, that my breast had been torn open, my heart and vitals taken from thence and thrown over my left shoulder, carried into the Valley of Jehosaphat, there to become prey to the wild beasts of the field and the vultures of the air [some lodges say, "my heart plucked out and placed on the highest pinnacle of the temple, there to be devoured by the vultures of the air"] ere I had conspired in the death of so good a man as our Grand Master Hiram Abiff." The third had been the voice of Jubelum, louder and more lamenting than the others, "Ah, Jubela and Jubelo, it was I that struck him harder than you both! It was I who gave him the fatal blow! It was I who killed him! Oh, that my body had been severed in twain, my bowels taken from thence and burned to ashes, the ashes scattered to the four winds of heaven, that there might not be the least track or trace of remembrance among men, or Masons, of so vile and perjured a wretch as I am."

The search party returns to the rocks, captures the three fugitives, and takes them to King Solomon. Kneeling before the king, all three plead guilty and are sentenced to the punishments out of their own mouths. With much clatter and scuffling, the three are taken out of the lodge room, and the candidate, still wrapped in his blanket, hears the groans and cries coming from outside the room. Then he hears a voice announce to the king that the sentences have been carried out.

Next, Solomon orders the twelve Fellow Crafts to search for the grave of Hiram Abiff, telling them that when they find his body to check carefully for any revelation of the Master's word, or any key to it. Looking for the spot where the acacia had been pulled up, the searchers "discover" the initiate, still in his blanket "grave" in his role as Hiram Abiff. As they open the grave, they are overcome by the stench of the putrefying body and put their hands out in front of them, palms downward (emulating the dueguard of this degree), to ward off the smell. Probing the body, they discover nothing but the ribbon and jewel about his neck, which they take back to King Solomon, reporting that they could find no clue to the Master's word, which, apparently, is now lost forever. (Some lodges say that the faint letter G appeared on the breast of the decomposing body.)

Turning to Hiram, king of Tyre (the lodge treasurer), Solomon decrees that the first sign given and the first word uttered at the grave shall become part of the rule of the Master Mason's degree until That-Which-Was-Lost is discovered by future generations. All then move to the "grave" and encircle it. King Solomon, upon his first view of the body, raises his hands, palms forward (in the Grand Hailing Sign of Distress of the Master Mason), and cries, "Oh, Lord my God, is there no help for the widow's son?" Then the king asks that the body be raised from the grave by the grip of the Entered Apprentice, but is told that the flesh leaves the bone when that grip is tried. Then he asks that the body be raised with the grip of the Fellow Craft, but that grip, too, fails to raise the body. Finally, Solomon says that he will try, personally, to raise the body from the grave by using the "Lion's Paw," the grip of the Master Mason. Applying the grip (and assisted by several members of the lodge), he raises the candidate's body to a vertical position and arranges that the candidate's right foot is inside the right foot of Solomon, their right knees pressed together, their left hands on each other's backs, with their mouths close to each other's ears. In some jurisdictions, the Worshipful Master, as King

Solomon, whispers to the candidate the Master's word *mahabone* and has him whisper the word back, cautioning the new Master that the word must only be passed in this position, called the "five points of fellowship." As the newly raised Master Mason learns the Master's word, the blindfold is removed.

Stepping back, the Worshipful Master explains that the five points of fellowship are: *Foot-to-Foot*, to indicate that a Master Mason will go out of his way, on foot if necessary, to assist a worthy brother; *Knee-to-Knee*, as a reminder that in his prayers to the Almighty, the Master Mason remembers his brother's welfare as well as his own; *Breast-to-Breast*, as a pledge that each Master Mason will keep in his own breast any secrets of a brother when given to him as such, murder and treason excepted; *Hand-to-Back*, because a Master Mason will always be ready to reach out his hand to support a brother and to defend his character and reputation behind his back, as well as to his face; and *Mouth-to-Ear*, because a Master Mason will always endeavor to caution and to give good advice to an erring brother in the most friendly manner, pointing out his faults and giving him timely counsel so that he may ward off approaching danger.

Partly because the newly raised Master Mason could hardly be expected to have completely grasped the story of Hiram Abiff encumbered by a blindfold and wrapped in a blanket, the entire "historical account" of the murder of the Grand Master is delivered to him, with detail added. He is told that, after Hiram was pulled from the grave by King Solomon, he was buried beneath (sometimes "near") the *Sanctum Sanctorum* of the temple, which was being built to house and honor the Ark of the Covenant. He is told that, according to Masonic tradition, a beautiful monument (now lost) was built to honor the memory of Hiram Abiff. It consisted of a beautiful virgin weeping over a broken column, with a book open before her. In her right hand she held a sprig of acacia; in her left, an urn. Behind her stood Time, counting the ringlets in her hair. It is explained that the broken column represents the unfinished temple, as well as the unfinished life and task of Hiram Abiff. The book is the eternal record of the Grand Master's virtues and accomplishments. The sprig of acacia symbolizes his immortality and the urn holds his ashes, while the figure of Time reminds us that time, patience, and perseverance accomplish all things. All this, the initiate is told, is the reason why the

Master Masons' lodge is known as the Sanctum Sanctorum of Freemasonry.

The new Master is shown many of the Masonic symbols, with their explanations, none of which is known to have existed in Secret Masonry. (Americans will be most interested in the All-Seeing Eye, the symbol of the Supreme Being, the Great Architect of the Universe, because it appears on every U.S. one-dollar bill, above a topless pyramid, a Masonic symbol for the unfinished Temple of Solomon.)

Thus ends the initiation of the Master Mason, most interesting of the three degrees to us because it contains the unexplained allegory that gave Freemasonry its central identification with the construction of the Temple of Solomon. Because it freely departs from the biblical account, it most certainly hides clues as to the origins of the Masonic order. Now it was time to address the mysterious words, terms, symbols, and Old Charges of Secret Masonry, beginning with the special Masonic vocabulary that down through the centuries has helped to set it apart from all other organizations, and by the use of which Masons all over the world instantly recognize each other.

CHAPTER 17

MYSTERY IN LANGUAGE

From the initiation rituals of the three basic craft degrees of Masonry had been gleaned a number of words and terms whose true meanings had been lost over the centuries. These are words and terms unique to Masonry, such as *tyler, cowan, cable-tow, due-guard,* and *Lewis,* plus the Scottish "Mason's word" *mahabone,* to which we could add a mythical Scottish mountain, Mount *Heredom.* There was *Abiff,* the surname of the allegorical master builder of the Temple of Solomon, and the *Juwes,* the murderers of Hiram Abiff named *Jubela, Jubelo,* and *Jubelum.* There have been numerous attempts on the part of Masonic writers to force this vocabulary into a relationship with the workings of medieval stonemasons, but the attempts were strained and those explanations are rejected today by serious Masonic researchers, so that each of these terms remains an unsolved mystery.

It appeared that if there was anything to the hypothesis that the fugitive Knights Templar were the dominant factor in fourteenth-century Masonry, that hypothesis could first be tested on the basis that the Templars were a French-speaking order. The answers that could not be found in English might be there in medieval French. At once one encounters the very basic problem that exists in tracing old French words and phrases from their current usage in English: In the course of time, pronunciation affects spelling and spelling affects pronunciation. We have seen that the very Norman name *de Burghe* became the very Irish *Burke,* just as the very French name *Saint Clair* became the very Scottish *Sinclair.*

Today, tourists in London are sometimes confused when their concierge tells them that the china shops they seek are on "Beecham" Place, which they walk right by because the sign at the top of the road reads "Beauchamp." The Templars, too, furnish an example in their extensive property in Lincolnshire, which was known as Temple Bruer. In medieval French, *bruer* (pronounced Broo-Ay) meant "heath." Gradually, some of the locals began pronouncing the name from its spelling, then the spelling changed to match the new pronunciation, so that today some maps of the area identify that location as "Temple Brewer," and the conclusion is often drawn that this was a place at which the Templars made beer.

As for turning French words into known English words, perhaps no such conversion is more common than the tennis player's term for a zero or goose-egg score. Few who cry out "forty-love" realize that the tennis term "love" began as *l'oeuf,* the French word for egg.

With all of these possibilities in mind, the search began for Masonic answers in medieval French. The first word searched was "tyler," but none of the few French words beginning with *ty* made any sense in the Masonic context. We decided to try a phonetic approach, since the sound of *ty* in French is spelled *tai,* and the answer emerged in the French word *tailleur,* which means "one who cuts." The word root had supplied the medieval English word *taille* (pronounced "tie"), which meant a tax, or the "cut" taken by the government. In an anglicized variation, it had provided the word *tithe,* the "cut" that goes to the church. From *tailleur de vêtement,* "one who cuts clothing," came our word "tailor." Seeing its various distortions in other English words, we could accept that *tailleur* could evolve into "tyler" (which is almost exactly how the Londoner pronounced "tailor"). In practice, "the cutter" seemed a perfectly acceptable designation for a man who stands outside the door (or in the woods) with a drawn sword in his hand.

The Tyler had as his primary duty the protection of the lodge from "cowans and eavesdroppers." The usual Masonic explanation is that the word *cowan* was an old Scottish term for a stonemason not yet skilled enough to be admitted to the guild. Upon investigation, we could not find *cowan* in any compendium of old Scottish words, and we knew that the Lowlanders of Scotland in the Middle Ages were linguistically more akin to the English than to the Gaelic-speaking Highlanders; the common people used the English tongue and the Norman-French nobles, who constituted the bulk of the Lowland aristocracy, used the French. Once again, the French language produced a sensible solution in the word *couenne* (pronounced "koo-WAHN"). Its meaning is an "ignoramus" or "bumpkin," so it is possible that the word was indeed applied to an unskilled laborer in Scotland, but its use was by no means limited to that application, nor was it limited to Scotland. Further, this derivation was supported by the French *couarde* (koo-ard), which came into English as "coward." The Tyler, then, was protecting the lodge meeting against the ignorant (cowans) and the curious (eavesdroppers).

The term *due-guard*, the sign a Mason gives to identify himself in any craft degree, was also there in French, in a term that had been truncated over the years. The French term for a protective gesture is *geste du garde*, which gradually shortened to *du garde*, with the spelling anglicized to "due-guard." Should this appear too speculative, consider that the same transition with truncation has taken place a number of times as French terms gradually became absorbed into the English language. A close parallel exists in a tightly woven fabric developed by the weavers of Nîmes in France. It was known as *serge de Nîmes*, then *serge de Nim*, and still later the first word was dropped, so that the term survives in English simply as "denim."

The Masonic term *Lewis* for a son of a Mason was a bit more difficult: There is no word in any French dictionary beginning with the letters *lew*. Then we recalled that several English dialects, including the speech once common to London, frequently reversed the sounds of *v* and *w*. That inversion provided the answer in the French plural word *levées* as used in an agricultural context, which would have been pronounced "lewis" by many Englishmen. The meaning of the word is virtually synonymous with "scions." It means "sprouts," a sensible designation for sons and heirs.

By far the most troublesome challenge lay in trying to find a French root for *Hiram Abiff*. The word *Abiff*, supposedly the surname of the murdered Master Mason who was in charge of the construction of the Temple of Solomon, is not from the Hebrew and it is not English. It was not to be found in French, either, in a review of every French word beginning with the letter *a*. Then I noticed an anomaly in the initials frequently used in Masonic writings to provide a level of secrecy. Most of the Masonic documents use the initials HA for Hiram Abiff, but some of the older works referred to him as HAB. Did this mean that at some point his name had been Hiram A. Biff? Tackling the French dictionaries again, the answer was found in the verb *biffer*, which means to strike out or eliminate. The Masonic term was not a name, but a designation: *Hiram à Biffe* simply means "Hiram who was eliminated."

We could find no evidence that anyone had ever seriously attempted to find real significance in the names of the Juwes, the three men who had beaten and killed Hiram Abiff, which is not surprising since the names Jubela, Jubelo, and Jubelum at first appear to be akin to childish wordmaking from meaningless syllables, like Tweedledee and Tweedledum. The search in old French, however, proved that our first impression was wrong. The French word *jubé* means a "rood screen," the screen in a medieval church which stood at the entrance to the chancel, the area east of the nave that included the choir. In those days a large crucifix was mounted on the rood screen, so-called because *rood* is an ancient Saxon word for cross.

It was in front of this jubé, this screen and crucifix, that the public penance set by the priest was often carried out. Rather than a typical current penance of a dozen Hail Marys, the medieval penance might mean hours of prayer, or even a beating, with bare knees on rough stone. More to the point, in religious orders such as the Knights Templar, it was at the jubé that the physical punishments or penances of monks and friars were effected, including the whippings prescribed by their rules. The jubé was the site of public punishment of sin. This meaning lives today in the French colloquial term *venir à Jubé*, literally "to come to the jubé," which is defined as to submit, to get one's just desserts. It is in that sense of punishment and retribution that the word *jubé* lives on in Masonic ritual. To memorialize the fates of the three attackers of Hiram Abiff, who were duly punished for their crime and sin by the judgment of King Solomon, the originators of the allegory might have called them Jube One, Two, and Three, but chose to differentiate by using the feminine, masculine, and neuter suffixes by naming them *Jube*la, *Jube*lo, and *Jube*lum. The collective term, the *Juwes*, undoubtedly began as the *Jubes*. With no English equivalent, the names of Those-Who-Were-Punished point directly to a French-speaking order and to a medieval time frame.

The Scottish term *intrant* for the Entered Apprentice is obviously dialect for "entrant," originally a French word which kept the same meaning as it became an accepted word in English. It seemed reasonable that an earlier title for a new member was Entrant, and that in the push to identify the fraternity with medieval guilds, whose beginners were called apprentices, the Masonic term would have become *Entrant* Apprentice, which verbal rendering would gradually have reduced to the smoother sound of Entered Apprentice. Without such an explanation, there is no easy understanding of the term Entered Apprentice (as opposed, for example, to a non-Entered Apprentice, an unlikely status). Actually, the very use of the word "apprentice" is evidence of its addition at a much later date, perhaps even as late as the passage of Secret Masonry into Public Masonry, because it violates a basic tenet of secret societies. New members of secret societies are confined to a small group of new and low-level members until their trustworthiness is beyond doubt, so that they can betray only a minimum number on their own low entry level, whether maliciously or by accident. To bolster that security, entry-level initiates are led to believe that they are full-fledged members fully acquainted with the leaders of the society. Ideally, they don't even suspect that there are higher levels and much more important members and superiors totally unknown to them. The use of the title "Apprentice" destroys that leadership security because it makes it obvious that there are levels above, so it is most unlikely that the word was ever used in the days when secrecy at every level of the order was vital.

The Scottish "Mason's word" is *mahabone*, which defied all of our attempts to find its origin in the French language, although the French *bon* is frequently found in English as *"bone,"* as in London where the original French name *Marie le Bon* lives on in the name of Marylebone. We came up with one possible explanation, but it is highly speculative. In the ritual for the initiation of a Master Mason, the candidate is told that this degree will make him "a brother to pirates and corsairs." We have already seen that this special brotherhood probably stems from the Templars who took the order's fighting ships and opted for the hazardous life and livelihood of the freebooter. In that period, the greatest pirate port on the north African coast was the city of Mahdia. Just as Madrid under Moorish rule was called Mahadrid, Mahdia was formerly known as Mahadia. If this great corsair city welcomed and sheltered the fugitive Templars and their ships, it could well have been known as "Mahadia the Good," or *Mahadia le Bon,* which over centuries of strictly verbal communication could easily have changed to *mahabone.* Admittedly, that is pure speculation, not a piece of evidence, although it is reasonably certain that if an original meaning is ever proven it will confirm that the Scottish syllable "bone" came from the French *bon.*

The term *cable-tow* seemed to hold no French connection, since it is made up of two good English words, but there was the annoying fact that in its English meanings it makes no sense as applied to Masonic ritual. In English, a cable is a heavy rope or hawser at least ten inches in diameter. As a unit of British measure, a cable length is a distance of one hundred fathoms or six hundred feet. But turning to medieval French, we found a completely different meaning. The French word *cable* (pronounced KAH-bluh) came directly into that language from the Latin word *capulum.* The meaning in both Latin and French is "halter," precisely the use in Masonic ritual as the candidate is led through the ceremonies by means of a rope wrapped around part of his body as a halter, and which lengthens to a lead line, together comprising the Masonic "cable-tow." What apparently happened is that the term was used for the massive ropes required to tie down, or "halter" a ship, and the original animal meaning was eventually lost to the nautical.

A term unique to Scottish Masonry is *Mount Heredom,* a mythical mountain said to be near the town of Kilwinning, home of the "Mother Lodge" of Freemasonry in Scotland. No plausible explanation of *Heredom* has been brought forth, so we tried to find an answer in French.

To begin with, the suffix *dom* could be French or English, both deriving from the Latin *domus*, the word that gave us "domicile." It originally meant a geographic location, so that the king*dom* was the area ruled by a king. Later, it came to mean a state of being, rather than a place, so that free*dom* meant the state of being free. The suffix seemed clear, but what did *Here* mean? There is no way to be conclusive, but we did find one answer that made sense. The old French word *héraudie* means heraldry. *Heraudom*, easily anglicized to *heredom*, would indicate the place or state of being noble. Ex-Templars, who had to be of the knightly class as exemplified in their right to heraldic armorial bearings, but now living under assumed identities, could well have wanted to preserve a symbolic memorial of their social status.

Establishing the origin of these lost words of Masonry in the French language solves a number of minor Masonic mysteries but does not, of course, conclusively establish any direct association with the Knights Templar. It certainly does, however, add weight to the hypothesis of the Templar connection, which it does not do for the old claim of Masonic beginnings in the construction of Solomon's temple, or the current claims to origins in medieval guilds of stonemasons; in neither of those contexts would the participants have been French-speaking. What it does establish is a social stratum tied to the Norman-French upper classes, and a time frame. It was not until the year 1362 that a law was passed in England that all trials would thenceforth be conducted in the English language, so that the participants would understand what was going on. The French-language roots of the lost words of Masonry indicate the strong probability that the society was in existence in the first half of the fourteenth century, another point that contributes to the feasibility of origins associated with the Templars, who fled from arrest by church and state in that very period.

A more direct Masonic connection to the Templars could be found in the French word by which the knights addressed each other. The Templars of all classes called each other *frère*, or "brother," not *chevalier*, or "knight," as do the modern Masonic Templars who address one officer, for example, as "Sir Knight Generalissimo." The Templars addressed their own military commander (they didn't have a generalissimo) as *Frère Maréchal*, or "Brother Marshal." The French term for Freemason is *Franc-Maçon*, which would probably have been anglicized into "Frank Mason" (remembering that in Masonic verbal communications the name Pythagorus had degenerated into "Peter Gower"). On the other hand, the French term for brother Mason is *frère Maçon*. Anticipating the example of C. S. Forester, who had English officers and men alike in one of his Horatio Hornblower stories pronounce *frère* as "freer," the anglicizing of *frère Maçon* would have produced "Freer Mason" and later, for easier speaking, the smoother Free Mason. Indeed, much of the old Masonic literature does employ the term "brother mason," and we can find no fourteenth-century precedent for any organization that consistently referred to fellow members as brothers, except for the various religious orders, which, of course, included the Knights of the Temple.

The Masonic term *lodge* may not seem to contain any mystery because the world has adopted the Masonic definition. Whether one turns to the original definitions of the English *lodge*, the medieval English *logge*, or the French *loge*, the meaning is the same. A lodge is a place to sleep, and sometimes to eat as well. Nowhere outside Freemasonry was it ever a cell or chapter, or a group of men joined by fraternal bonds. That meaning, however, which was revealed for the first time when the Masons came public in 1717, has now become an accepted part of the language. *The Random House Dictionary of the English Language* gives several definitions of *lodge*, including "the meeting place of the branch of a secret society" and "the members comprising the branch." Thus we hear of an Odd Fellows Lodge and a Moose Lodge and easily lose sight of the fact that this purely Masonic use of the word provides an important clue to just what those Secret Masons were doing. It is generally accepted that in ancient Masonry the only formal meetings were those called to conduct an initiation. Even then, there would have been no formal "lodge" room, but rather a few men gathered in secret with sentries, or Tylers, posted for their protection. The meeting would have been as brief as possible in consideration of the business at hand. That is not a "lodge" in the original sense.

Masonic historians have told us that the itinerant guild masons, traveling from job to job, stayed and met in "lodges" to review their work and to discuss their guild business, but now we know that the guild concept was largely fantasy. So what was a "lodge" to an ancient Secret Mason? Exactly what the word means and has always meant: a place to eat and sleep for brother Masons on the move or on the run. These were men who had secrets that could cause them to lose life and property. They had taken bloody oaths not to betray one another, and had sworn to help one another. An Old Charge of Masonry says that if a brother comes to you, give him "work" for two weeks, then give him some money and direct him to the next lodge. Why the assumption that he will need money? Because he is running, and hiding. What he got was not the allegorical "work," but actual *lodging*. After he had a chance to rest, to exchange news, and after he had determined that this was not a safe harbor where he could settle down, he was given some money and put on the road to the next Masonic "lodging" in the direction in which he was headed. He would be told the tavern, the farm, the blacksmith shop, or even the church where he should present himself at the next stop, making himself known by the secret signs, perhaps even by the catechism, "Are you a traveling man?" "Yes, I am." "Where are you traveling?" "From west to east."

Another Old Charge fitting this situation warned that whenever a "visiting" brother went "into the town," he must be accompanied by two local brothers to "witness" for him. Those witnesses and the money for his pocket were extremely important to the traveler. In medieval England the vagrant was not only jailed but liable to be painfully whipped before being sent on his way. Under the Tudors the time came when the penalty for the third offense of vagrancy was death.

All through the oaths and the Old Charges we see emerging a mutual aid and protection society, protecting men who could die if caught. The word *lodge* provides strong support for that contention, because nothing is more important to the man on the run than safe lodging, especially when backed up by funds and directions for the next leg of the journey, and ultimate assistance in finding a place at which to stop running. Since the brothers themselves were scattered, it would be natural to think of the society geographically in terms of the "lodging" at Maidstone or the "lodging" at York. Those providing that lodging, and the gifts of funds, would think of themselves as centered on that facility. The lodging would normally be the only place at which traveling underground Masons would meet their local brothers, not in a meeting room but in the cellar, the attic, the hut in the woods, or wherever safe, secret lodging was provided.

The transition from the old meaning to the new is easily understood. The place selected to provide lodging for the brother on the run would have been the most secure and secret place the local members could provide, perhaps an attic loft or a cellar reached by means of a trapdoor. The primary function of this secret space would have been as a "lodge" for the brother on the move or in hiding. It would have had a secondary function as well, because when the local Masons had to meet, the most secret and secure place they knew of for their gathering would be the local "lodge" room. As time passed and there were no longer brothers to be hidden and fed in the "lodge," its original purpose fell away, and only its function as a secret meeting room remained. As even the memory of the original use faded, an entirely new meaning for the term came into use; it was defined as the place of the cell meeting, or the collective members of that cell.

It may be an aid to a better understanding of the actual gatherings of ancient Secret Masonry to consider the secret meetings held in their camps by Masons who were prisoners of war in World War II. Not only had Freemasonry been outlawed by the Fascist governments, but no prison-camp commander would tolerate a secret society functioning in his prison, for whatever purpose. Punishment for all participants would have come swiftly. There were no altars or candles, no pillars, no trestle-board; indeed, no lodge room. None was necessary. The circle on the floor could be scribed in the dirt or marked on the floor with chalk or water. There was none of the tedious repetition found in the modern lodge meeting, and the rapid order of business was conducted in whispers. The Tyler, in his traditional role of lookout, was no ornamental functionary but a most vital official, quick to warn of the approach of any cowan or eavesdropper, especially if clad in a German or Japanese uniform. Here for a brief period was the true secret society, whose very existence had to be kept secret. These meetings probably came closer to the reality of ancient lodge meetings than any other Masonic functions of the past two centuries, especially because they met only for a very specific purpose, as briefly as possible, and were motivated by mutual protection and assistance.

There was one more mystery word in Masonry, the word *Mason* itself, which we decided to consider only after careful study of the central feature of Masonic ritual, the legend of Hiram Abiff.

In the meantime, it would be necessary to address the symbols and the "clothing" of Masonry, along with aspects of the rituals of initiation, to see how they fit with the hypothesis of a Templar connection with Freemasonry. As it turned out, they not only fit the hypothesis, they virtually proved it.

CHAPTER 18

MYSTERY IN ALLEGORY AND SYMBOLS

We have seen the candidate for Masonic initiation prepared for the ceremony by being partially undressed, relieved of all metal objects, and bound with a rope, the *cable-tow*. The blindfold is common to almost all secret societies, since no initiate can be permitted to see the faces of the members until he has taken the oath and been admitted. (In some societies the initiate is not blindfolded, but all members in the room are masked or hooded.) The other aspects of the preparation, however, have specific Masonic significance.

Today, the candidate relieved of metal gives up his loose change, his keys, perhaps a money clip, a cigarette lighter, cuff links, or a gold ball-point pen. In the fourteenth century, and later, the metal a candidate was likely to have on his person would have been limited to money, edged weapons, and perhaps a piece of protective armor or chain mail. (The guild worker would have been limited to a few coins.) The lack of clothing, of money, and of weapons, with a rope halter wrapped around him, all speak to a common condition, which might well have been summed up and described to him in these words: "You have come to us bound, half-naked, and defenseless. You have no money with which to feed and lodge yourself, no armor to ward off the blows of your enemies, no weapons with which to defend yourself.

"Take comfort from the fact that all of your brothers are sworn to help you. If you are naked, we will clothe you. If you are hungry, we will feed you. We will shelter and protect you from your enemies. We will keep your secrets. Your call for help will never go unanswered.

"You, too, have sworn. If a brother in need comes to you, you will protect and shelter him. You will defend his good name. You will keep his secrets, just as you have sworn to keep all of the secrets of our brotherhood that have been and will be revealed to you."

All of this makes good sense for a secret society, but has no reasonable place in the building trades. It speaks to men who have enemies, and who may very well expect to need help, proven by the fact that the initiate is taught the secret ways to solicit that help. Even in the dark, or out of the sight of those who might come to his aid, he has a spoken distress appeal, "Oh, Lord my God, is there no help for a Son of the Widow?" For times when he is in full view of others, he is taught the Grand Hailing Sign of Distress to be used in seeking aid. That sign, with both hands raised in the air, gives away its age, because the hands are held exactly as they would be in response to a gunman's demand, "Hands up!" If such a gunman gave that command to ten people in a bank, or six people getting out of a stagecoach, all would appear to be giving the Grand Hailing Sign of Distress of a Master Mason. Such a sign would only have been created and used before the days of a highwayman with a handgun, which attests to its antiquity.

None of this, of course, points directly to any group connected with the Knights Templar, but merely to a secret society of fugitives or people at risk of becoming fugitives, or of those with such strong sympathies for the transgressors that they are willing to risk their lives and property to help them. The motivation to join and to participate in the risks would have required very strong feelings and total commitment, and in the years following the papal orders for their arrest and torture, the fugitive Templars were certainly such a group.

Turning to certain symbols of Freemasonry, however, there are much more direct Templar connections. It was important to stay with the "clothing" of Masonry and certain aspects of the rituals rather than with the "furniture" of the modern lodge room, because secret meetings "on high hills and in deep valleys," or in barns and cellars, certainly did not include an altar, candlesticks, columns, or chairs. Nor would they have included the Holy Bible (which still brings criticism to Freemasonry today for referring to the Holy Book as an item of the "furniture" of a lodge room). In the period we are examining, individuals did not have Bibles, at least not legally. The elements they could have had were the circle, the mosaic pavement, and the compass and square.

The circle that is at the center of the Masonic lodge is in four parts: first, the circle itself; then the point in the center of the circle; and then two parallel lines, one on each side of the circle. In Masonic lore the circle is the boundless universe, the point in the center is the individual Mason, and the lines on two sides of the circle are the staffs of St. John the Baptist and St. John the Evangelist.

Now let's have a medieval Mason prepare the meeting place. He will brush back the leaves and fallen twigs to make a clear area. He will cut two sticks, say, four feet long. He will hold or tie them at one end, spreading them at the other end to make a crude compass. Holding the end of one stick firmly to the ground, he will rotate the other to scratch a circle in the dirt. The end that was held in place will necessarily leave a point in the center of the circle. Placing the two sticks on either side of the circle, he will have created the total symbol. Active minds and the passage of time will imbue the point with important symbolic meaning of its own, as they will also do for the two sticks. At one point in the ritual, the Masons in attendance will walk around the circle, a reverential act now known as the "circumambulation of the lodge."

Can the Knights Templar provide any solution to the mystery of the circle and the circumambulation? Easily. Initiation ceremonies of the Knights of the Temple took place in their own churches, which were usually circular in shape to emulate the Church of the Holy Sepulchre in Jerusalem. While it is true that not every Templar church was built in a circle, certainly most of those in Britain were. Significantly, the most important Templar church in Britain, the one consecrated in A.D. 1185 by Heraclius, patriarch of Jerusalem, the one still standing today in the Temple area of London, was built in a perfect circle.

As to circumambulation, a feature of the medieval church was the procession of priest and parishioners around the church. A few years ago I attended a Christmas service at Lincoln Cathedral at which the Anglican priest reminded the congregation of this ancient custom, which he now asked be repeated as part of this festal service. At that, the priests, the acolytes, the choir, and the entire congregation rose and joined in one great procession throughout the cathedral, singing carols as they went. When the Templars processed around their circular churches they had only one way to move: in a circle, just as today's Masons process in their "circumambulation" of the lodge.

It is also interesting to note that since a compass is required to scribe a circle, the compass was probably a feature of the society before its members began to call themselves "Masons," and may even have made some small contribution to the evolution of that particular cover story.

As for the Masonic mosaic pavement, it could have been indicated on the ground by scratching a checkerboard, or by using any black and white material. Strangely, there is no rule as to the size of the squares or the number of squares. In all probability, the symbolism began as one white square and one black, because carrying a mosaic, or the materials to make one, would have been difficult to explain if discovered, making it an unnecessary risk. The Templar basis for this symbolism is simple and direct. The battle banner of the Knights Templar, the *Beau Séant,* was a vertical design consisting of a black block above and a white block below. The black block signified the black world of sin the Templar had left behind, and the white block symbolized the pure life he had adopted as a soldier for Christ. Masonic historians don't even try to speculate as to the origin of their mosaic pavement, usually saying no more than that "it came from the east." They are right. It did, from the battle flag of the Templars, which, if repeated over and over, makes a very effective black and white mosaic.

Another mystery that found a solution in the Order of the Temple was the "clothing" of Freemasonry. The primary item, of course, is the Masonic apron, the first item received by the Entered Apprentice at his initiation and the first Masonic symbol explained to him. Today that apron has come to be lined, trimmed, fringed, and decorated with badges and symbols, but in ancient Masonry it was not a manufactured apron at all. It was an untrimmed white lambskin tied around the waist. This lambskin has been proclaimed by Masonry to be a badge of innocence and purity, derived from the work aprons worn by the members of the stonemasons' trade in the Middle Ages. Quite apart from the fact that it is difficult to see purity and innocence as vital qualifications for a stonemason in the Middle Ages, there appears to be no evidence whatsoever that those craftsmen ever wore sheepskin aprons, and for the researcher there is no shortage of contemporary drawings and paintings of men working at the construction of stone castles and cathedrals.

We could, however, see a very direct tie to the Knights Templar. It may be remembered that their Rule forbade any personal decoration except sheepskin, and further required that the Templar wear a sheepskin girdle about his waist at all times as a reminder of his vow of chastity, a context within which purity and innocence are vital. The lambskin would have been a very effective and secure item of secret ceremonial and remembrance, because in the wool-based economy of England in the Middle Ages, the possession of a lambskin would not have been looked upon with suspicion. As an item of common fraternal livery it would have been innocuous, but it would have had very direct significance as each man tied this remembrance of the Templar Rule about his waist to participate in the ceremonials of Secret Masonry.

The situation is different with the other item of Masonic clothing, the gloves. These were not an article of common clothing in the Middle Ages, and possession of them might well have aroused suspicion, or at least have drawn attention to the wearers, for which all secret societies hold a strong aversion. Gloves were not easy to make and were expensive, so generally were worn only by the knightly class and the higher clergy. Even today gloves are bestowed as part of the religious ceremony that makes a priest a bishop, and the high clergy have oversize rings made that can be worn over gloves; the gloves are retained as symbols of power. As for the medieval stonemasons, we could find no documentation or illustration of their wearing of gloves.

There is, however, a strong Templar connection. Their Rule required that the Templar priests wear gloves at all times to keep their hands clean "for when they touch God" in serving Holy

Communion. The priests who participated in the secret society might have worn their gloves at ceremonies as a remembrance of their own part of the Templar Rule, or at one time gloves may have been worn by a lodge chaplain, but it is very doubtful that in Secret Masonry every brother brought a pair of gloves to a meeting of his lodge—at least not until the later years, when gloves became a standard item of common dress.

The white robe worn at Masonic initiations is perhaps too common a garment to try to use it to trace origins, except to mention that the Templar rule specified a pure white mantle as the knight's principal item of clothing.

As for mysterious phrases from Secret Masonry, we have already addressed the one most puzzling to Masons themselves, the assertion that the Master Mason's degree makes a man "a brother to pirates and corsairs." We have been able to come up with no possible origin of that assertion other than the brotherhood with those Templars who took the order's fighting ships to sea as pirates and corsairs.

Another puzzling phrase identifies the Mason as a traveling man traveling from west to east. All Templars started in the west, and to fulfill their mission and their vows they had to travel to the east, the Holy Land. The Freemasons, as symbolic Masons whose task it is to finish or rebuild the allegorical Temple of Solomon, must also symbolically journey eastward to that temple. The importance of that allegorical journey is emphasized by its inclusion in a secret catechism of identification.

There is one other dramatically graphic connection between the Knights of the Temple and Freemasonry that is difficult to deny as specific evidence of that connection. The Masonic oaths are taken on the compass and square, which are resting on top of a Holy Bible. Those Bibles were not available to individuals in the Middle Ages, which leads us to conclude that the oaths were formerly taken on some symbol, apparently the compass and square. If those earliest Masons were indeed fugitive Templars or their descendants, that symbol might well have been the Seal of Solomon, which strongly resembles the Seal or "Star" of David, except that one equilateral triangle is outlined and the other is solid. But Masonry has been defined by its own writers as "a science of morality, veiled in allegory and illustrated by symbols." As such, and as a secret society anxious to remain secret, it would not be likely to use a known symbol in its literal sense. The literal symbol would need to be "veiled in allegory," so that it looked like one thing to the outside world but represented quite another to the initiated. It is not difficult to draw the veil of allegory over the literal Seal of Solomon, which looks like this:

To completely change the appearance and meaning of that seal, one needs to do no more than leave out the horizontal bars and then it looks like this:

Suddenly we see the compass and square, and only minor modifications are required to give the new symbol the surface appearance of those tools. And thus the easily identified Seal of Solomon, a symbol well known to and holding special meaning for the Knights of the Temple of Solomon, becomes an innocuous representation of two simple tools of the stonemason. Over the centuries the secret meaning was totally lost and the symbolic meaning survived to encourage the gradual concoction of fantasy origins for the Masonic order in nonexistent guilds of masons.

If someone should cry "Coincidence!" one must recognize the unlikelihood of a coincidence within a coincidence. Note the position of the "legs" of the compass derived from the Seal of Solomon, with one leg above the "square" and one beneath it, exactly the juxtaposition of the compass and square as they are presented for the oath-taking in the Fellow Craft degree, once the degree of full membership in the Masonic brotherhood.

But some may ask about the modern compass and square with the letter G in the center. How does that tie in with the Templars? The answer is simple: It doesn't. We must remember that before Masonry became public in 1717 there were no graphic representations of the compass and square, no jewels, no imprints, no signs, no bumper stickers. And no letter G.

The matter, however, must be addressed in any serious research into Masonic origins because of the almost reverent attitude of modern Masonry for that letter G, which members are taught stands for Geometry. The Mason first learns of the importance to Freemasonry of the science of geometry in the lecture following the initiation ceremony of the Fellow Craft degree. He learns that geometry is the most important science to architecture, and the only science by which one can measure and appreciate the universe. He learns that sometimes the word *geometry* is even used as a synonym for Freemasonry, as it was in the first Masonic constitution of 1723. Its importance to modern Masonry is unquestioned, but where did it fit in ancient Secret Masonry?

The first clue came in the manner of its presentation to the new Fellow Craft Mason. Geometry has no part at all in the initiation ritual and is presented only as a part, albeit a very important part, of the lecture that follows. This almost ensured that it had been layered on at some point, but why?

The answer lay in what has emerged as the true purpose of Secret Masonry, the mutual protection of men at odds with church and state, particularly when the state religion was Roman Catholicism. As shall be seen further in the investigation into the religion of Freemasonry, disagreement with the teachings of the church, and fear of punishment by the church, were the factors that kept Freemasonry alive, and desperately secret, for several centuries. Then came a time near the beginning of the seventeenth century when science and mathematics began to take hold of men's minds, to stir their imaginations, and to invoke new theories, new experiments. The church was caught unawares. Ideas were being promulgated that high church officials had neither the time, the knowledge, nor the inclination to absorb and evaluate. Scientific findings seemed to conflict with literal scriptural interpretations, and as such were unacceptable. The church felt called upon to defend its own presentation of the Word of God and to discipline this new breed of dissenter.

We can look back smugly now and wonder how such a thing could ever have happened. Yet if we don't look back at all but just look around, we find similar situations existing today, but now it's not the Roman Catholics. Protestant fundamentalists operate colleges awarding advanced degrees, including a doctoral degree in creation science, for the study of a literal interpretation of the biblical Book of Genesis that proves that the world is not much over four thousand years old. Accordingly, creation science rejects the modern teachings of geology, anthropology, paleontology, archaeology and linguistics, and scoffs at the practice of carbon dating.

In 1987, in a town near my home in Kentucky, the local newspaper reported that members of the county school board had called on an elementary school teacher at her home. She was told that if she ever again dared to repeat the sin she had committed that week, it could mean her discharge from the school. Her sin? She had shown children a National Geographic film about dinosaurs that spoke of an earth millions of years old, in direct violation of the revealed Word of God.

Now the struggle is social, and when it breaks out into the community, as in banning textbooks in Louisiana, it is a matter for the law courts. In the seventeenth century, the church *was* the court in matters of religion and morality. The upstart scientists found themselves in grave danger of ecclesiastic punishment. The most famous case of all, of course, was that of Galileo Galilei, the Italian astronomer and telescope builder, who announced that he had discovered that the sun does not move around the earth, but, to the contrary, the earth moves around the sun. To the church, this was blatant blasphemy, for did not scripture say that at one point the sun had stopped in its orbit around the earth? To avoid harsher punishment and to obtain his release from the papal prison, Galileo recanted and swore that he had been wrong, so he was merely banished to his own village for the rest of his life, forced to live out his days in fear of speaking the truth.

Other men of science saw the point but would not abandon their scientific curiosity, and so there was a new source of recruits for the Freemasons in Britain, men who had reason to meet to share their ideas and findings in secret, away from the eyes and ears of the church. Men of science in London, Oxford, and Cambridge met in secret in what has been termed an "invisible college," which now appears to have existed in secret Masonic lodges in those areas. Their first known secret meeting was held in 1645, just three years after the death of Galileo. The man destined to become their most famous member, Sir Christopher Wren, was just thirteen years old at the time. By 1660, the group felt secure enough in the apparently Protestant reign of Charles II to petition the crown for a royal charter, which was granted in 1662. The name they chose was The Royal Society of London for the Improvement of Natural Knowledge, but they were known simply as the Royal Society and are still so called today.

When Freemasonry came public in 1717, just fifty-five years later, it appeared that the Royal Society was virtually a Masonic subsidiary, with almost every member and every founding member of the Royal Society a Freemason.

Before the public revelation of Masonry, however, an event had occurred that had distracted the men of science from theory and bent them in the direction of an immediate need. In September of 1666 a devastating fire swept through London, destroying most of the City. The need to rebuild from the ashes was so urgent that in the following year Parliament passed laws designed to encourage all classes of building tradesmen to come to London. There they could earn citizenship and become freemen of London, and no guild membership was required.

Sir Christopher Wren, a Freemason who had been a founder of the Royal Society at the age of twenty-eight, was not an architect by training. He was a geometrician of some fame and had been a professor of astronomy at Oxford University. In this time of great national need, he found an overwhelming demand and appreciation for his services in the rebuilding of London. Eighty-seven churches had been destroyed in the Great Fire and Wren acted as supervising architect for fifty-one churches built to replace them.

It was his knowledge of geometry that gave Wren his greatest triumph, the rebuilding of St. Paul's Cathedral. When the observer sees the great dome of St. Paul's against the London sky, he is not usually aware that the visible dome is simply a lead-covered timber shell. The shell is held up by a concealed brick cone that provides all the support. The dome seen from below is simply a decorative, nonsupporting cavity built inside the bottom of the brick cone. The support of the great dome was a triumph of solid geometry. St. Paul's was completed in 1711, just six years before Masonry came out into the sunlight.

For the fifty-year period just before Masonry revealed itself, these men of science, the engineers, mathematicians, architects, and geometers, were the heroes of the day, exerting great influence on the Masonic order to which most of them belonged. Nor were the Scottish Masons left out, because shortly after the Great Fire of London, a similar fire had ravaged Edinburgh, prompting the passage of a law decreeing that from that date forward all buildings built in that city must be built of stone.

A picture helps to summarize the story. There is a great painting in Wren's final architectural achievement, the Naval Hospital at Greenwich, a project conceived by Queen Mary and built after her death by the Protestant King William. It is an allegorical painting of William and Mary on their thrones, surrounded by many figures. Below them, cherubs hold a drawing of St. Paul's, a tribute to the hospital's architect. Another cherub holds a compass in one hand and a square in the other. A short distance away, the papal tiara lies on the ground.

The constitution for the Grand Lodge was written in London, where these men of science and architecture were most prominent and influential members. They put their mark on Masonry forever, by instilling it with the importance of their own work. They linked geometry to Masonry and added the G to the compass and square. Their own use of Freemasonry, their reverence for geometry and architecture, become a central feature of Public Masonry, although the propensity to dramatize and fantasize caused them to fix the entry of Geometry into Masonry at the building of Solomon's temple, forgetting that at that time neither the word *geometry* nor the letter G as yet existed. Their science had nothing whatever to do with the origins of Masonry, but has a role in remembrance of the days when science had need of what Secret Masonry could bestow upon its members, that all-important protection from their common enemy.

What did have to do with the origins of Masonry were the more ancient symbols of the craft: the lambskin apron and gloves, the circle on the floor, the mosaic pavement, the circumambulation of the lodge, and the compass and square hidden in the Seal of Solomon, all of which tied directly to the Knights of the Temple in ways that were clear and direct.

Now it was time to examine the most troublesome aspect of Freemasonry, the brutal penalties of the oaths of initiation.

CHAPTER 19

MYSTERY IN BLOODY OATHS

The most controversial mysteries of Freemasonry, and the most inspirational to anti-Masons, are the penalties that are included in the oaths taken with each degree. The vocabulary of condemnation has been exhausted, as the Masonic oaths have repeatedly been branded as bloody, brutal, horrible, repugnant, illegal, atheistic, anti-Christian, sickening, and so on. Indeed, to have one's tongue torn out by the roots, heart plucked from the breast, body cut in two with entrails burned to ashes, appears to be overkill, literally, and is unquestionably against the law of any land in which Freemasonry functions, as well as against the tenets of any of the religions whose members are welcomed into the brotherhood. At one point, the public shock and revulsion at the revelation of the Masonic penalties came close to destroying the order entirely in the United States, based as it was on allegations of murder.

On March 13, 1826, Captain William Morgan of Batavia, New York, signed a contract for the printing of a book that he said would reveal the secret grips, signs, and rituals of Freemasonry. In the consternation that broke out among the local members of the order, the printer's shop was set on fire and, in what he termed an act of harassment, Morgan was arrested and jailed for nonpayment of debt. An anonymous benefactor paid the debt for him, but as Morgan left the jail he was seized by men waiting out front and forced into a coach that immediately dashed off on the road north. He was taken to the abandoned Fort Niagara and held there as a prisoner. That much was confirmed later when five Masons confessed to the abduction and confinement. The Masonic version was that he was released, or escaped, and fled to Canada, while the anti-Masonic story was that his captors had taken Morgan out on the river in a boat, where he was tied to heavy stones and rolled overboard. No body was ever recovered, but the public, and many Masons, were convinced that Morgan had been murdered in an attempt to protect Masonic secrets.

As arrests were made and a trial set, the public learned that the local sheriff, the judge, and some of the jurors were Masons. The sheriffs of the towns through which the kidnappers had passed were Masons. So was the secretary of state of the United States, and it came out that New York Governor DeWitt Clinton was a past Grand Master. It appeared that Freemasonry might be functioning as an underground government.

Impromptu Masonic conventions were called at which the murder of Morgan was condemned, and thousands of practicing Freemasons resigned from the order. An Anti-Masonic party was organized as a third political party in the United States, with formal fund raising, its own newspapers, and the first national convention at which a nominee for president was selected. The most vocal champion of the Anti-Masonic party was Congressman John Quincy Adams, who had served as the sixth president of the United States. Masons claimed that the alleged murder of Morgan was just an excuse for Adams to attack Freemasonry, that he was bitter that he had been denied a second term as president because of the popularity and political machinations of Freemason Andrew Jackson.

Whatever the reasons, Adams passed up no opportunity to condemn Freemasonry, alleging that the murder of Morgan had been in line with the murderous oaths of the Masonic order. He appealed to all Freemasons to abandon the order and to help abolish it once and for all, since it was totally incompatible with a Christian democracy. He wrote so many letters against Masonry that they can, and do, fill a book. In a letter to Edward Ingersoll on September 22, 1831, the ex-president summed up his attitude toward the Masonic oaths and their impact on the brotherhood:

"Cruel and inhuman punishments are equally abhorrent to the mild spirit of Christianity, and to the spirit of equal liberty. The infliction of them is expressly forbidden in the Bill of Rights of this Commonwealth, and yet thousands of her citizens have attested the name of God, to subject themselves to tortures, which cannibal savages would instinctively shrink from inflicting.

"It has therefore been in my opinion, ever since the disclosure of the Morgan-murder crimes, and of the Masonic oaths and penalties by which they were instigated, the indispensable duty of the Masonic Order in the United States, either to dissolve itself or to discard forever from its constitution and laws all *oaths*, all *penalties*, all *secrets*, and as ridiculous appendages to them, all *mysteries* and *pageants*."

Nor, as the chief celebrity spokesman for the Anti-Masonic party, was Adams in favor of accepting the idea put forth by some that the Morgan affair was the result of the actions of a few Masons acting independently, with no central planning or approval. That attitude might let Freemasonry as a whole off the hook, to the detriment of the party. In a letter to Richard Rush of York, Pennsylvania, Adams gave some political advice:

"With a view to the ultimate object of Anti-Masonry, *the abolition of Masonry in these United States*, it appears to me to be an important point gained, if we produce on the public mind a full conviction that those crimes have been committed, and that *Masonry* is responsible for them."

For a while it appeared that Adams would have his wish, as the Masons who resigned the order in the furor of the Morgan murder allegations were not replaced by new recruits. Morgan's book was published by the burned-out printer, who restored his shop and printed the book the following year, 1827, under its extraordinary copyrighted title, *Illustrations of Masonry by one of the Fraternity who has devoted Thirty Years to the Subject. "God said, Let there be Light, and there was Light."* Its revelation of the bloody oaths accelerated the events of the next few years, including the growth of the Anti-Masonic party. Among its unintended markets were Masters of Masonic lodges, who purchased the book to aid in staging ceremonies, since Freemasonry still maintained the rule of verbal communication only, and Morgan's book provided the first "guide book" to help administer the complex rituals of initiation. It is still published today, under the much shorter (and much more sensational) title of *Freemasonry Exposed.*

The Anti-Masonic party dwindled away in a generation, and American Masonry was soon rebuilding, but criticism of the Masonic oaths was still alive and well. In 1869, an anti-Masonic book was published by the Reverend C. G. Finney, the president of Oberlin College in Ohio. Where the concerns of Adams about the Masonic penalties were primarily political, Finney's concerns were religious. In his preface, setting forth his reasons for writing the book, Finney stated in part, "I wish, if possible, to arouse the *young men* who are Freemasons, to consider the inevitable consequences of such a horrible trifling with the most solemn oaths, as is constantly practiced by Freemasons. Such a course must, and does, as a matter of fact, grieve the Holy Spirit, sear the conscience, and harden the heart." In a chapter headed *"Awful Profanity of Masonic Oaths,"* after a discussion of the penalties, Reverend Finney wrote:

> "But I get sick of pursuing these loathsome and blasphemous details; and I fear I shall so shock my readers that they will be as wearied as I am myself. In reading over these oaths, it would seem as if a Masonic lodge was a place where men had assembled to commit the utmost blasphemy of which they were capable, to mock and scoff at all that is sacred, and to beget among themselves the utmost contempt for every form of moral obligation. These oaths sound as if the men who were taking and administering them were determined to annihilate their moral sense, and to render themselves incapable of making any moral discriminations, and certainly, if they can see no sin in taking and administering such oaths under such penalties, they have succeeded, whether intentionally or not, in rendering themselves utterly blind, as regards the moral character of their conduct. By repeating their blasphemy they have put out their own eyes."

Then the good Reverend, in the best traditions of zealotry, went over the edge and past the truth.

> "Now these oaths mean something, or they do not. Masons, when they take them, mean to abide by them or they do not.

If they do not, to take them is blasphemy. If they do mean to abide by them, they are sworn to perform deeds, not only the most injurious to society, to government, and the Church of God of any that can well be named, but they swear, in case of the violation of any point of these obligations, to seek to have the penalties inflicted on the violator. In other words, in such a case, they swear to commit murder; and every man who adheres to such obligations is under oath to seek to accomplish the violent death, not only of every man who shall betray the secrets, but, also, of everyone who shall violate *any point* or *part* of these obligations."

A very emotional presentation, but totally false. No Mason swears to *inflict* the penalties, but only invites them down on his own head. There has never been any indication whatsoever of just what person or power is supposed to carry out the penalty, and since the oath is taken on the Holy Bible it is highly likely that God was being asked to take on that responsibility. Such requests were common in the Middle Ages and are not unknown today. How many times in history has someone said, "May God strike me dead if I am not telling the truth!"? We remember Pope Gregory VII, at the celebration of his victory over the Holy Roman Emperor, as he picked up a piece of the consecrated host and asked that God choke him to death on the bread if he had done anything wrong. And we remember the fate of Judas Iscariot in the Book of Acts. He purchased a tract of land with the thirty pieces of silver he had received for the betrayal of Jesus Christ. As he stood on that "Aceldama" ("the field of blood") Judas fell to the ground headlong. His stomach swelled up and burst, spilling his entrails on the ground. In fixing the penalty for the Master Mason's degree, it may well have been considered that God Himself had decreed disemboweling as the appropriate punishment for betrayal.

To fully understand the Masonic oaths in context, we must ask ourselves why men, and governments, so often have asked that other men swear in the name of God, with their hands on the Holy Bible. Such oaths were considered a guarantee of truth, or a guarantee that an agreement would be fulfilled. Why feel reassured when a witness gives an affirmative answer to the question, "Do you swear that the testimony you are about to give is the truth, the whole truth, and nothing but the truth, *so help you God?*" The answer, much more so in times past than now, was pure, raw fear. A man who broke an oath made before God and on the Holy Bible risked eternal damnation, perpetual agony that we are told would far surpass any punishment as simple as having the tongue or heart torn out. A Freemason takes the oath on the Holy Bible, swearing by his faith in God, and so is theoretically subject to whatever penalty God chooses to apportion to one who breaks an oath sworn in His name. *In addition,* he invites down on his own head a specific punishment for betrayal of his brothers or their secrets. If we agree that the hell-fire of damnation will be more agonizing and of infinitely longer duration than the penalty the candidate voluntarily calls down upon himself, we may wonder why the lesser, voluntary penalty gets all the attention. It can only be because the threat of damnation for oath-breaking has lost its power—plus, of course, the erroneous belief that the candidate is also swearing to inflict such punishment with his own hands on some brother Mason transgressor, one of the most common and enduring misconceptions about Masonry.

The final aspect of the penalties for breaking the Masonic oaths is the frequent charge that the punishment does not fit the crime. Why should there be such bloody mutilations, including death, for revealing secrets available to anyone with a library card and a modicum of curiosity? The answer to that takes us back into the years of Secret Masonry in the centuries before 1717, when the secrets of Masonry were not available to the public, and when the betrayal of a brother Mason could very possibly mean his torture and death.

Ex-President Adams may have been correct when he said that "cannibal savages would instinctively shrink from inflicting" penalties such as those of the basic Masonic degrees, but the civilized Christians in the fourteenth century had no problem with those very punishments, and worse. As to tearing out the tongue, it may be recalled that during the Black Death the king of France decreed the loss of the tongue for a third offense of blasphemy, the first two offenses having caused the offender to have his upper and lower lips sliced away. Slitting the throat was an established method of getting rid of prisoners and others and was a form of civil capital punishment in the east. Even today, in the museum at the capital of the Moslem Khanate of Kiva, there are actual photographs of this punishment being carried out by law in the 1920s.

Finally, the Master Mason's penalty, which appears at first glance to be unsurpassedly bloody, proves to be far less cruel and gory than its legal equivalent in the proper time frame. The Masonic penalty is to have the body cut in two, the entrails burned, and the ashes scattered. Yet we saw in the judicial vengeance after the Peasants' Rebellion legal executions related to but far more cruel than the Masonic version. Cutting the body in two brings death, and the subsequent burning would be purely ceremonial. Following the instructions of Chief Justice Tresilian, royal executioners made openings in rebels' stomachs, drew their entrails out of their bodies, and allowed them to drop onto charcoal braziers to burn while the victims were still alive to watch and suffer. Then the rebels had their heads cut off and were quartered, their bodies cut into five pieces, not two.

Does this comparison justify the Masonic penalty? Of course not, because such brutality is totally beyond our experience and comprehension; but one must wonder what kind of comfort, what kind of threatened punishment, would make a man feel that he should completely trust another, when that other man could betray him to the kinds of punishments meted out by the medieval mind. Burning at the stake was selected as the punishment of choice for heresy not because it lent itself to ceremonial but because a burn was the most painful experience they knew, and burning to death was the ultimate agony, emulating hell itself. What would be the appropriate retribution for a man who betrayed another to that fate, or to the whole gamut of physical torture? When Pope Clement V ordered that in the questioning of the Templars the Inquisitors should "spare no known means of torture," he by definition declared that no punishment known could exceed that which he had ordered.

In the context or providing a measure of security for Templars in hiding, the violent penalties make very good sense, and it is in that time frame and under those circumstances that the mysteries of the Masonic penalties stop being mysteries. We have seen by now that the ancient society was a mutually protective brotherhood, sworn to help other men whose feelings, whose convictions, were at odds with the established church. The essence of that protection was that they be sheltered from being discovered, philosophically as well as geographically. When a man joined the order in those days, he was putting his life and property into the hands of any man who saw his face or knew his name. In such circumstances the penalties could not be taken lightly, and some who thought to earn a reward or settle a private grievance by turning informer may very well have been punished, though not in keeping with the literal penalties. I, for one, doubt that any mission was ever undertaken to convey a tongueless dead body, with its throat cut, a hundred miles to the seashore in order to bury it where the tide ebbs and flows twice in a twenty-four-hour period. If a traitor was indeed ever executed, he would more likely have been buried six feet under a village pigsty. The actual penalties were probably somewhat symbolic for purposes of oath taking, but were of no value unless the initiate was absolutely convinced that *some* such penalty would be visited upon him if he violated that oath.

The mystery that remains is why the Freemasons have clung to the recitation of these penalties long after they were unnecessary and had ceased to make sense, and long after any Mason believed that such penalties were a real possibility. The only answer is tradition. In a rapidly changing world there is comfort and security in being part of things that do not change. If part of that tradition is strange, or secret, or only half-understood, the drama is increased, as is the important feeling that one is a part of a very special group. No Mason believes that the penalties of his oath will be visited upon him, and every candidate would hurry out of the room if ever told that he must help to inflict those penalties on someone else.

Unfortunately for Masonry, the bloody penalties will continue to be a focal point of attack until it is recognized that a tradition loses nothing and even gains by being identified as a tradition, a fact which even now is the subject of occasional Masonic conferences throughout the English-speaking world. Nothing would be lost if at the appropriate point in the ritual the Master of the lodge would say to the initiate: "You have sworn an oath before your God and on the Holy Book of your faith, and now we ask that you repeat another oath, not to be sworn to by you, but to be spoken aloud by you in a Rite of Remembrance. So that you never forget our ancient brothers who risked their lives and their property, who risked obscene tortures to work in secret for freedoms that you now enjoy in public, you will repeat the oath taken in those days; an oath which recites a penalty for betrayal that, as brutal as it may seem, was not as brutal as those penalties which might be inflicted upon the betrayed brother. Let it ever remind you of the risks that the brothers before you were willing to take for those of us who came after."

That kind of a preamble would in no way detract from the solemnity of the occasion, and should remove the Masonic penalties from the anti-Masonic stream of incessant criticism.

Upon analysis, the penalties of the Masonic oaths reveal to us that they originated in a medieval time frame, when the betrayal of a brother could reveal that he was guilty of crimes that could subject him to the loss of his life and his property. Those legal punishments were specific and were levied for heresy and treason at a time when heresy *was* treason. The Masonic penalties were products of their times. The protection of heretics by secrecy fits with the heretical acceptance of men of all religious beliefs, as it fits with the fugitive Knights of the Temple who rejected the church that had rejected them and subsequently extended the hand of brotherhood and assistance to those of similar convictions, in a secret society kept alive by a growing stream of dissenters from a church ever more greedy for wealth and power.

CHAPTER 20

MYSTERY IN RELIGIOUS CONVICTIONS

Freemasons vehemently deny that Masonry is a religion, and it isn't, but the primary requirement for membership is certainly religious in nature. The candidate must assert his belief in a monotheistic Supreme Being and must also believe in the resurrection and immortality of the soul. How the individual Mason perceives and worships the Supreme Being in which he believes is his own business, as is the means by which he hopes to attain immortality, and no brother Mason is permitted to attempt to dissuade him from those beliefs. To reinforce that rule, the discussion of religious beliefs is forbidden in the Masonic lodge.

The emphasis on a monotheistic God is taken seriously. A few years back a British lodge in India wanted to initiate a prominent Hindu, to which objections were raised based on the allegation that Hinduism is pantheistic, with Vishnu, Siva, Kali, and a number of other deities. The matter had to be taken back to London for consideration by the Grand Lodge, where agreement was finally reached that these apparently separate deities were simply symbolic manifestations of aspects of one Supreme Being. The Hindu was welcomed into the order.

Freemasons also glorify the Temple of Solomon as the first

temple built to a monotheistic God (which may warrant an apology to Abraham). The Roman Catholic church understandably
takes issue with the Masonic monotheistic concept, since the
church recognizes only the triune God of the Holy Trinity. Actually, the Masonic perception of God may be the only monotheistic perception in all of Christianity, because Masonic teachings
make no mention of a devil or Satan. Most Christians are taught
that there are at least two deities: God, who is the embodiment
of all that is good; and Satan, who embodies all that is evil. To
deny the existence of Satan is of course heretical, and to identify
him as the God of Evil probably is, too, but whatever his role,
Masonry takes no note of it. Barring whatever personal beliefs
any individual Mason may hold on the subject, Masonry appears
to hold that a man's shortcomings are the results of his own moral
failures, not of a demonic evil that presses him to live in the sin
he was born to.

Similarly, the Masonic leaning is to encourage the individual to
advance toward the hope of resurrection and immortality
through personal merit and acts of charity, a concept that also
upsets certain established Christian creeds which maintain that
salvation is not attained through personal morality and good
works, but only through belief in Christ. Since it is an order open
to men of many creeds, however, the answer of Freemasonry
would be that they take no issue with that pathway to salvation,
nor with any other religious tenet held by any Mason: He may
believe the teachings of any organized religion, or he may even
have religious convictions that are his alone—as did Thomas Jef-
ferson and John Locke—so long as he believes in a Supreme
Being. On that basis, Masonry has welcomed Jews, Moslems,
Sikhs, and others, all of whom take the oaths on their own Holy
Books.

This policy of accepting as brothers men of many different
faiths, especially non-Christians, has been the focus of frequent
attacks on Masonry, some of which are going on today (taking no
notice of the fact that the same criticism could be leveled at the
World Council of Churches). In their tolerance, even acceptance,
of men of all faiths, however, it should not be thought that the
basic Masonic requirement of belief in a Supreme Being is in any
way a cursory rule of the order. When French Masonry
announced in 1847 that belief in God would no longer be a

requirement for membership and that atheists would be welcome in French lodges, they were promptly disavowed by British and American Masonry and all formal ties summarily severed.

The acceptance of men of all faiths is also taken seriously, as Prussian Masonry learned at about the same time. When the English Grand Lodge in 1846 investigated complaints that Jewish Masons were being denied entrance to lodge meetings, the Grand Lodge of Berlin replied that they had determined to limit their Masonry to Christians only, without specifically noting that the Jews were the only non-Christians among them. The British Grand Lodges immediately disavowed all relationships with the Prussian, which brought them back into line, so that once again Jewish Masons were welcomed (or at least admitted) to Prussian lodge meetings.

A basic analysis of the Masonic attitude toward religion is that far from being a religion unto itself, it is a teaching that enables men of varying religious beliefs to come together, and stay together, in a fraternal society. The Old Charges of ancient Secret Masonry allude to men who had differences of religious opinion, at a time when both secular and church law would tolerate no such differences. All men were to be of just one universal belief which was decreed, taught, and enforced by the only legally allowable church, the Church of Rome. The Masonic Old Charges reveal that there were men at odds with the teachings of Rome, sympathetic and protective toward each other. What we see in Masonry is provision for aid and protection for those whose beliefs placed them in grave danger, and since the betrayal of a Secret Mason's "secrets" might cost him his life and property, we must assume that the secrecy and mutual protection that were central to the order provided shelter from the highest established authority. In consideration of the acceptance of brothers of variant religious beliefs, it appears that the authority to be feared most was the church, although usually that authority was welded to the state. Even as late as the reign of Queen Elizabeth I, over three hundred Catholics went to the headsman's block because they stayed with their Roman faith, although the legal charge was "treason against the crown."

Today, the concept of a society that will accept men of any religious belief appears very ordinary, so commonplace that it hardly merits any attempt at dramatization. It is difficult for any of us, raised in a social atmosphere in which freedom of religion is so matter-of-factly accepted and legally enforceable, to imagine a time when freedom of worship was unimaginable and expressly forbidden. Secular monarchs felt that a universal religion, practiced to the exclusion of all others, was vital to the efficient government of the people, and in the western world in the fourteenth century that religion could be none other than the Roman Catholic faith. Blatant heretics had to be killed off so that they would not infect others and so break down the fabric of the orderly autocratic society. In the century before the suppression of the Templars, a papal crusading army of over thirty thousand men had butchered tens of thousands of people of all ages and both sexes in the Albigensian Crusade against the Cathar heretics in southern France, a conflict that gave rise to the most shocking quote in religious history. The military commander about to attack the city of Béziers asked how his troops could differentiate between the heretics and the loyal Catholics among the fifteen thousand men, women, and children in the city. The papal legate replied, "Kill them all. God will recognize his own." Starting in 1209, the slaughter lasted until 1244. During that holy war, the zealous pursuit of Cathar heretics by the Spanish priest Dominic Guzman had enabled him to found the Dominican order. By 1229 that order had played a key role in the establishment of the Holy Office, officially known as the Holy Roman and Universal Inquisition. Its ferocious defense of the purity of the faith taught its victims the danger of even expressing doubts about the teachings of the Roman church. In that atmosphere, the Masonic willingness to accept the holder of any belief or mode of worship in bonds of brotherhood was a capital offense, which made Freemasonry a very high-risk organization to which to belong. The desire to be part of such a group meant a dedication, a commitment to the concept of errors in the teachings and practices of the one established church. Those found guilty of such a commitment would have been guilty of both heresy and treason, giving true meaning to the Masonic Old Charge that a Mason should reveal no secret of a brother Mason that might cost him his life and property.

It is not difficult to relate the fugitive Templar to this dangerous commitment, as, indeed, it is extremely difficult to think of any other organization that had the Templar motivation to originate such a philosophy. The Templar knights, their priests, and their sergeants were all members of a religious order under the direct command of the pope. When they were rejected by the pope, arrested, and for five years imprisoned, tortured, and burned at the stake, they lost their contact and intercessor with God. If the pope rejected them, and their response was to reject the pope, what kind of Christians could they be? Certainly not Roman Catholics. Would they accept the teaching that abandonment by the pope meant abandonment by God? Or when their panic died down and hatred grew to take its place, might they decide that it was the pope, not they, who had sinned against God? If they retained their belief in God but rejected the authority of the papacy and the teachings of the church about the role and authority of the church, they were among the first to sow the seeds of protest, but not necessarily all in the same way. Some may simply have wanted to reject *this* pope. Others may have rejected the very concept of the papacy, or the validity of its self-avowed delegation of supreme spiritual and temporal authority on earth from Jesus Christ through Peter. Certainly in the confusion and panic of their rejection they would not individually have come up with a universal response to their common dilemma. What they did have in common was a desire to remain free, to seek help, and to give help in a mutual pact to shelter one another. In order to feel safe, to extract and trust oaths of secrecy and brotherhood, they would trust only the man who could swear before God. Those who rejected God and could not swear such an oath would not be trusted, so atheists could not become part of the protective brotherhood.

What the secret society needed was men who would affirm their belief in God, with a desire for brotherhood strong enough to accept any man's personal religious persuasion as secondary to their principal goal of survival. Ample demonstrations all about them that religious differences could drive men apart, even set them at each other's throats, led to the Masonic rule that would prohibit proselytizing and abolish religious argument, or even religious discussion, from the meetings of the brotherhood.

All of this meant leading double lives, because both secular and spiritual law required, on pain of punishment, that every man be a devout and practicing member of the church. To the outside world, he must appear law-abiding, attend mass regularly, and pay his tithes to the church without question. His dissension, and his aid to other dissenters, must be in secret, because such dissension was a serious crime against the state and the most serious crime against the church. Such a society might seem doomed to die along with its founders, but it was born at a time when dissension in Britain was just beginning to make itself heard, and on the basis of the old rule that "the enemy of my enemy is my friend," there was no shortage of recruits over the centuries to come, as a brief examination will show.

The fourteenth-century dissenters are often classed as the forerunners of the Protestant Reformation, but they were in reality more reactionaries than reformers. They had no new ritual or doctrine to suggest to the church, but rather wanted the church to return to earlier principles. Men like the priest John Wycliffe resented those church teachings that were formed long after the death of Christ. They could find no scriptural basis for a pope, for the doctrine that the bread and wine of the mass turn into the actual body and the actual blood of Jesus Christ, or for the storehouse of merit based on the virtues of Christ and His Mother that the church could sell for silver and gold. Their fervent desire was not to establish a new church, but rather to have the old one back. For its part, the church had declared that in many ways the *teachings* of the church, the points reasoned out by the church leaders over many centuries, were more important than actual scripture. It was decreed that any doubt or rejection of the *teachings* of the church was heresy equal to that of doubt or rejection of scripture itself and was subject to the same punishment. That made heresy much more common and much easier to establish.

One of those teachings was that the church followed Christ in being quick to forgive, but also followed God Himself in His actions after the fall of Adam and Eve, when He meted out the punishments of ultimate death, disease, and the need to work for one's living. The punishments were applicable not just to the guilty parties, Adam and Eve, but to all mankind forever, a concept designated by the church as the doctrine of original sin. It said that God offers forgiveness to all but *requires* punishment, the essence of the Sacrament of Confession, Punishment (*Penance*), and Absolution. This absolute requirement that sin be punished made it even more risky for any secret protester or dissenter. The only guarantee of maximum security was maximum secrecy, so that the only safe shelter or assistance that one man could offer to another had to be tendered under the heaviest cloak of secrecy that minds could devise, and many of the Templar minds had been trained in exactly that direction.

It was a period when the Holy See was preoccupied with the extension of its own wealth and power, including the imposition of supreme autocratic power over the priesthood. When Archbishop Hunthausen of Seattle stated in 1986 that bishops of the church should have more autonomy, he was merely relieved, temporarily, of some of his duties. In the fifteenth century, a bishop who made that same suggestion was promptly arrested and thrown into an ecclesiastic prison for seven years. Bishops had indeed been autonomous for hundreds of years after the death of Christ. Then there came a time when the bishop of Rome declared that since his was the diocese of Saint Peter himself, he was surely the most important bishop of the church, and the bishop of Rome became "first among equals." Then the Roman bishops asserted stronger authority as the direct inheritors of the authority of Saint Peter, to whom had been entrusted the keys of the Kingdom of Heaven, styling themselves the vicars of Saint Peter. Taking even stronger positions as their power grew, they styled themselves the vicars of Christ and asserted themselves as the autocratic rulers of the entire church hierarchy. Pope Gregory VII (1073–1085) announced, after a thousand years of the Christian church, that henceforth only the bishop of Rome could use the title of *papa* or pope, and ordered that all secular princes were henceforth required to kiss the pope's foot, a gesture of reverential humility they were not to extend to any other bishop. As we have seen, Boniface VIII later made the papal position even stronger by declaring that it was a condition of salvation that every human being on earth should be subject to the Roman pontiff.

With the new power came new teachings. Pope Gregory, who had taken a vow of chastity as a monk before being raised to the Throne of Peter, was strong in his feelings that priests should not be married, but he fell victim to the revenge of the Holy Roman Emperor before he could enforce his ruling with papal discipline. It remained for Urban II, the pope who had called the First Crusade, to put teeth in the papal condemnation of clerical marriage. He ordered that all secular lords should demand of all married priests in their domains that their wives be put aside. The punishment ordered for those who refused was that the reluctant priest's wives were to be forcibly seized and sold into slavery. Many priests felt entitled to object, because scripture said that Christ had cast demons out of Peter's mother-in-law. That was clear scriptural evidence that Saint Peter, the founder of the church, was a married man, so why shouldn't his successors and followers also be married?

And there we find a clue to why dissension was so often expressed or led by the clergy. They were the only ones who had direct access to scripture as a basis for their disagreements with the church, especially in the area of "teachings" of the church that could not be supported by direct scriptural reference but were the results of clerical reasoning. One of these that stirred up a great deal of dissension was the reasoning that since Christ and His Mother were in all ways perfect and totally virtuous, they had stored up in the eyes of God an infinite amount of blessings. This Treasury of Merits, also called the Treasury of the Church, was declared to be completely under the control of the pope, who could draw upon that boundless inventory of virtue at his own discretion. Units of this merit could be bestowed as rewards, as to the Crusaders, but could also be sold, a practice that led to strong objections from many clerics, including Wycliffe, John Hus, and Martin Luther. These sales of "indulgences" were enabled by another reasoned teaching of the church, the concept of purgatory, a spiritual holding pen required because no human being is perfect and perfection is required to enter the kingdom of heaven. Purchasing units of time from the Treasury of the Church could shorten the purgatorial cleansing period by hundreds, even thousands of years, an income source that angered many of the lower clergy.

One more area of clerical protest, although it does not complete the whole catalog of dissension, is worth setting forth because it created several areas of protest based on a single theme: the church teaching of transubstantiation. This teaching says that in the sacrament of Holy Communion the bread becomes the actual body of Jesus Christ and the wine becomes His actual blood. It cannot be that different pieces of bread become different parts of His body, so it was agreed that each piece of bread, each crumb of bread, becomes the whole body of

Christ, while the form remains that of bread. Any secular examination, by taste, by microscope, by qualitative and quantitative
analysis can be expected to show that the bread is bread because
the *form* remains the same. The *substance* of the bread, however,
becomes the whole and actual body of Jesus Christ, hence the
term *transubstantiation.* The first protest was that the ceremony
of the Last Supper was one of remembrance, not an actual group
consumption of twelve bodies of Christ. Could such a thing be
when Christ Himself was sitting right there at the table with his
disciples? The next protest on this theme was that in his ordina-
tion the priest was empowered to perform the miracle of transubstantiation as a delegation to the priest of authority given exclusively to the church by Jesus Christ through Peter. This meant
that no one other than an ordained priest of the Church could
serve mass.

The third protest may have been the strongest of all, against
the claim that every priest of the church had the right and the
power to give orders to God, which God had no choice but to
obey. It seemed that the subservience of the church to God had
been at least partially reversed, and nowhere was that right of the
church to give orders to God stronger or more dramatic than in
the priest's role in Holy Communion. That language may seem
strong to some, so let a priest say it. In his *Faith for Millions,*
Father John A. O'Brien of Notre Dame University, expressed it
this way:

> "The supreme power of the priestly office is the power of con-
> secrating. 'No act is greater,' says Saint Thomas, 'than the conse-
> cration of the body of Christ.' In this essential phase of the sacred
> ministry, the power of the priest is not surpassed by that of the
> bishop, the archbishop, the cardinal or the pope. Indeed, it is equal
> to that of Jesus Christ. For in this role the priest speaks with the
> voice and authority of God Himself.
>
> "When the priest pronounces the tremendous words of conse-
> cration, he reaches up into the heavens, brings Christ down from
> his throne, and places Him upon our altar to be offered up again
> as the victim for the sins of man. It is a power greater than that of
> monarchs and emperors: it is greater than that of saints and angels,
> greater than that of Seraphim and Cherubim. Indeed, it is even
> greater than the power of the Virgin Mary: For, while the Blessed
> Virgin was the human agency by which Christ became incarnate

a single time, the priest brings Christ down from Heaven, and renders Him present on our altar as the eternal Victim for the sins of man—not once but a thousand times! The priest speaks and lo! Christ, the eternal and omnipotent God, bows His head in humble obedience to the priest's command."

It is this miraculous power, plus such powers as the right to forgive sins with the assurance that God will accede to the priest's judgment, that sets the priest apart from all other men, and in spite of all the rifts and protests, the church dedication to this role of the church and its priests has not diminished over the centuries. For example, in the attempts to bring the Church of England back into the Roman fold, compromises have been made, such as permitting a married Anglican priest who leaves his faith to become a priest of the Roman Church to keep his wife. On the other hand, in preparation for an Anglican conference to be held at Lambeth Palace in 1988 that would discuss, among other things, the union of the churches, the Vatican sent word in advance that the Roman teachings of transubstantiation must be accepted in their entirety and would in no way be the subject of compromise or negotiation.

In our contemplation of the religious attitudes of Freemasonry, of the possible birth of those attitudes among the suppressed Templars and their successors, and of a continuing supply of Masonic recruits in need of secrecy and protection in view of their religious convictions, it is the timing of these protests that interests us, not their validity. All of these protests, and more, were voiced by the priest John Wycliffe in the fourteenth century during the period just before and after the Peasants' Rebellion in England, as well as by the followers of the priest John Ball, who played a strong and direct role in that conflict.

The timing of the Templar suppression was right on target with the introduction of annates, or payments due to the Holy See for newly bestowed benefices, a form of tax passed on to the detriment of the parish priest. It coincided with the start of the Babylonish Captivity that saw the Holy See transferred from Rome to Avignon. It came at just the time that the papal court of Clement V exploded into a supermarket for the sale of indulgences.

It also came close to the time when the first great organized dissension against the church teaching was born in the followers of the teachings of Wycliffe, the Lollards, who were driven underground where they survived for centuries in what historians have called "secret cells" all over Britain, cells about which almost nothing is known. Their separate existence asks us to believe that there were two separate secret societies with cells, or lodges, all over Britain, both in opposition to the established church, both offering assistance and safe hiding for their members. Apparently it has not occurred to anyone that the two networks of secret cells may have been just one.

In any event, the suppression of the Templars came at a time of unrest and unhappiness in the lower clergy, at the beginning of the first great wave of English protest against the church, during the reign of a king whose rule generated so much dissension and disorganization that it bordered on anarchy. In all, an ideal time at which to form a secret society in which to hide from the vengeance, or even the knowledge, of the established church.

Nor was the suppression of the Templars the only event of the times to strike fear into opponents of the church. Those gentlest of men, the Spiritual Franciscan friars, felt the wrath of the Holy See at almost the same time. Saint Francis had taken the position that Christ and the apostles were poor men who had deliberately chosen lives of poverty as part of their lives of service. The early Franciscan lived on the food the faithful were willing to put into his bowl. The high churchmen were quite willing that the Franciscans live at a near-starvation level, but angrily resented the friars' suggestion that the clergy, the bishops, the cardinals, and even the pope himself should follow Christ's example and put away material things, the acquisition of which at that time was a high church preoccupation. The friars were told to abandon this stupid idea that Christ was poor, and most did. But a small group, who became known in Italy as the *Fratelli*, or Little Brothers, and to the rest of the world as the Spiritual Franciscans, refused to cast aside this basic teaching of their saintly founder. "If Christ walked," they asked, "why do bishops ride?" Their continual preaching embarrassed and angered the pope and his bishops, and in 1315 the Spiritual Franciscans were declared guilty of heresy and excommunicated. A number of them were burned alive in 1318, just four years after the burning of Jacques de Molay. These men were humble, dedicated religious, not warrior-monks.

If they could die for such a minor dissension, whose life was safe? Any honest disagreement with any teaching of the church was bound to be linked to honest fear.

There can be no other explanation for a secret organization in Britain that was supplied with new recruits generation after generation for four hundred years of total secrecy.

And yet, the origin of Masonry and the preservation of the order in centuries of religious difference may be thought to not solve all of the Masonic mysteries relating to religion, because of certain Masonic events after Freemasonry had come public.

The first of these was the drafting of a constitution for the Grand Lodge, which was first completed in 1723. It was largely the work of James Anderson, and in it Dr. Anderson said on the subject of the religion of Masons, "'Tis now thought more expedient only to oblige them to that Religion to which all men agree, leaving their particular opinions to themselves." Anti-Masons have stated that by this sentence Anderson had "de-Christianized" Masonry, as though before that date Masonry had been limited only to followers of Jesus Christ, of which there is no evidence. Quite to the contrary, there is an indication that the thought of a "Religion to which all men agree" did not originate with Dr. Anderson, who in any event could hardly have unilaterally imposed a personal religious belief upon the entire order.

Years earlier, Anthony Ashley Cooper, earl of Shaftesbury, had had an exchange with a lady at a social gathering. The earl said, "Men of sense are really of but one religion." "Pray, my lord, what religion is that which men of sense agree in?" "Madam," replied the earl, "men of sense never tell it." Lest this be shrugged off as yet another coincidence, it should be noted that Lord Shaftesbury, a leading deist of his day, was in all probability a Freemason himself. He was the patron of John Locke, who prepared a suggested constitution for Shaftesbury's proposed new colony of South Carolina. Locke suggested that each citizen of the new colony be required to publicly avow belief in a Supreme Being, with laws protecting each man from any interference in the manner in which he chose to worship that Supreme Being. In addition, no man would be permitted to sue another for money damages. Both of these are purely Masonic concepts. Shaftesbury died in 1683, forty years before Dr. Anderson recited Shaftesbury's stated religious belief in the Masonic constitution in 1723. The accusation that Freemasonry was deliberately de-Christianized in 1723 is patently false, but revealing in that it demands of Masonry that it become more like a religion, that it limit its membership to Christians only, to the exclusion of Jews, Moslems, and others, a move that in a secular fraternal society would strike a great blow for bigotry.

The last confusion of religion and Masonry is the injection of religious atmosphere and ceremony into the lodge room and on public display. The move out of the tavern and into the purpose-built lodge room saw the introduction of organ music and the composition of hymns to be sung by the brothers. There were Masonic funerals held in full Masonic regalia. Some of these took place in Protestant churches, where as the minister finished his service the Masons took over with their own rites. On the one hand, it might be said that these were generic services, showing that men of many creeds found common ground on which they could worship together. On the other hand, services conducted in a House of God in the presence of a congregation, complete with hymns and prayers, would justify any public perception that Masonry is a religious order. In recent years, Masons have been told to abandon the practice of public services in Masonic regalia, in order to tone down that religious image.

In summary, the religious requirements of Freemasonry are quite simple: a belief in a Supreme Being, and freedom from any interference with, or even persuasion against, the individual Mason's belief. Freemasonry can safely be asserted to *not* be a religion, on a simple basis. Religious creeds generally are believed by their adherents to be completely *right*. That means that they believe that all other creeds are, at least to some extent, wrong. The position of Masonry is the opposite, in that it acknowledges that there is some truth in all men's perception of God and declines to assert that any one belief is perfect.

As to criticisms of Masonry based on perceptions of its attitudes toward religion, they generally state that: (a) Freemasonry is a religion, (b) Freemasonry is not enough like a religion and should adopt the principles of the Christian creeds (depending upon the Christian principles embraced by the critic), or (c) the bloody oaths of Masonry are repugnant to God as well as to the law.

Testing the Templar hypothesis against the religious aspects of

Freemasonry, however, it was clear that nothing about the Masonic beliefs was contrary to the attitudes to be expected of a group that had been broken and cast aside by the Roman church, and that the Old Charges of Masonry clearly indicated a mutual protection society that not only permitted but provided shelter for those at odds with the established church. More specifically, while we had seen other group-destruction by the church on the continent in its domestic crusades against heresy, no group other than the Knights of the Temple had received that treatment from the church in Britain, and until after 1717 there is no evidence of Freemasonry anywhere other than in the British Isles.

That geographic isolation of Freemasonry over many generations was in itself a Masonic mystery supportive of the hypothesis of Templar origins because the Templars in Britain alone had been given the advantage of three months warning of their impending arrests, and Britain, with its unique attitudes toward the Church of Rome, had never permitted the Inquisition to set up shop on its side of the Channel.

There remained another mystery, and that was the significance of the period centered on the year 1717. Why had Freemasonry not declared itself fifty years earlier, or fifty years later? Conclusions that Templar-based Masonry had been kept alive by men at odds with the established Roman church needed that final test for validity. Something important had to have happened in the few years before 1717 that deprived Freemasonry of its need for secrecy, and perhaps even of its very purpose.

That important date would be addressed, but only after a deeper look into the most important ritual of Masonry, the allegory of the murdered Master.

CHAPTER 21

EVIDENCE IN THE LEGEND OF HIRAM ABIFF

In searching for answers in the allegory known as the legend of Hiram Abiff, it was necessary to bear in mind that in Secret Masonry the Master Mason was a master of men, not a master of an art or craft. The bulk of the Masonic order had been made up of Fellows, the full members, and of Entrants, those whose discretion and trustworthiness were not yet acceptable enough to merit their invitation to full membership. Most of those Entrants would have known only those brother Masons who were in their own cell, or lodge. The Masters were the masters of territory or of lodges, which required that they maintain communication with one another. This communication, and even the occasional secret general assembly, would have been absolutely necessary for the important matter of standardization—for arriving at common agreements as to hand and arm signals, passwords, and catechisms by means of which a brother Mason could seek help and by which members could identify one another with some sense of security. When it is even suspected in a secret society that security has been breached, those secret signs must be changed, with meetings held to make the change and then to spread the word. Also, in order to direct a brother on the run to the next lodge, it was obviously necessary that someone know the locations of those other lodges, at least on a regional basis. Thus, the Masters were at the same time the most important and the most dangerous members of the fraternity. Brothers whose acquaintances were limited to their own individual cells could betray no more than the membership of that single cell, whether in their cups or on the rack; but a Master could jeopardize the very existence of the society by revealing the names of other Masters, all of whom possessed much broader information, including the names and locations of still other Masters. That would be the reason why only the Master had need for a Grand Hailing Sign of Distress and a special call for help when in the dark, or just out of sight of assistance: "Oh, Lord my God, is there no help for a Son of the Widow?"

Every Master *was* the "widow's son." He was the continuation of the Master-line that had apparently been broken with the death of the first Grand Master, Hiram Abiff. In the initiation drama he had been assigned the role of Hiram Abiff, whose mantle, thus assumed, became the central feature of the candidate's role in the secret society. In that same role he would emulate Abiff, who had died rather than give up the secrets of the Master Mason. In that role he would thwart the effects of the attack by three assassins who had wanted those secrets badly enough to kill, not caring that the murder of Hiram Abiff meant an end to the building of the unfinished temple.

That continuation of the function of the Grand Master and temple architect, a kind of immortalization of a dream kept alive by those to come after him, was symbolized by the branch of acacia, a symbol of immortality much older than Christianity. To ancient peoples, the weather and the reactions of crops were the determinates of life and death, of good living or near starvation during the year ahead. The changes in seasons, too much or too little rain, and crop-killing frosts were much more understandable and more easily addressed in religious worship than were total mysteries such as molds, fungi, and animal diseases, which were usually ascribed to witchcraft or the evil eye. With no fresh food to look forward to and no means to preserve the food they had, the most dreaded season was winter, when the days grew shorter as the Power of Darkness each day gained ground over the Power of Light. As though to maximize their misery, every bush, tree, and plant died. All, that is, except the evergreen. It stayed bright and green and so had to be occupied by a spirit stronger than the Power of Darkness, preserving life until the sun could manage its inevitable, but temporary, victory. That strong spirit helped to bridge the gap from autumn to spring, preserving the thread of life. In some areas, an evergreen tree was cut down in order to bring the good spirit into the house, where the branches were draped with gifts, a tradition of the old natural religion which we still preserve at Christmastime. Thus the evergreen became a symbol of immortality, and one of those evergreens was the acacia.

The acacia would have been selected as the symbol of Hiram Abiff's "immortality" for very specific reasons. It was of acacia wood that God ordered that the Ark of the Covenant be made, the ark that was to be housed in the Sanctum Sanctorum of Solomon's temple, where the Grand Master made his plans for the next day's work. The acacia was also the host of a special breed of mistletoe with a flame-red flower. Not only was that mistletoe—which not only stayed green, but actually bore its fruit in the winter—a strong symbol of immortality in itself, but many believe that the acacia, covered with a blanket of fiery mistletoe blossoms, was the "burning bush" of the Old Testament. In addition, the Egyptian acacia bears a red and white flower, a reminder of the Templar colors, based upon a white mantle with red cross.

Hiram Abiff's immortality lies not in the eternal existence of his soul in some heavenly kingdom, but in the minds and bodies of those Masters who came after him, men charged to take his place and to finish what the mythical Grand Master had begun. Their duty was to make the plans and direct the "workmen," the Entrants and Fellows of the Craft, in achieving Abiff's goal, the completion of the Temple of Solomon.

All this has only the vaguest connection with the biblical account. According to scripture, Hiram was not an architect but a master worker in brass and bronze. He was not murdered but lived to see the temple completed and then went back to his home. The clues to Masonic origin and purpose are found in the allegorical legend, not in the scriptures.

As we search British history to find an unfinished temple as a basis for an exclusively British secret society, we find just one answer, in the religious order that often called itself by that simple name alone: the Temple. Jacques de Molay and his predecessors signed documents over the title *Magister Templi*, Master of the Temple. And *that* temple, taking its name from the Temple of Solomon, certainly was left unfinished upon the murder of its masters, who also had been tortured to reveal their secrets by three assassins who ultimately destroyed them. Not Jubela, Jubelo, and Jubelum, but Philip the Fair of France, Pope Clement V, and the order of the Knights of the Hospital of St. John of Jerusalem. Many who have read only the Catholic church's summations of the Templar suppression may object, stating that only the king of France could be considered the "assassin" of the Knights Templar, having done all of the dirty work and having coerced a weak pope to help him. True, that is the church's usual version to this very day, but the historical facts speak somewhat to the contrary, if we look again at events described earlier in this book.

When Edward II of England declined to torture the Templars, the pope could have thrown the problem back to Edward's father-in-law, the king of France: No one forced Clement V to dispatch ten church torture specialists to London. The pope could have lived with the acquittal of the Templars on Cyprus: No one forced him to demand a new trial, or to dispatch a torture team with the power to draw upon the local Dominicans and Franciscans if extra help was required. Nor did the king of France prevail in his desire that one of his family be made the head of a combined Hospitaller/Templar order, with full access to their combined wealth. And if Clement V had been merely a timorous puppet pope with Philip pulling the strings, as church historians would have us believe, the kings of France would have been the new owners of the Templar properties in France, not the Hospitallers. The pope was much tougher, or at least much more obstinate, than we have been led to believe and it would appear that he had contrived a plan of his own in concert with the Hospitallers.

That order has managed to escape any criticism in the matter of the Templar suppression, but apparently only because it had kept a low profile throughout, probably for the very good reason that its role and its rewards had been worked out in advance. It is well known that the papacy was in favor of a union of the Templars and Hospitallers and had already determined that Foulques de Villaret, master of the Hospitallers, would be the Grand Master of the combined orders. The Templars, at their headquarters on Cyprus, had heard of the serious intent to combine the orders and had taken the time to prepare a written rebuttal. The Hospitallers, at their own headquarters on that same island, must have received the same information, yet they prepared no rebuttal, written or verbal. In fact, de Villaret managed to stay away from the meeting in France altogether, with no recorded papal criticism for his absence. That was undoubtedly because his presence wasn't needed and because there was no point in chancing a confrontation between the two orders, especially since the pope was already dedicated to looking after the interests of the Hospitallers. Not only did the Hospitallers offer no objection to the concept of the merger, but they made no attempt whatever to speak up for their brother warrior-monks as they were arrested and tortured. They simply stayed out of it and bided their time, until Clement V, much to the anger of King Philip, declared that all of the confiscated Templar property would go to the Knights Hospitaller and that all released Templars could be taken into the Hospitaller order, thereby achieving *de facto* the union he had been planning all along, with full Hospitaller approval and cooperation. If one looks for motive, the Hospitaller order was the major beneficiary of the suppression of the Templars, as had probably been planned from the beginning. The pope and the Hospitallers together thwarted the aims of Philip of France, and there should be no doubt that the Hospitallers rank as one of the three assassins of the Order of the Temple.

An interesting point about the legend of Hiram Abiff is that in it, the three assassins have already been punished, have been "brought to the Jubé." Certainly there were wars with France before and after the Templar suppression, and it becomes increasingly probable that the punishments meted out to the Hospitallers during the Peasants' Rebellion, including the murder of their prior, were acts of vengeance carried out under the cover of a political disturbance. As for punishment of the Holy See, the Templar-spawned underground movement was probably the most effective enemy the church had in the British Isles before, during, and after the Reformation. Over five hundred years after the Templar suppression, popes were still condemning Freemasonry for welcoming members of all religious faiths and for failing to acknowledge Roman Catholicism as the one true church. In

Secret Masonry, religious dissenters and protesters had an organization that would help them, hide them, and provide communication with others of their kind, and as the years went by, conflicts between popes and kings, between popes and the people, and between popes and their own priests provided a river of recruits for a secret society that permitted them to worship God in their own ways. All three assassins of the Order of the Temple had reason to regret their actions against the bearded knights.

A major mystery of the Legend of Hiram Abiff is the identity of "that which was lost." Some Masonic historians take the allegory literally, almost always a mistake, and state that what was lost was the "word" of the Grand Master, or the "secrets" of the Master. What the Templars had lost, literally, was their wealth, respect, and power. What the allegory suggests was lost was the architect, the planner who was needed to finish the temple and provide the leadership to move forward. The man being initiated as a Master by acting out the murder is being turned into another Hiram. Every Master takes that role, and *becomes* Hiram (a name by which Masons sometimes address each other). He *is* the "son of the widow," and it is *his* task to replace that which was lost: the leadership, the direction, the work required to "finish" the building of the (Order of the) Temple, which was brutally stopped by beatings and murder. Now, of course, that leadership, that elevation to the role of one of the supreme leaders of the society, has been changed. Every Mason has the opportunity to become a Master, and the initiate may be somewhat confused that what appears to him to be just another degree on his ladder of progress in Masonry should be so emphatic about the means of seeking and providing help, and so emphatic about the need to guard his brother Master Masons' secrets.

In summary, the legend of Hiram Abiff tells us that it is not a coincidence that two organizations found their central identification in the Temple of Solomon, because one group gave birth to the other. It explains the purpose of the successor group, the Freemasons, by recounting, allegorically, the fate of the prior group, the Order of the Temple. The temple was left unfinished because of the murder of the Grand Master. The man being exposed to this legend in his initiation takes the role of the Grand Master and then assumes his task, the completion of the Temple. In this sense, the Freemason is neither an "operative" mason with tools in his hands nor a "speculative" mason who joins a guild of masons as a nonworking member. Rather, he is a *symbolic* mason, whose building task is not connected to any actual building but is concerned only with the survival and growth of the symbolic temple, the Order of the Poor Fellow-Soldiers of Christ and the Temple of Solomon: the Knights Templar.

As the true origins of Masonry were obscured by time and then lost altogether, the Freemasons were left with the allegory only, and they created a fantasy world by accepting that allegory as factual. One Masonic writer was awestruck that Masonry had preserved for over two thousand years these details of the building of the Temple of Solomon which had escaped the authors of the Old Testament. The legend of Hiram Abiff was taught not as legend but as a recitation of historical fact.

Along with the acceptance of Hiram Abiff as a real person, Freemasonry for generations taught that the order had been founded among the workmen who built the Temple of Solomon. That building became a focal point for Masonic reverence and respect. Artists' renderings of Solomon's temple came to decorate the walls of Masonic temples, and some Masons made pilgrimages to the site. Some managed to bring back to their lodges a piece of stone from the Temple Mount or from nearby quarries, relics that were displayed proudly with all of the aura of religious relics. Even today, long after Masonry shifted its claims of origin from the construction of the temple to the medieval guilds of stonemasons, there are Masons firmly convinced that their order began in the building of that temple.

Finally more sober minds did prevail, and Masonry did come to acknowledge that the story of Hiram Abiff was not factual but was an important piece of Masonic mythology. Its acceptance as fact had caused the whole fraternity to bend in the direction of the building trades and had led them to identify every common stonemason's tool as a Masonic symbol, to identify the Supreme Being as the Great Architect of the Universe, to teach that Masons had built the great Gothic cathedrals, and to include details of architecture and building in the Masonic rituals.

Now that the story of Hiram Abiff has been recognized as legend, not fact, all of the building-trade symbolism generated by the literal acceptance of the story remains, and that symbolism serves to confuse origins and purposes because it has become imbued with a reality and antiquity it does not have. In the absence of written records, centuries of time played their inevitable role of obscuring beginnings and purposes, and the rush to embrace the building trades built a screen few cared to look behind. The symbolism born of allegory was accepted as factual.

The mystery is simply this: If the story of Hiram Abiff and the Masonic role in the building of Solomon's temple are acknowledged as myths, how did that temple become central to Masonic ritual and legend? Certainly medieval stonemasons provide no answer to that question, and as the medieval guild theory itself falls away, there appears to be no answer to that mystery ... except one. The temple that is so honored and revered by Freemasonry is not a building but is the only other order that ever identified itself with that building; the Knights of the Temple.

CHAPTER 22

MONKS INTO MASONS

We have seen that there are only two organizations that have found their principal identifications in the Temple of Solomon: Freemasonry and the Crusading Order of the Temple. The great mass of circumstantial evidence has clearly indicated that the common identification was no mere coincidence, but rather that the secret organization was born in the ashes of the public organization that had been condemned by both the church and state in an era of the most brutal bodily punishments. The only way the hunted Templars could continue to stay in contact with each other and help each other was in the darkest secrecy. That state of secrecy required no great adaptation for Templars, to whom secrecy was part of their vows and of their Rule. Every Templar was subject to swift punishment if he revealed any portion of the Rule of the order, or any part of the proceedings of their chapter meetings, which were kept secret by means of guards stationed outside the meeting room, their swords at the ready.

Fortunately, the circumstances of the time, as outlined earlier, were in their favor. Three months before their mass arrests in France at dawn on Friday, the thirteenth of October, 1307, the throne of England had passed to its weakest and most pitiable king, Edward II. The result of that monarch's weakness, confusion, and procrastination had been to provide the condemned Templars in England with a three-month warning period during which to make plans. When their arrests finally did go forward in January 1308, the king was off to France to get married, having left his homosexual lover behind as regent. And at the same time that the English Edward II was setting his kingdom on the pathway to effective anarchy, Robert Bruce in Scotland was pulling his people together, preparing to take the state of war between England and Scotland from a stalemate to the ultimate Scottish victory at Bannock Burn. He would welcome any fighting man in flight from the English dominions in Britain or on the continent. Having ignored the papal directive to arrest the Templars in Scotland, he had made that country a haven for Templars on the run.

As for the English people at that time, they had seen the French enemy handpick a pope and had watched the shift of the Holy See from Rome to Avignon. Thus the Templar suppression had coincided with the Babylonish Captivity of the papacy, a situation that aroused and maintained the suspicions and concerns of the English populace. They had no incentive to help the pope, who appeared to be acting as a tool of their national enemy Philip of France, in his quest to find and torture the military monks he had condemned. Had the matter of the Templars been put to rest quickly, the fugitive monks and their comrades might simply have helped one another in a cursory fashion, based on the hasty needs of the occasion as they arose. The suppression dragged on, however—Grand Master de Molay was burned almost seven years after the initial arrests in France—and this delay gave the loose threads of contact among the fugitives time to mature into strong bonds of brotherhood. The formal organization that developed provided a base from which to establish a permanent institution, fed by a ceaseless flow of dissenters and protesters against the church.

Although claims have been made that the Masonic secret society originated in the builders of Solomon's temple or medieval guilds of stonemasons in Britain, along with other suggestions even more fanciful, no beginning other than the Knights Templar provides such clear explanations of the lost meanings of the Masonic symbols of the circle and the mosaic on the lodge room floor, or the lambskin apron and gloves that comprise the "clothing" of Masonry. The compass and square appear allegorically as the unfinished Seal of Solomon, directly symbolizing the unfinished temple. The compass and square hidden in the Seal of Solomon provide a graphic link impossible to ignore, a link between the major badge of Freemasonry and the interruption of the building of Solomon's temple in the legend of Hiram Abiff, as symbolized by the "unfinished" Seal of Solomon.

That legend, which is the central feature of Masonic ritual, adds credence to the Templar origin, especially since it is based upon an allegorical temple whose construction was halted because of the beating and murder of Grand Master Hiram Abiff. We know that the real Temple of Solomon was fully completed and in use for several centuries. The Temple of Solomon that was *not* completed can only be the Order of the Poor Fellow-Soldiers of Christ and the Temple of Solomon, the Knights Templar. The dead master is replaced by the initiate who is raised to the degree of Master Mason. He not only "becomes" Hiram Abiff in the ritual drama, but also assumes the Grand Master's interrupted objective, the completion of the temple, by keeping the secret society alive and growing, symbolically rescuing the Order of the Temple from the cessation ordered for it by king and pope.

The legend also gives the Grand Master the title of Master Builder, and the allegory of the construction of the temple provided the basis for the eventual cover story of the secret society as a society of stonemasons. These were *symbolic* masons, completing in secret a symbolic temple that the world believed had been destroyed. That cover story was used as additional cover to preserve the Old Charges and Landmarks of Masonry as though they were the rules for the conduct of a medieval guild of masons. The rules of the ancient guilds are well known and they bear little relationship to the Old Charges of Masonry, which are clearly structured to support a secret society of mutual protection. No guild required that one protect the secrets of a brother that might cost him his life or property if discovered, nor with a locally chartered guild was there ever any call to provide "employment," lodging, and pocket money for brothers from other local guilds passing through.

That risk of life and property was not a loose, undefined fear, but a very specific punishment set by the church. The papal Council of Toulouse in 1229 had decreed that any man who harbored a heretic was to lose his property and be punished; any

house where a heretic was found was to be demolished and the
land under it to be confiscated by the church; and finally, heretics
and their protectors were to be sentenced to death. It is clear,
then, that the secret of a brother that could cause the loss of his
life and property was that he was guilty of heresy, a charge that
was never leveled against any craftsmen's guild. The ancient
guilds were almost militantly religious, and all clung overtly to the
established Roman Catholic church. None could have had, or
would have wanted, a code of religious toleration that provided
full brotherhood to those whose opinions were in any way at odds
with the teachings of the church.

Any excommunicated individual would have had a problem in
his personal relationship with God once his connection to the
Church had been severed, but he would have had to work out the
problem only to fit his personal needs. The Templars, however,
were cut off by the church as a group. It was unlikely that a common ground of dissent or protest would be arrived at quickly, but
the need for a belief in God *was* immediately necessary to give
substance to mutual oaths of secrecy and support. Their first concern would have been saving lives, not souls, and a solution to the
immediate need for binding oaths was found in the insistence
upon an avowed belief in God, without any requirements as to
the individual's mode of worship or his attitudes toward the established church. Surrounded as they were by massive evidence of
the capacity of religious differences to drive men to blood lust,
the fugitives desperately needed to negate religious differences in
order to hold their group tightly together. The answer lay in banning all religious arguments, or even discussions, as each man's
own beliefs were accorded full respect by his brothers.

Today the Masonic creed says that admission is available to
men of all religious faiths, but that would not have been the original concept in the fourteenth century, a period shortly after all
the Jews had been driven from Britain by Edward I but before the
advent of clearly identifiable Protestant sects. There was only one
religious faith, the Roman Catholic, so the religious differences
could only have been those of varying protests against teachings
of the church, dissent from its scriptural interpretations and "rea-
sonings," and rejection of the life-styles and materialism of the
church hierarchy. The Templar rejection by the church, accompanied as it was by the sort of ferociously brutal punishments that

engender hatred and a desire for revenge, provided a very clear foundation for a secret society with that religious philosophy, which cannot be approached by any other event or organization in British history. Adding weight to this conclusion is the fact that the Crusading Templars were among the few groups in Europe that had actually experienced and encouraged religious tolerance. The Great Mosque at Acre had been converted into a Christian cathedral but had provided an area for Moslem worshipers as well. On the other side of the city, the mosque by Oxen's Well was maintained for Moslems but provided a place of worship for Christian visitors. One is hard pressed to even fantasize a medieval Christian church in Europe that would have permitted Jewish services on its premises or have allowed a synagogue to have a crucifix. In that time and place, the very thought of tolerance was intolerable, and illegal.

Finally, the discovery of the lost meanings of Masonic terms in medieval French gives vital support to the hypothesis of the birth of Masonry in the French-speaking Knights Templar, and provides a matching time frame. There remained no reasonable doubt that Freemasonry had originated in the plight and the flight of the Knights of the Temple, an organization uniquely equipped to form a secret society quickly, since so much of their own order had functioned in secrecy with codes, passwords, and its own spy system.

It may seem that there is a great leap from the Templar suppression in 1307 to the public revelation of Freemasonry in 1717 with no evidence of any Masonic existence within that four-hundred-year span, but that is not true. Evidence does exist, but since no historian even suspected a Masonic connection, much of that evidence has been passed over with no connection made. Consider again the Peasants' Rebellion of 1381, with its hints of Masonry and its Templar-related mysteries, such as the concentration of the vicious attacks on the property of the Hospitallers; the incredibly easy seizure of the Tower of London for no known purpose but the murders of the archbishop of Canterbury and the prior of the Hospitaller order; the special protection of the central Templar church as the rebels burned down all of the buildings around it. Then there is the haunting evidence of rebel leaders who confessed to being members of a Great Society which no historian has even attempted to define. Once the origin of Masonry in the fugitive Templars' secret society is accepted, it is easy to conclude that the Great Society that set Walter to direct the rebellion, and called him "the Tyler," was the direct descendant of the Templar fugitives and the predecessor of the secret society of Freemasonry.

That precise time period also provided the bridge to the next evidence of Masonic existence, in the rebel priests and others who were influenced by the protests against the church and its hierarchy by the English priest John Wycliffe. Followers of the Wycliffe doctrines of dissent and protest formed what historians say was a separate secret society known by outsiders as the *Lollards*, or "mumblers" (as some were seen mumbling prayers as they walked along). Archbishop Courtenay, who became the leading churchman in England as successor to the archbishop whose head had been lopped off by Wat Tyler, identified the existence of the Lollard group in the spring of 1382, less than a year after the Peasants' Rebellion. He drove them out of Oxford and attempted to crush the entire movement. Lollardy, however, survived his efforts, and those of other civil and church leaders, for the next two centuries by the expedient of going underground. The Lollards conducted business in "conventicles," or secret meetings, in a network of cells throughout the country, and they somehow gained the support of certain members of the aristocracy, especially the knightly class. No historian seems able to tell us much about these cells beyond the fact that they did exist, that the movement stayed alive until well into the Protestant Reformation (to which it contributed much), and that the Lollards did erupt into overt action on several occasions over the years, most dramatically in the revolt led by Sir John Oldcastle in 1414. It does not appear to be reasonable that two secret societies existed side by side in all of those relatively small towns in Britain with no relationship between them, especially when each had as a central theme the provision of "lodging" to hide brothers from the wrath of the state religion. It must be considered quite likely that there was just one such far-flung secret society in Britain, and that the secret Lollard cells of early Protestants and the secret society that evolved into Freemasonry were largely one and the same, or at least closely related. If so, Secret Masonry had a major role in the Protestant Reformation in Britain with which it has never been credited.

If the concept that Masonic lodges were actually based on Lollard cells seems too wildly speculative, one might consider certain Lollard activities in and around Leicester, as chronicled by Henry Knighton, a canon of Saint Mary's Abbey in that city. The following is a series of direct quotations from those chronicles, extracted for the sake of brevity. The italics have been added.

"William Smith, so called from his trade . . . renounced all pleasure as . . . he taught the alphabet and did clerking. Various knights used to go round protecting him from any harm for his profane teaching, for they had zeal for God but were uninstructed, for they believed what they heard from the false prophets. . . . They would attend the sermon with sword and buckler to stop any objections to the blasphemy.

"One Richard Waytestathe, priest, and this William Smith, used to have spells at *St. John Baptist's chapel* outside Leicester near the leper hospital. Here other sectaries *met for their conventicles* [secret meetings] . . . for here was a *hostelry and lodging* for that kind of visitor and there they had a school of malignant doctrines and opinions and a clearing-house of heresy. The chapel had been dedicated to God, but it was now an asylum for blasphemers who hated Christ's church.

"There was at Leicester a priest called William de Swynderby who the people called a hermit because he once lived as such. . . . He joined up with William Smith at *St. John Baptist's* by the leper hospital and associated there with other Wyckliffes . . . he levelled [his sermons] against the clergy saying they were bad, and, as the rest of the sect, said parishioners need not pay tithes to the impure, to non-residents, or those prevented from teaching and preaching by ignorance or inaudibility, for the other Wyckliffes said tithes were a voluntary gift and payment to evil-livers was connivance. He also preached that *men might ask for payment of debt but not sue or imprison for it,* that excommunication for nonpayment of tithes was extortion and that one who lived contrary to God's law was no priest, though ordained.

"John Bukkyngham, Bishop of Lincoln, had wind of this and promptly suspended him from all preaching in chapel, church or graveyard, excommunicating any who would listen to him and sending notice of this to various churches. . . . The bishop summoned him to appear in Lincoln Cathedral. . . . There he was publicly convicted of heresies and errors and richly deserved to be food for fire.

"That day the pious Duke of Lancaster *happened to be at Lincoln* and he often protected the Lollards, for their smooth tongues and faces tricked him and others into thinking them saints of God. *He persuaded the Bishop to give William a different sentence....*"

And so once again we are faced with a battery of what some may choose to label coincidences, but which might just as easily be termed items of circumstantial evidence. A group of protesters against the church and its clergy was based on a chapel named for St. John the Baptist, a patron saint of Freemasonry. They held secret meetings. They preached against the use of lawsuits for payment of debt, a basic Masonic precept. They provided "lodging" to itinerant travelers who shared their point of view. They were protected by local knights. When one of their number was condemned to be burned alive for heresy, a royal duke just "happened" to be on hand to persuade, or coerce, the bishop of Lincoln to reduce the sentence. Taken all together, it would appear that a Masonic "lodge" was active at Leicester toward the end of the fourteenth century.

For more possible circumstantial evidence we can leap all the way to the seventeenth century, to an event that occurred generations after Lollardy is believed to have totally disappeared, although what happened seems strangely related to the happenings at Leicester.

In her authoritative history of a portion of the reign of Charles I entitled *The King's Peace, 1637–1641,* C. V. Wedgwood had included this interesting anecdote: It seems that William Laud, Anglican archbishop of Canterbury, had become concerned about reports of the increasing number of secret meetings—"conventicles"—throughout the kingdom during the prior year. Finally his patience ran out with the arrest of a man named Trendall who was in London, far from his home, preaching against the hierarchy of the church. The archbishop determined to burn Trendall at the stake, as an example to others, but it had been a generation since a heretic had been burned in England. Laud wrote to the elderly archbishop of York for details on how to stage the ceremonial execution, but it never took place. Somehow Mr. Trendall escaped his fate. All that seems to be known of him was that he was said to have been a *stonemason* from Dover.

We have seen John Locke incorporate Masonic charges in the

constitution he wrote for the proposed colony of South Carolina over half a century before Freemasonry came public, including a prohibition against lawsuits for money damages. (It may be no more than another of the dozens of coincidences we have had to contend with, but South Carolina became a bastion of Freemasonry in the United States, which it still is. The city of Charleston was the port of entry for what became Scottish Rite Masonry when it was introduced from France.)

Going back behind Locke and Laud to a period over a century before Freemasonry was revealed, we find ample Masonic evidence in the writings of Sir Francis Bacon, a scientist, philosopher, and politician at the courts of Elizabeth I and James I. His essays never disagree with Masonic principles, nor with the Masonic attitudes toward science and religion. In keeping with the Mason's admonition to correct a brother's errant ways firmly but in friendship, and yet always speak well of a brother and enhance his reputation, Bacon wrote: "And certain it is, that the Light that a man receiveth by counsel from another, is drier and purer than that which cometh from his own understanding and judgment . . . the best preservative to keep the mind in health is the faithful admonition of a friend." And, "A man can scarce allege his own merits with modesty, much less extol them; a man cannot brook to supplicate or beg. . . . But all these things are graceful in a friend's mouth, which are blushing in a man's own."

Much, much more to the point, Bacon wrote a piece called "The New Atlantis," which was published in 1627, the year after his death. The work contains Bacon's concept of Utopia, an unknown island guided by a learned society, told from the view of a shipwrecked gentleman. He has one of the officials explain: "'We of this island of Bensalem,' (for so they call it in their language) 'have this; that by means of our solitary situation; and of the laws of secrecy, which we have for our travelers, and our rare admission of strangers; we know well most parts of the habitable world, and are ourselves unknown.'"

Bacon then prophesies the "Invisible College" of scientific Masons who founded the Royal Society, and whose first "known" meeting took place in 1645, although this story suggests that it may have been before that. In recounting the history of the secret island, the official tells of a great and ancient king who had provided wise laws for his people: "'Ye shall understand (my dear friends) that amongst the excellent acts of that king, one above all hath pre-eminence. It was the erection and institution of an Order or Society, which we call *Salomon's House*; the noblest foundation (as we think) that ever was upon the earth; and the lanthorn of this kingdom. It is dedicated to the study of the works and creatures of God. Some think the founder's name to be a little corrupted. . . . But the records write it as it is spoken. So I take it to be a denominate of the king of the Hebrews, which is famous to you, and no stranger to us.'"

It is further explained that every twelve years (reminding us of the twelve Fellows that Solomon sent, in parties of three, to search for Hiram Abiff) two ships sail out into the world in search of learning: "'That in either of these ships there should be a mission of three of the Fellows or Brethren of Salomon's House whose errand was only to give us knowledge of the affairs and state of those countries to which they were designed, and especially of the sciences, arts, manufactures and inventions of all the world; and withal to bring us books, instruments and patterns in every kind. . . . '"

Then Bacon puts it all squarely into a Masonic summary: "'But thus you see we maintain a trade not for gold, silver or jewels; nor for silks; nor for spices; nor of any other commodity of matter; but only for God's first creature, which was Light.'"

As a sidelight on religion in the mystic kingdom, Bacon cites that Jews live on the island, that they are free to practice their religion without being forced to convert, and that they in return "give unto our Savior many high attributes." He learns of this from a Jewish merchant named Joabin, whose name Bacon seems to have concocted from *Jachin* and *Boaz*, the names of the pillars that flanked the entrance to Solomon's Temple, names that also have been applied to secret Masonic handgrips. All of which leads to the firm conclusion that Freemasonry was there, mingling with the likes of Drake, Hawkins, and Raleigh at the court of Elizabeth I, and thwarting, both secretly and publicly, the Catholic ambitions of the Jesuits and of Philip of Spain to return England to the authority of the Roman church.

Many more clues to the existence and activities of Secret Masonry will surely surface, if only a few students of British history can be encouraged to have one mental band tuned to the wavelength of the Masonic connection.

Of course, in contrast to the almost total lack of recognized historical documentation of Secret Masonic existence, those familiar with Masonic history know that there were frequent claims, after Masonry came public, of a Templar connection with Freemasonry. We have seen one of them in the short-lived "Strict Observance" Masonry, which claimed that fugitive Templars had traveled to Scotland, where they teamed up with a guild of stonemasons. Another claim, which also arose in France, was that while in prison Jacques de Molay had signed a document naming one Johannes Marcus Larmenius his successor as grand master of the Templars, and that since that date there had been a secret unbroken succession of grand masters. This was all set forth in a document called *The Charter of Transmission of Larmenius,* now proven to have been a blatant forgery. It is currently housed in the Mark Masons' Hall in London. Others saw the Templar connection to Masonry in Ramsay's Oration, although Ramsay never mentioned the Templars by name. Some Masons rejected the assertions of a Templar connection as a Jesuit plot to injure Freemasonry, because at the time the Templars were believed to have been guilty of all of the charges of arrogance, subversion, and heresy that had been heaped upon them. That belief in Templar guilt stayed alive and was dramatized when Freemason Sir Walter Scott made the Knights of the Temple—and especially their English master—the sinister villains of his popular novel *Ivanhoe,* and cast the Templar grand master in the Holy Land as a completely evil man in *The Talisman.* It remained for later historians, studying the trials of the Templars, to determine that they had not been enemies of the church but rather its victims.

Somehow the ancient relationship of the Templars and Freemasons had been kept alive as a concept, but with no documentable proof. The response of some of those convinced of the concept was to try to create proof, and as those proofs were proven false the Templar connection lost all credibility. One theory proposed, for example, was that the Templars had deliberately chosen the al-Aqsa Mosque as their headquarters because it was on the site of the Temple of Solomon, and that in their secret meetings the Templars were keeping alive the order of Freemasonry, which had been founded in the building of that temple. When it became clear that Masonry had no connection whatsoever with the construction of the actual Temple of Solomon, the

Templar connection, too, was exposed as a spurious claim. Over time, the attempts to link Masonry with the Knights of the Temple by fantasy and forgery seemed to kill off any chance of discovering the true source of Masonic origins and directed Masonic researchers to ever more far-fetched allegations of origins in the *Steinmetzen* (stonemasons) of Germany, the Culdees, the Essenes, and the Druids, for none of which does the tiniest wisp of evidence exist.

Out of the explosion of French Masonry following Ramsay's Oration did evolve the "Masonic Orders of Chivalry," including a series of side degrees in Masonic orders of the Knights of Malta and the Knights of the Temple. The original order of the Knights of Malta, its name changed from the earlier Hospitallers of St. John, still exists today, recognized by the Vatican as a sovereign state and headquartered in Rome in a palace conveyed to the order as a part of the property confiscated from the Templars. Apparently Ramsay's contention that the Masonic Crusaders had effected an alliance with the Knights of Malta was taken as justification for creating a new Order of Malta as a part of Freemasonry. As for the Masonic Knights Templar, they first appeared in Germany, then spread to France and, with variations, were established in the United States before 1770 and in Great Britain by 1778. None of those orders were based on the true origin of Masonry in the flight of the Templars from the clutches of Pope Clement V. Although the Masonic Templar orders do teach the story of the Templar suppression and have "degrees of vengeance" centered on revenge for the death of Jacques de Molay, our research has indicated that a Freemason is actually closest to "being" a Knight of the Temple when he is raised to the degree of Master Mason in the ritual based on real events—even though remembered only allegorically—rather than in an order made up long after the fact and containing no knowledge or recognition of the true bond between Templarism and the birth of the Masonic order. It is an interesting point that the appeal to membership in the Masonic Orders of Chivalry is that the initiate is made a knight. Actually, whether admission was sought to either of the original orders of the Knights of the Temple or the Knights of Malta (Hospitallers), an unyielding requirement was that the candidate already be of the knightly class. What his membership did was not to make a man a knight, but to make a knight a monk, a transformation that would not appeal to the bulk of today's fraternal members. Furthermore, we have not dwelt on the side degrees beyond the basic "Blue Lodge" of Craft Masonry because they do not relate to any of the mysteries of pre-1717 Secret Masonry; nor, as "made up" societies, do they have any unsolved mysteries of their own, nor any direct connections with either ancient Secret Masonry or the original Knights of the Temple. Those connections stop with the three basic degrees of Craft Masonry.

As to that basic Craft Masonry, how might it be affected by the discovery that it evolved from a protective society of fugitive Templars, and not from medieval guilds of stonemasons? Should present workings be abandoned? Of course not. The stonemason cover story is an important part of Masonic tradition. Back in the days when Christianity had to function as a secret society, it adopted a cover story of being "fishermen." The preservation of that cover in symbolism and song, even in church decoration, enriches the fabric of religious tradition, as does the allegorical presentation of the church as shepherd to a flock, as Christ said, "Feed my sheep." All traditional symbolism and ritual should remain intact, although acceptance of the findings in this book would require changes in aspects of the Masonic lectures. Those changes would amplify and enrich the traditions of the order and might even enhance membership by being able to cite origins that are at the same time more sensible and more exciting than those recited to new members today. Secrets that save a man's life are much more to be respected than secrets of a trade, and a secret recognition signal is more dramatic when used to identify a blood brother than to validate a fellow chisel owner. The Old Charges, too, move from behind the cover story to be exposed as the basic rules for a brotherhood based on the preservation of life itself. Nothing about Templar origins detracts from Masonry. In fact, much is added, especially in the areas of understanding about Masonry's birth, its purposes, and the fabric of religious freedom that was important enough in its time that men would risk their lives and liberty for centuries on end under the shelter of the common goals that forge true brotherhood. They placed their lives in each others' hands with vows of security, secrecy, and support. And it might not hurt to remind the brotherhood that the world is not yet in such a state that we can assume that freedom of religion is universally accepted and so need not be maintained as a central purpose of the order, as it was in the days of Secret Masonry. As far as that basic principle is concerned, the unfinished Temple of Solomon is still unfinished.

CHAPTER 23

THE PROTESTANT PENDULUM

In reviewing with Freemasons and others the conclusion that the central purpose of Secret Masonry had been the protection of its members from discovery and punishment by the established Church, several asked how that objective could have held Secret Masonry together for the two centuries after Henry VIII took England away from the supremacy of the Roman church, a period during which such secret protection was no longer necessary. Why would Masons need to wait two hundred years, until 1717, to make themselves known? It turned out to be a common perception, at least in the United States, that England had stopped being Catholic during the reign of Henry VIII and had become irrevocably Protestant, as though by the throwing of a switch. A brief look at the religious climate in Britain from the first break with Rome to 1717 should make clear the answer to the important question of the timing of Freemasonry's abandonment of total secrecy.

On August 22, 1485, King Richard III of England lost his throne, and his life, at the Battle of Bosworth. The victor was Henry Tudor, the Welsh earl of Richmond, who ascended the throne as King Henry VII. He had to solidify his position not only at home, as the new king, but among the nations of Europe as well, as the founder of a new dynasty. His first effective move at home was to marry Elizabeth of York, the heiress to his greatest rivals at home. Looking to the continent for alliances, he was eager to make a strong affiliation with the new Spanish power that had been created by the marriage of King Ferdinand of Aragon to Queen Isabella of Castile, who together were acquiring more territory by pushing back the Moors in Spain. He was delighted to arrange the betrothal of his eldest son, Prince Arthur, to the Princess Catherine of Aragon, daughter of Ferdinand and Isabella. His younger son Henry was trained for service in the Church, which was tantamount to an alliance with Rome. His daughter Margaret was married to King James IV of Scotland. His daughter Mary was betrothed to the much older king of France, who died just months after their marriage. She then married the duke of Suffolk, a union that produced the tragic Lady Jane Grey.

Henry Tudor's major European alliance appeared to shatter upon the death of Prince Arthur, who died of tuberculosis in 1502. The second son, Henry, was now heir to the throne, but he could not maintain the alliance with Ferdinand and Isabella by marriage to his brother's widow because the church held that marriage to an in-law was as much incest as marriage to a near blood relative. The answer was for Henry VII and Ferdinand to join forces to get a papal dispensation setting aside that church policy, and they were successful. The English throne went to the eighteen-year-old Henry VIII in 1509, and within six weeks he married the widowed Catherine of Aragon with the blessings of the Holy See.

The firm establishment of the Tudor dynasty was just as much a preoccupation for him as it had been for his father, but Henry VIII and his queen just did not seem capable of producing a healthy male heir. In eighteen years of marriage the queen experienced a series of stillbirths and miscarriages. Just one son had survived the pangs of birth, in 1511, only to die a month and a half later. Then in 1516 a daughter was born and survived and appeared healthy, living on as the Princess Mary. Finally Henry conveniently convinced himself, and tried to persuade others, that God was denying him a male heir as a punishment for the grievous sin of marrying his brother's widow. His solution was to petition Pope Clement VII to rescind the earlier papal dispensation that had permitted the marriage outside the rules of the church, an act that would set aside his unproductive long-term marriage to Catherine of Aragon. It would also render the birth of the Princess Mary illegitimate.

Henry might have had his way, but his timing was bad. The emperor Charles V had invaded Italy and was in Rome with an army. He was not about to let the pope cancel out the legal marital status of the queen of England, who was his aunt. The argument raged for five years, during which time Henry VIII determined to and did marry Anne Boleyn, the mother of the future Queen Elizabeth I.

The failure of Cardinal Thomas Wolsey, Henry's lord chancellor, to arrange the rescission of the papal dispensation brought about his downfall, to the great satisfaction of many at the English court. Wolsey's power had been great and his greed was legendary. Over a thousand servants catered to his needs at a number of palaces, including the magnificent Hampton Court Palace, which he had built for himself with both church and state revenues. He had enriched his illegitimate son with church benefices that brought that fortunate young man an incredible income of over twenty-seven hundred pounds a year, more than enough to arouse the envy and the enmity of barons and earls. And then there was the question of land: The church never seemed to be able to get enough of it, and seldom parted with any, even by sale. It was given land, it purchased land, and it seized land as fines and punishments. That land remained largely untaxed, and much of its revenues went to Rome or to absentee holders of English benefices.

The point is that Henry alone could not have broken with Rome, but in the atmosphere surrounding the church in England he had support at every level of society. Nor did Henry VIII have in mind a Protestant church when he broke with Rome. He considered himself a very devout Catholic in all but papal supremacy. He was proud to have been awarded the title Defender of the Faith by Pope Leo X as a reward for his scholarly treatise *In Defense of the Seven Sacraments*, a work that categorically exposed and condemned the heresies of the Augustianian monk Martin Luther. He reinforced support for burning at the stake as the proper punishment for disavowal of the doctrine of transubstantiation. What Henry wanted was an English ("Anglican") Catholic church administered by the ruler of England, rather than a Roman Catholic church administered by a foreign pope.

Protesters and dissenters from the Catholic doctrine in England had every bit as much to fear from Henry VIII as they did from Clement VII. The pope declared that the subjects of Henry VIII would no longer enjoy papal protection from enslavement by their fellow Christians, and that any conqueror of the English was now free to sell them in the slave markets. Henry did permit the publication and distribution of the Bible in English, but came to regret it. He later tried to limit its use to privileged classes, but it was too late: Another generation had tasted the fruit of the Tree of Knowledge, and wanted more.

And then there was all that land. The courtiers around Henry VIII never tired of reminding him how many supportive knights, barons, and earls could be maintained by a redistribution of that almost unfathomable wealth, over a third of the land surface of the whole country. Then, too, they pointed out that every monastic center could be depended upon to plot and subvert to return England to the supremacy of Rome. The religious communities had little to offer in rebuttal, since generations of idle "country club" living with armies of serfs, villeins, and servants had made many indolent and often blatantly immoral. In 1536 and 1539 the monasteries were dissolved. The king did not keep all of the lands for the crown but sold major holdings at bargain rates to his followers, thus locking in their determination to keep England separate from Rome. The profit taking produced a great anti-Roman euphoria in the largest transfer of land titles since William the Conqueror in 1066.

Those landholders provided a solid backing for Henry's son, Edward VI, who came to the throne in 1547 at the age of ten. He ruled for just six years and died short of his sixteenth birthday, but of his own tendencies and those of his advisors, he opened the doors to Protestant reformation. He repealed the laws of heresy. It was in the second year of his reign that England saw the publication of Archbishop Cranmer's English-language *Book of Common Prayer*, which presented a program of uniform worship in the English church that diverged enough from the Roman practice to cause an almost immediate armed rebellion in the southwest of England.

As the young king was dying of tuberculosis, his principal "protector," the duke of Northumberland, used the king's devotion to church reform to implement a scheme of his own. Based on the fact that Edward's half-sister Mary, the heiress to the throne, was a staunch Catholic, Northumberland got Edward VI to designate his cousin Lady Jane Grey as heiress to the crown. She stood only fifth in line of succession but ranked first in Northumberland's schemes, for he had arranged her marriage to his own son.

Death claimed Edward VI in 1537. Henry VIII had left England Anglican Catholic. Edward VI had moved it off-center in the direction of Protestantism.

The duke of Northumberland's plan to be the real power behind Queen Jane I fell apart in little more than one week, and it cost him his head. Lady Jane Grey sat on the throne of England for just nine days before being ousted by the superior claim of Henry's daughter Mary, who ruled for five years as Queen Mary I, but who is almost always referred to as "Bloody Mary." The new queen had gained support by promising religious tolerance and, more important, by assuring the great lords that they would not have to return the monastic lands they had acquired at such great advantage. She kept the latter promise but completely disregarded the former. She canceled the anti-Roman laws initiated by her father and brother and restored the English church to the supremacy of Rome in a spirit of ruthless dedication. She saw opposition to the Roman church as treason as well as heresy. She burned the Anglican bishops Latimer and Ridley at the stake at Oxford in 1555, permitting them the mercy of sacks of gunpowder hanging from their necks, and burned Archbishop Cranmer at the same location the following year. Elizabeth I would order three hundred executions in her forty-five-year reign. Mary managed to match that record in three. Seeking a Catholic monarch to rule beside her, she married the king of Spain and insisted that he reign as king of England and not as prince consort, a concept that not even her Catholic subjects could easily accept because of their fears of Spanish political domination. Mary created a reign of terror, with burnings and beheadings that drove dissenters from the Roman church deeper into secrecy than ever before.

One of the heads that was expected to drop at any moment was that of Mary's younger sister Elizabeth, a secret Protestant who preserved her life by adopting the attitude of total servility and by having mass said every day in her country home. She was determined that no more devout Catholic should be found anywhere in England, her only hope of protection from her bloody sister.

Accordingly, it was assumed by almost everyone, including the pope, that as she ascended the throne as Queen Elizabeth I she would continue to maintain the Roman church's exclusive position in England. Negotiations actually went forth to attempt her betrothal to Philip of Spain, a champion of the church. But bit by bit, Elizabeth's true feelings came out as she organized her court around her. She reinstated the anti-church laws of her father and brother, which Queen Mary had set aside, and was ultimately excommunicated by the pope, who decreed that Catholic Englishmen no longer owed her any allegiance or obedience. The definitive break with the church gave Elizabeth three determined Roman Catholic enemies; one to the north, one to the south, and one underground.

The threat from the north was possible assassination, because the heiress to the throne in the event of Elizabeth's death was her cousin, Mary Stuart, Queen of Scots, who was a staunch Catholic and could count on aid from the church and from the continental Catholic monarchies. A rebellion broke out in 1569, led by the Catholic earls in the north of England, and the next few years saw a wave of plots to assassinate the English queen. In 1586 Mary Stuart foolishly allowed herself to get involved with a group headed by an angry Catholic named Anthony Babington, who extracted a pledge from his followers to murder Elizabeth. Although Elizabeth attempted to avoid personal involvement, Mary Queen of Scots was arrested for high treason and executed the following year.

The enemy to the south was King Philip of Spain, His Most Catholic Majesty, who was intellectually dedicated to pulling down the heretical queen of England and economically exasperated by the sea-going successes of Drake, Hawkins, Grenville, and Raleigh, who had successfully challenged the supremacy of Spain in the Americas. Just to teach the English a lesson would not do. All that would do was the invasion and total conquest of the island kingdom and its total return to Rome. By May of 1588, Philip was ready. He had assembled a naval force of a hundred and thirty ships, including Portuguese and Venetian galleys. His intent was to transport twenty thousand soldiers, then pick up sixteen thousand more from the Spanish Netherlands, and proceed to invade the south coast of England. Fortunately for England, the Spanish Armada was poorly planned, poorly led, and unlucky. The English wreaked havoc with their faster craft and longer-range guns, and the winds favored their fire-ships. As the Spanish broke for home by sailing north around Scotland and Ireland, they were broken up by the fierce "Protestant Gale" off the rocky coasts and suffered more from the weather than from the enemy. The anti-Roman population of England rejoiced in the confidence that God was on their side.

The third enemy was not so easy to blow away. This was the Jesuit order, dedicated and well trained, which prepared numbers of its Soldiers of Christ specifically for covert service in England, where they were to organize local Catholics, provide leadership, and pull Elizabeth down from her heretical throne, by her death if necessary. In some cases they moved openly in disguise, as stewards or other servants of the Catholic nobility. Many stayed hidden, serving mass in Catholic houses, ready to run to their secret hiding places, or "priest-holes," upon the approach of priest-hunting pursuers. Many of these hiding places were extraordinarily ingenious, but none more so than those planned and built in the homes of loyal Catholics by the master of priest-holes, Nicholas Owen. He was captured, tortured, and finally executed in 1606, but his unusual services were not forgotten. He was canonized as a saint of the Roman Catholic Church over three hundred and sixty years later, in 1970.

England under Elizabeth I leaned more toward the Protestant, but much more Protestant than she had in mind. As far as she went, she had subjects who wanted to go further. Some rejected not only the over-lordship of the Church of Rome but the rule of the English church by the throne as well. Thus Elizabeth's reign saw the birth of Puritanism and of the concept of the "presbytery," the rule of the congregation by its own ministers and elders. The Puritan backlash against the rich ceremonials, vestments, and decoration of the churches introduced a note of stern compassionless austerity into the new Protestantism. Their influence spread, in Parliament as well as throughout the towns and villages. For them, the Anglican church and its hierarchy were not only too much like the Roman Catholic denomination but were contrary to scripture. But they were very like the medieval popes in one thing: They asserted the right to determine morality, coupled with the right to punish those who departed from that determination.

That was the religious situation that Elizabeth left upon her death in 1603: the Roman Catholics subdued, the Anglican Catholics in control of the court, the new Protestants on the rise. It was a turmoil that led to more turmoil and ultimately to civil war. In the meantime, the House of Tudor gave way to the House of Stuart and the union of the English and Scottish crowns in a monarch of whom Thomas Macaulay said, "He was made up of two men—a witty, well-read scholar who wrote, disputed and harangued, and a nervous, driveling idiot who acted."

James VI of Scotland was the son of Mary Queen of Scots and a great-grandson of Henry VII. The Stuart dynasties of England and Scotland came together in him when he assumed the English crown as James I upon the death of Queen Elizabeth in 1603. He was happy to leave the irritating Presbyterians, who were expanding rapidly in Scotland, but less than joyful at the expanding Puritan sect he found in England. As for himself, he was content to serve as governor of the Anglican church, although he glorified that role more than did those around him when he wrote, "Kings are breathing images of God on earth."

Secret Catholic opposition continued from Elizabeth's reign, complete with assassination plots, culminating in the scheme of a group of Catholics who rented a coal cellar under the parliamentary chamber. They stacked the cellar with barrels of gunpowder, planning to blow up the king and the entire Puritan-Anglican Parliament on its opening day, November 5, 1605. The plot was discovered, the gunpowder removed, and a conspirator, Guy Fawkes, was arrested and executed. The only explosion caused by the Gunpowder Plot was one of intensified anti-Catholic anger. To this day, people all over England remember Guy Fawkes each November 5 with fireworks and with bonfires on which they burn a stuffed figure of a man. Today everyone seems to assume that the figure is that of Guy Fawkes, having forgotten that until a few generations ago the height of Guy Fawkes Day excitement in many villages in England was the burning of the pope in effigy.

James I did not get along with the House of Commons, nor with the growing number of Puritans in it, but he did allow himself to be persuaded that individual Britons would benefit from Bible study. He authorized a group of scholars to translate the

Bible into English, and his "King James Version" of the Bible became an instant best-seller. To this day it remains the best-selling book ever printed. Unfortunately for his point of view, it enhanced the cause of Protestantism. Men could read, ponder, debate, and band together with others who came to similar scriptural conclusions, conclusions that in James's time sometimes led to persecutions such as that which launched the journey of the Mayflower during his reign.

When he died in 1625, James I left a combined British kingdom that had experienced new hatred and fear of Roman Catholicism. The Anglican Catholic church was the official state religion, but the new Protestant movements were flexing their muscles in the shires and especially in the House of Commons.

His successor, King Charles I, has been described as "a saintly young man of twenty-four." Saintly he may have been, but he lived all his life as though the real world was just off there in a fog where he couldn't quite make it out. He married the very Catholic Princess Henrietta Maria of France, and apparently couldn't grasp why his Anglican barons and parliamentarians expressed concern over the influx of foreign Catholics to the English court. At odds with the House of Commons, which alone could impose taxes, Charles raised crown funds with ingenious schemes of his own, such as imposing heavy charges for the bestowal of knighthood, then imposing heavy punishments on the wealthy gentlemen who declined the expensive honor. His chief advisor on religious matters was Archbishop Laud, who worked to restore complex ritual and elaborate vestments to the English church, precisely opposite the view of the Puritan parliamentarians. Laud imposed his ritualistic ideas on the church in Scotland, and the result was an armed revolt. Charles I rejected the assertions of Parliament that they had any say over the structure or conduct of the Anglican church, and that they had any control over the military. In his view, the church and the army belonged to the king alone. The dissension grew until the day in January of 1642 when the king entered the House of Commons with an armed guard, intending to personally arrest five of its members. None of them was in attendance, and all that Charles got in return for his dramatic interruption of the proceedings was a royal dressing down from the Speaker. (His words were apparently heard, for no British sovereign has crossed the threshold of the House of Commons from that day to this.) By August of that year, the situation had degenerated into a state of civil war, with Charles I on one side backed by the church, Oxford University, and the rural gentry of the north and west. On the other side, the Puritanical House of Commons could call on the wealth of the trading cities of the south, including London. Charles had the backing of ideas; the Commons had the money. With it, they created a New Model Army under a fellow member, Oliver Cromwell, which finally defeated the royal forces in 1646. To cement that victory, they determined to place the king on trial. To his credit, Charles I defended himself with clear logic and royal dignity, but with no apparent grasp of the fact that he had not been placed on public display to be tried, but to be found guilty. Tourists today are shown the window through which the king was brought from the banqueting hall of his new palace of Whitehall on January 30, 1649, to a high scaffold where his head was chopped off in view of the crowd in the street. A few days later the Commons voted to abolish the monarchy as "unnecessary, burdensome and dangerous to the liberty, safety and public interests of the people." The king's heir, who would become Charles II, was living in exile in Catholic France. The country he would one day rule was now firmly, even rigorously, Puritan.

Cromwell, who ruled as virtual dictator with the title of lord protector, had no room in his heart or mind for tolerance and set out to prove just how joyless a religion can be. Endless laws were passed against such practices as labor on the Sabbath, and stiff penalties were imposed for profanity, creating an atmosphere that depressed the people and disgruntled the army. Cromwell had the strength of will and the devotion to discipline necessary to hold such a society together, but the task was beyond his son, who took over the mantle of government upon the death of his father in September 1658. Finally the army stepped in, deposed the ineffective young protector, and invited Charles II to come home to his crown. He arrived in London on his thirtieth birthday, May 29, 1660.

Charles II was a secret Catholic but had sense enough to realize that his best course to hold on to the crown was to provide a strong force for moderation and tolerance, working against such proposals as the exclusion of all except Anglican Catholics from government service. Rumors have persisted that Charles II had made a secret treaty with the king of France in which he had agreed to work to return Britain to the Roman church, in exchange for a large sum of money. Those rumors were given substance very recently in 1988, when Lord Clifford of Chudleigh declared that he was going to auction off some old documents from the archives of his family. They included a signed copy of the agreement under which Charles would work to return Britain to the Roman church in exchange for a payment of 1.2 million gold *livres*. (There is no record that the sum was ever paid.)

The most dramatic event of Charles's reign was the Great Fire of London in 1666. Once more, the mood of the people was inflamed against the Catholic church as rumors were spread, and believed, that the fire was started by agents of the pope. Nell Gwynn, one of the king's mistresses, saved herself by declaring to an angry mob that blocked her path, "Good people, I am the *Protestant* whore!" The king's own true feelings came out during the last hours of his life in February 1685, when at his request a Catholic priest was brought up the back stairs to administer the last rites of the church.

Throughout the final years of his reign, Charles II had been repeatedly asked to exclude his younger brother James from the succession, because James was a devout Roman Catholic. The courtiers wanted the king's illegitimate son, the duke of Monmouth, who was just as strong a Protestant. Charles consistently refused, so that upon his death the crown passed to a determined Catholic monarch, James II. Monmouth did make a try for the throne, landing in the West Country, where he tried to promote a rebellion. His forces were quickly put down, but the people were shocked by the brutality of the punishments levied by Judge George Jeffreys. Men were executed, branded, and sold into bondage to the Caribbean sugar planters. One villager was executed for selling some fish to the rebels, a matter in which the poor man had no choice whatever. That brutality carried over into the government, where a new wave of Protestant persecutions was launched. James II replaced government officials, including admirals and generals, with his Catholic appointees. He also prosecuted seven Anglican bishops.

The existence of Freemasonry during the reign of Charles II has been well documented, and in the succeeding reign of James II it could only have grown, with the king himself as the master catalyst for recruitment. By his unrelenting campaign to return the Roman church to supremacy in Britain by any means available to him, James drew all of the anti-Roman sects together for the first time in a common cause. There were plots and schemes and secret meetings, and we can be certain that, as the best-established secret society, Freemasonry was playing a major role.

The people bided their time, however, because there was no heir. The Catholic crown would die with James II. Then in June 1688 the queen give birth to a son, and the king declared that the boy's education and upbringing would be in the care of the Jesuits. Protestants started the rumor that the succession was a Jesuit plot, that there was no crown prince, and that the baby had been smuggled into the royal bedchamber in a warming pan.

Finally a group of Protestant leaders, which included the bishop of London, decided to act. They turned to Mary, James's own daughter, who had married her cousin William of Orange, a nephew of Charles II. Together they were the strongest female and male claimants to the throne after the newborn son of James II. More important, William was the leader of the Protestant Dutch against the Catholic Louis XVI of France. On the premise that the baby was not the true son of James II, William and Mary were invited to share the English throne. As William arrived on Guy Fawkes Day, November 5, 1685, the support for James II fell away. It was just thirty-two years before Masonry would make itself known in London in 1717.

Sixteen years later, in 1701, a law was passed that excluded from the throne all except members of the Church of England, and a religious settlement was reached to guarantee limited freedom of religious worship to non-Anglican Protestants (the "nonconformists"). Significantly, this was the end of the divine right of kings in Britain. It was clear now that Parliament would decide who occupied the royal seat.

Although William purported to espouse religious tolerance, one blot on his record speaks to the contrary. He required that all of the leaders of the Catholic clans of Scotland sign documents of submission. The leader of a small group of the MacDonald clan in the valley of Glencoe missed the deadline by a few days, as he beat his way through a winter storm to sign for his people. The price paid is remembered as the Massacre of Glencoe, a highland bloodbath in which all ages and both sexes were butchered as punishment for the tardiness of their chief. Religious feelings remained high, and William's death was ceremoniously remembered for years after it occurred. He died from injuries sustained when his horse stumbled in a molehill at Hampton Court, and Jacobites gratefully memorialized the mole with the quiet toast, "To the little gentleman in black velvet."

Thus, in 1701, the crown passed to Anne, Protestant daughter of James II, whose thirty-seven-year-old body had been battered by seventeen pregnancies, none of which resulted in a living heir to the throne.

Queen Anne, the last of the Stuarts, was an unspectacular sovereign, but a number of spectacular events occurred during her reign. The wave of continental victories under the duke of Marlborough established new respect for British military prowess. The Royal Society flourished with men of letters and science, such as John Locke and Isaac Newton, and Freemason Sir Christopher Wren continued to express his genius in the restoration of St. Paul's Cathedral. In 1707 the Act of Union between England and Scotland combined those crowns irrevocably and formed Great Britain.

As to religion, Anne was firmly Church of England and even yielded up royal funds to increase the livings of the lower clergy, a grace those gentlemen called "Queen Anne's Bounty." In Rome, the Holy See still remembered his family's loyalty and willingly played host to the man who would have been James III. There were still Jacobite plots in Britain to restore the Roman Catholic claimants to the throne, but such restoration would need to be by force, since it was expressly prohibited by law. In 1689 James II and his son had specifically been denied the succession by an act of Parliament that stated categorically that no Roman Catholic or spouse of a Roman Catholic could occupy the British throne. Then, in 1701, Parliament had been even more specific. In the Act of Succession they decreed that after Queen Anne the crown would pass to the nearest Protestant relative of the House of Stuart. That turned out to be Sophia, a granddaughter of James I, who was married to the elector of Hanover.

Thus, upon Anne's death in 1714, Sophia's son founded the Hanoverian dynasty in Britain as King George I. He never bothered to learn English and spent more time at home in Germany than at his court in London, but it didn't matter anymore. The country was ruled by Parliament, as the new monarchy took shape and Robert Walpole became England's first prime minister.

In the following year the long-awaited Jacobite rebellion was launched and was a short-lived dismal failure. It was put down so quickly that it was over before James could arrive in Britain to join it. The Jacobite cause, the struggle to return Britain to the Roman church, was effectively broken—just two years before four Masonic lodges in London decided to reveal themselves to the world. Now, indeed, Freemasons had no more need for secrecy, no reason to hide from the establishment, or to plot against the establishment. Freemasonry had *become* the establishment.

CHAPTER 24

THE
MANUFACTURED
MYSTERIES

This book has dealt with the major mysteries of the Ancient Order of Free and Accepted Masons, most of which have been mysteries to the Masons themselves, and has provided sensible solutions to almost all of them, in support of the principal conclusion of this research—that the origins of Masonry lie in the members and friends of the order of the Knights Templar who fled arrest and torture by king and pope. However, we are aware that many will feel that this book is incomplete because it does not deal with Masonic mysteries and problems that they have read or heard about: What about Masonic devil worship? What about the Masonic responsibility for corrupting the Vatican into the biggest financial fraud of our time? How about the secret infiltration of law enforcement and government? The KGB connection?

Our first thought was to ignore these, because they are "mysteries" that do not emanate from the ritual, the history, or even the legends of Freemasonry. Rather, they have been alleged and fostered, even promoted, by anti-Masonic writers. In recent years, more and more anti-Masonic opinion arose, especially in Britain, that appeared to be based upon a book titled *The Brotherhood*, by

British journalist Stephen Knight. In 1976 Mr. Knight attracted worldwide attention with his book *Jack the Ripper—The Final Solution*, which purported to solve the Jack the Ripper murders in London by proving that they were perpetrated, then covered up, by prominent Freemasons, and that the bloody mutilations of the victims were in keeping with the penalties of the Masonic oaths. The book resulted in newspaper headlines and was covered by radio and television. A fictionalized version of the story was made into a movie called *Murder By Decree*, which had Sherlock Holmes solve the mystery and confront the guilty Masons.

As a sequel to this publishing success, Mr. Knight wrote *The Brotherhood*. The subtitle on the hardback book was *The Secret World of the Freemasons*. The paperback edition carried the more sensational subtitle, *The Explosive Exposé of the Secret World of the Freemasons*. First published in 1984, the book caused a sensation in Britain and elsewhere. Mr. Knight was quickly elevated to the position of the leading authority on the evils and potential evils of Masonry and must stand as the most influential anti-Mason of this century. As such it was inevitable that his book be studied to see whether his research had turned up any meaningful information that might lead to solutions of the Masonic mysteries, or shed new light on the origins of the order. His book provided no help in either of those areas but was fascinating because it did provide a capsule study of how information can be colored and twisted, how facts can be changed by stating them incompletely or out of context, and the extent to which someone could go to force data to fit a preconceived conclusion. This book has criticized Masonic historians for trying to force everything about the order into the preconceived concept of origins in the medieval stonemasons, so in fairness it should criticize the same technique when used by their detractors.

Mr. Knight never tells his readers his own position, so before examining some of the Masonic mysteries that he has implanted in his readers, let me state that I am not and never have been a Freemason and am not and never have been a Roman Catholic. I freely invite the careful scrutiny and critique of either of those groups relative to what I found in the analysis of *The Brotherhood*.

First, let's deal with the most damning of his conclusions about Masonry, in a chapter called "The Devil in Disguise?" In this chapter Mr. Knight cites the papal encyclical *Humanum Genus*, an extraordinary document issued in 1884 by Pope Leo XIII. Mr. Knight says, "Leo XIII classed Freemasonry as a grouping of societies in the 'kingdom of Satan.'" What the pope actually said was that the Salvation Army, the Baptist church, the Buddhists, and the Mormons—in fact, every member of the human race who was not a Roman Catholic—was part of the "kingdom of Satan." But lest I seem to interpret, let Leo XIII speak for himself:

> "The human race [Humanum Genus], after, by the malice of the devil, it had departed from God, the Creator and Giver of heavenly gifts, divided itself into two different and opposing parties, one of which assiduously combats for truth and virtue, the other for those things which are opposed to virtue and to truth. The one is the Kingdom of God on earth—that is, the [Catholic] Church of Jesus Christ; those who desire to adhere to which from their soul and conducively to salvation must serve God and His only begotten Son with their whole mind and their whole will. The other is the kingdom of Satan, in whose dominion and power are all who have followed his sad example and that of our first parents."

And just how did the pope say that Freemasonry fit into this great non-Catholic kingdom of Satan? "In our days, however, those who follow the evil one seem to conspire and strive all together under the guidance and with the help of that society of men spread all over, and solidly established, which they call Free Masons."

Mr. Knight further states of Pope Leo XIII: "He qualified Masonry as subversive of Church and State." What the pope actually complained of was the *separation* of church and state, but once again, we'll let the pope speak for himself, remembering that when he uses the word *church*, he means the Roman Catholic church only:

> "They [Masons] work, indeed, obstinately to the end that neither the teaching nor the authority of the Church may have any influence; and therefore they preach and maintain the full separation of the Church from the State. So law and government are wrested from the wholesome and divine virtue of the Catholic Church, and they want, therefore, by all means to rule States independent of the institutions and doctrines of the Church."

Since *Humanum Genus* is only about fifteen pages long, we assume that Mr. Knight read it all and is aware that its major theme is an argument against the idea of democracy, and against the theory of separation of the Catholic church from temporal authority over every state. The pope was horrified at the idea that people should make laws to govern themselves rather than be obedient to the rulers who were given divine command when anointed by the church. Far-fetched? Leo XIII states it (the italics are mine): "To recognize, as she [the church] does, *the divine right of command*, concedes great dignity to civil power, and contributes to conciliate the respect and love of subjects." In 1884, the Holy See still favored autocratic monarchs anointed by the church and who recognized the temporal authority of the church. In that respect, *Humanum Genus* was every bit as much a condemnation of the Constitution of the United States as it was of Freemasonry, as comes out in a catalog of sins of which Masonry is accused:

> "The sect of the Masons aims unanimously and steadily also at the possession of the education of children. They understand that a tender age is easily bent, and that there is no more useful way of preparing for the State such citizens as they wish. Hence, in the instruction and education of children, they do not leave to the ministers of the [Catholic] Church any part either in directing or watching them. In many places they have gone so far that children's education is all in the hands of laymen: and from moral teaching every idea is banished of those holy and great duties which bind together man and God."

The accusations get stronger, as Masons are equated with "naturalists."

> "The principles of social science follow. Here naturalists teach that men have all the same rights, and are perfectly equal in condition; that every man is naturally independent; that no one has a right to command others; that it is tyranny to keep men subject to any other authority than that which emanates from themselves. Hence the people are sovereign; those who rule have no authority but by the commission and concession of the people; so that they can be deposed, willing or unwilling, according to the wishes of the people. The origin of all rights and civil duties is in the people or

in the state, which is ruled according to the new principles of liberty. The State must be godless; no reason why one religion ought to be preferred to another; all to be held in the same esteem.

"Now it is well known that Free-Masons approve these maxims, and that they wish to see governments shaped on this pattern and model needs no demonstration."

That's what the "kingdom of Satan" was doing in *Humanum Genus*: it was depriving the church of authority and privilege, and sometimes property as well, by replacing church-approved sovereigns with democratic rule. We must remember the date of this letter, April 20, 1884. The Holy See had just lost the Papal States in Italy to the new kingdom of Italy, so that Leo XIII was the first pope in centuries to be only a priest and not a king as well. Mexico had been taken over by a revolution led by Benito Juárez, whose new Mexican government had taken away church lands, outlawed convents and monasteries, and forbidden the sending of church funds to Rome, all while remaining staunchly Catholic, but telling the pope that his mission on earth was spiritual and pastoral, not economic and political. Untold wealth had been lost by the church in South America as the result of revolutions under Simón Bolívar and José de San Martín. *Humanum Genus* blamed naturalists, men who wanted to substitute reasoning for the teachings of the church and who taught that laws should be made "by just the consent of the governed." Yes, the pope did accuse Freemasons of "religious indifference," as Mr. Knight reports, but he fails to report that the church is actually condemning this Masonic acceptance of men of all religious beliefs in the face of the fact that all religions except Roman Catholicism had been declared false: "By opening their gates to persons of every creed they promote, in fact, the great modern error of religious indifference and of the parity of all worships, the best way to annihilate every religion, especially the Catholic, which, being the only true one, cannot be joined with others without enormous injustice."

There was nothing nefarious or subversive on the pope's part. Leo XIII was a troubled man. He felt deeply the great losses in church power, privilege, and wealth brought on by the democratic revolutions and developed such profound mistrust that he kept all of the gold of the Vatican in a box under his own bed. He truly believed that democracy was evil, part of the "kingdom of Satan," and that the Catholic church had a right and duty to oversee every secular government. Nor did that attitude die with him. As recently as April 1948 the official Jesuit publication, *Civilità Cattolica*, made it clear that when Catholics in any country are in the minority, the church will ask for religious freedom for all; but when the majority is Catholic, all other creeds will be denied legal existence. Leo XIII would have agreed with the Jesuit statement:

"The Roman Catholic Church, being convinced, through its divine prerogatives, of being the only true church, must demand the right of freedom for herself alone, because such a right can only be possessed by truth, never by error. As to other religions, the Church will certainly never draw the sword, but she will require that by legitimate means they shall not be allowed to propagate false doctrine. Consequently, in a State where the majority of the people are Catholic, the Church will require that legal existence be denied to error, and that if religious minorities actually exist, they shall have only a *de facto* existence without opportunity to spread their beliefs. . . . In some countries, Catholics will be obliged to ask full religious freedom for all, resigned to cohabitate where they alone should rightfully be allowed to live. But in doing this the Church does not renounce her thesis, which remains the most imperative of her laws, but merely adapts herself to *de facto* conditions, which must be taken into account in practical affairs."

And there we have the apparently irreconcilable difference between Freemasonry and the Roman Catholic Church. A central feature of Masonry is the acceptance of men of all religious creeds, including Catholicism, while the Roman church believes that its faith alone is right, and that when able to do so it has a divine duty to suppress all others. Each organization believes strongly in its own position, and a compromise seemed impossible until Pope John XXIII, in his Second Ecumenical Conference, urged expanded dialogue with other creeds. Of course, that was long after the battery of papal condemnations of Masonry cited by Mr. Knight. Those condemnations are almost totally political and economic. They contribute nothing to Mr. Knight's thesis that devil worship has its place in Freemasonry. Of course, in *The Brotherhood* he does speak of "a more sinister situation in Rome, where I have evidence that the Vatican itself is infiltrated by

Freemasons." Why didn't he give us *that* exciting information? Was there no room in the book? Was there no room in his book to explain that the celebrated papal condemnation of Freemasonry called *Humanum Genus* was guilty of gross error? It condemns Masonic teachings of the separation of church and state, government by the people, civil marriage, and teaching of children by laymen rather than priests, but none of those things is specifically espoused by Freemasonry, which leaves choices in such matters entirely to the individual members. The pope simply confused Freemasonry with all non-Catholics. In any event, *Humanum Genus* contributes nothing in the way of evidence of Masonic devil worship.

Actually, Mr. Knight found all of the evidence of Masonic devil worship he needed in the revelation of the "ineffable name of God" as disclosed in the initiation rites of the Royal Arch degree. He decided, and declared, that this name, which is apparently an acronym meant to symbolize the Masonic acceptance of men of all faiths, is incontrovertible proof of the existence of a separate and easily identifiable God of Masonry. Although nothing whatsoever is mentioned in the Masonic ritual other than the name itself, Mr. Knight has figured out the "true nature" of the Masonic god he has created. That "ineffable name" is *Jahbulon*, which has been stated to be a name made up of three syllables standing for Jehovah, Baal, and On, or Osiris. Some Masons trying to "break the code" of the name arrived at this conclusion, although by no means is the interpretation universally accepted by Masonic historians. Mr. Knight happily accepted the interpretation, because it served his purpose in attempting to prove that Satan has a role in Freemasonry. As to the name *Jahbulon*, Mr. Knight says that it is "not a general umbrella term an individual Freemason might choose, but a precise designation that describes a specific supernatural being." In setting the nature of that specific Masonic god, he speaks to just one syllable, that *bul* stands for Baal. He then points out that a sixteenth-century demonologist described Baal as a devil with the body of a spider and heads of a man, a toad, and a cat. *That* certainly sounds like a specific deity.

The problem is that Baal is not a name: It is a title, and its use does not pinpoint a specific deity. We do not know that the Baal who had his altar overturned by Gideon was the same as the Baal who was challenged to a duel with Jehovah by Elijah, or that either was the same deity worshiped in Lebanon at the Temple of the Sun at Baalbek.

Simply, *Ba'al* is a Hebrew word that means lord or master. Numerous deities were addressed by that title in the Middle East, but their names have not come down to us. It would have caused great confusion if the English translators of the Old Testament had translated *ba'al* into the English word *lord*, so they left the word in Hebrew. To the reader in English it appears to be a name rather than the honorific title it is, a title that is still used in the Jewish faith. For example, one who can work miracles in the name of God is known as a *Ba'al shem*, the lord (or master) of the Name. Perhaps the most famous of these was the *Ba'al shem Tov*, the Ukrainian rabbi who founded the Hasidic movement in Poland, so if you meet a husky young man in a long black coat with no necktie, with a full beard and ringlets hanging beneath a black hat, don't run the risk of telling *him* that *Ba'al* means the Devil.

What happened, of course, was not much different from Pope Leo XIII's contention that any rival to the Roman Catholic church was a member of the kingdom of Satan, except that in the case of "Baal" it was any rival of Jehovah. At one point a number of Israelites were following an unnamed "lord," rather than Jehovah, and to put the matter to a test Elijah ordered that each faction should kill a bullock and put it on a pile of wood, then ask their god to light the fire. Four hundred and fifty priests of "Ba'al" prayed earnestly all day, even cutting and slashing themselves in personal sacrifice, to get their god to act, but nothing happened. Then Elijah, who had his wood watered down for good measure, called on Jehovah, who responded with bolts of lightning that lit Elijah's fire. In a great burst of religious fervor and gratitude, Elijah had his followers immediately murder the 450 rival priests.

Quite apart from the fact that if there is one miracle that Satan should be able to muster up it should be to start a little fire, the Jews did not accuse Jehovah's rival of being the Devil, but rather denigrated him by calling him the lord over nothing, the Lord of the Flies or—in Hebrew—*Ba'al-zbub*. Over a thousand years later some impassioned Christians decided that any rival of Jehovah had to be the Devil and anglicized the Hebrew Lord of the Flies to Beelzebub, which they declared to be a name of Satan. All of which is terribly contrived, motivated by the viciousness that often asserts itself in religious disagreements. However, it does nothing to produce the tiniest bit of evidence that there is even a hint of devil worship in Freemasonry, especially since the assumption that Jahbulon means Jehovah, Ba'al, and Osiris is itself pure conjecture. No one knows for certain what it means, or even how the name was originally pronounced before it underwent changes from centuries of strictly verbal communication. For example, I have seen the last syllable spelled *on, om,* and *un.* Might it have started out as *am?* If it did, someone may have taken the last syllable from a name God revealed to the Israelites: *I am.* If the original name had been Jahbaalam, since *Ba'al* is Hebrew for "lord," it would then be a name made up of three different names for Jehovah. I am not claiming new evidence, just pointing up the possibilities and the reasonable doubts. In *The Brotherhood,* Stephen Knight had no doubt at all as he wrote, "If Christ was an acceptable part of Freemasonry even to a non-Christian, why not the devil as well? Unacceptable as he might be to most initiates, he has his place."

And so we begin to see a typical source of the "manufactured mysteries" of Freemasonry (and many other institutions), those that are concocted not for analysis but for destruction, and *The Brotherhood* by no means stops with Masonic devil worship. In another chapter entitled "The Italian Crisis," Mr. Knight writes about the involvement of the pope's own bank in the greatest financial fraud of this century, a catastrophic papal scandal that still isn't over. Yet in Mr. Knight's book the matter escapes any hint of church scandal, being described as a "Masonic conspiracy."

The basis for his characterization of the conspiracy as "Masonic" is a former Masonic lodge known as *Propaganda Due,* or P2, a lodge originally formed by the Italian Grand Orient as a lodge of research. In 1975 an Italian fascist named Licio Gelli was made the Venerable Grand Master of P2, and the following year that lodge was disavowed and suspended by the Grand Orient of Italy, so whatever it was, P2 ceased to be an official Masonic organization. Gelli converted the shell of P2 to his own purposes and those of his associates, eventually using it to build a network of secret cells of powerful politicians, bankers, and publishers throughout Italy. It was all done in complete secrecy, and with no authorized Masonic connections whatever.

Soon after P2 was thrown out of official Italian Masonry, Gelli brought in Michele Sindona, the leading financial advisor to the Vatican. Then, in 1977, Sindona brought in Roberto Calvi, head of the Banco Ambrosiano in Milan, which was closely associated with the papal bank, one of its major shareholders. Until the fall of Mussolini's government, it had been necessary for any borrower, or even depositor, to prove that he or she was a Roman Catholic before being able to do business with the Banco Ambrosiano. Calvi brought to the table his most valued contact, the *Instituto per lo Opere di Religione*, the Institute for Religious Works (the "IOR"), a financial institution often erroneously referred to as the "Vatican bank." The IOR belongs not to the Vatican city-state, but to the pope alone. As its name indicates, the Institute's function is to receive deposits from Catholic organizations and individuals, then loan the money out at nominal rates on favorable terms to finance the construction of Catholic schools, churches, and orphanages around the world. At the time of the scandals, and until 1989, the IOR was run by Archbishop Paul Marcinkus, a native of Cicero, Illinois, and a long-time friend and former bodyguard of Pope John Paul II.

After Calvi was in with Gelli and Sindona, the Banco Ambrosiano helped to set up foreign shell companies, including ten in Panama, which were controlled by the papal bank. Then the Banco Ambrosiano loaned these shells up to one and a third *billion* dollars. The papal bank also put in funds of its own, but no one in Rome will even hint at the amount or purpose of these extensive secret fundings. All that is known is that some of the money was used to buy and prop up the share value of Banco Ambrosiano.

When the Italian banking officials grew suspicious, Calvi and the archbishop exchanged letters. Marcinkus gave the banker "comfort letters" asserting that the foreign shell companies were indeed under the direct or indirect control of the papal bank, and Calvi responded with letters asserting the IOR did not really owe the one and a third billion dollars. Both men knew that the loans were uncollectable and the exchange of letters of little value. As the government closed in, Calvi's ultimate solution was to hang himself from Blackfriars Bridge in London, his pockets full of cash and rocks, although suspicions of murder still surface. Calvi's death triggered an exhaustive investigation and the Banco Ambrosiano collapsed. The papal bank is said to have lost over 450 million dollars in the debacle.

In spite of the huge losses, its controlling interest in the offshore companies, and its total involvement in the biggest financial fraud of this and perhaps any other century, the Holy See would answer no questions, nor would it provide any documentation as to the participation of the papal bank or of Vatican officials. Early in 1987, Archbishop Marcinkus was indicted by the Italian government for fraudulent bankruptcy. The Holy See would not produce Marcinkus to answer the charges, and he could not be extradited, for a very interesting reason.

Back in 1929, the year in which Licio Gelli had joined Mussolini's Black Shirts, the Italian dictator effected the Lateran agreements with the Holy See, an arrangement known as the Italian *Concordat*. In exchange for Vatican support, Mussolini agreed that Italy would have no laws that were not in keeping with church teachings, which is why Italian law did not permit divorce and why the Vatican had censorship control over all books, magazines, and newspapers in Italy. Mussolini gave in to the Vatican demand that cardinals of the church be accorded all of the rank, respect, and privileges of princes of royal blood. He founded the Vatican fortune by agreeing to pay 92 million dollars as compensation for the loss of the Papal States, so that the church had a substantial pot of cash with which to buy when the rest of the world was pressured to sell at the very start of the Great Depression. Il Duce also agreed that the Vatican would be recognized as a completely separate sovereign state, totally independent from Italy or anyone else, and leaving Italy with no right of extradition. This proved useful to many during World War II, as Hitler also recognized the Concordat between his ally Mussolini and the Vatican, so that many aristocrats and others with the right connections were able to gain asylum from the Nazis in the Vatican, although they had to live out the war by carefully staying within the boundaries of the 108-acre Vatican state.

That's exactly what Archbishop Marcinkus did when he learned that he had been indicted by the Italian government. The Italian process servers and arresting officers were not allowed in, and the archbishop did not set foot outside the Vatican for the five months that the issue of authority over him was being argued up to the Italian Supreme Court. Finally, in July 1987, that court decided that the Italian government had no authority to issue an indictment concerning acts performed inside another sovereign state, a conclusion that was universally expected. (The Observer of London met the news with the facetious comment, "Surprise, surprise.")

The really big shock was that the papal bank agreed to pay and paid over to the Banco Ambrosiano the incredible sum of 244 million dollars, while denying any guilt, or even any material involvement, in the great fraud. Together with the reputed loss of 450 million dollars, this means that the affairs between the papal bank and the Banco Ambrosiano cost the Catholic church almost 700 million dollars, over ten times the 1987 operating loss that Catholics all over the world were asked to make up with extra donations, and with no explanations given the faithful for the gross mismanagement of the funds they had given or deposited in the past. The padlocks of total secrecy have been vigorously clamped on every aspect of the scandal by the Holy See, leaving little doubt as to the one "secret society" involved in this disgrace.

That is what happened, but as described in Mr. Knight's *The Brotherhood* it is not a Vatican scandal at all, but a *Masonic* scandal. His allegation is based on nothing more than the fact that, on the secular side of the affair, a clandestine group was involved that *called* itself a Masonic lodge, but was not. His chapter *"The Italian Crisis"* begins with the sentence, "A Masonic conspiracy of gigantic proportions rocked Italy to its foundations in the summer of 1981." He reports that Gelli extracted government and personal secrets from members to be used for blackmail and calls the production of those secrets "Masonic dues." He refers to "the corrupt Freemasons in Italy's armed forces."

As to the hanging of Calvi from London's Blackfriars Bridge, Mr. Knight reported that the death was found to be a suicide, but added a rumor that he had heard (or embellished), that Calvi "had been ritually done to death by Freemasons, a Masonic 'cable-tow' around his neck and his pockets filled, symbolically, with chunks of masonry, the location of the murder being chosen for its name—in Italy the logo of the Brotherhood is the figure of a Blackfriar." I suggest the embellishment of this rumor (if such a rumor exists) because I have not been able to find that the figure of a Blackfriar is the logo of Italian Masonry, although, in keeping with the custom of Masonic lodges having names, there is one lodge in Italy called by the plural form of that name, *Frati Nere* (Black Brothers). Another point of all this that didn't seem to bother Mr. Knight was the matter of motive. Why would Freemasons bother to run the risk of murdering the Italian banker? Others may have had motive: officers of the Banco Ambrosiano; those involved in the Vatican-controlled companies that got the loan proceeds; anyone who received any of that money; anyone with a strong need to cover up; but none of the possible motives points to Freemasonic involvement. As to the Vatican itself, Mr. Knight not only perceived the affair as a Masonic scandal, rather than a Vatican one, but he further considered that the Vatican was a possible victim of further Masonic wrongdoing, citing "Freemasonry's penetration not only of the Roman Catholic church, but the Vatican itself." His conclusions, however, were not accompanied by a single shred of proof.

But wait, he is not through yet. Wrapped up in all this, Mr. Knight also sees "the KGB penetration of Freemasonry." In *The Brotherhood* he very flatly claims, "The Soviet espionage machine has made a priority of infiltrating every kind of organization in every country of the world. Its prime target, in every country where it existed, was inevitably Freemasonry." *Its prime target!*

One of the countries in which Freemasonry exists is Switzerland. "Through an intermediary," wrote Mr. Knight, "I asked former KGB spy Ilya Grigevich Dzhirkvelov, who defected to the West in 1980, about Freemasonry." Mr. Dzhirkvelov apparently knew nothing about Freemasonry, so Mr. Knight covered his disappointment by pointing out that most of Dzhirkvelov's thirty-five years as a KGB agent were spent in Switzerland, where there are only fifty-two Masonic lodges. Remember that Mr. Knight has said that in every country *where it existed,* Freemasonry was the *prime target* of the KGB, yet here he is in contact with a KGB agent who has operated for most of his life in a small country with fifty-two Masonic lodges, and the man has nothing to say about Freemasonry. Didn't they cover their *prime target* in Dzhirkvelov's training? But the intrepid Mr. Knight wouldn't give up, and had the former spy comment on what *Mr. Knight had to say* about Freemasonry, and found so much triumph in the reply that he gave it two lines of italics: "Dzhirkvelov . . . said that if Freemasonry was such an important part of the Establishment as I said, *there was no doubt at all that the KGB was exploiting it, even to the extent of instructing its British recruits to become Masons."* Just as the KGB might instruct recruits to become scoutmasters, to be active in local charities, to join a smart country club or the Lions or Rotary Club, or to make any other moves that would make them appear to be substantial and respected members of the community.

There was even more "hard evidence" to come.

Mr. Knight met a recently retired intelligence officer in true secret service fashion by a fish pond on the first floor of a bank. As *The Brotherhood* puts it: "He had agreed to meet me only on the understanding that we not discuss matters covered by the Official Secrets Act. He was not a Freemason. He said that he had never been aware that Freemasonry could be an advantage in government service, nor felt the need to be a Mason to advance his career. He added, 'But perhaps that is because I never thought about it.'

"He told me that he had never come across a case of the KGB using Freemasonry in England, and added, 'But of course that does not mean that it has not happened.'" How's that for evidence substantiating the charge that Freemasonry is the prime target of the KGB?

Just one more example to put to rest the Masonic "mystery" of its alleged involvement with the Soviet spy system. In the British Intelligence Service, the overseas department is MI6, while the domestic security section is MI5. In *The Brotherhood*, Mr. Knight tells us, "As I learned from a former Home Secretary . . . it is forbidden for any member of either of the intelligence services to be a Freemason." But further on he also says, "According to the evidence now available the undoubted 'jobs for the brethren' aspect of British Freemasonry has been used extensively by the KGB to penetrate the most sensitive areas of authority, most spectacularly illustrated in the years since 1945, by placing spies at the highest levels of both MI5 and MI6." Unfortunately, Mr. Knight didn't put those two bits of information adjacent, as they are here, so most of his readers missed the point that the KGB have successfully used Freemasonry to place spies in the upper reaches of two departments where Freemasons aren't allowed. Trying to figure out that logic could give one a severe headache.

In summary, Mr. Knight's definitive conclusions about the KGB connection with Masonry are based on his conviction that Freemasons enjoy undue preferment and advancement, and that, therefore, any spy organization would want to take advantage of that situation. Yet he was not able to give one clear-cut example in the thirty-four pages of that section of his book, entitled *"The KGB Connection."* That is another Masonic mystery manufactured by Mr. Knight, or perhaps we have been deceived by the two KGB defectors whose books appeared in the spring of 1988: *Secret Servant: My Life with the KGB and the Soviet Elite,* by Ilya Dzhirkvelov (the same former spy whom Mr. Knight contacted through an intermediary), and *On the Wrong Side: My Life in the KGB,* by Stanislav Levchenko. Neither author mentions Freemasonry as the prime target of the KGB. In fact, neither of them mentions Freemasonry at all.

In reality, Mr. Knight's allegations of a KGB connection with Freemasonry are simply an extension of the major thesis of *The Brotherhood,* which is favoritism and job preferment among Masons, to the detriment of the rest of society. He sees Masonic preferment everywhere, but in his book he has a terrible time proving it. The reason is that, although there is indeed a great deal of actual preferment in all facets of life in every country of the world, much of it exists in the minds of those who feel that they have been passed over and wronged—a natural reaction of all except the most self-deprecating, as we instinctively look outside ourselves for explanations of our shortcomings. If a Catholic boss promotes a Catholic worker, a Protestant rival for the post may belabor his wife with a condemnation of religion-based favoritism. If a Catholic salesman tries to make a big sale to a Jewish-owned firm and loses it to a rival Jewish supplier, he may well tell his own superior, "You know how those Jews are—they stick together." Although blacks have often had the short end of the stick in American industry, the promotion of a better-qualified white man will often generate accusations of racism at work, whether true or not.

Barring the unwarranted complaints of the losers, is there still actual favoritism in the workplace or in government? Absolutely. But it can't be laid at the feet of any one segment of society, although, as a group, politicians would have to carry the greatest burden of culpability for the misuse of their appointment power.

Until quite recently in the United States, the chairman of the winning political party was automatically appointed as postmaster general after the election, as though his consummate ability as a politician equated with the ability required to manage a multibillion-dollar business. Even President Kennedy got in the act when he declared that, after due deliberation, he had decided that his younger brother was the best qualified man in the United States for the post of attorney general. In many cases, as with President Kennedy, it is the desire to be surrounded by people with whom one can easily relate that prompts such decisions. A few years ago in the advertising business, the story was reported that a very major manufacturer of pasta products interviewed a number of advertising agencies. The Italian-born owner and president sat through all of the presentations as bright young men presented the results of their market research and consumer analyses, followed by beautiful layouts and TV storyboards. The final presentation shocked everyone in the room because from beginning to end it was entirely in Italian, which was only understood by one man in the group. As the Italian-speaking account executive finished, the president announced that his agency would have the account. "But, sir," one of his executives complained, "just because they speak Italian doesn't mean that they understand our marketing problems." "Maybe not," replied the happy owner, "but it means they understand *me!*" An obvious case of linguistic preferment.

Another point that must be made about job preferment is that it is eagerly sought by those who expect to benefit from the advancement shortcuts it provides. In my younger days I was employed at a company owned by one Jewish family, and the majority of the top executives were of that faith. One day we were introduced to a young man just out of the university who had been hired by the company president himself and not by the personnel manager. After a few days the new man confided to the rest of us that we should not take it personally if, in a few weeks, he was made head of the department. He explained that he had been president of the Jewish fraternity at his university, where our company president was a director, and that they belonged to the same temple. He had been brought in to be pushed rapidly upward. He apparently thought that this connection also precluded any need to work, and within ninety days he was gone, almost in a state of shock. He had missed the point that what he had was not a guarantee but a *contact*, which meant he had been given a crack at an opportunity, not at a secure future. That is what associations mean to many—the contacts one can make at church, in amateur theatricals, in a fraternal society, or in a business club.

In fact, many organizations, contrary to the avowed Masonic point of view, openly tout the business contacts one will make as a reason for joining, and many fully expect those contacts to pay off. Some time ago my secretary came to tell me that there was a man in the reception area who would not give his name but told her to inform me that he was an old college fraternity brother of mine. I immediately stopped what I was doing to take the time to reminisce with an old friend. I could not place his face, but kept talking. Finally I said, "I'm terribly embarrassed, but I just don't seem to remember you. What years were you at Miami University?" "Oh," he answered, "I didn't go to Miami, I went to Arizona State" (roughly two thousand miles away). He explained that as part of a new marketing program at the company for which he sold life insurance, each salesman had submitted the name of his college fraternity and the company had responded with names of all the members in his sales territory. "We thought you'd like to buy your insurance from a fraternity brother." He was wrong.

Nor is this approach limited to individuals. A Catholic developer in a city near my home had an idea: With a heavily Catholic population in that area, he would build a small shopping center and rent only to Catholic merchants, and then the local Catholic population would give preferment to those stores. He actually named it "The Madonna Center." The whole concept was a complete failure as spiritual brotherhood lost out to quality, price, and selection.

The point is that job and business preferments certainly do exist, but not to the extent that prospective beneficiaries might like to think. It is an area of human activity about which it can truly be said that after all's said and done, there's a great deal more said than done. To the end of time men will hope to use the contacts they make in the Ancient Order of Hibernians, the Caledonian Society, the Sons of Italy, the Knights of Columbus, the Lions Club, and Freemasonry. But I have heard or seen no evidence, including in the pages of *The Brotherhood*, that Masonic preferment is any better or worse than that of any other fraternal organization. People will persist in leaning in the direction of people they know; members of any nationalistic, ethnic, or religious group will continue to feel more comfortable with their own kind; and people will continue to find a way to do business with and give jobs to people they like and trust, just as people will avoid doing business or stop doing business with people they don't like or don't trust. And bet on the fact that no manager is going to risk his own career, or make his own job harder, by hiring an incompetent man because he sits in the next pew, belongs to the same luncheon club, or shares the same secret handgrip.

Now suppose, given all of that, I want to accuse one group of insidious preferment that amounts to corruption, as Mr. Knight seems to want so desperately in *The Brotherhood*. I could go to Boston, identify high-ranking Catholic police officials over the past few decades, and check how many Catholics were currently on the force to prove job preferment. Then I could check to see how many police officers had been found to be taking kickbacks or involved in other illegal activities, identify which of them was Catholic, and present the findings as a Catholic conspiracy to fill and corrupt the police department. I could do the same thing to establish Baptist guilt in Birmingham, Alabama, and Mormon-based corruption in Utah.

By no means can Mr. Knight be accused of manufacturing the "mystery" of Masonic job preferment and the cover-up of brother Masons' corrupt acts. Those allegations have been around a long time. But Mr. Knight did take the lead in dragging them into the present and into the public press, with conclusions based on some of the most misleading writing I have ever seen. After reading *The Brotherhood* for the first time I was confused by the staggering accusations and conclusions based on flimsy or incomplete data. Upon reading it the second time I became embarrassed at what had slipped by me the first time in the smooth flow of language. For example, in the prologue Mr. Knight reports that two brothers in publishing, who had already made a substantial payment to him, announced that they would forfeit their advance because they had decided not to publish his book. The publisher reported that "although neither he nor his brother was a Freemason, their father . . . was a senior member of the Brotherhood and in deference to him they would not publish it." Clear enough. The two publishing brothers were *not* Freemasons. On the next page, Mr. Knight sums up this situation, stating, "If the incident does not demonstrate the direct power of Freemasonry over the Fourth Estate, it does offer a vivid example of the devotion that Freemasonry so often inspires in its initiates, a devotion that is nothing less than religious." What *initiates?* According to the book, these men weren't devoted Masonic initiates at all, having clearly stated that they were not Freemasons. The incident is not a "vivid example" of anything except that two brothers chose not to make money at the expense of their father's feelings. However, what it is indeed an example of is quite something else.

Having illustrated a unique brand of logic, let's take a final look at the deep knowledge on which this critique is based. I shall quote just one paragraph of *The Brotherhood*'s condemning knowledge of the inner workings of Freemasonry. The paragraph is complete, the parenthetic italics are mine:

"Much of masonic ritual centers on murder. [*Wrong: In the three complex rituals of Craft Masonry, there is one symbolic murder in one degree.*] At the 3rd Degree, the victim is Hiram Abiff, mythical architect in charge of the building of Solomon's temple. The ceremony involves the mimed murder of Hiram by three Apprentice Masons [*wrong: They are three Fellow Craft Masons*], and his subsequent resurrection. [*Wrong: Hiram did not rise from the dead. He was simply exhumed and buried in a different grave.*] The three Apprentices [*wrong again*] are named Jubela, Jubelo and Jubelum—known collectively as the *Juwes*. In Masonic lore, the Juwes are hunted down and executed [*wrong: They are hunted down and taken prisoner, then brought to King Solomon for judgment*] 'by the breast being torn open and the heart and vitals taken out and thrown over the left shoulder' [*wrong: Only one of the three Juwes was sentenced by Solomon to that punishment*], which closely parallels the details of Jack the Ripper's *modus operandi.*"

As for that last statement, Mr. Knight's earlier anti-Masonic book *Jack the Ripper: The Final Solution* was devoted to proving that the Ripper murders were Masonically motivated and Masonically covered up by Sir Charles Warren, commissioner of the Metropolitan Police. Mr. Knight was so fond of his most dramatic piece of damning evidence that he repeated it in *The Brotherhood*. His claim is that a chalked message had been found on a wall near the site of the fourth Ripper murder. It read: "The Juwes are The Men That will not be blamed for nothing." He reports that when Sir Charles heard of this message he hurried to the spot and washed it away. He tells us: "Warren . . . knew only too well that the writing on the wall was telling the world, 'The *Freemasons* are the men that will not be blamed for nothing.'" That gives Mr. Knight the distinction of being the first writer on Masonry in 270 years to state that the word *Juwes* is synonymous with "Freemasonry." Everyone knowledgeable about Masonry, which includes all who have read this book, knows that the word Juwes is synonymous with the *enemies* of Freemasonry, the murderers of the Grand Master Hiram Abiff.

I just could not believe that this was a book that had shaken up a government. It had shaken me up, but for a totally different reason. I was awestruck that Mr. Knight could summon up from some great reservoir of *chutzpah* the testicular diameter required to identify himself in *The Brotherhood* as a "neutral observer." After all, if a "neutral observer" asserts accusations of unfair advancement in business and government, corruption of the police and the judicial system, a connection with the KGB, an infiltration of the Vatican in a conspiracy to commit the biggest financial fraud of our time, responsibility for the Jack the Ripper murders, and the undoubted worship of the Devil, what is left for an *enemy* to assert?

CHAPTER 25

THE UNFINISHED TEMPLE OF SOLOMON

On February 11, 1988, a group of high-ranking Freemasons gathered in the Oval Office of the White House. They were assembled to honor and to be honored by President Ronald Reagan. First, Mr. Reagan received a certificate of honor from the Grand Lodge of Washington, D.C., then was made an Honorary Scottish Rite Mason. The third honor was the highest, as Mr. Voris King, imperial potentate of the Ancient Arabic Order of Nobles of the Mystic Shrine, named the President of the United States an honorary member of the Imperial Council of the Shrine.

The Shrine, the most visible aspect of Freemasonry in the United States, had come a long way. Just a generation ago Shriners' conventions had caused alarm and concern; editorials were written against grown men who apparently felt that it was hilariously funny to drop a bag of water from a hotel window onto the head of an unsuspecting pedestrian below. Shriner-time was party-time.

Then some wise men found a way to harness and redirect that exuberant energy, with great success. The focus was children, and the result was a network of twenty-two Shrine Hospitals for Crippled Children, including nineteen orthopedic hospitals and three burn centers. Research plays an important role as well: Twenty years ago a child whose body was 30 percent covered with first-degree burns would most certainly die, whereas today a child with twice that coverage will survive, thanks to Shrine-funded research. Perhaps the most remarkable aspect of these hospitals is that they have no patient billing department. No child waits for treatment while its parents establish their ability to pay or document their insurance coverage, because there is no charge, ever. And when the Shrine Circus comes to town to raise money for those hospitals, seats are set aside for children from local orphanages and broken homes—and the gift does not stop there. Individual Shriners pick up the children and return them after the show. At the circus they dip into their own pockets to make certain that their wide-eyed charges have all the cotton candy, popcorn, and lemonade they can hold. And that Shrine clown helping to make their visit extra memorable may be your neighborhood banker. Taken altogether, the shift in Shrine direction and purpose to the achievement of unassailable good works is an outstanding example of the effectiveness of leadership and the inherent willingness of men to exert themselves physically and financially for a cause they can believe in.

That being the case, one might ask why this book has not directed more attention to the better-known side degrees of Masonry, such as Scottish Rite and York Rite Masonry. The answer is simply that the origin and organization of those Masonic systems are well known and contain no forgotten mysteries. The real mysteries lie only at the heart of the original "Craft" or "Blue Lodge" Masonry of the Entered Apprentice, Fellow Craft, and Master Mason, the truly secret society whose origins and purposes appeared to have been lost forever in the passage of time and the vagaries of whispered verbal transmission.

That atmosphere of mystery carries over into the public view, as any "secret" society arouses the curiosity, enmity, and envy of those who are not in it, and even more so if they are not even eligible. One price that such societies pay is that, in the absence of knowledge of their workings, the society as a whole must bear the stigma of acts of individual members. The "Molly Maguires," for instance, who terrorized the Pennsylvania coal fields by burning down the houses and cutting the ears and noses off the mine superintendents who fired their drunken brothers, were all members of the Ancient Order of Hibernians, and it took the Hibernians a time to convince the world that the mutilations were not officially sanctioned. Similarly, Masonry has reeled under attacks upon the order brought on by the acts of individual members, such as the alleged murder of Captain William Morgan. Another such event involved what was then the whole Mormon population of the country.

Not far from Morgan's home in Batavia, New York, was the town of Manchester, the home of a young man named Joseph Smith, who founded the Mormon church. Smith based his new church on instructions and two golden plates that he said had been given to him by the angel Moroni just a little more than a year after Morgan's disappearance. He started at Palmyra, New York, but was driven out and moved his congregation to Ohio, where he was driven out again and finally settled at Nauvoo, Illinois. The town mushroomed in size and Freemasonry grew right along with it, with many Mormons swelling the Masonic ranks. Alphonse Cerza, a Masonic historian, reported that by 1843 there were five Mormon Masonic lodges at Nauvoo, all of which were suspended by the Grand Lodge for irregularities in their conduct. The Mormon lodges ignored the suspensions, adding to the tension already mounting between Mormons and local Christians—including non-Mormon Freemasons—on the subject of polygamy.

What happened next is disputed. The anti-Mormon local population erupted one night into a rage that saw mobs shooting and beating, burning down Mormon houses and barns, triggering a chain of events that led to the murder of Joseph Smith. His successor, Brigham Young, condemned the local Freemasons for the attack, branding them the agents of Satan. He decreed that any Mormon who refused to abandon Masonry, or chose to become a Mason, was subject to summary excommunication from the Mormon church. The Masons, on the other hand, claimed that the Freemasons of Nauvoo had nothing to do with the savage attacks. For their part, the Mormons decided to leave the United States altogether, heading west until they reached the Mexican territory of Utah. The Masons ultimately decided that Mormonism was incompatible with the principles of Freemasonry, and for many years no Mormon could become a Freemanson; but in 1984 the Grand Lodge of Utah made peace with the Mormons and today many Mormons are Freemasons.

A few years later, during the War Between the States, Masonic officers and men found themselves facing their Masonic brothers on the other side. There are many Civil War legends of help rendered in response to Masonic signs of distress, but the most significant event happened just after the war was over. Angered by the erosion of their way of life and the enforced growing political power of men who had been their slaves until the war was lost, a group of Southerners decided to fight back by means of a secret society. Many of them were Freemasons, who drew upon their knowledge of Masonic rites to develop a ritualistic infrastructure for the society that was to save the South through the maintenance of white supremacy. They adopted the circle of the lodge as their formal meeting arrangement for members, named their society for it, and demonstrated their educational level by using the Greek word for "circle," which is *kuklos*. The pronunciation and spelling quickly became Ku Klux, and they styled themselves as the Knights of the Ku Klux Klan, as terms of chivalry were introduced into the ritual. The single All-Seeing Eye of Masonry became the Grand Cyclops. There were hand signals, secret passwords, secret handgrips and recognition signals, even a sacred oath, all adapted from Masonic experience. Some Klansmen even boasted of official connections between the Klan and Freemasonry.

A society that had begun as the Southerners' only recourse against the postwar invasion of the South quickly degenerated into something else. Violence took hold, with beatings, lynchings, and even torture, so it was decided by the leadership that the Klan should be disbanded. In 1869 the Grand Master and former Confederate cavalry general Nathan Bedford Forrest issued his only General Order, which was for all Klans to disband and disperse. It was too late. The general's order was ignored by many who still smarted under the humiliation of defeat in the war, and what they felt was the even greater humiliation of its aftermath. As the violence grew, and the target for Klan hatred widened in scope from blacks to Jews, to Catholics, to all foreign-born, the talk of the Masonic connection continued. Finally, state Masonic Grand Lodges in both North and South felt called upon to declare publicly their total rejection of the philosophy, the motives, and the actions of the Ku Klux Klan.

Nevertheless, a shadow had been cast on Freemasonry in the

minds of many, and it was not helped by the attitude of many Masons toward the black community. True, there is a very light sprinkling of blacks in Masonry, but the number is just a fraction of a fraction of one percent of total membership. One Mason explained to me that this was because the Old Charges of Masonry state that no man could become Mason who was not "a free man born of a free mother," and all American blacks are directly descended from slaves. He had no response to the point that the Old Charges do *not* say that a Mason must be a free man born of a free great-great-grandmother.

An older shadow on Masonic racial attitudes is an influential but almost unknown network of Masonic lodges that is very much a part of the black establishment across the United States but remains unrecognized by white Masons. It is known as Prince Hall Masonry, after its founder, a free black who appears to have served as a soldier in the Revolutionary War. Before that conflict, he and fourteen other blacks had been made Freemasons by a traveling military lodge, No. 441, of the British 38th Regiment of Foot, stationed at Boston. When the regiment pulled out of the area, the lodge left its resident black brothers with a permit which allowed them to hold meetings, but not to take in initiates or to award degrees.

The war made certain that the British military lodge would not return to Boston, so Prince Hall subsequently made application to the Grand Lodge of England, which issued a warrant on September 29, 1784, for African Lodge No. 459. Although very much an official Masonic lodge, No. 459 was not recognized by white Masonry in the United States. It finally responded to the exclusion by beginning to issue charters to lodges in other black communities, and even warranted traveling military lodges that existed within black military units in the Civil War, and later in both world wars. Prince Hall Masonry gradually spread across the country and expanded into side degrees, in much the same manner as white Masonry. It eventually became one of the most influential yet least known pillars of the black community, especially in the South, with over a quarter of a million members.

From time to time discussions do come up in Masonic conferences about giving full recognition to the Prince Hall lodges, but those in favor have never been able to muster up a majority for affirmation. Masons declare that they are not racist, but it is difficult to wrap one's mind around the concept of a *limited* universal brotherhood.

Another barrier to "universal" brotherhood has been the relationship between Masons and Catholic societies and the Catholic church, although this has changed much in recent years, especially since the Second Vatican Council. No longer do clerics so strongly implement the instructions of Pope Leo XIII in *Humanum Genus* to "insist that parents and spiritual directors in teaching the catechism may never cease to admonish appropriately children and pupils of the wicked nature of these sects [the Freemasons], " and the children were so taught. One Catholic attorney told me that in his parochial elementary school, in the 1950s, the sisters lectured against Freemasonry in the classroom. In his case, there was a Masonic temple only two blocks away, and pupils who had to pass that way to and from school were told to avert their eyes as they passed by, to avoid looking at the house of the anti-Christ. (In fairness, it was not all one-sided. Twenty years earlier my Presbyterian mother had pointed out to me, then a child of seven or eight, that Catholic churches and monasteries were so often built on hilltops because the grounds were to be used as artillery positions when the Catholics would attempt to take over the country.)

Leo XIII also recommended that societies be formed to give the "working man" an alternative to Freemasonry. He urged that they be "invited to good societies that they may not be dragged into bad ones" and expressed his approval that such societies were already being formed. He may have had in mind the fact that just two years before, at Hartford, Connecticut, Father Michael J. McGiveny had formed a society of Catholic men of Irish descent that took the name "Knights of Columbus." A fraternal organization, complete with secret meetings, passwords, and degrees, the society was founded to meet the needs of Irish Catholics who found themselves in virtual ethnic ghettos surrounded by a sea of anti-Catholic Protestants and, as they openly stated, to provide a Catholic alternative to Freemasonry. The concept took hold, and today it is estimated that there are over 1.3 million Knights of Columbus in the United States, with additional members in Mexico, Canada, and the Philippines.

Both fraternal societies grew during the early years of this century. The Masons and the Knights of Columbus never came to blows, but they attacked each other constantly in every other way. The conflict between them became most dramatic in Mexico, in what the Knights of Columbus refer to as their "Mexican Campaign" against the "communists," as they called the anti-church ruling party of the country. The revolutionary victories in Mexico had deprived the Catholic church of extensive properties and most of the traditional church privileges. Religious orders were outlawed and elementary school teaching was forbidden to clerics and religious. There had been a complete separation of church and state and priests were not permitted to vote, being regarded as citizens of a foreign state, with their primary loyalty owed to the Vatican.

By 1925 there were thousands of Knights of Columbus in Mexico, determined to fight the anti-Catholic laws and to return Mexico to Rome. They even tried to run religious schools but were suppressed. Finally, many of the Knights joined with other Catholic laymen to form the *Liga Nacional*, the National League for the Defense of Religious Liberty. The league in turn formed the nucleus of an armed rebellion against the government. The rebels dedicated their allegiance to *Cristo Rey*, Christ the King, for which they were referred to as the *Cristeros*. Mexican Freemasons fought in the government ranks, while many Mexican Knights took to the field of battle as *Cristeros*. Back in the United States, funds and support were gathered for the two sides by Masons and Knights alike. The rebellion raged from 1926 to 1929, and ultimate brutal treatment for the defeated *Cristeros* was guaranteed by their use of assassination as a weapon for attempted victory. In 1927 two members of the *Liga Nacional*, one a Jesuit priest, were executed without trials for the attempted murder of President Alvaro Obregón, who did not escape the assassins' bullets when another attempt was made the following year. As the rebellion was put down, the *Cristero* prisoners were summarily shot.

The threshold of the Great Depression in America saw a resurgence of the Ku Klux Klan, which many of the Knights of Columbus tied to Freemasonry. Mutual antagonism threatened to produce more violence, but already cracks were beginning to appear in the great religious wall that separated the Knights and the Masons, based on their common ground of American nationalism. The Knights had set up service organizations in Europe during World War I, by which time they had already instituted a fourth degree based on patriotism. After the war they decided to donate an equestrian statue of Lafayette to the city of Metz in France, as a symbol of gratitude and brotherhood, and were immediately attacked by some of their fellow Catholics. Their critics declared that Lafayette had been a Freemason and therefore should not be honored by any loyal Catholic. The strongest and most vociferous condemnation of the project came from the societies of German-American Catholics, some of whom accused the Knights of trying to create a "Freemason saint." The Knights had to make a decision. They concluded that while they were loyal Catholics, they were also loyal Americans. They could not embrace a policy that rejected contributions to American history by Freemasons, since this would mean eliminating George Washington, Benjamin Franklin, John Hancock, and dozens more. The tribute went forward and the bronze statue was dedicated to the memory of the aristocratic French Mason on August 6, 1920. After the ceremony, a delegation of Knights went to Rome for an audience with Pope Benedict XV, who put the conflict to rest with the comment that complete devotion to one's country is not incompatible with Catholic ideals.

It would be foolish to maintain that animosity no longer exists between the Freemasons and Catholic fraternal societies such as the Catholic Order of Foresters, the Ancient Order of Hibernians, and the Knights of Columbus, but there certainly has been a marked improvement in recent years. In 1967 high officials of both Craft and Scottish Rite Masonry actually sat down at the table with major leaders of the Knights of Columbus to discuss their common goals of morality, patriotism, and law and order. Actually, they had more in common than that. Both orders had been severely criticized for the juvenile physical "hazing" that often found its way into initiation ceremonies, and both had been accused of job preferment and political influence. Having read Stephen Knight's condemnations of preferment in Freemasonry, I was interested to see that Christopher J. Kauffman, in his officially recognized *Faith and Fraternalism: The History of the Knights of Columbus,* wrote: "There were of course, also those men who joined the Order primarily for economic and political reasons. However, because these reasons are common motives for membership in any fraternal organization, they are not unique traits of the Knights of Columbus."

As fraternal societies are learning to live with each other, they are also having to live with the fact of declining membership. Freemasonry is still the largest fraternal order in the United States, and in the world, but recruitment has fallen away in the past few years and many members have simply dropped out. Unavoidably, as times change the needs of men also change. During the great periods of expansion, as the English-speaking people moved out around the globe, Freemasonry had provided important social services. Whether being transferred to Hong Kong, seeking employment at a South African mine, or debarking at San Francisco during the great gold rush, the solitary Freemason did not have to remain lost and lonely for more than the day or two it took to make contact with local Masonic brothers, who guided him, helped him if he had trouble, and put in a good word for him in the right places. And his Masonic membership also ensured his social status.

How important that could be was dramatically illustrated in the early history of Australia. It is well known that its early "colonization" was by thousands of convicts, but it is not so well known that the army units sent down under to guard the convicts took their Masonry with them in their traveling military lodges. Technically, the convict who had served out his time could avail himself of all the opportunities of a new land, but whether he built a business of his own, or a substantial farming operation, he and his family, perhaps for several generations, had to live with the stigma of penal servitude, firmly fixing them at a lower level of the social scale. All that was required to change that status was for the ex-convict to be accepted into a Masonic lodge, which put him at once in the position of sworn brotherhood with officers of the garrison, leading citizens, and members of the government. This advantage was not available to the many Irish ex-convicts, whose Roman Catholicism precluded the Masonic ladder to social acceptance. Australia took to Freemasonry, and there are over three thousand lodges there now.

The social status of Freemasonry in Britain has been assured in years past by the patronage of the royal family, but that, too, may be changing. Prince Charles is the first British male heir to the throne to reject Masonry in almost two hundred years. The explanation most frequently given, but unconfirmed, is that Charles has been influenced against Masonry by his father, Prince Philip, who bitterly resented the pressure brought to bear on him to become a Freemason by his father-in-law, King George VI. Philip did join but remained totally inactive, so the present Grand Master is the royal cousin, the duke of Kent.

It must not be thought, however, that the vows of brotherhood created a great melting pot in which class distinctions disappeared. When the duke of Sussex became Grand Master of the United Grand Lodge, he suggested that a lodge be assembled made up entirely of peers of the realm, so that he might have a "proper" lodge to serve as Worshipful Master. Royal patronage did, however, make it much easier to have Masonic lodges in naval and military units, and lodge rooms in such venerable institutions as Scotland Yard and the Bank of England.

In addition to the royal rejection by the Prince of Wales, British Masonry is still smarting under the residue of the attacks on the order by Stephen Knight and others, as witness a ten-minute bill introduced (unsuccessfully) to the House of Commons in June 1988, intended to curtail the acceptance of Freemasons into the Metropolitan Police.

It's too early to evaluate the success of its efforts, but the United Grand Lodge of England has made some attempts to counter the bad press. One of them, begun in 1986, was a program of free public tours of Freemason's Hall, but unfortunately some of the press coverage of those tours was insulting and facetious (and at least partially fictitious). For example, an article in the *Illustrated London News* of November 1987, entitled "Temple of Horrors," featured an illustration of thousands of bats flying from Freemason's Hall. It ostensibly reported the tour from a woman's viewpoint. After sharing her observations on the odors of the Hall ("halitosis, brilliantine and furniture polish"), the author introduces just two of her fellow visitors, both Americans. One is described as a "Freemasoness"—the first I've ever heard of—who of course has spiked heels that clack on the marble floor, and who at one point is observed stroking statues of Jonathan and David. The other American is a Texan who chews gum incessantly and responds to the conductor's comments with "Wowee" and "Gee whiz." (I have known a lot of Texans, who certainly have mastered some of the most ingenious epithets and pungent expletives in the English-speaking world, but I never heard one say "Wowee" or "Gee whiz." Perhaps Gomer Pyle is still running on British TV). As the group stops to examine a star set in the floor, the reporter observes that she would not be surprised to "see the Prince of Darkness himself burst up through the lapis lazuli star with red smoke swirling from flared nostrils." Passing a closed door, she speculates on the possibility that chickens are having their heads cut off on the other side. It is difficult to imagine what such a style of reporting does for the publication's readers, but perhaps it prompted waves of laughter from the author's own circle of friends, which is frequently the primary objective of that form of journalism. Such articles should also set minds at ease that Freemasonry does not control the free press in Britain.

In earlier times Freemasonry had been a powerful force for religious freedom. The newly formed United States was made up of colonies in which bigotry and religious intolerance were part of the way of life. Colonies had their own state religions, and the State of Connecticut remained officially Congregationalist until 1818. Roger Williams fled religious intolerance in Massachusetts to found Rhode Island, and even the Catholic Calverts only got their charter for Maryland by agreeing that the state religion would be Anglican Catholicism. Virginia was militantly Church of England, with laws calling for the public whipping of Baptist and Methodist ministers who dared to preach sermons to their followers. Under the pressure of that persecution, a number of those congregations left Virginia for the wooded wilderness of the American Southeast, where they still hold sway. Nor could the Roman Catholics be condemned in any way for this bigotry in the Land of the Free, for they comprised less than one percent of the population in 1776. It was up to the disparate Protestants to work things out for themselves, and by no means were they all in favor of the proposed religious freedom to be guaranteed in the Bill of Rights. The Masonic affiliations of many of the men who fought for those rights indicate that they took seriously their vows to uphold the principle that how a man chose to worship God was his own business.

As useful as Freemasonry may have been to its members in the past, however, the major issue for the order today is where does it go from here? The concentration on individual morality and group charity has not halted the erosion of recruitment, as young men more frequently decline to follow their fathers and grandfathers into the Craft. One problem may be that, in an increasingly permissive and materialistic society, the concepts of personal morality, personal pride, and personal honor may appear antiquated. If so, a program needs to be launched to bring them back, not just as concepts but as real modes of behavior. If Freemasonry could help to do that, it would be doing us all a great favor, caught as we are in a society in which substantial monetary gain seems to modify the social and moral stigma of crime. The man who steals a five-thousand-dollar automobile is a thief, a crook, and an outcast, but the man who steals 20 million has no shortage of cocktail invitations. A friend paid thirty dollars to take me to dinner to hear a highly successful ex-convict predict the future of the world economy, and after the lecture questions were put to him by the audience—largely made up of bankers, brokers, and businessmen—in an atmosphere of attentive respect. Prison is not as dull for the man who commits his crimes on Wall Street or on Pennsylvania Avenue, because he can occupy his hours writing a book against a substantial advance from his publisher and correspond with his agent about subsequent paid lectures and television talk-show appearances. In such a climate, any force for a resurgence of personal morality would be most welcome.

Much more unique to Freemasonry, and of potential benefit to all, is its ancient tradition against litigation. Each year the United States sees the birth of 3.8 million babies and 8 million lawsuits. It has been reported that of all of the men and women practicing law on the face of the earth, over 60 percent are in the United States. Recently, in the Kentucky county in which I live, a drunken driver at the wheel of a pickup truck drove head-on into a church bus, which burst into flames and killed twenty-seven people. In the ensuing weeks I heard as much conversation about the lawsuit potential of the accident as I did about the shocking deaths of twenty-four innocent youngsters.

In response to the proliferation of litigation, the rapidly rising costs of liability insurance have affected the cost and even the availability of vital goods and services. In one community in Georgia, the doctors practicing obstetrics and gynecology announced that they would no longer accept any patient who was an attorney, wife of an attorney, or employee of a law firm, all from a growing and realistic fear of malpractice suits. The unfortunate expectant mothers were forced to drive about seventy miles to Savannah for prenatal care and childbirth. Even the gentle laws of hospitality suffer, and one becomes frightened to let neighbors and guests use a swimming pool or ride a horse, or to let their children climb a tree.

The Freemasons could provide a great service if they would bring their ancient attitudes toward litigation into the light and into the public forum. Their old rules say that lawsuits are the settlement of last resort, and that—even then—the suit should be for restitution only, and not for money damages. While it is clear that the Masonic attitudes were designed for relationships among the fraternity, and by no means anticipated the types of litigation we see today, the Old Charge is quite clear that men are to try all other remedies before seeking the redress of the courts. Three million men asserting that point of view publicly, and to their legislators, could exert a powerful influence and force. Some such force is necessary, before a situation that is already running wild degenerates to the point that an increasingly aggressive society, motivated primarily by the achievement of material success, launches more and more planned monetary attacks that draw upon a confusing complexity of laws which no one man could ever hope to memorize, much less understand.

Even more important to the whole world would be for Freemasonry to publicly promulgate and work for its Old Charges regarding bonds of brotherhood among men of all religious faiths, as well as the exhortations to its members that each should give time and active support to his own faith. As this book is being written, religion, the love of God, is still the major problem in many lands. It is the basis for political turmoil, terrorism, and outright war and carries the potential for much more of the same in the future. The Sikhs in India, who want their own state in the Punjab, made the intensity of their feelings known by the assassination of Prime Minister Indira Gandhi, and felt the punishment of machine guns turned loose on their sacred Golden Temple at Amritsar. The Indian army dispatched Hindu troops to Sri Lanka to help put down an uprising of Buddhist Tamils. Khomeini proved that religion could be a stronger force than welfare programs and high-tech weaponry as he overthrew a government and then sent hundreds of thousands of his Shi'ite followers against the equally militant Sunnis of Iraq. Both sides were ready to die over what had

begun as a difference of opinion over which of Mohammed's relatives had the right to inherit his leadership of Islam. The situation became even more divisive in Beirut when, in May 1988, pro-
Iranian Shi'ites battled pro-Syrian Shi'ites with tanks and
machine guns, until hundreds of coreligionists lay dead and mutilated in the streets.

The Russians thought that they had effectively blocked the
young people of Central Asia from the Islamic faith of their
fathers by reducing the number of *meddresseh*, or Moslem semi-
naries, from over four hundred to just two. Antireligious lectures
were delivered in the schools and, for good measure, antireligious
posters were mounted in Moslem shrines ("Praying to God,"
reads one of them, "is like asking that two plus two please not
equal four"). But in the early stages of the war in Afghanistan, to
which they had sent Uzbek troops—Moslem descendants of the
Mongols—the Russians were surprised when the Uzbeks and the
Afghan guerrillas shouted to each other from behind their rocks,
"Brother, we are both Believers and Sons of the Prophet. Why do
we try to kill each other for these Russians?" The Uzbeks had to
be withdrawn from combat, and the Russians must have pondered how these young men in their twenties could consider
themselves Moslems when the total machinery of government,
schools, and government-controlled media had consistently
pounded into them that there is no God.

In Britain, church membership has fallen off sharply, and bishops of the Church of England have questioned the miracles of the
New Testament. In northern Europe, more people stay away
from church than attend. In Japan, a wave of anti-Semitism is
gaining momentum with books, articles, and even posters in the
Tokyo subway. In Greece, it has been proposed that most of the
wealth of the Orthodox church be place under government control.

In Switzerland in 1988, Archbishop Lefebvre happily
embraced excommunication from the Roman church for himself
and his thousands of followers around the world as he consecrated four bishops against the express orders of the Holy See. He
declared his determination to return the church to its status
before what he termed the "heretical" changes of the Second
Vatican Council (1962–65). Membership in the priesthood in the
United States has also declined sharply, and the membership of

religious orders has dropped from a peak of over one hundred thousand to little more than six thousand in 1988. Catholic schools have been closed and churches shut down for lack of priests to lead them. Nor will women be permitted to fill that gap in the Catholic church, because it has been determined that although women may be accorded larger roles in the church, they will never be ordained as priests. (They are not alone in this: In October 1987 Southern Baptist churches ousted an entire congregation that had selected a female pastor, citing scriptural reference that women cannot have authority over men.)

Pope John Paul II has not hesitated to chastise church dissidents, but dissension continues unabated, particularly in regard to marriage within the priesthood, the role of women, abortion, the use of condoms to prevent AIDS, birth control, and homosexuality. Nor has he resolved the problems of the communist priests in Latin American politics, even though he has forbidden their activities.

In the United States, the Ku Klux Klan is apparently alive and well, militantly antiblack and anti-Catholic. The image of television evangelists has been tarnished, perhaps beyond repair, by the personal conduct of some of their number. In 1987 the U.S. Supreme Court reversed the decision of a federal judge in Louisiana that violated the constitutional precept of the separation of church and state: In March, U.S. District Court Judge W. Brevard Hand had ruled against what he termed "secular humanism"— the attempt to teach moral behavior on a secular rather than a religious basis. He ordered forty-four textbooks removed from the schools, including two home economics books for budding homemakers. No more could the story of George Washington and the cherry tree be used to teach a moral lesson. "If this court is compelled to purge 'God is great, God is good, we thank him for our daily food' from the classroom," said the judge, "then this court must also purge from the classroom those things that serve to teach that salvation is through one's self rather than through a deity." Also in 1987, the U.S. Supreme Court struck down as unconstitutional a state law that required state schools to teach "creationism"—the literal creation story from the Book of Genesis—along with the theory of evolution. The ruling seriously angered Protestant fundamentalists, who have also expressed their objection to the Supreme Court's three-part standard for school programs: The program must have a purely secular purpose; it cannot have the effect of advancing the cause of any religion; and it must avoid entangling the government in religious matters. In the meantime, another appeal is waiting to be heard, in which a federal judge in Tennessee decided that fundamentalist children should be excused from having to read classroom books that violate their religious beliefs, citing portions of *The Diary of Anne Frank, Cinderella,* and *The Wizard of Oz.*

We have spoken here of fundamentalist Moslems, fundamentalist Catholics, and fundamentalist Protestants, and one more group must be cited. With the Iran-Iraq war in a state of uncertain truce and the Soviets withdrawn from Afghanistan, the most potentially explosive situation left in the world may be wrapped up in the fundamentalists in Israel, who can complicate either or both of two very vital issues. First is the matter of the uprisings in the Occupied Territories (where even a prime minister described the local residents, some of whose families may have been there for ten generations, as "foreigners"). It is important for Israel to be recognized as a democracy, especially in its relations with the United States, and even with many American Jews. To preserve that impression, it must find a way to deal with the substantial non-Jewish population it has acquired in military victories. To achieve its overriding ambition of preserving a purely Jewish state, Israel cannot allow those non-Jews equal voting rights, which would permit them a substantial voice in the Knesset. To many Israelis, the solution is to give up some of the conquered territory, as the lesser of two catastrophes. Others are angered at the thought of such a move, and some even mention that Israel does not yet have all of the land that God originally gave to His chosen people. The hard-right fundamentalists have tougher solutions, such as simply expelling the Moslem population and replacing it with Jewish settlers, a move that would risk the condemnation of the rest of the world and perhaps war as well.

The other problem in Israel brings us right back to Freemasonry, because it is squarely centered on the original site of the Temple of Solomon on Mount Moriah, the Temple Mount in Jerusalem, the birthplace of the Knights Templar. Perhaps no spot on earth cries out for the brotherhood of men of different religions more than the site of the original Temple of Solomon, in a situation so tense that some writers have speculated that it could well trigger World War III. And for the first time in this book, we are not discussing allegories based on the temple, but the real temple, on the Temple Mount in Jerusalem.

It is of vital importance to three great religions—Judaism, Islam, and Christianity. King David had the vision to build a great house of God and purchased the threshing floor of Ornan, on Mount Moriah, for the building. It remained for his son, Solomon, to actually construct the temple, which took seven years to complete, in the tenth century B.C. In 587 B.C. Jerusalem fell to the Babylonians under King Nebuchadnezzar, when the temple was stripped of all its valuables and then burned to the ground.

About fifty years later Babylon was taken by the Persians, who permitted the Jews to return from exile to the practice of their religion. The Persians named one Zerubbabel as governor, who with the encouragement of the high priest Joshua determined to build a second temple on the same site. It was a sizable structure, but without the magnificence of Solomon's offering. It was completed about 515 B.C. and served for centuries, but not without pain and conflict and change of ownership.

In 168 B.C. the king of Syria, Antiochus Epiphanes, failed in his attempt to subdue Egypt but ravaged the Jewish territory between, giving the temple its darkest days of desecration. Circumcision was outlawed, punishable by death, as was any celebration of the Jewish sabbath. As a deliberate humiliation of the Jews, whose dietary laws prohibited pork, Antiochus had an altar built on the Temple Mount for the sacrifice of swine.

None of this was lost on a guerrilla band of militant Jews who operated in the hills under a man named Mattathias. The band became known as the Maccabees, or the "hammerers." Upon the death of Mattathias, command passed to his son Judas (or Judah). The enemy so underrated this military genius that before one major battle the opposing general arranged for the sale of the Jewish army to slave dealers, only to have his own army defeated by the Maccabees, whom they overwhelmingly outnumbered. One victory followed another until the Maccabees had taken Jerusalem. Going to the temple to offer their prayers of thanksgiving and to relight the sacred menorah, they discovered just a tiny bit of consecrated oil. It would take eight days to go through the ritual required to consecrate more, while the amount on hand

would last less than a day. They went ahead anyway, and witnessed a miracle as the small amount of oil burned for eight days
and nights until the new oil was ready, a miracle still remembered
in the celebration of Hanukkah, the Feast of Lights.

But the Romans were coming, and their conquest of Jerusalem
kept the holy city away from Jewish control for over two thousand
years until the Six Day War in 1967. It was King Herod, the
Roman appointee, who undertook to expand and beautify the
second temple. It would be larger than Solomon's temple, and to
accommodate its expanded foundations a massive retaining wall
was built on the southwest side of the Temple Mount. It was in
the colonnaded courtyard of this expanded temple that Jesus
Christ walked and taught His disciples. This newest temple had
the shortest life, as it was totally destroyed by the Romans in the
civil strife of A.D. 70. All that remains of the elaborate structure
is part of the retaining wall, now called the Western Wall, or the
Wailing Wall.

Although Israel got possession of Jerusalem in 1967, they have
been reluctant to take possession of the Temple Mount. It is still
policed by Moslems, because instead of a Jewish temple to God,
the mount is crowned with two mosques built during the days of
Islamic rule, including the famous mosaic-covered, gold-topped
Dome of the Rock. This situation is a matter of dissension and
disagreement among Israelis. Most are willing to leave well
enough alone for the moment; but at the other end of the spec-
trum are fundamentalists, such as the *Gush Emunim,* "the Faithful," who find that attitude as intolerable as the idea of Moslems
worshiping on the very site of the temple of God, while Jews are
restricted to the foundation wall below. Meir Kahane, the American rabbi who heads the far-right Kach fundamentalists, has no
problem with the Moslems. He simply says that they should all be
driven out of Israel, after which the problem of the Temple
Mount could be easily dealt with.

These groups and others want a Jewish temple on the Temple
Mount, preferably on the very site of the Temple of Solomon.
Why else would there be a program to teach ancient temple ritual
at the Orthodox seminary Yeshivah Ateret Hacohanim? The
overriding question for the world is whether any of these groups
prevail to the point that they actually consider tearing down the
mosque of the Dome of the Rock to make way for a new temple.

This would undoubtedly arouse the wrath of every Moslem in the world, who hold the site sacred as the place where Mohammed ascended the ladder to the very throne of Allah. There is no way to predict the violence—from sporadic terrorism to outright war. Any Moslem ruler who declined to join in would be risking his throne.

Yet to the Jews, this low hill in Jerusalem, this Temple Mount, is the most sacred place on earth. The Temple of Solomon predates Christianity by a thousand years and Islam by many more. And to the Christian, too, the place where Christ debated and taught, and drove out the money-changers, is sacred ground. The Catholic church has suggested that Jerusalem become an international city, a concept which may have merit, but which does not solve the problem. It is not the city itself but the few sacred acres of Mount Moriah that sit at the center of the controversy. Can the followers of three great religions, three great ways to worship God, find a way to come together in peace and brotherhood in this tiny space? This is the place where, more than anywhere else, the central religious attitude of Freemasonry could be applied with the most beneficial effect to the rest of the world, where men who avow their beliefs in a Supreme Being could meet in brotherhood and bear full respect for the other man's mode of worship.

To achieve that goal on the Temple Mount would be a monumental task. Should there be one tripartite temple for all? Is it practical to leave the Dome of the Rock as it is, but build a Jewish temple and a Christian shrine on the mount, all connected with a common courtyard or plaza? A sensible plan needs to be made and then sold: to Israel, because it controls the land and desires a temple; to Moslems, because they will be concerned over any desecration of the Dome of the Rock; and to Christians, who are denominationally splintered, so that an interfaith group might be required to administer the Christian portion.

Just mounting a move in that direction might help to thwart the plans of those willing to risk war in a maniacal game of king-of-the-hill, to set their God above other gods, whichever of the three He may be. Whoever wins, men will die, and it is time that men stopped dying, and killing, over how merciful, compassionate, and all-caring is their God. Churches have said, and are still saying, that their followers cannot be Freemasons, because to acknowledge all religions is to denigrate the "true religion" by equating it with all the other false ones, so I am certainly not suggesting that all men become Freemasons. What I am suggesting is that about 5 million Freemasons in the world, who do accept brotherhood with men of all faiths, in that spirit might take the lead in solving the problem of the Temple Mount by combining their religious attitudes with their veneration of the Temple of Solomon, to the benefit of the whole world. It would be a long and expensive journey from west to east, but it would give new meaning to each man shaping himself into the perfect ashlar ready to take its place in the Temple of God. It would be a wonderful way to complete the unfinished Temple of Solomon and to complete a full-circle circumambulation back to the very first purpose of their predecessor Knights of the Temple, the safe passage of all pilgrims to that holy place.

Appendix

(Following is an English translation, from the original Latin, of the encyclical Humanum Genus, the strongest and most comprehensive papal condemnation of Freemasonry, promulgated in 1884.)

THE MASONIC SECT

LEO, POPE, XIII.

*To all venerable Patriarchs, Primates, Archbishops, and Bishops
in the Catholic world who have grace and communion with
the Apostolic See:*

VENERABLE BROTHERS:

Health and the Apostolic Benediction!

THE HUMAN RACE, after, by the malice of the devil, it had departed from God, the Creator and Giver of heavenly gifts, divided itself into two different and opposing parties, one of which assiduously combats for truth and virtue, the other for those things which are opposed to virtue and to truth. The one is the Kingdom of God on earth—that is, the Church of Jesus Christ; those who desire to adhere to which from their soul and conducively to salvation must serve God and His only begotten Son with their whole mind and their whole will. The other is the kingdom of Satan, in whose dominion and power are all who have followed his sad example and that of our first parents. They refuse to obey divine and eternal law, and strive for many things to the neglect of God and for many against God. This twofold kingdom, like two states with contrary laws working in contrary directions, Augustine clearly saw and described, and comprehended the efficient cause of both with subtle brevity in these words: "Two loves have made two states: the love of self to the contempt of God has made the earthly, but the love of God to the contempt of self has made the heavenly." (De Civ. Dei, lib. xiv., chap. 17.)

The one fights the other with different kinds of weapons, and battles at all times, though not always with the same ardor and fury. In our days, however, those who follow the evil one seem to conspire and strive all together under the guidance and with the help of that society of men spread all over, and solidly established, which they call Free-Masons. Not dissimulating their intentions, they vie in attacking the power of God; they openly and ostensibly strive to damage the Church, with the purpose to deprive thoroughly if possible Christian people of the benefits brought by the Saviour Jesus Christ.

Seeing these evils, we are compelled by charity in our soul to say often to God: "For lo! Thy enemies have made noise; and they that hate Thee have lifted up the head. They have taken malicious counsel against Thy people, and have consulted against Thy saints. They have said: Come and let us destroy them, so that they be not a nation." (Ps. lxxxii., 2-4)

In such an impending crisis, in such a great and obstinate warfare upon Christianity, it is our duty to point out the danger, exhibit the adversaries, resist as much as we can their schemes and tricks, lest those whose salvation is in our hands should perish eternally: and that the kingdom of Jesus Christ, which we have received in trust, not only may stay and remain intact, but may continue to increase all over the world by new additions.

The Roman Pontiffs, our predecessors, watching constantly over the safety of the Christian people, early recognized this capital enemy rushing forth out of the darkness of hidden conspiracy, and, anticipating the future in their mind, gave the alarm to princes and people, that they should not be caught by deceptions and frauds.

Clement XII. first signalized the danger in 1738, and Benedict XIV. renewed and continued his Constitution. Pius VII. followed them both; and Leo XII., by the Apostolic Constitution—*quo graviora*—recapitulating the acts and decrees of the above Pontiffs about the matter, validated and confirmed them forever. In the same way spoke Pius VIII., Gregory XVI., and very often Pius IX.

The purpose and aim of the Masonic sect having been discovered from plain evidence, from the cognition of causes, its laws, Rites and commentaries having come to light and been made known by the additional depositions of the associated members, this Apostolic See denounced and openly declared that the sect of Masons is established against law and honesty, and is equally a danger to Christianity as well as to society; and, threatening those heavy punishments which the Church uses against the guilty ones, she forbade the society, and ordered that none should give his name to it. Therefore the angry Masons, thinking that they would escape the sentence or partially destroy it by despising or calumniating, accused the Pope who made those decrees of not having made a right decree or of having overstepped moderation. They thus tried to evade the authority and the importance of the Apostolic Constitutions of Clement XII., Benedict XIV., Pius VII., and Pius IX. But in the same society there were some who, even against their own will, acknowledged that the Roman Pontiffs had acted wisely and lawfully, according to the Catholic discipline. In this many princes and rulers of States agreed with the Popes, and either denounced Masonry to the Apostolic See or by appropriate laws condemned it as a bad thing in Holland, Austria, Switzerland, Spain, Bavaria, Savoy, and other parts of Italy.

But the event justified the prudence of our predecessors, and this is the most important. Nay, their paternal care did not always and everywhere succeed, either because of the simulation and shrewdness of the Masons themselves, or through the inconsiderate levity of others whose duty required of them strict attention. Hence, in a century and a half the sect of Masons grew beyond expectation; and, creeping audaciously and deceitfully among the various classes of the people, it grew to be so powerful that now it seems the only dominating power in the States. From this rapid and dangerous growth have come into the Church and into the State those evils which our predecessors had already foreseen. It has indeed come to this, that we have serious fear, not for the Church, which has a foundation too firm for men to upset it, but for those States in which this society is so powerful—or other societies of a like kind, and which show themselves to be servants and companions of Masonry.

For these reasons, when we first succeeded in the government of the Church, we saw and felt very clearly the necessity of opposing so great an evil with the full weight of our authority. On all favorable occasions we have attacked the principal doctrines in which the Masonic perversity appeared. By our Encyclical Letter, *quod apostoloci muneris*, we attacked the errors of Socialists and Communists; by the Letter, *Arcanum*, we tried to explain and defend the genuine notion of domestic society, whose source and origin is in marriage; finally, by the letter which begins *Diuturnum*, we proposed a form of civil power consonant with the principles of Christian wisdom, responding to the very nature and the the welfare of people and Princes. Now, after the example of our predecessors, we intend to turn our attention to the Masonic society, to its whole doctrine, to its intentions, acts, and feelings, in order to illustrate more and more this wicked force and stop the spread of this contagious disease.

There are several sects of men which, though different in name, customs, forms, and origin, are identical in aim and sentiment with Masonry. It is the universal center from which they all spring, and to which they all return. Although in our days these seem to no longer care to hide in darkness, but hold their meetings in the full light and under the eyes of their fellow-men and publish their journals openly, yet they deliberate and preserve the habits and customs of secret societies. Nay, there are in them many secrets which are by law carefully concealed not only from the profane, but also from many associated, viz., the last and intimate intentions, the hidden and unknown chiefs, the hidden and secret meetings, the resolutions and methods and means by which they will be carried into execution. Hence the difference of rights and of duties among the members; hence the distinction of orders and grades and the severe discipline by which they are ruled. The initiated must promise, nay, take an oath, that they will never, at any way or at any time, disclose their fellow-members and the emblems by which they are known, or expose their doctrines. So, by false appearance, but with the same kind of simulation, the Masons chiefly strive, as once did the Manicheans, to hide and to admit no witnesses but their own. They seek skillfully hiding places, assuming the appearance of literary men or philosophers, associated for the purpose of erudition; they have always ready on their tongues the speech of cultivated urbanity, and proclaim their charity toward the poor; they look for the improvement of the masses, to extend the benefits of social comfort to as many of mankind as possible. Those purposes, though they may be true, yet are not the only ones. Besides, those who are chosen to join the society must promise and swear to obey the leaders and teachers with great respect and trust; to be ready to do whatever is told them, and accept death and the most horrible punishment if they disobey. In fact, some who have betrayed the secrets or disobeyed an order are punished with death so skillfully and so audaciously that the murder escaped the investigations of the police. Therefore, reason and truth show that the society of which we speak is contrary to honesty and natural justice.

There are other and clear arguments to show that this society is not in agreement with honesty. No matter how great the skill with which men conceal it, it is impossible that the cause should not appear in its effects. "A good tree cannot yield bad fruits, nor a bad tree good ones." (Matt. vii., 18.) Masonry generates bad fruits mixed with great bitterness. From the evidence above mentioned we find its aim, which is the desire of overthrowing all the religious and social orders introduced by Christianity, and building a new one according to its taste, based on the foundation and laws of naturalism.

What we have said or will say must be understood of Masonry in general and of all like societies, not of the individual members of the same. In their number there may be not a few who, though they are wrong in giving their names to these societies, yet are neither guilty of their crimes nor aware of the final goal which they strive to reach. Among the associations also, perhaps, some do not approve the extreme conclusions which, as emanating from common principles, it would be necessary to embrace if their deformity and vileness would not be too repulsive. Some of them are equally forced by the places and times not to go so far as they would go or others go; and yet they are not to be considered less Masonic for that, because the Masonic alliance has to be considered not only from actions and deeds, but from general principles.

Now, it is the principle of naturalists, as the name itself indicates, that human nature and human reason in everything must be our teacher and guide. Having once settled this, they are careless of duties toward God, or they pervert them with false opinions and errors. They deny that anything has been revealed by God; they do not admit any religious dogma and truth but what human intelligence can comprehend; they do not allow any teacher to be believed on his official authority. Now, it being the special duty of the Catholic Church, and her duty only, to keep the doctrines received from God and the authority of teaching with all the heavenly means necessary to salvation and preserve them integrally incorrupt, hence the attacks and rage of the enemies are turned against her.

Now, if one watches the proceedings of the Masons, in respect of religion especially, where they are more free to do what they like, it will appear that they carry faithfully into execution the tenets of the naturalists. They work, indeed, obstinately to the end that neither the teaching nor the authority of the Church may have any influence; and therefore they preach and maintain the full separation of the Church from the State. So law and government are wrested from the wholesome and divine virtue of the Catholic Church, and they want, therefore, by all means to rule States independent of the institutions and doctrines of the Church.

To drive off the Church as a sure guide is not enough; they add persecutions and insults. Full license is given to attack with impunity, both by words and print and teaching, the very foundations of the Catholic religion; the rights of the Church are violated; her divine privileges are not respected. Her action is restricted as much as possible; and that by virtue of laws apparently not too violent, but substantially made on purpose to check her freedom. Laws odiously partial against the clergy are passed so as to reduce its number and its means. The ecclesiastical revenue is in a thousand ways tied up, and religious associations abolished and dispersed.

But the war wages more ardently against the Apostolic See and the Roman Pontiff. He was, under a false pretext, deprived of the temporal power, the stronghold of his rights and of his freedom; he was next reduced to an iniquitous condition, unbearable for its numberless burdens until it has come to this, that the Sectarians say openly what they had already in secret devised for a long time, viz., that the very spiritual power of the Pope ought to be taken away, and the divine institution of the Roman Pontificate ought to disappear from the world. If other arguments were needed for this, it would be sufficiently demonstrated by the testimony of many who often, in times bygone and even lately, declared it to be the real supreme aim of the Free-Masons to persecute, with untamed hatred, Christianity, and that they will never rest until they see cast to the ground all religious institutions established by the Pope.

If the sect does not openly require its members to throw away of Catholic faith, this tolerance, far from injuring the Masonic schemes, is useful to them. Because this is, first, an easy way to deceive the simple and unwise ones and it is contributing to proselytize. By opening their gates to persons of every creed they promote, in fact, the great modern error of religious indifference and of the parity of all worships, the best way to annihilate every religion, especially the Catholic, which, being the only true one cannot be joined with others without enormous injustice.

But naturalists go further. Having entered, in things of greatest importance, on a way thoroughly false, through the weakness of human nature or by the judgment of God, who punishes pride, they run to extreme errors. Thus the very truths which are known by the natural light of reason, as the existence of God, the spirituality and immortality of the soul, have no more consistence and certitude for them.

Masonry breaks on the same rocks by no different way. It is true, Free-Masons generally admit the existence of God; but they admit themselves that this persuasion for them is not firm, sure. They do not dissimulate that in the Masonic family the question of God is a principle of great discord; it is even known how they lately had on this point serious disputes. It is a fact that the sect leaves to the members full liberty of thinking about God whatever they like, affirming or denying His existence. Those who boldly deny His existence are admitted as well as those who, like the Pantheists, admit God but ruin the idea of Him, retaining an absurd caricature of the divine nature, destroying its reality. Now, as soon as this supreme foundation is pulled down and upset, many natural truths must need go down, too, as the free creations of this world, the universal government of Providence, immortality of soul, fixture, and eternal life.

Once having dissipated these natural principles, important practically and theoretically, it is easy to see what will become of public and private morality. We will not speak of supernatural virtues, which, without a special favor and gift of God, no one can practice nor obtain, and of which it is impossible to find a vestige in those who proudly ignore the redemption of mankind, heavenly grace, the sacraments, and eternal happiness. We speak of duties which proceed from natural honesty. Because the principles and sources of justice and morality are these, a God, creator and provident ruler of the world, the eternal law which commands respect and forbids the violation of natural order; the supreme end of man settled a great deal above created things outside of this world. These principles once taken away by the Free-Masons as by the naturalists, immediately natural ethics has no more where to build or to rest. They only morality which Free-Masons admit, and by which they would like to bring up youth, is that which they call civil and independent, or the one which ignores every religious idea. But how poor, uncertain, and variable at every breath of passion is this morality, is demonstrated by the sorrowful fruits which partially already appear. Nay, where it has been freely dominating, having banished Christian education, probity and integrity of manners go down, horrible and monstrous opinions raise their head, and crimes grow with fearful audacity. This is deplored by everybody, and by those who are compelled by evidence and yet would not like to speak so.

Besides, as human nature is infected by original sin and more inclined to vice than to virtue, it is not possible to lead an honest life without mortifying the passions and submitting the appetites to reason. In this fight it is often necessary to despise created good, and undergo the greatest pains and sacrifices in order to preserve to conquering reason its own empire. But naturalists and Masons, rejecting divine revelation, deny original sin, and do not acknowledge that our free will is weakened and bent to evil. To the contrary, exaggerating the strength and excellency of nature, and settling in her the principles and unique role of justice, they cannot even imagine how, in order to counteract its motions and moderate its appetites, continuous efforts are needed and the greatest constancy. This is the reason why we see so many enticements offered to the passions, journals, and reviews without any shame, theatrical plays thoroughly dishonest; the liberal arts cultivated according to the principles of an impudent realism, effeminate and delicate living promoted by the most refined inventions; in a word, all the enticements apt to seduce or weaken virtue carefully practiced—things highly to blame, yet becoming the theories of those who take away from man heavenly goods, and put all happiness in transitory things and bind it to earth.

What we have said may be confirmed by things of which it is not easy to think or speak. As these shrewd and malicious men do not find more servility and docility than in souls already broken and subdued by the tyranny of the passions, there have been in the Masonic sect some who openly said and proposed that the multitudes should be urged by all means and artifice into license, so that they should afterward become an easy instrument for the most daring enterprise.

For domestic society the doctrine of almost all naturalists is that marriage is only a civil contract, and may be lawfully broken by the will of the contracting parties; the State has power over the matrimonial bond. In the education of the children no religion must be applied, and when grown up every one will select that which he likes.

Now Free-Masons accept these principles without restriction; and not only do they accept them, but they endeavor to act so as to bring them into moral and practical life. In many countries which are professedly Catholic, marriages not celebrated in the civil form are considered null; elsewhere laws allow divorce. In other places everything is done in order to have it permitted. So the nature of marriage will be soon changed and reduced to a temporary union, which can be done and undone at pleasure.

The sect of the Masons aims unanimously and steadily also at the possession of the education of children. They understand that a tender age is easily bent, and that there is no more useful way of preparing for the State such citizens as they wish. Hence, in the instruction and education of children, they do not leave to the ministers of the Church any part either in directing or watching them. In many places they have gone so far that children's education is all in the hands of laymen: and from moral teaching every idea is banished of those holy and great duties which bind together man and God.

The principles of social science follow. Here naturalists teach that men have all the same rights, and are perfectly equal in condition; that every man is naturally independent; that no one has a right to command others; that it is tyranny to keep men subject to any other authority than that which emanates from themselves. Hence the people are sovereign; those who rule have no authority but by the commission and concession of the people; so that they can be deposed, willing or unwilling, according to the wishes of the people. The origin of all rights and civil duties is in the people or in the State, which is ruled according to the new principles of liberty. The State must be godless; no reason why one religion ought to be preferred to another; all to be held in the same esteem.

Now it is well known that Free-Masons approve these maxims, and that they wish to see governments shaped on this pattern and model needs no demonstration. It is a long time, indeed, that they have worked with all their strength and power openly for this, making thus an easy way for those, not a few, more audacious and bold in evil, who meditate the communion and equality of all goods after having swept away from the world every distinction of social goods and conditions.

From these few hints it is easy to understand what is the Masonic sect and what it wants. Its tenets contradict so evidently human reason that nothing can be more perverted. The desire of destroying the religion and Church established by God, with the promise of immortal life, to try to revive, after eighteen centuries, the manners and institutions of paganism, is great foolishness and bold impiety. No less horrible or unbearable is it to repudiate the gifts granted through His adversaries. In this foolish and ferocious attempt, one recognizes that untamed hatred and rage of revenge kindled against Jesus Christ in the heart of Satan.

The other attempt in which the Masons work so much, viz., to pull down the foundations of morality, and become co-operators of those who, like brutes, would see that become lawful which they like, is nothing but to urge mankind into the most abject and ignominious degradation.

This evil is aggravated by the dangers which threaten domestic and civil society. As we have at other times explained, there is in marriage, through the unanimous consent of nations and of ages, a sacred and religious character; and by divine law the conjugal union is indissoluble. Now, if this union is dissolved, if divorce is juridically permitted, confusion and discord must inevitably enter the domestic sanctuary, and woman will lose her dignity and children every security of their own welfare.

That the State ought to profess religious indifference and neglect God in ruling society, as if God did not exist, is a foolishness unknown to the very heathen, who had so deeply rooted in their mind and in their heart, not only the idea of God, but the necessity also of public worship, that they supposed it to be easier to find a city without any foundation than without any God. And really human society, from which nature has made us, was instituted by God, the author of the same nature, and from Him emanates, as from its source and principle, all this everlasting abundance of numberless goods. As, then, the voice of nature tells us to worship God with religious piety, because we have received from Him life and the goods which accompany life, so, for the same reasons, people and States must do the same. Therefore those who want to free society from any religious duty are not only unjust but unwise and absurd.

Once grant that men through God's will are born for civil society, and that sovereign power is so strictly necessary to society that when this fails society necessarily collapses, it follows that the right of command emanates from the same principle from which society itself emanates; hence the reason why the minister of God is invested with such authority. Therefore, so far as it is required from the end and nature of human society, one must obey lawful authority as we would obey the authority of God, supreme ruler of the universe; and it is a capital error to grant to the people full power of shaking off at their own will the yoke of obedience.

Considering their common origin and nature, the supreme end proposed to every one, and the right and duties emanating from it, men no doubt are all equal. But as it is impossible to find in them equal capacity, and as through bodily or intellectual strength one differs from others, and the variety of customs, inclinations, and personal qualities are so great, it is absurd to pretend to mix and unify all this and bring in the order of civil life a rigorous and absolute equality. As the perfect constitution of the human body results from the union and harmony of different parts, which differ in form and uses, but united and each in his own place form an organism beautiful, strong, useful, and necessary to life, so in the State there is an infinite variety of individuals who compose it. If these all equalized were to live each according to his own whim, it would result in a city monstrous and ugly; whereas if distinct in harmony, in degrees of offices, of inclinations, of arts, they co-operate together to the common good, they will offer the image of a city well harmonized and conformed to nature.

The turbulent errors which we have mentioned must inspire governments with fear; in fact, suppose the fear of God in life and respect for divine laws to be despised, the authority of the rulers allowed and authorized would be destroyed, rebellion would be left free to popular passions, and universal revolution and subversion must necessarily come. This subversive revolution is the deliberate aim and open purpose of the numerous communistic and socialistic associations. The Masonic sect has no reason to call itself foreign to their purpose, because Masons promote their designs and have with them common capital principles. If the extreme consequences are not everywhere reached in fact, it is not the merit of the sect nor owing to the will of the members, but of that divine religion which cannot be extinguished, and of the most select part of society, which, refusing to obey secret societies, resists strenuously their immoderate efforts.

May Heaven grant that universally from the fruits we may judge the root, and from impending evil and threatening dangers we may know the bad seed! We have to fight a shrewd enemy, who, cajoling Peoples and Kings, deceives them all with false promises and fine flattery.

Free-Masons, insinuating themselves under pretence of friendship into the hearts of Princes, aim to have them powerful aids and accomplices to overcome Christianity, and in order to excite them more actively they calumniate the Church as the enemy of royal privileges and power. Having thus become confident and sure, they get great influence in the government of States, resolve yet to shake the foundations of the thrones, and persecute, calumniate, or banish those sovereigns who refuse to rule as they desire.

By these arts flattering the people, they deceive them. Proclaiming all the time public prosperity and liberty; making multitudes believe that the Church is the cause of the iniquitous servitude and misery in which they are suffering, they deceive people and urge on the masses craving for new things against both powers. It is, however, true that the expectation of hoped-for advantages is greater than the reality; and poor people, more and more oppressed, see in their misery those comforts vanish which they might have easily and abundantly found in organized Christian society. But the punishment of the proud, who rebel against the order established by the providence of God, is that they find oppression and misery exactly where they expected prosperity according to their desire.

Now, if the Church commands us to obey before all God, the Lord of everything, it would be an injurious calumny to believe her the enemy of the power of Princes and a usurper of their rights. She wishes, on the contrary, that what is due to civil power may be given to it conscientiously. To recognize, as she does, the divine right of command, concedes great dignity to civil power, and contributes to conciliate the respect and love of subjects. A friend of peace and the mother of concord, she embraces all with motherly love, intending only to do good to men. She teaches that justice must be united with clemency, equity with command, law with moderation, and to respect every right, maintain order and public tranquillity, relieve as much as possible public and private miseries. "But," to use the words of St. Augustine, "they believe, or want to make believe, that the doctrine of Gospel is not useful to society, because they wish that the State shall rest not on the solid foundation of virtue, but on impunity of vice."

It would, therefore, be more according to civil wisdom and more necessary to universal welfare that Princes and Peoples, instead of joining the Free-Masons against the Church, should unite with the Church to resist the Free-Masons' attacks.

At all events, in the presence of such a great evil, already too much spread, it is our duty, venerable brethren, to find a remedy. And as we know that in the virtue of divine religion, the more hated by Masons as it is the more feared, chiefly consists the best and most solid of efficient remedy, we think that against the common enemy one must have recourse to this wholesome strength.

We, by our authority, ratify and confirm all things which the Roman Pontiffs, our predecessors' have ordered to check the purposes and stop the efforts of the Masonic sect, and all these which they establish to keep off or withdraw the faithful from such societies. And here, trusting greatly to the good will of the faithful, we pray and entreat each of them, as they love their own salvation, to make it a duty of conscience not to depart from what has been on this point prescribed by the Apostolic See.

We entreat and pray you, venerable brethren, who co-operate with us, to root out this poison, which spreads widely among the Nations. It is your duty to defend the glory of God and the salvation of souls. Keeping before your eyes those two ends, you shall lack neither in courage nor in fortitude. To judge which may be the more efficacious means to overcome difficulties and obstacles belongs to your prudence. Yet as we find it agreeable to our ministry to point out some of the most useful means, the first thing to do is to strip from the Masonic sect its mask and show it as it is, teaching orally and by pastoral letters the people about the frauds used by these societies to flatter and entice, the perversity of its doctrines, and the dishonesty of its works. As our predecessors have many times declared, those who love the Catholic faith and their own salvation must be sure that they cannot give their names for any reason to the Masonic sect without sin. Let no one believe a simulated honesty. It may seem to some that Masons never impose anything openly contrary to faith or to morals, but as the scope and nature is essentially bad in these sects, it is not allowed to give one's name to them or to help them in any way.

It is also necessary with assiduous sermons and exhortations to arouse in the people love and zeal for religious instruction. We recommend, therefore, that by appropriate declarations, orally and in writing, the fundamental principles of those truths may be explained in which Christian wisdom is entertained. It is only thus that minds can be cured by instruction, and warned against the various forms of error and vice, and the various enticements especially in this great freedom of writing and great desire of learning.

It is a laborious work, indeed, in which you will have associated and companioned your clergy, if properly trained and taught by your zeal. But such a beautiful and important cause requires the co-operating industry of those laymen who unite doctrine and probity with the love of religion and of their country. With the united strength of these two orders endeavor, dear brethren, that men may know and love the Church; because the more their love and knowledge of the Church grows the more they will abhor and fly from secret societies.

Therefore, availing ourselves of this present occasion, we remind you of the necessity of promoting and protecting the Third Order of St. Francis, whose rules, with prudent indulgence, we lately mitigated. According to the spirit of its institution it intends only to draw men to imitate Jesus Christ, to love the Church, and to practice all Christian virtues, and therefore it will prove useful to extinguish the contagion of sects.

May it grow more and more, this holy congregation, from which, among others, can be expected also this precious fruit of bringing minds back to liberty, fraternity, and equality; not those which are the dream of the Masonic sect, but which Jesus Christ brought into this world and Francis revived. The liberty, we say, of the children of God which frees from the servitude of Satan and from the passions, the worst tyrants; the fraternity which emanates from God, the Father and Creator of all; the equality established on justice and charity, which does not destroy among men every difference, but which, from variety of life, offices, and inclinations, makes that accord and harmony which is exacted by nature for the utility and dignity of civil society.

Thirdly, there is an institution wisely created by our fore-fathers, and by lapse of time abandoned, which in our days can be used as a model and form for something like it. We mean the colleges or corporations of arts and trades associated under the guidance of religion to defend interests and manners, which colleges, in long use and experience, were of great advantage to our fathers, and will be more and more useful to our age, because they are suited to break the power of the sects. Poor working-men, for besides their condition, deserving charity and relief, they are particularly exposed to the seductions of the fraudulent and deceivers. They must, therefore, be helped with the greatest generosity and invited to good societies that they may not be dragged into bad ones. For this reason we would like very much to see everywhere arise, fit for the new times, under the auspices and patronage of the Bishops, these associations, for the benefit of the people. It gives us a great pleasure to see them already established in many places, together with the Catholic patronages; two institutions which aim to help the honest class of workingmen, and to help and protect their families, their children, and keep in them, with the integrity of manners, love of piety and knowledge of religion.

Here we cannot keep silence concerning the society of St. Vincent de Paul, celebrated for the spectacle and example offered and so well deserving of the poor. The works and intentions of that society are well known. It is all for the succor and help of the suffering and poor, encouraging them with wonderful tact and that modesty which the less showy the more is fit for the exercise of Christian charity and the relief of human miseries.

Fourthly, in order more easily to reach the end, we recommend to your faith and watchfulness the youth, the hope of civil society. In the good education of the same place a great part of your care. Never believe you have watched or done enough in keeping youth from those masters from whom the contagious breath of the sect is to be feared. Insist that parents, and spiritual directors in teaching the catechism may never cease to admonish appropriately children and pupils of the wicked nature of these sects, that they may also learn in time the various fraudulent arts which their propagators use to entice. Those who prepare children for first communion will do well if they will persuade them to promise not to give their names to any society without asking their parents' or their pastor's or their confessor's advice.

But we understand how our common labor would not be sufficient to outroot this dangerous seed from the field of the Lord, if the Heavenly Master of the vineyard is not to this effect granting to us His generous help. We must, then, implore His powerful aid with anxious fervor equal to the gravity of the danger and to the greatness of the need. Inebriated by its prosperous success, Masonry is insolent, and seems to have no more limits to its pertinacity. Its sectaries bound by an iniquitious alliance and secret unity of purpose, they go on hand in hand and encourage each other to dare more and more for evil. Such a strong assault requires a strong defence. We mean that all the good must unite in a great society of action and prayers. We ask, therefore, from them two things: On one hand, that, unanimously and in thick ranks, they resist immovably the growing impetus of the sects; on the other, that, raising their hands with many sighs to God, they implore that Christianity may grow vigorous; that the Church may recover her necessary liberty; that wanderers may come again to salvation; that errors give place to truth and vice to virtue.

Let us invoke for this purpose the mediation of Mary, the Virgin Mother of God, that against the impious sects in which one sees clearly revived the contumacious pride, the untamed perfidy, the simulating shrewdness of Satan, she may show her power, she who triumphed over him since the first conception.

Let us pray also St. Michael, the prince of the angelic army, conqueror of the infernal enemy; St. Joseph, spouse of the most Saintly Virgin, heavenly and wholesome patron of the Catholic Church; the great Apostles Peter and Paul, propagators and defenders of the Christian faith. Through their patronage and the perseverance of common prayers let us hope that god will condescend to piously help human society threatened by so many dangers.

As a pledge of heavenly graces and of our benevolence, we impart with great affection to you, venerable brethren, to the clergy and people trusted to your care, the Apostolic benediction.

Given at Rome, near St. Peter, the 20th of April, 1884, the seventh year of our pontificate.

LEO, PP. XIII.

Bibliography

Adams, John Quincy. *Letters on the Masonic Institution*. Boston; 1847.

Addison, C. G. *The Knights Templars' History*. New York; 1875.

Aston, Margaret. *Lollards and Reformers*. London; 1984.

Aston, Trevor, ed. *Crisis in Europe 1560–1660*. New York; 1967.

Attwater, Donald, ed. *A Catholic Dictionary (The Catholic Encyclopaedic Dictionary)*. New York; 1953.

Bainville, Jacques. *History of France*. New York; 1926.

Barber, Richard, *The Knight and Chivalry*. New York; 1982.

Baring-Gould, S. *Curious Myths of the Middle Ages*. London; 1877.

Barraclough, Geoffrey. *The Medieval Papacy*. New York; 1968.

Bassett, John S. *A Short History of the United States*. New York; 1931.

(Bell Publishing Co.). *The Lost Books of the Bible*. New York; 1979.

Bennet, H. S. *Life on the English Manor*. Cambridge; 1971.

Berton, Pierre. *The Comfortable Pew*. New York; 1965.

Bohmer, Heinrich. *Luther in Light of Recent Research*. Trans. Carl F. Huth, Jr. New York; 1916.

Boorstin, Daniel J. *The Discoverers*. New York; 1985.

Brailsford, H. N. *The Levellers and the English Revolution*. Ed., C. Hill. London; 1961.

Briggs, Asa. *A Social History of England*. London; 1963.

Bryant, Arthur. *King Charles II*. London; 1931.

Bryant, M. Darrol, ed. *The Future of Anglican Theology*. New York; 1984.

Buchan, John. *The Massacre of Glencoe*. London; 1985.

Campbell, G. A. *The Knights Templars*. New York; (n.d.)

Campbell-Everden, William P. *Freemasonry and its Etiquette*. New York; 1978.

Cardinale, Hyginus E. *Orders of Knighthood, Awards and the Holy See.* Gerards Cross, Bucks.; 1983.

Ceram, C. W. *Gods, Graves and Scholars.* New York; 1951. (Orig. publ. 1949.)

Chambers, Michael. *Chambers' Guide to London, the Secret City.* London; 1974.

Chesneaux, Jean. *Peasant Revolts in China.* London; 1973.

Churchill, Winston S. *The Birth of Britain.* New York; 1956.

———. *The New World.* New York; 1956.

Clunn, Harold P. *The Face of London.* London; 1960.

Cohen, J. M. and M. J. *The Penguin Dictionary of Quotations.* Middlesex; 1960.

Collins, James A., ed. *Book of the Scottish Rite.* Cincinnati; 1895.

Commynes, Philippe De. *The Universal Spider.* London; 1973.

Cook, Ezra A. *Revised Knight Templarism Illustrated.* Chicago; 1986.

Cooper-Oakley, Isabel. *Masonry and Medieval Mysticism.* London; 1977. (Orig. publ. 1900.)

Costain, Thomas B. *The Three Edwards.* New York; 1958.

Dawley, Powell Mills. *Chapters in Church History.* New York; 1950.

Delderfield, Eric R. *Kings and Queens of England.* New York; 1966.

Ditchfield, P. H. *English Villages.* London; 1901.

Dobson, R. B., ed. *The Peasants' Revolt of 1381.* London; 1970.

Draffen, George, of Newington, ed. *Masons and Masonry-Selected Articles from the Grand Lodge of Scotland Year Books 1953–72.* London; 1983.

Dupuy, R., and Trevor N. *The Encyclopedia of Military History.* London; 1970.

Erbstosser, Martin. *Heretics in the Middle Ages.* Leipzig; 1984.

Ernst, Jacob. *Illustrations of the Symbols of Masonry.* Cincinnati; 1868.

Evans, Joan, ed. *The Flowering of the Middle Ages.* New York; 1985. (Orig. publ. London, 1966.)

Fellows, John. *The Mysteries of Freemasonry.* London; 1860.

Finney, Rev. C. G. *The Character, Claims, and Practical Workings of Freemasonry.* Cincinnati; 1869.

Foxe, John. *Foxe's Book of Martyrs.* Ed. Marie G. King. New York; 1968. (Taken from Foxe's original *History of the Christian Martyrs.* Publ. ca. 1583.)

Fraser, Antonia. *Cromwell: The Lord Protector.* New York; 1975. (Orig. publ. London, 1973.)

Frere, A. S., ed. *Grand Lodge 1717–1967.* Oxford; 1967.

Fuller, J. F. C. *The Decisive Battles of the Western World: 480 B.C.–1757.* 2 vols. London; 1970.

Funk, F. X. *History.* 2 vols. Trans. Luigi Cappadelta. London; 1913.

Gabrieli, Francesco, ed. and trans. *Arab Historians of the Crusades.* Trans. from the Italian E. J. Costello. Berkeley, Calif.; 1969.

Geoffrey Of Monmouth. *History of the Kings of Britain.* Trans. Sebastian Evans. New York; 1958. (Orig. publ. 1912.)

George, Dorothy. *England in Transition.* London; 1953.

Gibbon, Edward. *The Decline and Fall of the Roman Empire.* London; 1960.

Gies, Frances. *The Knight in History.* New York; 1984.

Gies, Joseph and Frances. *Life in a Medieval Castle.* New York; 1979.

————. *Life in a Medieval City.* New York; 1981. (Orig. publ. 1969.)

Girouard, Mark. *The Return to Camelot: Chivalry and the English Gentleman.* London; 1931.

Gould, Robert F. *The History of Freemasonry.* 3 vols. Edinburgh: (n.d.)

Gray, Robert. *A History of London.* New York; 1985.

Greene, Samuel D. *The Broken Seal, or Personal Reminiscences of the Morgan Abduction and Murder.* Boston; 1872.

Greer, Thomas H. *A Brief History of Western Man.* New York; 1968.

Hamill, John. *The Craft: A History of English Freemasonry.* London; 1986.

Hay, Douglas, Peter Linebaugh, John G. Rule, E. P. Thompson, and Cal Winslow. *Albion's Fatal Tree.* London; 1975.

Heer, Friedrich. *The Medieval World: Europe 1100–1350.* Trans. J. Sondheimer. London; 1963.

Helms, L. C. *Twice Told Tales: A Masonic Reader.* Richmond, Va.; 1985.

Hilton, R. H., and H. Fagan. *The English Rising of 1381.* London; 1950.

Hilton, R. H., and T. H. Aston, eds. *The English Rising of 1381.* Cambridge; 1984.

Hinnells, John R., ed. *The Penguin Dictionary of Religions.* Middlesex; 1984.

Hole, Christina. *A Dictionary of British Folk Customs.* London; 1978.

Housley, Norman. *The Avignon Papacy and the Crusades 1305–1378.* Oxford; 1986.

Hutchinson, William. *The Spirit of Masonry.* New York; 1982. (Orig. publ. 1775.)

Huxley, Aldous. *The Devils of Loudun.* New York; 1965.

Jarrett, Derek. *England in the Age of Hogarth.* London; 1974.

Jenkins, Elizabeth. *Elizabeth and Leicester.* London; 1972.

Joinville and Villehardouin. *Chronicles of the Crusades.* Trans. M. R. B. Shaw. Middlesex; 1963. (New York, 1985.)

Jones, Bernard E. *The Freemason's Guide and Compendium.* London; (n.d.)

Kauffman, Christopher J. *Faith and Fraternalism: The History of the Knights of Columbus 1882–1982.* New York; 1982.

Kavanaugh, Fr. James. *A Modern Priest Looks at his Outdated Church.* New York; 1967.

Keen, Maurice. *Chivalry.* New Haven; 1984.

Kelen, Betty. *Muhammad: The Messenger of God.* New York; 1975.

Kenny, Anthony, ed. *Wycliffe in his Times.* Oxford; 1986.

Knight, Stephen. *Jack the Ripper: The Final Solution.* London; 1976.

_____. *The Brotherhood.* London; 1985.

Knowles, David. *Bare Ruined Choirs.* Cambridge; 1976.

Koenigsberger, H. G., and G. L. Mosse. *Europe in the Sixteenth Century.* New York; 1968.

Ladurie, Emmanuel Leroy. *Montaillou: The Promised Land of Error.* Trans. Barbara Bray. New York; 1979.

Lewis, Roy, and Angus Maude. *Professional People in England.* Cambridge, Mass.; 1953.

Macaulay, Thomas B. *The History of England from the Accession of James II.* 5 vols. New York; 1856.

Mansfield, Peter. *The Arabs.* New York; 1980.

Martin, Malachi. *The Decline and Fall of the Roman Church.* New York; 1981.

_____. *Rich Church Poor Church.* New York; 1984.

Mayer, Hans Eberhard. *The Crusades.* Trans. John Gillingham. Oxford; 1988.

Meltzer, Milton. *Slavery: From the Rise of Western Civilization to Today.* New York; 1977. (Orig. publ. in 2 vols. 1971.)

Mitchell, Donald G. *English Lands Letters and Kings from Elizabeth to Anne.* New York; 1890.

Moncrieffe, Sir Iain. *Royal Highness-Ancestry of the Royal Child.* London; 1982.

Moote, A. Lloyd. *The Seventeenth Century: Europe in Ferment.* Lexington, Mass.; 1970.

Morgan, Capt. William. *Freemasonry Exposed.* Chicago; 1986.

Morris, Jan. *The Oxford Book of Oxford.* Oxford; 1978.

Nettl, Paul. *Mozart and Masonry.* New York; 1987.

Newhall, Richard A. *The Crusades.* New York; 1963. (Orig. publ. 1927.)

Nicholas, David. *The Medieval West.* Homewood, Ill.; 1983.

O'Brian, Rev. John A. *The Faith of Millions: The Credentials of the Catholic Church.* Huntington, Ind.; 1958.

O'Connor, Richard. *The Spirit Soldiers.* New York; 1973.

Pagels, Elaine. *The Gnostic Gospels.* New York; 1981.

Palmer, Alan. *Kings and Queens of England.* London; 1976.

Parker, Thomas W. *The Knights Templars in England.* Tucson, Ariz.; 1963.

Partner, Peter. *The Murdered Magicians.* Rochester, Vt.; 1987.

Pick, F. L., and G. N. Knight. *The Pocket History of Freemasonry.*
————. *The Freemason's Pocket Reference Book.* London; 1953. Revised F. Smyth, 1965 and 1983.

Platts, Graham. *Land and People in Medieval Lincolnshire.* Lincoln; 1985.

Poundstone, William. *Big Secrets.* New York; 1983.

Powell, E., and G. M. Trevelyan, eds. *The Peasants' Rising and the Lollards.* London; 1899.

Powell, James M. *Anatomy of a Crusade 1213-1221.* Philadelphia; 1986.

Powell, K., and C. Cook. *English Historical Facts 1485-1603.* London; 1977.

Quennell, Marjorie and C. H. B. *A History of Everyday Things in England 1066-1499.* London; 1919.

Randel, William P. *The Ku Klux Klan.* Philadelphia; 1965.

Read, Jan. *The New Conquistadors.* London; 1980.

Rebold, Emmanuel. *A General History of Freemasonry in Europe.* Trans. J. F. Brennan. Cincinnati; 1866.

Redding, M. W. *Scarlet Book of Free Masonry.* New York; 1880.

Richardson, Jabez. *Monitor of Free-masonry.* Chicago; (n.d.)

Roberts, Allen E. *Freemasonry in American History.* Richmond, Va.; 1985.

Ross, Frank, Jr. *Arabs and the Islamic World.* New York; 1979.

Rowley, Trevor, and John Wood. *Deserted Villages.* Princes Risborough, Bucks.; 1982.

Rowse, A. L. *Oxford in the History of the Nation.* London; 1975.

Runciman, Sir Steven. *A History of the Crusades.* 3 vols. Cambridge; 1951.

Rundle, R. N. *Scenes from Stuart England.* London; 1978.

Russell, Bertrand. *Why I Am Not a Christian.* London; 1957.

Sadler, Henry. *Masonic Facts and Fictions.* Wellingborough, Northants; 1985.

Sampson, Anthony. *Anatomy of Britain Today.* New York; 1965.

Scott, A. F. *Everyone a Witness: The Plantagenet Age.* New York; 1976.

Scott, Sir Walter. *Ivanhoe.* New York; 1982. (Orig. publ. 1819.)

Seward, Desmond. *The Hundred Years War.* New York; 1984.

————, *The Monks of War.* Frogmore, St. Albans; 1974.

Smith, Elwyn A., ed. *The Religion of the Republic.* Philadelphia; 1971.

Smurthwaite, David. *Battlefields of Britain.* Exeter; 1984.

Stillson, Henry Leonard, ed. in chf. *History of Freemasonry and Concordant Orders.* Boston; 1900.

Stubbs, J. W. *Freemasonry in my Life.* London; 1985.

Theis, Dan. *The Crescent and the Cross.* New York; 1978.

Tierney, B., D. Kagan, et al., eds. *Great Issues in Western Civilization Since 1500.* New York; 1968.

Towers, Eric. *Dashwood: The Man and the Myth.* London; 1986.

Trevelyan, G. M. *History of England.* London; 1926.

Tuchman, Barbara W. *A Distant Mirror: The Calamitous 14th Century.* New York; 1978.

Turnbull, Stephen. *The Book of the Medieval Knight.* London; 1985.

Van Gordon, John H. *Ancient and Early Medieval Historical Characters in Freemasonry.* Lexington, Mass.; 1986.

_____. *Biblical Characters in Freemasonry.* Lexington, Mass; 1982.

_____. *Medieval Historical Characters in Freemasonry.* Lexington, Mass.; 1987.

_____. *Modern Historical Characters in Freemasonry.* Lexington, Mass.; 1985.

Vaughn, Richard, ed. and trans. *Chronicles of Matthew Paris: Monastic Life in the Thirteenth Century.* Gloucester; 1986.

Waite, Arthur E. *A New Encyclopaedia of Freemasonry.* New York; 1970.

Walkes, Joseph A., Jr. *Black Square and Compass.* Richmond, Va.; 1981.

Webber, Ronald. *The Peasants' Revolt.* Lavenham, Suffolk; 1980.

Webster, Nesta H. *Secret Societies and Subversive Movements.* London; 1924.

Wedgwood, C. V. *The King's Peace, 1637–1641.* London; 1955.

_____. *The King's War 1641–1647.* London; 1958.

_____. *The Trial of Charles I.* London; 1964.

Wells, H. G. *The Outline of History.* 2 vols. New York; 1930.

Wilken, Robert L. *The Myth of Christian Beginnings.* New York; 1971.

Williams, Ann. *The Crusades.* Harlow, Essex; 1975.

Wilmshurst, W. L. *The Meaning of Masonry.* (Orig. publ. London, 1927.)

Winkler, Paul. *The Thousand-Year Conspiracy.* New York; 1943.

Wolf, Eric R. *Peasants.* Englewood Cliffs, N.J.; 1966.

Wolf, John B. *The Emergence of European Civilisation.* New York; 1962.

Yates, Frances A. *The Occult Philosophy in the Elizabethan Age.* London; 1979.

Index